T0173076

Digital Gaming Re-imagines the Middle Ages

Digital gaming's cultural significance is often minimized much in the same way that the Middle Ages are discounted as the backward and childish precursor to the modern period. *Digital Gaming Re-imagines the Middle Ages* challenges both perceptions by examining how the Middle Ages have persisted into the contemporary world via digital games as well as analyzing how digital gaming translates, adapts, and remediates medieval stories, themes, characters, and tropes in interactive electronic environments. At the same time, the Middle Ages are reinterpreted according to contemporary concerns and conflicts, in all their complexity. Rather than a distinct time in the past, the Middle Ages form a space in which theory and narrative, gaming and textuality, identity and society are remediated and reimagined. Together, the essays demonstrate that while having its roots firmly in narrative traditions, neomedieval gaming—where neomedievalism no longer negotiates with any reality beyond itself and other medievalisms—creates cultural palimpsests, multiply layered transtemporal artifacts. *Digital Gaming Re-imagines the Middle Ages* demonstrates that the medieval is more than just a stockpile of historically static facts but is a living, subversive presence in contemporary culture.

Daniel T. Kline is Professor of English at the University of Alaska, Anchorage, USA.

Routledge Studies in New Media and Cyberculture

Digital Gaming Re-imagines the Middle Ages

Edited by Daniel T. Kline

Routledge
Taylor & Francis Group

LONDON AND NEW YORK

First published 2014
by Routledge
711 Third Avenue, New York, NY 10017

Simultaneously published in the UK
by Routledge
2 Park Square, Milton Park, Abingdon, Oxon OX14 4RN

*Routledge is an imprint of the Taylor & Francis Group,
an informa business*

Library of Congress Cataloging-in-Publication Data

Digital gaming re-imagines the Middle Ages / edited by Daniel T. Kline.
    pages cm. — (Routledge studies in new media and cyberculture ; 15)
  Includes bibliographical references and index.
(alk. paper)
 1. Computer games.   2. Video games.   3. Middle Ages—Computer
games.   I. Kline, Daniel T.
  GV1469.15.D538 2013
  794.8—dc23

ISBN: 978-0-415-63091-7 (hbk)
ISBN: 978-0-203-09723-6 (ebk)

Typeset in Sabon
by Apex CoVantage, LLC

Printed and bound in the United States of America by Publishers Graphics,
LLC on sustainably sourced paper.

For Wendy

Contents

PART III
Case Study 1—*World of Warcraft*

PART IV
Case Study 2—*Dante's Inferno*

PART V
Theoretical and Representational Issues in Medieval Gaming

Figures and Table

TABLE

FIGURES

Acknowledgments

The editor would like to thank Boydell and Brewer for permission to reprint portions of Harry J. Brown's "Baphomet Incorporated: A Case Study in Neomedievalism," originally published in *Studies in Medievalism* 20 (2011), pages 1–10. The editor would also like to thank Electronic Arts for permission to use the image of Dante and the Master and Fellows of Corpus Christi College, Cambridge, for permission to reproduce the strip-map of traveling to Jerusalem, Matthew Paris's *Chronica Majora* (CCC MS 26). Finally, the editor would like to thankfully acknowledge the use of the lines from *Purgatorio* by Dante Alighieri, translated by Robert Hollander & Jean Hollander, translation copyright © 2003 by Robert Hollander and Jean Hollander. Used by permission of Doubleday, a division of Random House, Inc. Any third-party use of this material, outside of this publication, is prohibited. Interested parties must apply directly to Random House, Inc. for permission.

Introduction

"All Your History Are Belong to Us": Digital Gaming Re-imagines the Middle Ages

Daniel T. Kline

DANTE AT THE BAR

In June 2011, in a 7–2 vote the U.S. Supreme Court ruled in *Brown v. Entertainment Merchants Association* that a California law designed to protect children from violent video games violated the First Amendment: "Like the protected books, plays, and movies that preceded them, video games communicate ideas—and even social messages—through many familiar literary devices (such as characters, dialogue, plot, and music) and through features distinctive to the medium (such as the player's interaction with the virtual world). That suffices to confer First Amendment protection."[1] Not only a political milestone, the Supreme Court decision in *Brown v. Entertainment Merchants Association* marks a moment of cultural maturity for video gaming. No longer just kid's stuff, gaming earned $18 billion in 2010 and has become a major economic force.[2] On one hand, gaming has reached a level of artistic maturity on a par with other fine arts.[3] On the other hand, although the decision affirms gaming's right to constitutional protection, it nonetheless reproduces the stereotype that gaming, particularly games portraying violence, is somehow base and unsophisticated. Writing for the majority, Justice Antonin Scalia notes that although the *Inferno* has moments of graphic violence, "Reading Dante is unquestionably more cultured and intellectually edifying than playing Mortal Kombat. But these cultural and intellectual differences are not *constitutional* ones. Crudely violent video games, tawdry TV shows, and cheap novels and magazines are no less forms of speech than The Divine Comedy, and restrictions upon them must survive strict scrutiny."[4] He argues that because many classic children's books, such as Grimm's fairy tales, and required high school texts, such as Homer's *Odyssey* and Dante's *Inferno*, "contain no shortage of gore," video games differ only in degree rather than in kind from other, earlier forms of art and entertainment.[5]

Dante's great medieval work receives Justice Scalia's approbation, instituting in the Supreme Court decision a hierarchy of taste while protecting the content of lesser artistic productions: "Even if we can see in them 'nothing of any possible value to society . . . , they are as much entitled to the protection of free speech as the best of literature.'"[6] Yet the great medieval work, the *Commedia,* achieves recognition in *Brown v. Entertainment Merchants,* because it is both a violent *and* a classic text that warrants protection. Even the U.S. Supreme Court perceives the medieval period as a time of blood and barbarity, a Dark Ages. For Scalia, the medieval itself serves as a kind of cultural shorthand for a violent and brutal but romantic and courtly culture where honor is achieved through bloodshed and personal valor; that is, Dante may be more edifying but no less brutal than *Mortal Kombat.* However, in 2010 Dante's *Inferno* itself was released as an action-adventure video game, *Dante's Inferno,* where players no longer read about and follow Dante's journey through Hell with Virgil as his guide. Instead, they take on the character Dante, now reconfigured as a violent crusading knight, as he hacks and hews his way through the nine rings of Hell to rescue Beatrice's soul from Lucifer, encountering a host of barbaric punishments along the way. According to the Supreme Court, *Dante's Inferno* deserves the same First Amendment protection as Dante's *Inferno.*

In his majority opinion, Scalia briefly traces the development of children's entertainments from gruesome fairy tales to dime novels, radio programs, movies, television, and musical lyrics, and he notes how at each point the Supreme Court eventually opposed censorship and provided First Amendment protection. Implicit in Scalia's argument is the cultural unease that accompanies each new form of media and the fear over the new media's ability to influence children negatively.[7] Scalia's linear account of artistic development depends upon a narratological assessment that equates the storylike content of books, movies, radio, TV, and video games, but in his dissent Justice Breyer notes that, in conjunction with the State of California's argument, "A typical video game involves a significant amount of physical activity. . . . And pushing buttons that achieve an interactive, virtual form of target practice (using images of human beings as targets), while containing an expressive component, is not just like watching a typical movie."[8] In other words, according to Breyer, although games, like books and other forms of entertainment, incorporate character, plot, setting, action, and point of view, gaming brings something new to the table, a physically interactive experience that goes beyond purely narrative forms. In terms of theoretical approaches, critics who study games with tools adapted from narrative fiction tend to show the continuity of gaming to previous artistic forms, whereas the ludologists (*ludi* is Latin for "games") seek to identify gaming's unique characteristics.[9] The essays in *Digital Gaming Re-imagines the Middle Ages* take both narratological and ludological approaches to gaming, seeking textual and thematic continuities with earlier texts and examining the unique technological and ludic manifestations of contemporary gaming.

MEDIEVALISM AND NEOMEDIEVALISM: TRANSLATION, ADAPTATION, REMEDIATION

The title of this introduction, "'All Your History Are Belong to Us': Digital Gaming Re-imagines the Middle Ages," deliberately contains a grammatical oddity that might be off-putting for those new to gaming but harbors a clue for long-time gamers as to the key concerns of the volume. "All Your History Are Belong to Us" plays upon a *meme*—a unit of culture or a concept or image that spreads virally,[10] often via the Internet—as derived from a mistranslated Japanese phrase from the 1991 video game *Zero Wing*. In the opening cutscene to *Zero Wing*, an evil character proclaims "All your base are belong to us" to say that his forces have taken over all friendly territory, which must then be reconquered as part of the gameplay.[11] The mangled translation from Japanese into English has served as a touchstone for gamers ever since. "Mistranslation" is after all still a form of translation, and, like books and movies, gaming has developed its own history, genealogy, and forms of digital translation. *Digital Gaming Re-imagines the Middle Ages* is first of all concerned with contemporary video games as they appropriate and translate the raw material of the Middle Ages for interactive gameplay while going beyond simple storytelling to incorporate narrative as well as audio, visual, haptic, and kinesthetic elements into coherent interactive worlds. *Digital Gaming Re-imagines the Middle Ages* is not only interested in the complex processes of translation from one period of history to another but also the transformation of narratives and genres, social issues, and cultural questions from the medieval to the contemporary era, as in Dante's makeover from a spiritual pilgrim in the medieval *Inferno* to a vengeful warrior in the modern game. *Digital Gaming Re-imagines the Middle Ages* therefore:

- Shows how medieval stories, themes, characters, and tropes persist into the present and are transformed in the contemporary world of digital gaming;
- Demonstrates how these features of medieval culture are creatively reimagined and reinterpreted for contemporary audiences and purposes; and
- Reveals that in these processes of reinterpretation, digital gaming preserves and even extends something essentially *medieval* in the modern period.

Thus, the distinctions between medieval and modern collapse as the medieval roots of these modern electronic compositions are revealed, and these contemporary adaptations complicate the notions of 'medieval' and 'medievalism.' Rather than medieval texts and cultures being perceived as *premodern,* contemporary gaming is *postmedieval,* sharing an essential heritage with medieval textual and iconographic traditions.

Medievalism, the postmedieval analysis and usage of medieval phenomena, is a growing academic field, with a well-established tradition in textual and historical study, and it is gaining attention in the examination of popular culture, especially film.[12] *Neomedievalism* has come to describe gaming's unique approach to medieval material.[13] Contemporary medievalism's examination of popular culture looks back to Umberto Eco's 1986 essays, "Dreaming the Middle Ages" and "Living in the New Middle Ages," in particular his taxonomy of "Ten Little Middle Ages,"[14] and to the efforts of Leslie J. Workman and *Studies in Medievalism* to define itself as a field.[15] Building upon Workman's endeavors, Tom Shippey, defines *medievalism* as "Any post-medieval attempt to re-imagine the Middle Ages, or some aspect of the Middle Ages, for the modern world, in any of many media; especially in academic usage, the study of the development and significance of such attempts."[16] Eco's ten postmedieval appropriations of the medieval period oscillate between "fantastic neomedievalism and responsible philological examination."[17] Clarifying the form of medievalism found in contemporary gaming, Richard Utz argues that "*Neomedieval* texts no longer strive for the authenticity of original manuscripts, castles, or cathedrals, but create pseudo-medieval worlds that playfully obliterate history and historical accuracy and replace history-based narratives with simulacra of the medieval, employing images that are neither an original nor the copy of an original, but altogether Neo [*sic*]."[18] Neomedieval games thus are marked by a double vision, looking toward medieval originals but through intermediate sources like *Dungeons & Dragons,* with little regard for medieval realities. The contributors to *Digital Gaming Re-imagines the Middle Ages* variously use the term *neomedieval, pseudomedieval,* and *medievalist* to refer to these digital worlds.

Eco's valorization of "responsible philological examination" and consequent disparagement of "fantastic neomedievalism," those new (*neo*) versions of medieval predecessors like Las Vegas's Excalibur casino, betrays what Linda Hutcheon calls "the (post-) Romantic valuing of the original creation and of the originating creative genius that is [also] clearly one source of the denigration of adapters and adaptations."[19] Like contemporary gaming, the medieval period knew no such possessiveness concerning 'original sources' but instead conserved its received materials, freely combining original matter with contemporary adaptations, commentaries, paraphrases, and revisions. Dante made the ancient poet Virgil his guide to the afterlife, freely uniting his own period with that earlier one without regard to anachronism, and Dante placed himself shamelessly in the company of the great epic poets. In contrast, post-Romantic culture valorizes the lone genius, artists who create wholly original works out of their own imaginative fecundity, but disparages 'derivative' works or those that wear their sources visibly. As Hutcheon notes, "this negative view [of adaptation] is actually a late addition to Western culture's long and happy history of borrowing and stealing or, more accurately, sharing stories."[20] In reassessing the positive role of derivative works, Hutcheon defines *adaptation* as "An acknowledged transposition of a recognizable other work or works, a creative *and* an interpretive act of appropriation/salvaging, [and] an extended intertextual engagement with the adapted work."[21] The pleasure and production of adaptations are, to use Michael Alexander's term, "inherently 'palimpsestuous' works, haunted at all times by their adapted texts."[22] The ink on ancient and medieval parchments could be scraped off and the vellum reused for a new text, often leaving traces of the earlier copy, and the resultant multiply-layered document is termed a 'palimpsest.' Neomedieval games convey this 'palimpsestuous' pleasure, not only revealing the hidden layers of earlier texts but also providing a fresh gloss on already-known narratives. As a literary text, Dante's *Inferno* has canonical status and an elevated reputation that is not diminished by *Dante's Inferno,* the game, but knowing Dante's *Inferno* can make playing *Dante's Inferno* much more enjoyable because of its (in)fidelity to the original; that is, its adaptive novelty. With a palimpsest, the original text never disappears—it simply fades to the background—and this multiple layering gives neomedieval games a special appeal. Game makers have used the medieval past to lend credence to their plotlines, to make exotic their characters, to romanticize their settings, and to give authority to their efforts. The medieval period is not something in the distant past but a present reality, a treasure trove whose contents can be ceaselessly reconfigured for current needs. "Our penchant for appealing to it [the medieval past]," writes Gwendolyn Morgan, "echoes closely the medieval poets citing real and invented classical authorities for their own art."[23] To differing degrees, the essays of *Digital Gaming Re-imagines the Middle Ages* demonstrate the palimpsestuous desire of contemporary video games and the delicious pleasure of playing them.

It is clear then that digital gaming expands the parameters of traditional narrative arts through computer technology and physical interaction with that technology. David J. Bolter and Richard A. Grusin's concept of *remediation* argues that new media finds its significance in refashioning or *remediating* old media types, and their distinction between *transparency* and *hypermediacy* provides a starting point for conceptualizing the experiential range of technological usage in gaming, or more simply, the relationship of the media and the message, or the form and the content.[24] Both types of remediation strive for immediacy of experience, but *hypermediacy* involves the experience of the technology as an artifact, whereas *transparency* strives for the artifact's (or technology's) disappearance. Neomedieval games vacillate between hypermediacy and transparency to the degree that they make game players aware of the created nature of the game interface; that is, the conscious presence of the processes of representation. What separates gaming from other media technologies is their degree of *immersion,* or the highest level of transparent immediacy, so that players experience the game world as fully as possible and forget that they are playing a game. Hutcheon notes that reading a story, watching a film, and playing a game each engages an audience in differing degrees of "immersion, identification, and distance," but she equally recognizes that the game player "becomes at once protagonist and director in a way no performance spectator or reader ever can. . . . Instead of just interpreting, the player intervenes" and feels "physically present in the mediated environment, rather than in our real world."[25] The pleasure of immersion and remediation is only intensified by the player's familiarity with the sources of the neomedieval games themselves.

ORGANIZATION OF *DIGITAL GAMING RE-IMAGINES THE MIDDLE AGES*

Investigation into gaming and medievalism, however, is still nascent.[26] *Digital Gaming Re-imagines the Middle Ages* sits at the intersection of medieval studies, literary and cultural theory, new media studies, and the emerging discipline of gaming studies. Neomedieval gaming includes within its purview elements of print, film, TV, and other games in digital media to extend and to transform the dynamics of those other, older media, for gaming reconfigures the traditional distinction between author and reader (or user) by making players the authors of their own experiences within the game world. The neomedieval does not strive for historical authenticity but for digital legitimacy and game-world coherence. Successful neomedieval games create a "heterocosm" (literally "other world") that enjoys more "truth-of-coherence" (or consistency within the internal game world) than "truth-of-correspondence" (or fidelity to the external source).[27] With neomedieval gaming, however, the external source might not be a medieval text but rather other forms of postmedieval and neomedieval content, each palimpsestuously related to 'authentic' medieval texts. In Amy Kaufman's words, "The neomedieval idea of the Middle Ages is gained not through contact with the Middle Ages, but through a medievalist intermediary: Tolkien's *Lord of the Rings* series, T. H. White's *Once and Future King*. . . . Neomedievalism is thus not a dream of the Middle Ages, but a dream of someone else's medievalism. It is medievalism doubled up upon itself."[28] Neomedieval games likewise engage multimodal forms of literacy beyond print. With the increasing pervasiveness of digital media in everyday life, gaming itself has become a new form of literacy, or "meaning making extended well beyond traditional reading and writing to include the multimodal, culturally and socially situated experience that included all the elements (i.e., modes) that are part of the meaning making process, including 'image, gaze, gesture, movement, music, speech, and sound-effect'"[29] as well as visual, iconographic, spatial, and technological expressions.[30] To that multimodal list we might include the gestural, haptic, and kinesthetic dimensions of gaming. For gamers, these literacies are second nature within the heterocosm of the game world.

It would be a mistake, then, to assess neomedieval gaming according to its fidelity to an original text or its faithfulness to a 'real' medieval history, for such originary fantasies are themselves constructions of a different kind. Instead, coming from medieval studies, media studies, and gaming studies perspectives, the contributors to *Digital Gaming Re-imagines the Middle Ages* assess the kinds of cultural work performed by these games. The volume is broken into six parts. "Part One: Prehistory of Medieval Gaming" is composed of William J. White's "The Right to Dream of the Middle Ages: Simulating the Medieval in Tabletop RPGs." In Chapter 1, White examines four role-playing games (RPGs)—*Chivalry & Sorcery* (1977), *Fantasy Wargaming* (1981), *King Arthur Pendragon* (1985), and *Chronica Feudalis* (2009)—"in order to describe the 'dream of the Middle Ages' as role-playing simulation" (16). Tabletop RPGs are thus both an important precursor to digital gaming and an essential part of the gaming tradition.

"Part Two: Medieval Gaming Re-imagines Medieval Traditions" is composed of four essays, each concerned with a specific medieval text or topic. Chapter 2, Candace Barrington and Timothy English's "'Best and Only Bulwark': How Epic Narrative Redeems *Beowulf: The Game*," examines three sets of changes the game introduces into the *Beowulf* narrative to argue that "*Beowulf: The Game* has both the attributes that appeal to gamers as well as the ambiguity that allows for adjustments that correspond with interpretive moves medievalists make" (40). Chapter 3, Jason Pitruzzello's "Systematizing Culture in Medievalism: Geography, Dynasty, Culture, and Imperialism in *Crusader Kings: Deus Vult*," shows how "*Crusader Kings* models systems of cultural change in the Middle Ages" (45), for the game's "system of culture, religion, provinces, and characters creates multiple sites of conflict as well as interaction" (46). Chapter 4, Gregory Fedorenko's "The Portrayal of Medieval Warfare in *Medieval: Total War* and *Medieval 2: Total War*," "highlights certain revealing discrepancies between the idea as commonly understood by modern audiences on the one hand and 'total warfare' as evident in contemporaneous, medieval descriptions of conflicts on the other" (54). Chapter 5, Angela Tenga's "Gabriel Knight: A Twentieth-Century Chivalric Romance Hero," reveals how the "*Gabriel Knight* series reinterpret[s] the Grail legend and revive[s] the figure of the Arthurian knight in the guise of its unlikely hero—a lowbrow rogue, inveterate womanizer, third-rate novelist, and amateur sleuth" (67).

"Part Three: Case Study 1—*World of Warcraft*" is composed of four essays, each looking in detail at Blizzard's popular massively multiplayer online role-playing game (MMORPG). Chapter 6, Elysse T. Meredith's "Coloring Tension: Medieval and Contemporary Concepts in Classifying and Using Digital Objects in *World of Warcraft*," examines "the color classification system in *World of Warcraft*" to address "how in-game treatment of pixel-based artifacts mediates between certain capitalistic game structures and the nominally feudal and manorial setting to alter the overall gaming experience" (81). Chapter 7, Kristin Noone and Jennifer Kavetsky's "Sir

Thomas Malory and the Death Knights of New Avalon: Imagining Medieval Identities in *World of Warcraft*," suggests "that the medievalism of *World of Warcraft* is a conscious construction by its creators, relying on the game's ability to imaginatively embody both continuity with the past and a form of playful, postmodernist discontinuity, taking joy in its own additions to and alterations of the Arthurian legendarium" (93). Chapter 8, Jennifer C. Stone, Peter Kudenov, and Teresa Combs's "Accumulating Histories: A Social Practice Approach to Medievalism in High-Fantasy MMORPGs," examines "how high-fantasy MMORPGs provide contexts that hail players into longstanding motifs of neomedievalist gender practices, such as expectations for masculinity and femininity, chivalry, courtly love, and warfare" and investigates "moments of transgression, where medievalist historical structures of gender are exposed or questioned" (108). Chapter 9, Kim Wilkins's "'Awesome Cleavage': The Genred Body in *World of Warcraft*," takes the pun in the title to raise questions about gender and genre in *World of Warcraft* because "it references the medieval violence ubiquitous in these games; it references the way the female body is often depicted within them; and, as parody, it plays on generic expectations, and so implicitly or explicitly acknowledges the audiences that respond to and shape genres" (119).

"Part Four: Case Study 2—*Dante's Inferno*" is made up of four essays that examine the Visceral Games/Electronic Arts action-adventure game based upon Dante's great medieval work. Chapter 10, Bruno Lessard's "The Game's Two Bodies, or the Fate of *Figura* in *Dante's Inferno*," argues that the game allows "the notion of *figura* to survive in the world of digital gaming via its unvoiced demand to answer the Deleuzian question par excellence: What can a video game body do?" (134). Chapter 11, Oliver Chadwick's "Courtly Violence, Digital Play: Adapting Medieval Courtly Masculinities in *Dante's Inferno*," demonstrates that "By re-imagining Dante as a crusader-knight, and framing his digital performance within the courtly love paradigm, *Inferno* also becomes an adaptation of the courtly knight-lovers of Arthurian Romance" (148). Chapter 12, Timothy J. Welsh and John T. Sebastian's "Shades of Dante: Virtual Bodies in *Dante's Inferno*," examines "how Visceral's efforts to give weightiness to on-screen virtualities might be understood within Dante's incorporation of the impossible weight of the shades into a metaphysics of sin" (163). Chapter 13, Angela Jane Weisl and Kevin J. Stevens's "The Middle Ages in the Depth of Hell: Pedagogical Possibility and the Past in *Dante's Inferno*," establishes how "the creators at EA have taken an essential medieval figure (Dante) and the essential medieval narrative of the love quest, and a little bit of the Orpheus legend, and put them together with some science-fiction trappings, collapsing the Middle Ages into a unitary project in which any one element can be imposed on any other element" (176).

"Part Five: Theoretical and Representational Issues in Medieval Gaming" is composed of four chapters, each taking up broad thematic concerns. Chapter 14, Thomas Rowland's "We Will Travel by Map: Maps as Narrative

Spaces in Video Games and Medieval Texts," contends that "medieval maps, like video game maps, evoke and chronicle a certain sort of narrative experience as one reads them that seeks to present an understanding of the world as Creation, as a tool by which one can virtually travel this world, and finally as a piece of art" (191–92). Chapter 15, Michelle DiPietro's "Author, Text, and Medievalism in *The Elder Scrolls*," examines the use of texts in the game to demonstrate that "the bona fide seal of 'medievalism' in *TES* is not its heroes or its strongholds, but its books" (202). Chapter 16, Nick Webber's "Technophilia and Technophobia in Online Medieval Fantasy Games," engages "three themes: the notion of technophobia and the opposition between contemporary and medieval constructions of technology; the use of medieval games not as ways to represent the past but as ways of saying something about ourselves; and the way in which MMORPGs interpret and respond to contemporary attitudes to technology, in particular the technophilia of the societies that produce and play them" (214). Chapter 17, Harry J. Brown's "The Consolation of Paranoia: Conspiracy, Epistemology, and the Templars in *Assassin's Creed*, *Deus Ex*, and *Dragon Age*" argues that "Synonymous with occultism and secret knowledge since the nineteenth century, the Templars play a crucial role in these epistemological dramas, in each case constituting a regime of truth standing in opposition to the player's own attempt to control this knowledge" (237).

The volume concludes with "Part Six: Sociality and Social Media in Medieval Gaming" and Serina Patterson's Chapter 18, "Casual Medieval Games, Interactivity, and Social Play in Social Network and Mobile Applications." Casual social games are different from the games discussed elsewhere in the volume, and Patterson argues "that medieval social casual games on social networks and mobile devices form pseudomedieval fictional worlds constructed in part by online user relationships, which, in turn, project a digital fictionalization of the self through inclusion on user profiles, news feeds, and achievement boards; specifically, their visual user interfaces and group dynamics compose part of an individual's desired identity and status" (244–45).

CONCLUSION

Digital gaming's cultural significance is often minimized much in the same way that the Middle Ages are discounted as the backward and childish precursor to the modern period, as in Scalia's Supreme Court opinion. *Digital Gaming Re-imagines the Middle Ages* challenges both perceptions by examining how the Middle Ages have persisted into the contemporary world via digital games as well as analyzing how digital gaming translates, adapts, and remediates medieval stories, themes, characters, and tropes in interactive electronic environments. At the same time, the Middle Ages are reinterpreted according to contemporary concerns and conflicts, in all their complexity. Rather than a distinct time in the past, the Middle Ages form a space in which theory and narrative, gaming and textuality, identity and society are remediated and re-imagined. Together, the essays demonstrate that although having its roots firmly in narrative traditions, neomedieval gaming—where neomedievalism no longer negotiates with any reality beyond itself and other medievalisms—creates cultural palimpsests, multiply layered transtemporal artifacts. *Digital Gaming Re-imagines the Middle Ages* demonstrates that the medieval is more than just a stockpile of historically static facts but is a living, subversive presence in contemporary culture.

NOTES

1. *Brown, Governor of California, et al. v. Entertainment Merchants Association, et al.*, No. 08–1448, 2, http://www.supremecourt.gov/opinions/10pdf/ 08–1448.pdf (accessed August 15, 2011). See also *"Brown v. Entertainment Merchants Association,"* *Wikipedia*, http://en.wikipedia.org/wiki/Brown_v._ Entertainment_Merchants_ Association (accessed January 15, 2013).
2. "Supreme Court Violent Video Games Ruling: Ban on Sale, Rental to Children Unconstitutional," *The Huffington Post*, http://www.huffington-post.com/2011/06/27/supreme-court-violent-video-games_n_884991.html (accessed August 19, 2011).
3. As one measure, the Museum of Modern Art in New York recently added video games to its collection. See "Video Games: 14 in the Collection, for Starters," *Inside/Out: Museum of Modern Art Blog*, http://www.moma.org/ explore/inside_out/2012/11/29/video-games-14-in-the-collection-for-starters (accessed January 15, 2013). For an opposing view, see Roger Ebert, "Video Games Can Never Be Art," *Roger Ebert's Journal*, http://blogs.suntimes. com/ebert/2010/04/video_games_can_never_be_art.html (accessed January 15, 2013).
4. *Brown v. Entertainment Merchants Association*, 9n4.
5. *Brown v. Entertainment Merchants Association*, 9.
6. *Brown v. Entertainment Merchants Association*, 9n4, citing *Winters v. New York*, 333 US 507.
7. The same could be said, of course, of the current unease surrounding violent video games. See "Violent Video Games and Young People," *Harvard Mental Health Letter*, October 2010, http://www.health.harvard.edu/newsletters/ Harvard_Mental_Health_Letter/2010/October/violent-video-games-and-young-people (accessed January 15, 2013).
8. *Brown v. Entertainment Merchants Association*, 10–11.
9. See Gonzalo Frasca, "Simulation versus Narrative: Introduction to Ludology," *The Video Game Theory Reader*, ed. Mark J. P. Wolf and Bernard Perron (New York: Routledge, 2003), 221–36, and the work of Jesper Juul, particularly, "Games Telling Stories," *Game Studies* 1, no. 1 (2001), http:// www.gamestudies.org/0101/juul-gts/ (accessed August 18, 2011), and *Half-Real: Video Games between Real Rules and Fictional Worlds* (Cambridge, MA: MIT Press, 2005).
10. The term was coined by Richard Dawkins to describe "the idea of a unit of cultural transmission." See *The Selfish Gene*, 2nd ed. (Oxford: Oxford University Press, 1989), 192.
11. "All Your Base Are Belong To Us," *Wikipedia*, http://en.wikipedia.org/wiki/ All_your_base_are_belong_to_us (accessed August 18, 2011).

12. See, for example, Kevin J. Harty, *The Reel Middle Ages* (Jefferson, NC: McFarland, 2006) for a list of almost 600 medieval films and Laurie Finke and Martin B. Shictman, *Cinematic Illuminations: The Middle Ages on Film* (Baltimore: Johns Hopkins University Press, 2009).
13. See Carol L. Robinson on neomedievalism, "Some Basic Definitions," *MEMO: Medieval Electronic Multimedia Organization*, http://medievalelec tronicmultimedia.org/definitions.html (accessed August 24, 2011).
14. Umberto Eco, "Dreaming the Middle Ages" and "Living in the New Middle Ages," *Travels in Hyperreality*, trans. William Weaver (New York: Harcourt, 1986), 61–72 and 73–85. Eco's "Ten Little Middle Ages" are found on 68–72.
15. See Kathleen Verduin, "The Founding and the Founder: Medievalism and the Work of Leslie J. Workman," *Studies in Medievalism* 17 (2009): 1–27.
16. Tom Shippey, "Medievalisms and Why They Matter," *Studies in Medievalism* 17 (2009): 45.
17. Eco, "Dreaming the Middle Ages," 63. "Neomedievalism" has since taken on a political valence in relationship to neoconservatism and the breakdown of the post–Cold War world order. See Bruce Holsinger, *Neomedievalism, Neoconservatism, and the War on Terror* (Chicago: Prickly Paradigm Press, 2007).
18. Richard Utz, "Preface: A Moveable Feast: Repositionings of 'the Medieval' in Medieval Studies, Medievalism, and Neomedievalism," in *Neomedievalism in the Media: Essays on Film, Television, and Electronic Games*, ed. Carol L. Robinson and Pamela Clements (Lewiston, ME: Edwin Mellen, 2011), v.
19. Linda Hutcheon, *A Theory of Adaptation* (New York: Routledge, 2006), 3–4.
20. Hutcheon, *Adaptation*, 4.
21. Hutcheon, *Adaptation*, 8.
22. Cited in Hutcheon, *Adaptation*, 6.
23. Gwendolyn A. Morgan, "Medievalism, Authority, and the Academy," *Studies in Medievalism* 17 (2009): 56.
24. They use the terms *immediacy* and *hypermediacy* in *Remediation: Understanding New Media* (Cambridge, MA: MIT Press, 1999), but Bolter clarified the relationship of transparency and hypermediacy in a 2007 piece, "Digital Essentialism and the Mediation of the Real," in *Moving Media Studies: Remediation Revisited*, ed. Heidi Philipsen and Lars Qvortrup (Frederiksberg: Samfundslitterature Press, 2007), 202.
25. Hutcheon, *Adaptation*, 134–35.
26. See the essays on neomedievalism and gaming in *Studies in Medievalism* 16 (2008) and Robinson and Clements, *Neomedievalism in the Media*.
27. Hutcheon, *Adaptation*, 14.
28. Amy Kaufman, "Medieval Unmoored," *Studies in Medievalism* 19 (2010): 4.
29. Sandra S. Abrams, "A Gaming Frame of Mind: Digital Contexts and Academic Implications," *Educational Media International* 46 (2009): 337. The internal quotation is from Gunther Kress and Carey Jewitt, "Introduction," in *New Literacies and Digital Epistemologies: Vol. 4. Multimodal Literacy*, ed. Carey Jewitt and Gunther Kress (New York: Peter Lang, 2008), 1.
30. Abrams, "Gaming," 337–38.

Part I

Prehistory of Medieval Gaming

1 The Right to Dream of the Middle Ages
Simulating the Medieval in Tabletop RPGs

William J. White

> The [fantasy role-playing] campaign, then, is pervaded by the elements of feudalism. Players are urged to absorb as much of the "mental set" of the period as possible to permit role-playing that is authentic. To think as a 20th Century man while conducting a campaign based on feudal society is an unfortunate thing to do, as most of the fun of the thing will be lost.
>
> —Edward E. Simbalist and Wilf K. Backhaus,
> *Chivalry & Sorcery* (1977)

In an essay on the persistence of the Middle Ages in Western culture, Umberto Eco notes that the medieval is invoked in contemporary culture in a variety of ways and to mean a variety of things. In many cases, Eco observes, the invocation of the medieval is mere pretense: "There is no real interest in the historical background; the Middle Ages are taken as a sort of mythological stage on which to place contemporary characters."[1] Alternately, Eco continues, the idea of the 'medieval' may be used to convey something real, as shorthand for a variety of connotations: (1) the atavistically barbaric, (2) the culturally romantic, (3) the historically originary, (4) the artistically decadent, (5) the mystically Hermetic, or (6) the perennially philosophical—when it is not just a device for (7) the ironically self-parodical, à la Monty Python. Sometimes, however, the Middle Ages are indeed the object of sober and serious-minded philological reconstruction, by which Eco means a historiographically sophisticated redescription of medieval modes of thought, language, and action such as that of the Annales school.

Fantasy role-playing games (RPGs), part of a broader fantasy and science fiction fandom that is itself a component of "geek culture,"[2] happen to partake of the invidious division that Eco identifies, with medieval trappings frequently serving only vaguely thematic or pretense-play-enabling functions. In some cases, however—as when a game author is interested in the faithful replication in play of a Middle Ages–inspired game setting—the RPG text may constitute a primer on the reconstruction of the medieval in the service of a more satisfyingly 'realistic' game experience. This orientation to the in-game diegesis as a simulation of some other domain of experience, like a distant era or a foreign place, is called 'Right to Dream' play by some observers of role-playing gaming;[3] it is conceptually similar to the sort of imitative play known as *mimesis*.[4]

This chapter examines the discourse of the medieval within and around four tabletop RPGs that eschew some of the other conventions of 'traditional' secondary-world fantasy role-playing in order to pursue the 'Right to Dream' of the Middle Ages. These works can be seen as explicit efforts to simulate a medieval setting and include *Chivalry & Sorcery* (1977), *Fantasy Wargaming* (1981), *King Arthur Pendragon* (1985), and *Chronica Feudalis* (2009).[5] The various ways in which the medieval is implicated in each game-text—as sociopolitical ordering, as moral framework, as Arthurian structure of feeling, as system of interpersonal relations—are discussed and compared in order to describe the 'dream of the Middle Ages' as role-playing simulation. The epitextual reception of these games—particularly online discussion by fans regarding them—is also traced in order to understand the extent to which they are actually used to simulate the medieval.

TABLETOP ROLE-PLAYING AND DIGITAL GAMING

At this point, it may be necessary to mention that some game studies scholars take the position that nondigital forms of adventure gaming (board games, collectible card games [CCGs], tabletop RPGs, and live-action role-playing [LARP], for example) are outside the purview of their field, or at best are at its margins.[6] This position is understandable, because it allows those scholars to focus on the phenomena of particular interest to them, but it is also unnecessarily limiting as a matter of disciplinary boundary work, for a number of reasons.

The first is the increasing technological sophistication of digital games, which paradoxically makes the experience of play more similar to nondigital games than before. Online games, in particular, with their capacity to allow synchronous high-bandwidth communication among players, foreground the social and communicative aspects of play in ways that dramatically contradict the hoary stereotypes of gaming-as-alienation—and that bear strong similarities to the experience of tabletop play.[7] In a world of highly variegated mediated play, in other words, 'face-to-face' is just another medium. Insights produced in the study of one kind of play may thus be applicable to the other kinds, once differences in media characteristics are accounted for. The concept of *immersion*, for example, may serve as a powerful conceptual framework for understanding all kinds of participatory media.[8]

The second is the cultural entanglement of board gaming (e.g., *Arkham Horror* and *Settlers of Catan*), CCGs (e.g., *Magic: The Gathering* and *Pokemon*), tabletop RPGs (e.g., *Dungeons & Dragons*), and LARP (broadly defined to include sci-fi and comic-book character cosplay [costume play], creatively anachronistic RenFaire participation, and other forms of carnivalesque in-costume 'live-action role-playing') within a broader 'geek culture' that also includes digital games and digital gamers. Many of these activities, in other words, are enjoyed by the same set of people and are thus part of similar and related subcultural experiences.[9]

Third and finally, the historical role of tabletop RPGs as antecedent to and inspiration for many kinds of computer and online gaming has only recently begun to be explored as part of the cultural history of gaming and game design,[10] and further attention to this aspect of gaming's origins is thus warranted. More briefly, there are pragmatic, cultural, and historical reasons for regarding nondigital gaming as an integral part of the gaming scene, and so the scholarship of games and new media cannot limit itself to digital games only without fundamentally mistaking the object of its inquiry. As one game studies scholar has observed, such an extension of the field "is only a problem if we insist that 'digital' is an overriding category, which is both an arbitrary and a technology-fetishizing thing to do."[11]

WHAT IS ROLE-PLAYING?

The tabletop role-playing game emerged in the 1970s as an outgrowth of wargaming with miniature figurines—painted toy soldiers made of lead and arrayed in companies on a battlefield of model-scale terrain and made to fight "little wars"[12]—in which the focus of play shifted from the *military campaign* (i.e., a series of tactical tabletop battles in pursuit of an overall strategic objective) to the *dungeon crawl* (i.e., a sequence of ventures into the depths of an underworld in pursuit, largely, of in-game material gain). Early role-playing systems and supplements assumed a basic familiarity with the conventions of tabletop-miniatures wargaming even as they billed the game as something completely different.[13] What eventually became *Dungeons & Dragons*[14] was a creative amalgam that combined rules for medieval battles with game statistics for fantastic creatures and magical effects as well as the concept of dungeon exploration as the central activity of the game and the individual character (rather than the player's 'army' in aggregate) as the key instrumentality of play.[15] The transformation of the neutral referee who merely arbitrated rules and enforced game mechanical provisions mimicking the 'fog of war' (e.g., tracking the locations of hidden units) into an adversarial 'Dungeon Master' who created dangerous wilderness and dungeon settings for those individual player-characters to explore was also a central element in the origin of the tabletop role-playing game.[16]

Strict historical fidelity was not always a principle of those early Dungeon Masters, even though the appeal of fantasy gaming was understood to be potentially driven by an interest in medieval or military history as well as fantastic literature and mythology. Reading an account of the "first fantasy campaign"[17] more than 30 years after its publication, one 'old-school' gamer reports, "Gamers used to a more straitlaced and serious approach to world building will no doubt find much that offends their sensibilities (turnstiles to enter the dungeon, holy water hoses, souvenirs, etc.) and I'll admit that it's a fair bit more over the top than I'd ever use in my own campaign."[18]

Players, too, approached the game from different perspectives. In an interview for one of the earliest sociological accounts of fantasy role-playing games, M. A. R. Barker, the impresario of a fantasy campaign on the world of Tekumel,[19] describes the differences between two game groups: "The Thursday party is much more of a jolly kind of ha-ha game party, where you have adventures, and you go and you meet people and you do things, and you don't take it all that seriously. Whereas the party that comes on Monday night . . . all come here particularly because they're interested in the reality of Tekumel. They don't care if I ever open the book or ever use a table out of the book, they want to know how it really is on Tekumel."[20]

The range of aesthetic orientations or stylistic approaches that players bring to role-playing is an oft-remarked aspect of tabletop RPGs, and expert players have devoted some energy to making sense of this variety. The earliest attempts tried to catalog players according to their preferred style—the Combat Monster, the Pro from Dover, the Buddy, for example[21]—but soon enough there were efforts to develop more comprehensive and cogent explanations of role-playing as an activity. One of these, developed on a Usenet newsgroup in the 1990s, was called the "Threefold Model." It held that RPG play could be characterized according to the "group contract" that held among the players. 'Dramatism' valued the creation of a satisfying storyline; 'Gamism,' the negotiation of a sufficiently engaging player-level challenge; 'Simulationism,' the enactment of a coherent and internally consistent diegesis, or in-game reality. Based on the short description offered above, we can say only that M. A. R. Barker's Thursday group *may* have had mainly a Gamist orientation, but the sensibilities of his Monday night group seem perfectly Simulationist.[22]

The Threefold Model was taken up, modified, and further articulated in subsequent discussions in an online tabletop RPG design bulletin board called 'the Forge,' with 'Narrativism' replacing 'Dramatism' as the label for the story-oriented approach to play. The discussions on the Forge gave pride of place to Narrativism, defined as a concern in play for addressing an essential question or premise in order to create 'Story Now'; that is, making thematically resonant in-character decisions in the moment of play rather than going through the motions of a predetermined plot ('Story Before') or making narrative sense of a more-or-less random series of in-game events in their aftermath ('Story After'). And while Simulationism was not highly regarded by some Forge theorists, who read 'The Right to Dream' as bearing implications of childish wish-fulfillment and power fantasy,[23] it continued to attract ardent defenders. "Put aside what you think the story should be based on books and movies," advised Kim, "and instead think about the game-world as an alternate reality."[24]

GAMING THE MEDIEVAL

In the last quarter of the twentieth century, however, these understandings of the plurality of role-playing approaches were still inchoate. It was easy to look at how other groups played the game as doing it wrong and to want to produce one's own version of *Dungeons & Dragons* (*D&D*) that did it right. *Empire of the Petal Throne*, for example, emerged as one polyglot professor's attempt to build a coherent fantasy world with its own Southwest Asia–inspired languages, cultures, and mythologies as the backdrop for a *D&D* game. And although Barker's game was explicitly an effort to produce a secondary-world fantasy that stood in direct contrast to Middle Earth, other early RPG designers bent toward Simulationism wanted to delve deeper into the medieval European milieu evoked by Tolkien. The following subsections discuss each of four tabletop role-playing games in chronological order, attempting to find in each the particular set of 'game mechanics' (i.e., rules) that drive its attempt to simulate the medieval. Additionally, some discussion of the reception of each game is offered in order to assess the degree to which the vision of the medieval offered by the game is taken up by its audience.

CHIVALRY AND SORCERY: THE MEDIEVAL AS SOCIOPOLITICAL ORDERING

It seems clear that the creators of *Chivalry and Sorcery* approached role-playing primarily from a Simulationist point of view, inspired as they were by the example of M. A. R. Barker's *Empire of the Petal Throne*.[25] "To play FRP [fantasy role-play] is to engage in the creation of a group fantasy," announced coauthor Ed Simbalist in collection of essays by then-prominent RPG authors in the first issue of a 1979 fan magazine, "to produce the Grand Illusion of a world ethos by the deliberate suspension of one's disbelief."[26]

Though it would later become relatively obscure, in the earliest days *Chivalry and Sorcery* (*C&S*) could be regarded as "in some sense *D&D*'s major competition, in that it is also based loosely on the medieval period." Its main point of differentiation from *D&D* was that "while *D&D* deemphasizes social structure, *C&S* revels in it."[27] The rules encourage players to choose human characters rather than members of Tolkienesque fantasy races such as elves, dwarves, or halflings, because they "are not really part of daily life in human society and cannot hope to establish themselves as great lords beloved by their subjects. They are 'foreigners' and they are 'different,' two serious penalties to overcome in any feudal society."[28] The social features identified for human characters include "the social class of their fathers, their sibling rank within the family, their status in the family, and the vocation of their fathers."[29] These contribute to the character's overall social status, which may then "be modified by one's own deeds and experiences."[30]

Additionally, *C&S* gives characters an interpersonal resource called *influence*, taking the form of favors and debts of honor owed by other characters and defined as "the capacity of a character to win personal support from another character";[31] no such currency existed in *D&D*. The effect was to create a game where players had a strong sense of their character's biographical grounding. As one player put it, "If I really want to feel what my character is, then I'll play *C&S*."[32]

However, *C&S* received a mixed reception from players from the moment it appeared. Some appreciated the game as "realistic" and "internally consistent," whereas others found it "complicated" and "tedious" due to the complexity of its character-generation procedures as well as its rules for magic use.[33] Later, players would recall it as an "exercise in frustration" and "too complex" to teach others, one going so far as to describe it as "an incredibly complicated medieval fantasy heartbreaker with a bunch of non-cited historical stuff added in,"[34] although one long-time *C&S* game master suggested that by starting with a simple set of core rules and adding in more complex elements over time, he and his group were able to learn the game quite easily.[35] Even sociologist Gary Alan Fine, author of a seminal ethnography of the early role-playing scene and thus ostensibly a disinterested observer, found himself taking a mild stance on the merits of *Chivalry & Sorcery*. The detailed information about characters and their places in the world generated in *C&S* "would be counter-productive in *D&D*," he says, "which is focused on the adventure rather than the society."[36]

For some players, this was part of the game's charm, with the complexities of creating a character leading to player engagement with the game.[37] "*C&S* is not a game to be taken lightly; in fact, to play it at all requires much more attention than a game such as *D&D*," reports one old-school gamer. He goes on:

> C&S . . . had rules for chirurgeons [a thirteenth-century Middle English word for "surgeon"] with the ability to set bones and perform surgeries [instead of abstract, fungible "hit points" like *D&D*]. When coupled with the insanely detailed rules for building construction and magical research, most of the game was spent in "down time," with a focus on what the characters were doing when NOT adventuring. It was far more fun to make up characters and age them, never once doing any sort of dungeon delving. The system itself was designed for all the offscreen activities, and that has always been the appeal of C&S to me.[38]

In other words, the game was constructed so that players were motivated to avoid the risks of 'going on an adventure' in favor of fulfilling their expected social roles: nobles managed their domains, wizards created enchantments, priests oversaw their flocks, and others plied their trades (respectable or otherwise) in order to gain the experience that would allow them to advance in level. Notice how this pursues the Simulationist 'Right to Dream' by foregrounding the character as an individual occupying a specific place in the game world, rather than as the instrument of the player (as in Gamism) or the protagonist of a coherent narrative (as in Narrativism).

FANTASY WARGAMING: THE MEDIEVAL AS MORAL FRAMEWORK

Fantasy Wargaming (FW) was created, beginning in the late 1970s, by a group of wargamers and science fiction fans that included graduate students in history at Cambridge University who were motivated by a desire for a more historically grounded fantasy role-playing campaign.[39] Central to their efforts was a 'unified field theory' of magic that would provide an underlying rationale for the in-game operation of the supernatural, which they saw as the "heart of fantasy gaming."[40] "Religious and magical power were of the same type" in the Middle Ages, "but had different origins."[41] Magical spells were enabled by the witch's belief in herself; religious miracles came from the priest's belief in God. In each case, however, human will and belief were the central elements.

To be sure, social class in *Fantasy Wargaming* did play an important role in determining character abilities and effectiveness.[42] But it was not as fundamentally character defining as it was in *Chivalry and Sorcery*. Social mobility was built into *FW* via automatic increases in social class ranking at regular intervals upon advancing in level as well as through the possibility of 'buying up' into higher ranks by spending the character's adventuring loot. The moral and spiritual dimensions of characters were given much greater weight in the rules. In addition to the traditional *D&D* attributes of Strength (called Physique), Intelligence, Dexterity (called Agility), Constitution (called Endurance), and Charisma are Bravery, Faith, Greed, Selfishness, Lust, Piety, and Faith. These latter attributes serve mainly to determine the character's ability to withstand temptation and to avoid succumbing to vice.

Moreover, the character's adherence to the behavioral code of his or her religion (the 'Dark Age' options of Christianity, Satanism, or Teutonic paganism, where the term *Dark Ages* is used by the game's authors to evoke the medieval in Eco's sense of atavistic barbarism) determined his or her standing with the Higher and Lower powers, and thus the chance to plead successfully for divine or infernal intervention. The attribute of Piety "rises and falls according to your [character's] behavior, and the attention you pay your god. Behavior can be divided into virtues, which bring an increase in Christian piety, and sins, which bring about a corresponding decrease. For the Devil worshipper, the position is exactly reversed."[43] The dangers of moral transgression are real, with sinful behavior quantified according to its severity and subtracted from the character's Piety score. Once Piety is sufficiently low, "characters *will* receive an awful warning from the Higher powers [and] *may* also receive a visitation from the Devil, claiming their soul."⁴⁴ There are rules for a character's soul going to Heaven or Hell (which depends upon the character's Piety at death), becoming a saint or demon, and passing through Purgatory.

Most of the religion rules are couched in terms of the polarity of Christianity and Satanism, but provisions are also made for characters to worship the Norse gods, with the major differences being the classification of behavior as sinful or virtuous. Heroism and "sustaining honorable injury in the service of others" are the highest virtues, while "manslaughter in battle is not a sin unless one's opponent is the sort of person it's beneath one's dignity to kill."⁴⁵ Additionally, a calculation for a pagan to get into Valhalla at death is provided. Thus, the assumption of the reality of the supernatural allows the Dark Ages trappings of *Fantasy Wargaming* to produce a moral landscape characterized by the demands and nearly palpable presence of the heavenly, infernal, and pagan hosts as judges, guardians, and intercessors— encouraging players to react to the game world in a way the evokes medieval European cultural attitudes.

In general, this aspect of *Fantasy Wargaming* was not widely appreciated by players then or now. While regarded as a useful resource on the medieval period, it is held to be poorly written, badly organized, and confusingly formatted, for some to the point of unplayability. Some critics are put off by the invidious in-game distinctions made by the designers between sexes and among religions.⁴⁶ Very few of the gamers who discuss it in online forums have ever played it. "Most role-players have probably never heard of *Fantasy Wargaming*," observes one online discussion group participant. "Those who have probably think of it as the game which stats the Virgin Mary and [the Norse God] Balder."⁴⁷ This reference to providing in-game statistics for divine figures implies that there is something a little inappropriate about doing so, as if the game designer expected player-characters to do battle with the Virgin Mary (rather than call for her intercession).

KING ARTHUR PENDRAGON: THE MEDIEVAL AS ARTHURIAN STRUCTURE OF FEELING

In *King Arthur Pendragon,* the player-characters are Arthurian knights who fight their battles, pursue their quests, and live their lives while the events of the Arthurian legend play out as the backdrop to years, and even generations, of in-game play. Its designer, Greg Stafford, who also wrote an early and well-regarded competitor to *Dungeons & Dragons* called *RuneQuest,*⁴⁸ regards it as his "gaming masterpiece,"⁴⁹ and it has been recognized for its "unprecedented emphasis on epic, generational storytelling."⁵⁰ Stafford's recently published supplement for *Pendragon,* called *The Great Pendragon Campaign,* provides rule details for running a game in which the players begin as knights fighting in the wars of Uther Pendragon and end up as their grandchildren or great-grandchildren dealing with the aftermath of Arthur's death at the Battle of Camlann.[51] "Whole families of knights vie for Glory across the years from the Sword in the Stone to the final days of Camelot."[52]

Glory is a central game mechanic. Each character begins the game with a certain amount of Glory, reflected from the deeds of his forefathers, and seeks to accrue more through his own deeds so that he may progress from ordinary knight through the stations of notable and famous knight to become an extraordinary knight like Lancelot or Gawain. Knights may gain Glory from combat, through marriage, and from chivalrous acts of generosity, courage, or courtesy.

But because "the Arthurian tales are full of intense emotion, much of it uncontrolled,"[53] knights are also driven by in-game passions. Passions represent the commitment of the character to medieval mores and customs. They include "religion, love, hate, amor [i.e., courtly love], loyalty, envy, and anything else which the game will admit into the game."[54] For example, a character who encounters Queen Guenever for the first time must check to see if "the queen's regal beauty has instantly kindled a new Amor (Guenever) passion."[55] In play, when a character is confronted by a situation in which the passion is relevant, the player rolls to see if the character is moved by that passion to heights of inspiration, with consequent game-mechanical advantages; potential negative effects of succumbing to passion include becoming disheartened, melancholy, or mad. Sufficiently powerful passions are a source of Glory for the character as well.

Additionally, characters have 'traits,' presented as opposing pairs of personality features: chaste/lustful, energetic/lazy, generous/selfish, honest/deceitful, valorous/cowardly, and so forth. Characters are ranked for each trait on a spectrum that ranges from one to twenty. Traits work much like passions: when a situation presents itself to the character as an opportunity (or a temptation) to indulge a certain trait, the player must roll to see what sort of behavior the character exhibits. For example, when confronted with an enemy of notable prowess, the player might be required to make a 'valorous check' to avoid having his or her character turn tail and flee.

The effect of these rules is to embed the player-characters in the cultural perspective that underlies *Le Morte d'Arthur* and related Arthurian legends: the Dark Ages seen through late medieval eyes. "Drawing from every source in history and legend, *Pendragon* presents a matchless totality," an observer comments, "one of the rare role-playing books that stands as genuine scholarship."[56] What is being simulated in the play of this game is thus less a historical reality than a literary genre. Historically minded players seem to appreciate the game at this level. According to one *Pendragon* game master (GM), "the players were very much awed by the feeling of the game, they really got into the 'immersion' of seeing themselves as a band of young almost-knights . . . I think the players were all also very amused by the combination of history and legend that the setting comprises, the little historical details that made the setting come alive, and the importance of religion . . . to the atmosphere of dark-ages Britain."[57]

CHRONICA FEUDALIS: THE MEDIEVAL
AS SYSTEM OF INTERPERSONAL RELATIONS

Chronica Feudalis is one of many small-press games to have been published over the past decade as print-on-demand services have become increasingly economical[58] and an audience for 'indie games' has emerged.[59] It is much slimmer than the other three games discussed here, amounting to only 122 digest-sized pages, of which no more than seventeen are devoted to presenting medieval Europe as the game setting; it is 'rules light' in comparison as well.

Characters are created by selecting 'mentors' such as archers, knights, priests, peasants, outlaws, courtiers, monks, and other vaguely medieval archetypes. A character's mentors provide him or her with training in personal skills as well as 'tools' (a bow and arrow, a suit of armor, a crucifix, a pair of shoes, and so forth) that enhance the ability to use those skills. Additionally, those mentors serve as points of contact between the players and the fiction; they are a resource that may be drawn upon in play for information, aid, and succor as well as a potential source of fictional complications, as player-characters react to the needs of their mentors, who are important people in their lives.

Players also define 'Aspects' of the character; these are descriptive phrases that encapsulate the character's physical description or notable abilities, worldview, social rank and position, access to resources, and so forth. One character might be described as a "fearless knight," a "sword master," and the "protector of Lord Hugh," while another might have the Aspects "chaste cavalier," "sanguine temperament," and "For the love of my Queen!" Aspects can be invoked by either the player or the GM; the former when the Aspect provides a situational advantage; the latter, when it provides a disadvantage. For example, to be the "protector of Lord Hugh" might be advantageous when mustering one's courage to defend him from foes on the battlefield, but a liability when the Aspect requires one to interpose oneself between the young nobleman and an enemy's blade. Note that this allows (or requires) the players to build their own social, economic, psychological, and moral constraints into their characters, and so imagines a degree of historical knowledge being brought by players to the table rather than imposed upon players by the structure of the rules.

The game rules expect player-characters to come into conflict with GM-controlled non-player characters (NPCs) and advise the GM to create a 'relationship map' that shows patterns of sympathy and points of tension among those NPCs within which their characters will act. Reports of actual play describe games that make use of this technique to drive the action in the fiction, emphasizing power struggles and conflicts among characters with competing interests and goals rather than traditional heroic fantasy.[60]

WRITING THE DREAM OF THE MIDDLE AGES

These four games provide a longitudinal slice of a particular subgenre within tabletop RPGs, the medieval historical game. If they can in any sense be said to evolve, it is in growing increasingly focused and self-aware about the type of experience they are seeking to create. Whereas both *Chivalry & Sorcery* and *Fantasy Wargaming* presented themselves as describing 'how to play RPGs,' *Pendragon* and *Chronica Feudalis* explicitly set out to emulate a particular sort of fiction—Arthurian legends in the case of the former and modern historical fiction set in medieval Europe in that of the latter. Additionally, the audiences for those games are increasingly aware of the game as offering a choice about how and what to play for the time being, rather than as requiring a commitment to a particular philosophy of play, as seems to be the case for the earlier games.

All four games make an effort to describe the Middle Ages, or at least a version of them, as a way of introducing players to the game setting. The economic structures and imperatives of feudal society play an important role in *Chivalry & Sorcery* and *Pendragon*; they are slightly less important in *Fantasy Wargaming* (which seems to expect its characters to make their fortunes via dungeon crawling) and entirely abstract in *Chronica Feudalis*, which relies instead on GM-created relationship maps and other in-game setting information to provide the context of character action.

What is most interesting about these games is the way that game mechanics are employed to create a particular structure of incentives for players. In the case of *C&S* and *FW*, these structures seem almost inadvertent, as if the game designers were not quite aware of how the rules they created would shape in-game behavior. In the case of the latter two games, however, the authors describe particular game design choices as being motivated by goals for how the game is to 'feel' in play.[61]

Finally, the reliance on 'personality mechanics' (e.g., Bravery, Greed, and so forth in *FW*; passions and traits in *Pendragon*; Aspects in *Chronica Feudalis*) in three of the four games is suggestive, implying a vision of the medieval as *nonrational*, in the technical sense of not operating according to a strict calculus of utility maximization. Players are given incentives to act in 'inefficient' ways to keep the game going. In most of these games, in other words, players direct their characters to act not on self-interested instrumental grounds (as in *C&S*) but based on the dictates of psychological commitments and emotional connections that have been represented in terms defined by the games' rules. The ability to successfully 'dream of the Middle Ages,' as Eco would have it, would thus seem to be enabled by rules of play that layer the political economy of feudal society beneath the cultural ideals of the medieval era. An interesting further direction for inquiry would be to examine the phenomenological basis for a satisfying mimetic experience: is it rooted in an aesthetic appreciation of the experience as its first-person audience,[62] or in patterns of "parasocial" or imagined solidarity with the denizens of the game world?[63]

NOTES

1. Umberto Eco, "Dreaming of the Middle Ages," in *Travels in Hyperreality*, trans. William Weaver (New York: Harcourt, Brace, Jovanovich, 1986), 86.
2. J. A. McArthur, "Digital Subculture: A Geek Meaning of Style," *Journal of Communication Inquiry* 33 (2009): 58–70.
3. Emily Care Boss, "Key Concepts in Forge Theory," in *Playground Worlds*, ed. Markus Montola and Jaakko Stenros (Jyvaskyla, Finland: Ropecon ry, 2008), 232–47.
4. Roger Caillois, *Man, Play, and Games* (Champagne: University of Illinois Press, 2001).
5. Edward E. Simbalist and Wilf K. Backhaus, *The C&S Red Book* (Cambrose, Alberta: Gamestuff, 2000); Bruce Galloway, *Fantasy Wargaming* (New York: Stein and Day, 1981); Greg Stafford, *King Arthur Pendragon* (Oakland, CA: Chaosium, 1985); Jeremy Keller, *Chronica Feudalis* (Minneapolis, MN: Cellar Games, 2009).
6. Jesper Juul, *Half-Real: Video Games between Real Rules and Fictional Worlds* (Cambridge, MA: MIT Press, 2005).
7. T. L. Taylor, *Play between Worlds* (Cambridge, MA: MIT Press, 2006).
8. Evan Torner and William J. White, eds., *Immersive Gameplay* (Jefferson, NC: McFarland, 2012).
9. Henry Jenkins, *Fans, Bloggers, and Gamers* (New York: New York University Press, 2006); J. Patrick Williams, Sean Q. Hendricks, and W. Keith Winkler, *Gaming as Culture* (Jefferson, NC: McFarland, 2006).
10. Michael J. Tresca, *The Evolution of Fantasy Role-Playing Games* (Jefferson, NC: McFarland, 2011).
11. Espen J. Aarseth, "How We Became Postdigital," in *Critical Cyberculture Studies*, ed. David Silver and Adrienne Massanari (New York: New York University Press, 2006), 41.
12. H. G. Wells, *Little Wars* (Spring Branch, TX: Skirmisher Press, 2011).
13. Erik Mona, "From the Basement to the Basic Set: The Early Years of *Dungeons & Dragons*," in *Second Person*, ed. Pat Harrigan and Noah Wardrip-Fruin (Cambridge, MA: MIT Press, 2007).
14. E. Gary Gygax and Dave Arneson, *Dungeons & Dragons* (Lake Geneva, WI: TSR, 1974).
15. Tresca, *Evolution of Fantasy Role-Playing Games*, 60–62; Ron Edwards, "A Hard Look at Dungeons & Dragons," *The Forge*, http://www.indie-rpgs.com/articles/20 (accessed July 17, 2012).
16. Wilf K. Backhaus. "Once Upon a Time: The Secret History of RPGs," *Places to Go, People to Be*, http://ptgptb.org/0015/retro.html (accessed July 17, 2012).
17. Dave Arneson, *The First Fantasy Campaign* (Charlottesville, VA: Iron Crown, 1977).
18. James Maliszewski, "Retrospective: The First Fantasy Campaign," *Grognardia*, http://grognardia.blogspot.com/2009/04/retrospective-first-fantasy-campaign.html (accessed July 17, 2012).
19. M. A. R. Barker, *Empire of the Petal Throne* (Lake Geneva, WI: TSR, 1975).

20. Gary Alan Fine, *Shared Fantasy* (Chicago: University of Chicago Press, 1983), 145.
21. Aaron Allston, *Strike Force* (Charlottesville, VA: Iron Crown, 1988).
22. John H. Kim, *The Threefold Model FAQ*, http://www.darkshire.net/jhkim/rpg/theory/threefold/faq_v1.html (accessed July 19, 2012).
23. Ron Edwards, "All-out Dissection (LONG and BRUTAL)," *The Forge*, http://indie-rpgs.com/archive/index.php?topic=24.0 (accessed August 1, 2011).
24. John H. Kim, *Threefold Simulationism Explained*, http://www.darkshire.net/jhkim/rpg/theory/threefold/simulationism.html (accessed July 17, 2012).
25. Wilf K. Backhaus, "Readers' Forum," *Places to Go, People to Be*, http://ptgptb.org/0015/forum.html (accessed July 26, 2012).
26. Fine, *Shared Fantasy*, 121.
27. Fine, *Shared Fantasy*, 18.
28. Simbalist and Backhaus, *C&S Red Book*, 12.
29. Simbalist and Backhaus, *C&S Red Book*, 30.
30. Simbalist and Backhaus, *C&S Red Book*, 35.
31. Simbalist and Backhaus, *C&S Red Book*, 37.
32. Fine, *Shared Fantasy*, 19.
33. Fine, *Shared Fantasy*, 18–19.
34. Zomben, "Chivalry and Sorcery—Who Played It? How Was It?" *RPG.net Forums*, http://forum.rpg.net/showthread.php?425109-Chivalry-amp-Sorcery-Who-Played-it-How-was-it (accessed July 23, 2012).
35. Shane Devries, "History of C&S as I Know It," *Chivalry & Sorcery RPG Fan Site*, http://chivalrysorcery.myfastforum.org/History_of_C_amp_S_as_know_it__about14.html (accessed July 23, 2012).
36. Fine, *Shared Fantasy*, 18.
37. Devries, "History of C&S."
38. Brad Ncube, "Chivalry and Sorcery Playtest (Retroactive Analysis)," *Skull Crushing for Great Justice*, http://crushingskulls.blogspot.com/2011/07/chivalry-sorcery-playtest-retroactive.html (accessed July 26, 2012).
39. Mike Monaco, "Bruce Galloway's *Fantasy Wargaming*," *Swords & Dorkery*, http://mikemonaco.wordpress.com/bruce-galloways-fantasy-wargaming/ (accessed July 26, 2012).
40. Galloway, *Fantasy Wargaming*, 17.
41. Galloway, *Fantasy Wargaming*, 18.
42. Felix, "[Let's Read] *Fantasy Wargaming* (Seriously)," *RPG.net Forums*, http://forum.rpg.net/showthread.php?422199-Let-s-Read-Fantasy-Wargaming-(seriously) (accessed July 27, 2012).
43. Galloway, *Fantasy Wargaming*, 158.
44. Galloway, *Fantasy Wargaming*, 161.
45. Galloway, *Fantasy Wargaming*, 181.
46. David Johansen, "Bwahahaahahahah!!! I Have It and I Just Might Run It," *RPG.net Forums*, http://forum.rpg.net/archive/index.php/t-219474.html (accessed July 27, 2012); Lord Gorath, "*Fantasy Wargaming*, by Bruce Galloway," *Dragonsfoot Forums*, http://s123723500.websitehome.co.uk/forums/viewtopic.php?f=20&t=12045&sid=8e8145fafa73290de20b455f2a4db1b7 (accessed July 26, 2012); Siskoid, "RPGs That Time Forgot . . . *Fantasy Wargaming*," *Siskoid's Blog of Geekery*, http://siskoid.blogspot.com/2007/07/rpgs-that-time-forgot-fantasy-wargaming.html (accessed July 27, 2012); John "Omega" Williams, "*Fantasy Wargaming*: Hangins' Too Good for 'Em!!!" *RPG Geek*, http://rpggeek.com/thread/365078/fantasy-wargaming-hangins-too-good-fer-em (accessed July 27, 2012).
47. Felix, "[Let's Read] *Fantasy Wargaming*."

48. Greg Stafford, *RuneQuest* (Oakland, CA: Chaosium, 1978).
49. Greg Stafford, *Greg Stafford's Pendragon Page*, http://www.gspendragon. com (accessed July 30, 2012).
50. Allen Varney, "Greg Stafford, Mythmaker," *The Escapist*, http://www. escapistmagazine.com/articles/view/columns/days-of-high-adventure/6709- Greg-Stafford-Mythmaker#at (accessed July 30, 2012).
51. Greg Stafford, *The Great Pendragon Campaign* (Stone Mountain, GA: White Wolf Publishing, 2006).
52. Varney, "Greg Stafford, Mythmaker."
53. Greg Stafford, *King Arthur Pendragon*, 4th ed. (Oakland, CA: Green Knight Publishing, 1999), 199.
54. Stafford, *King Arthur Pendragon*, 199.
55. Stafford, *King Arthur Pendragon*, 202.
56. Varney, "Greg Stafford, Mythmaker."
57. John Tarnowski, "Actual Play: *Pendragon*," *The RPG Site*, http://www. therpgsite.com/showthread.php?t-10668 (accessed July 30, 2012).
58. Judith Rosen, "Distribution in a Digital Age," *Publishers Weekly* (April 16, 2012): 18–23.
59. Ron Edwards, "Understanding the Pool," http://adept-press.com/wordpress/ wp-content/media/Understanding_The_Pool.pdf (accessed August 1, 2011).
60. Eisenmann, "*Chronica Feudalis:* Witness," *RPG.net Forums*, http://forum. rpg.net/showthread.php?452092-Chronica-Feudalis-Witness (accessed July 31, 2012); Zac Dettwyler, "[Chronica Feudalis] Not What I Expected," *Abby's Place*, http://abbysgamerbasement.blogspot.com/2010/11/chronica- feudalis-not-what-i-expected.html (accessed July 31, 2012).
61. Jeremy Keller, "[Chronica Feudalis] Pinging Your Radar, Medievally," *Story Games*, http://www.story-games.com/forums/discussion/comment/234941 (accessed July 31, 2012); Stafford, "Greg Stafford's Pendragon Page."
62. M. M. Bakhtin, "Author and Hero in Aesthetic Activity," in *Art and Answer- ability*, trans. Vadim Liapunov (Austin: University of Texas Press, 1990); Markus Montola, "The Invisible Rules of Role-Playing," *International Journal of Role-Playing* 1, no. 1 (2008): 22–36.
63. Emile Durkheim, *The Division of Labor in Society*, trans. W. D. Halls. (New York: Free Press, 1984).

Part II

Gaming Re-imagines Medieval Traditions

2 "Best and Only Bulwark"·
How Epic Narrative Redeems
Beowulf: The Game

Candace Barrington and Timothy English

Anyone familiar with the Old English poem *Beowulf* who then plays *Beowulf: The Game* (2007) would be struck by the game's significant differences with the poem's narrative shape, its characters' motivations, and its thematic thrust.[1] Some of these differences are the consequence of the gaming environment. For instance, while Beowulf remains the central figure (with the player controlling the actions of Beowulf from a bird's-eye view as the legendary hero faces hordes of enemies), Hrothgar becomes a constant presence as the narrator. Unlike the poem and *Beowulf: The Movie* (the game's ancillary film), both of which present events achronologically, the game's linear interface presents events in sequential order to players, beginning with Beowulf's swimming race with Breca, an event the poem and the film recall in retrospect during a feast at Heorot.[2] Other differences between the poem and the game have less to do with the mechanics of gameplay and more to do with fulfilling expectations of the game's target audience. The resulting changes can be classified into three sets. The first set of changes fill some continuity gaps in the Old English *Beowulf*. As does the film, the game provides a backstory for Grendel and his mother, thereby explaining Hrothgar's paralysis in the face of great calamity and Beowulf's insistence that he single-handedly fight the dragon. The adaptations also depict the scops' early transformation of a flawed man's exploits into a hero's adventures of epic proportion. The game builds further on the desire for continuity by accounting for the lost years between Beowulf's investiture as a king and his final, fatal confrontation with the fire-breathing Wyrm. A second set of changes exaggerates aspects of the tale derived from the Germanic warrior tradition, rebarbarizing the Anglo-Saxons who exhibit much self-conscious sophistication in the poem. These two sets of changes work together to introduce a third, a thematic tension between a flawed, self-interested man and the perfect, selfless hero. The game underscores this tension through a series of choices the player makes for Beowulf. This essay will examine these three sets of changes and make two conclusions, one regarding purists' outrage over the perceived desecration of the ancient *Beowulf,* the other regarding gamers' rejection of a game that so manhandles *Beowulf* for the sake of pleasing them.

RE-IMAGINING CONTINUITY GAPS

The continuity gaps in *Beowulf* provide a prime opportunity for adaptations to adjust the narrative in order to suit expectations of contemporary audiences. *Beowulf: The Movie* filled many of these gaps, according to the screenwriter Roger Avary, by "remain[ing] true to the letter of the epic" while "read[ing] between the lines and find[ing] greater trust than had been explored before."[3] Not surprisingly, with its parallel title and its near coincident release, *Beowulf: The Game* incorporates most of them. In both, Hrothgar is seduced by Grendel's mother and sires the monster, thereby causing the enmity between the Danes of Heorot and the two Grendelkin. Burdened by his guilt, the aged Hrothgar (voiced in both by Anthony Hopkins) holds only a tentative grip on himself, his wife, and his once mighty kingdom; his wife, a young Wealtheow, aware of his monstrous bargain, alternates moodily between sad resignation and inexplicable flirtiness. Beowulf, in turn, is also seduced, and his spawn is the dragon, thus explaining to the early twenty-first-century audience why all three monsters belong in the same epic. Moreover, the inconsistencies among Beowulf's accounts of his exploits are embraced, demonstrating how legends aggrandize the original events. And the source of antagonism between Unferth and Beowulf becomes more than a mead-hall rivalry, deriving instead from the clash between pagan heroism and upstart Christianity, represented by Unferth, whose priestly robes and thin, dark, unhealthy appearance recall the conspiratorial Rasputin. In addition to these adaptations to the Anglo-Saxon text, the game also adds three more episodes, each explaining, in turn, the source of Beowulf's martial prowess, the long-term consequences of Beowulf's rivalry with Breca, and the events that filled the first fifty winters of Beowulf's kingship. As we will see, these changes often serve dual, triple, or even multiple purposes, working to make the narrative fit gamers' expectations for the mechanics of playing, reinforcing gamers' notions of medieval barbarism, and contributing to the thematic tension between the carnal and heroic.

In order to explain Beowulf's supernatural strength, the game commandeers the film's re-imagining of Grendel's mother as an otherworldly *femme fatale*. In the film and the game, Hrothgar falls prey to her allure and sires Grendel, a blood-drinking monster with the power of twenty men and the emotional maturity of an abandoned three-year old. Beowulf, too, is seduced by her. She promises he will achieve immortality through the legends repeated about his extraordinary exploits. As a result of this deal, he begets on her a monster even more terrifying than the mead-hall brawling Grendel: a fire-breathing dragon bent on destroying the entire kingdom. Beowulf's seduction by Grendelsmere happens in the film when the hero seeks her out after she attacks Heorot bent on revenge for Grendel's death. The game, however, introduces Beowulf's entrapment early, during the game's opening race between Breca and Beowulf when our hero is dragged

underwater by sea monsters. In this opening sequence of the game, Beowulf
meets Grendel's mother. She makes him her champion and imbues him with
great strength, a gift that he can choose to draw on at the cost of his virtue. The player then faces the sea snakes again but easily dispatches them
with Beowulf's new carnal strength. Not only does this addition account
for Beowulf's superhuman strength apparent from early in the poem, but it
also advances the gameplay in two ways. It introduces to the player first the
thematic tension that shapes much of the game and second the ability to call
upon extra resources, while requiring the player to calculate the cost of those
resources to future play. So, as gratuitous as this episode might seem to be,
it adds essential elements in the transition from film to game.

The years between Beowulf's investiture and the dragon's devastating
attacks, which both the poem and the film gloss over, the game fills with
a series of loosely related, episodic adventures drawn from Nordic, Gaelic,
and Greek mythology and epics. These adventures allow Beowulf to increase
his power as he protects and consolidates his kingdom. They begin with
Beowulf and his men rescuing scantily clad, blonde farm girls (repeatedly
identified as virgins by level labels and the instructions barked by Hrothgar) from giant kidnapping trolls who intend to deliver the girls to cultists
(resembling the Neanderthal invaders in *The 13th Warrior*), who, in turn,
plan to sacrifice the girls to a giant flaming wolf skeleton.[4] In order to defeat
the cult and kill the giant wolf skeleton, Beowulf receives from a village
witch both a magic talisman and guidance through the bogs to the cultists'
lair. Afterwards, Beowulf returns to Heorot, only to be criticized for resembling a wolf himself. Clearly, these continuity fillers are little more than
that— fillers. However, they become an uninhibited opportunity for inserting
desirable, barbaric violence gleaned from a wide range of ancient, medieval,
and contemporary sources.

The game continues to fill in those fifty winters by following up on the
antagonism between Beowulf and Breca, an adversary from his youth. Jealous and vindictive, Breca somehow allies himself with the Formor, a race of
small, hairy apes with goat heads, loosely based on the seafaring Fomoire
or Fomorians of Irish mythology. In the game they are the spitting image of
the apelike trolls in *Willow;* however, their existence is not explained, and
they serve no narrative purpose.[5] Breca's invasion is repelled in a sequence
where Beowulf retakes and holds a beachhead position. The player must use
Beowulf and his half dozen or so thanes to occupy a pair of trenches leading
up to a large wooden Celtic cross. Breca's Vikings and monsters, landing
on the beach in longboats, all make a beeline for the cross and attempt to
destroy it. In addition to providing a follow-up on the antagonism between
Breca and Beowulf, this episode in the game marks Heorot's abrupt transition from paganism to Christianity. The same witch who had previously
given Beowulf a runic talisman to guide him in the bog now gives him a
crucifix that magically opens certain doors. Wiglaf is cautiously optimistic
about their new religion, but Breca and the narrating Hrothgar both deride

Christianity as encouraging weakness. The tension between Christian and pagan values also corresponds loosely to the larger thematic tension between selfless heroic values and selfish carnal ones, though the paired values do not always line up.

Once Breca's invasion is repelled, the game continues to follow the two enemies when Beowulf takes ship and chases Breca to Iceland, where they meet in combat atop a cliff, and Beowulf kills Breca. Beowulf then takes his thanes and sails through *The Odyssey* and into the icy kingdom of Hel, where they fight their way through the underworld to the foot of a pinnacle where Hel's throne sits. Beowulf climbs to the top of the pillar, strangles the death-goddess—voiced by a sound-alike of the late Patricia Hayes in her role as Fin Raziel in *Willow*—and returns home. This sequence is perhaps the most baffling of any in the entire game. Beyond filling in Beowulf's lost years, the sequence provides another opportunity for incorporating a scattershot array of medieval Nordic elements.

REBARBARIZATION

As we have repeatedly seen, *Beowulf: The Game* is packed with a hodgepodge of elements taken from Greek, Germanic, and Norse mythology, as well as popular cinema and other hack-and-slash games. Because these barbarizing elements are seen as highly appealing to target audiences, game developers also exaggerate the perceived barbarisms originally found in the Old English epic by amplifying the hypermasculine debauchery of the meadhall and by overlaying it with an appalling sexism. All these elements build on a sense that the Middle Ages were a period in which the strong dominated the weak, men drank to excess, and women were forced to submit to men's desires.

Sometimes these inflated barbaric elements are a means to vary the gameplay. For instance, when the Geats first sail to the Danish coast, the player finds himself at the helm of a Viking longship, pounding drums and shouting encouragement at the rowers to fight through the waves and fog. To achieve this level's goals, the player must complete a sort of Simon-Says game in which a sequence of buttons flash on the screen and the player must repeat them correctly. At other times, these extravagantly medieval scenes add additional levels of play. When Beowulf lands on the beach of Denmark with Wiglaf and his Geatish thanes, they must fight their way through hordes of bandits up the cliffs and across the countryside towards embattled Heorot. Unlike in either the poem or the film, Beowulf and his Geatish troops are not met by a friendly Danish guard who escorts them unmolested to Hrothgar's court. Instead, the player fights between fifty and one hundred men in this sequence and encourages his thanes to roll boulders out of his way. Later, after Beowulf vanquishes Grendel, the player must spend another hour directing the hero to kill more bandits in the countryside. Similarly, the game introduces a new element by following the hero's prebattle boasts with a round of loud and bawdy song (which relies heavily on rhyming 'lass' with 'ass'). In this set of enhancements, neither narrative nor characters are complicated; instead, players receive heavy doses of barbarism.

CARNAL VERSUS HEROIC

Taken together, efforts to correct the continuity gaps and the rebarbarisms support the film's thematic exploration of the tension between a flawed, self-absorbed man and the perfect, selfless hero. This process begins when Beowulf receives the gift of great strength from Grendel's mother. Called the 'Carnal Mode,' this power is employed throughout the game as a means to show a philosophical crisis in the protagonist. The game embeds the structural tension when it makes the narrator from Hrothgar, who has undoubtedly been overwhelmed by the Carnal Mode, while keeping Beowulf, who fights the allure of the Carnal, the central figure controlled by the player. In every fight, the player chooses between drawing on either the respect of his loyal thanes to inspire them to victory or the bloody rage gifted by Grendel's mother. Activating Carnal Mode gives the player more powerful attacks and grants a bonus to quick-time events, yet that choice often causes the player inadvertently to kill his own allies.[6] The game is further structured to encourage players to focus on either the Carnal or Heroic aspects by giving experience points to unlock more powerful abilities at the end of each stage based on which mode the player uses to complete it.

Because Beowulf is tainted from the beginning by the Carnal Mode, the game does not allow the hero to emerge unscathed by his carnality. We see this phenomenon played out in the sequence after Beowulf's expedition to avenge Grendelsmere's attack on Heorot. Instead of the film's lengthy exposition wherein Beowulf returns to Heorot claiming that he has killed Grendel's dame (when, in fact, he has been seduced by her), and Hrothgar proclaims, before leaping to his death, that Beowulf should succeed him as the king of the Danes and the husband of Wealtheow, the game simply omits the transfer of power. Only a few seconds pass between the moment when Beowulf kneels in the troll-dam's cave and gives her Wealtheow's radiant dragon cup and the moment when Beowulf finds himself roughly awoken in Heorot by an irritated thane. The kingdom—suddenly his own—has come under attack. Beowulf mutters, "King? Of the . . . Danes?" and seems to have no recollection of the intervening time or the events that led him here. Wealtheow is now his wife and is also annoyed with him for having lost her golden cup. This continuity gap, though confusing, does have the effect of emphasizing the disastrous effects of Beowulf's carnal choice by juxtaposing his resubmission to Grendel's mother against the annoyance of his disenchanted subjects bringing news of the kingdom's turmoil. At the same time, it suggests that, unlike Hrothgar, Beowulf wakes up from the seduction before it is too late.

Once the intervening supplementary adventures are over and Beowulf's heroic status has been established, the rest of the game plays out to the end in much the same way as the film. That is, Beowulf returns to Heorot and seeks out the dragon, killing the wrathful reptile (which is also his offspring) by tearing out his heart. As the injured king bleeds out on the beach, his loyal, long-time companion Wiglaf arrives and offers to take him to a healer. Beowulf refuses and attempts to confess that he fathered the dragon with Grendel's mother. Wiglaf refuses to listen to him, saying, "the saga is already set." The king's body is laid atop a pile of gold in a longboat, set afire, and sent out to sea. Depending on whether the player focuses on heroic valor or carnal power, the tone of the game's final scene is slightly different. If the focus has been on heroic valor, then the respected and beloved king leaves behind a cautiously optimistic kingdom; if, however, the focus has been on carnal power, then the monster-slayer leaves the kingdom in disarray. This tension between the heroic and the carnal supplies one of the game's only direct references to lines from the original poem, a paraphrase of "Let whoever can / win glory before death. When a warrior is gone, / that will be his best and only bulwark (*wryce se þe mōte / dōmes ær dēaþe; þæt bið drihtguman / unlifgendum æfter sēlest*)" (1387a-89).

A NOTE TO GAME DESIGNERS

Because gaming journalism tends to describe the mechanics of a game rather than critique its content, any numerical rating tells us more about the way gamers judge its playability than the way they appreciate the storyline. Based on the numbers, critics and players generally agree that *Beowulf: The Game* is not very good. Metacritic.com, a criticism aggregator, averages the scores of twenty-three critics' reviews to rate the game at 51/100.[7] In a system where games scoring under 70 are generally not worth playing, this score indicates player frustrations with the poor quality of mechanical aspects of the game, such as fighting controls and user interface, and the simplistic and derivative nature of its combat system. Even what it does well, reviewers can point to games that do it better. For instance, some players loved the visceral, graphic combat—but *Conan* (2007) and *God of War* (2005–12) did it better; the artistic assets of the game—borrowed in part from the team working on the film—are beautiful and evocative, but *Skyrim* did it better.

To see what gamers thought of the content, we must turn to the written reviews, a task complicated by the intervening five years and the game's unpopularity: many reviews are no longer hosted online. What remains is generally negative—but perhaps not for what one would expect. For instance, reviewers forgive the juvenile barbarism in the game, with some even recommending that players turn to games such as *Conan* to sate their desire for violence. Instead, they criticize the game's reductive paraphrasing of the source text. According to IGN reviewer Charles Onyett, "the way the developers decided to make things so unnecessarily difficult to follow, especially considering they're offering a new angle on one of *the* classic works of Western literature, is an embarrassment to the medium of video games and their ability to convey weighty narrative concepts in unique ways."[8] His article (giving the game a score of 4/10) criticizes *Beowulf: The Game* for reducing the mighty Beowulf to a cheerleader as he encourages his thanes to push obstacles or row their boat. What remains of the other reviews upholds this appraisal, with varying degrees of forgiveness. The message to game designers seems to be that beyond chastising Ubisoft for developing such a flawed game, the reviewers were upset by the unnecessary departures from the medieval original.

Someone unfamiliar with how gaming and its audience have evolved over the years may have expected the players to find the epic's distant setting, alien culture, and complex thematic tensions too foreign or difficult to appreciate. Their objection to those things being diminished in *Beowulf: The Game* would indicate that the opposite is true. Despite some outliers at both ends of the spectrum, gamers are at least as educated as the general public, if not more so. It should be unsurprising that they disparage simplifying an adaptation of one of the foundational works of the Western literary tradition, or at least the classroom's standard anthologies of British literature. The medieval traits of the epic *Beowulf* that survive multiple iterations of translation from Old English poem to Hollywood feature film to video game are among its redeeming values. The modern player, against expectations, finds these ancient literary traits among the more familiar and embraceable features of the game.

This familiarity is due in no small part to the commonality of so many single-player games borrowing so much of their storytelling technique from the epic tradition, although few game designers would have the training to recognize this as their source. Some highly successful and popular game titles employ some of the same elements that *Beowulf: The Game* borrows from the Old English epic. For instance, *Fallout* (2008) and *Mass Effect* (2007), two series of futuristic role-playing games, require players to manage their character's heroic nature and reputation. In *Fallout 3* and *Fallout: New Vegas* (2010), the player's exploits, for good or ill, are broadcast over radio stations.[9] The radio host's role in narrating, sensationalizing, and editorializing the player's actions (which can range from generous to murderous, or somewhere in between), bears a more than passing resemblance to the role of the ancient scop. A similar device is employed in the *Mass Effect* franchise, where players' successes and failures become news items that they will overhear while visiting population centers as their career progresses.[10] Thus, the role of the scop in propagating and shaping Beowulf's reputation while he lives fits easily into a gamer's imaginative world.

These and many other games also include a mechanism whereby the player's reputation is tracked by various factions. Perhaps the most well-known is the ubiquitous reputation system in *World of Warcraft*.[11] By repeating various tasks and by representing factions in events such as jousting or clearing a dungeon, players accrue points towards achieving exalted status in the eyes of each faction (which number over fifty, more added regularly with each new content patch). This reputation, in turn, serves both as a gating aspect to progression in the game, by denying players access to some content until sufficient reputation is reached, and as a reward for the players' efforts, by providing such powerful items as equipment and recipes. Consequently, Beowulf's struggle for validation through heroic exploits strikes the modern player as very familiar.

Modern gamers would find very little in the Old English epic *Beowulf* that they would not enjoy seeing in a game. Many of the epic's themes have already found their way into highly acclaimed and well-received games. However, the primary constraint of the medium is still that a game must be entertaining. Like any new art form, it has evolved rapidly in the decades since its introduction. The ability to deliver narrative has increased meteorically from the days of *Pong* (1972) and *Super Mario Bros.* (1985) to modern titles whose narrative can last for upwards of fifty consecutive hours and often employ the talents of high-profile actors, such as Martin Sheen in *Mass Effect* and Anthony Hopkins in *Beowulf: The Game*. But developers learn that gamers can be unforgiving. In addition to the narrative and visual components, developers must strike the proper balance between innovation and familiarity with the game's controls. They must seamlessly combine tremendous amounts of code produced by large teams of software engineers and then carefully comb the result for errors and bugs. Because players must remain involved throughout the course of a game, they cannot skim paragraphs as they can during a boring section of a novel or play with their phones as they can during a bad scene in a movie. Consequently, players can feel more invested in a game than a film, whether that be love for a good game or frustration with a bad one.

A NOTE TO PURISTS

If *Beowulf: The Game* has been largely forgotten by gamers, it was largely ignored by medievalists. Although critics lamented the film's changes to the poem, they could not easily extend their regret to the game because playing the game requires a level of expertise that watching the film does not require. Nevertheless, based on similarities between the game and the film, Anglo-Saxonists' reactions would probably begin with assessments similar to those of the film, which see it as trivializing the epic for an adolescent audience.[12] Like the film, the game captures the problems inherent in adapting any foreign text—whether its alterity is the result of a barrier erected by centuries or by continents—no matter who makes the adaptation. Although the problems can be exaggerated in adaptations appealing to a popular audience, they can alert scholars that they should not be blind to the ways their own efforts are tainted by audience demands and cultural bias. In fact, if we consider *Beowulf* scholarship in light of the three dominant adaptations explored in this essay—continuity gaps, rebarbarization, and reconciliation of the carnal with the heroic—we can see that aspects of all three can be found in the interpretive moves made by scholars over the past 200 years.

By filling in the continuity gaps, the game makes a move embraced by critics who see that "[t]he curiously 'unfocussed' compositional organization of *Beowulf* renders the process of the poem's interpretation potential infinite, and is thus responsible for the endless deferral of the meaning of the poem."[13] When Beowulf awakens in the game to find himself with a queen, he finds himself in much the same situation that some scholars have placed him when they try to account for the poem's enigmatic inclusion at the hero's funeral of "*Gēatisc mēowle* / . . . *bundenheorde*," an older Geatish woman (lines 3150–1), who sings a litany of grief and fear. She appears after the poem's third monster—the dragon—has been defeated, after Beowulf dies, and after his funeral pyre has been built. With only thirty-two lines remaining to be related, the poem introduces this unnamed, minimally unidentified woman. Although—or because—the poem makes no mention of Beowulf's having a wife, scholars and translators once regularly identified this woman as Beowulf's wife. William Morris's 1895 translation calls her Beowulf's "sad wife," and Knut Stjerna conjectures that she is "the widowed queen," a speculation echoed a half century later by Kemp Malone.[14] Although none go so far as to equate this woman with Wealtheow, each critic demonstrates the sense that the poem has omitted essential information about Beowulf's life. By providing Beowulf with a queen, the game shares in these efforts to address an apparent oversight in the heroic king's biography.

Likewise, the game presents a biography for the Grendelkins. Usually, scholars begin and end by locating the sea monsters' ancestral affinity with Cain.[15] Though none posit that either Hrothgar nor Beowulf have a sexual relationship with Grendel's mere, and certainly no self-respecting Anglo-Saxonist would speculate that Grendel is Hrothgar's offspring, some scholarship has supported Dame Grendel as a formidable foe and as an alluring woman. In the middle of the twentieth century, Bonjour was considering the implications of "the sudden and startling surprise at the deadly hardness of the fight with Grendel's dam."[16] Not long after, Nora Chadwick argued that the poem uses ambiguous language to describe Grendel's mother, her actions, and her motivations; for example, *ides* could mean a "formidable" and "dignified woman."[17] More recently, Jane Chance has argued for the "erotic overtones" of the battle between Beowulf and Grendel's mother when she sits astride him.[18] By making Grendel's mother's sexual allure dangerous, the game brings together these two observations about the sea mere. And in significant ways, it mirrors Wendy Hennequin's contention that the poem never labels her as a monster, a cognomen brought to the fore in modern translations but not in the Old English text.[19] And yet, as preposterous as the result seems, it becomes another in the line of attempts to locate Grendel and his mother "within some type of historical reality."[20] When the game moves beyond an imaginary violent encounter between Germanic invaders and "primitive indigenous inhabitants," it provides a postcolonial reading with the added dimension of a sexual encounter and the resulting breed of offspring shunned by the dominant forces.[21] Though the result is unrecognizable to Anglo-Saxon scholarship, the monsters' genealogy presented by the game brings together several strands of credible scholarship.

In a spirit reminiscent of the nineteenth-century scholarship's energy spent identifying and stripping away the learned, Christian intrusions believed to have contaminated the original, pagan elements, the game works to intensify the barbaric elements associated with the pagan Danes.[22] Similarly, when the game borrows from a range of cultural elements resembling its audience's notions of barbaric violence, the game designers perpetuate arguments that *Beowulf*'s original redactor(s) show influence from the *Odyssey* and the *Aeneid*, positions held by some of the "most respected and prolific mediaeval scholars and philologists" of their generation.[23] For these scholars, it was an effort to elevate the poem's reputation by locating its ties to classical antecedents. For the game designers, it was an effort to infuse the poem with barbaric violence readily identified by its audience with European mythology and epics.

By foregrounding the use of the Carnal and Heroic Modes, the game looks for evidence and develops conclusions about Beowulf's character and motivations. The game is not content to see Beowulf as a one-dimensional heroic character but insists on presenting him as a man possessing virtues and vices competing with one another for dominance. Mid-twentieth-century critics rescued Beowulf from a one-dimensional interpretation, and later critics have further complicated that picture.[24] The Carnal versus Heroic aspect echoes, albeit reductively, Linda Georgianna's observation that "Beowulf's choices in the face of life's transitoriness come to seem extremely limited [. . . and] advances and retreats are equally illusory."[25] And it falls in line with a long lineage of efforts to locate the narrative's governing dichotomy, from Kaske's distinction between *sapeintia et fortitude* (wisdom and strength) to John Hill's *gravitas* and *celeritas* (weighty authority and impatient dispatch).[26]

With both these caveats to game designers and purists in mind, it is clear that *Beowulf: The Game* has both the attributes that appeal to gamers as well as the ambiguity that allows for adjustments that correspond with interpretive moves medievalists make. Players rejected *Beowulf: The Game* not because it source material was not appropriate, but because the gaming interface, the controls, and other mechanical aspects of the game failed to meet the quality of *Beowulf*. And if some medievalists would fault the game for its alterations to the original narrative, they will find that the game mimics many of the moves made by Anglo-Saxonists of the past century.

NOTES

1. *Beowulf: The Game*, Ubisoft (Ubisoft, 2007). References to *Beowulf* rely on Bruce Mitchell and Fred Robinson, eds., *Beowulf: An Edition*, rev. ed. (Malden, MA: Blackwell, 2006); Seamus Heaney, trans., *Beowulf*, bilingual ed. (New York: W. W. Norton, 2001).
2. Robert Zemeckis, dir., *Beowulf: The Movie* (Hollywood, CA: Paramount Pictures, 2007); Mitchell and Robinson, *Beowulf*, lines 530–81a; Heaney, *Beowulf*, lines 530–81.
3. Neil Gaiman and Roger Avary, *Beowulf: The Script Book* (London: Harper, 2007), 6.
4. John McTiernan, dir., *The 13th Warrior* (Burbank, CA: Touchstone Pictures, 1999). The movie is based on Michael Crichton's anthropological retelling of the story of Beowulf and Grendel: *Eaters of the Dead* (New York: Bantam, 1976).
5. Ron Howard, dir., *Willow* (Century City, CA: 20th Century Fox, 1988). For a sense of the similarities, see this clip from *Willow*: "Midgets, Trolls, and 2 Headed Dragons Oh My," http://www.youtube.com/watch?v=Hrb4n-x7CJ4&feature=youtube_gdata_player (accessed February 18, 2007).
6. A quick-time event (or QTE) is a type of gameplay mechanic that has become ubiquitous in the years since *Beowulf: The Game* was published. It is a sort of Simon-Says game where the player must rapidly and accurately repeat a sequence of buttons shown on the screen while the player-character performs a corresponding action. Although not universally embraced, QTEs allow the players to feel involved and in control even during unique, cinematic-scale events, such as Beowulf's battle with Grendel and the other monsters, grappling and hand-to-hand fights with the game's human adversaries, and even the seduction sequences with Grendel's mother.
7. "*Beowulf: The Game* for Xbox 360 Reviews, Ratings, Credits, and More—Metacritic," http://www.metacritic.com/game/xbox-360/beowulf-the-game (accessed June 28, 2012).
8. "*Beowulf* Review—Xbox 360 Review at IGN," http://xbox360.ign.com/articles/835/835410p1.html (accessed June 28, 2012).
9. *Fallout 3*, Bethesda Game Studies (Bethesda Softworks, 2008); *Fallout: New Vegas*, Obsidian Entertainment (Bethesda Softworks, 2010).
10. *Mass Effect*, Bioware (Demiurge Studies, 2007).
11. *World of Warcraft*, Blizzard Entertainment (Blizzard Entertainment, 2011).
12. Wally Hammond, "*Beowulf*," *Time Out*, http://www.timeout.com/film/reviews/84501/beowulf.html (accessed July 4, 2012); Andrew Osmond, "*Beowulf*," *Sight and Sound* 18, no. 1 (2008): 61–62; Manohla Dargis, "Confronting the Fabled Monster, Not to Mention His Naked Mom," http://movies.nytimes.com/2007/11/16/movies/16beow.html (accessed July 4, 2012); Michael Morpurgo, "Children's Author Michael Morpurgo on Beowulf," *Guardian*, http://www.guardian.co.uk/film/2007/nov/20/books forchildrenandteenagers.poetry (accessed July 9, 2012); Richard North, "Poetry in Motion," *Time Out*, http://www.timeout.com/film/features/show-feature/3815/Dr_Richard_North_on-Beowulf-.html (accessed July 9, 2012).
13. Natalia Breizmann, "Beowulf as Romance: Literary Interpretation as Quest," *Modern Language Notes* 113, no. 5 (December 1998): 1030.
14. William Morris and A. J. Wyatt, *The Tale of Beowulf* (London: Kelmscott Press, 1895), 273–74; Knut Stjerna, *Essays on Questions Connected with the Old English Poem of Beowulf* (Coventry, UK: Curtis and Beamish, 1912), 197; Kempe Malone, "Hildeburg and Hengest," *Journal of English Literary History* 10, no. 4 (December 1943): 271.

15. Robert L. Chapman, "Alas, Poor Grendel," *College English* 17, no. 6 (1956): 334–37; Oliver Emerson, "Legends of Cain, Especially in Old and Middle English," *PMLA* 21 (1906): 831–929.
16. Adrien Bonjour, "Grendel's Dam and the Composition of *Beowulf*," *English Studies* 30 (1949): 290–99.
17. Nora Chadwick, "The Monsters and Beowulf," in *The Anglo-Saxons: Studies in Some Aspects of the History and Culture Presented to Bruce Dickins*, ed. Peter Clemoes (London: Bowes, 1959), 172–73.
18. Jane Chance, "The Structural Unity of *Beowulf*: The Problem of Grendel's Mother," in *New Readings on Women in Old English Literature*, ed. Helen Damico and Alexandra Hennessey (Bloomington: Indiana University Press, 1990), 248–67.
19. Wendy Hennequin, "We've Created a Monster: The Strange Case of Grendel's Mother," *English Studies* 89, no. 5 (2008): 502–23.
20. Signe Carlson, "The Monsters of *Beowulf*: Creations of Literary Scholars," *The Journal of American Folklore* 80, no. 318 (December 1967): 363.
21. Carlson, "The Monsters," 363.
22. Francis Adelbert Blackburn, "The Christian Coloring in the *Beowulf*," *PMLA* 12 (1897): 205–25.
23. Tom Burns Haber, *A Comparative Study of the* Beowulf *and the* Aeneid (Princeton, NJ: Princeton University Press, 1931); R. W. Chambers, "*Beowulf* and the Heroic Age," in *Beowulf: Translated into Modern English Rhyming Verse*, trans. Archibald Strong (London: Constable, 1925), xxvi; Morris and Wyatt, *The Tale of Beowulf*; Jodi-Ann George, *Beowulf: A Reader's Guide to Essential Criticism* (Houndsmill, UK: Palgrave Macmillan, 2010), 24.
24. See, for example, Henry Bosley Woolf, "On the Characterisation of Beowulf," *Journal of English Literary History* 15, no. 2 (June 1948): 85–92.
25. Linda Georgianna, "King Hrethel's Sorrow and the Limits of Heroic Action in *Beowulf*," *Speculum* 62 (1987): 829–30.
26. Robert E. Kaske, "Sapientia Et Fortitudo as the Controlling Theme of *Beowulf*," *Studies in Philology* 55 (1958): 423–57; John M. Hill, *The Narrative Impulse of* Beowulf: *Arrivals and Departures* (Toronto: University of Toronto Press, 2009).

3 Systematizing Culture in Medievalism
Geography, Dynasty, Culture, and Imperialism in *Crusader Kings: Deus Vult*

Jason Pitruzzello

Anglia exterorum facta est habitatio et alicnigcnamm dominatio. Nullus hodie Anglus vel dux, vel pontifex, vel abbas; advense quique divitias ct viscera corrodunt Angliae; nee ulla spes est finiendse miseriae.[1]

[England has become thc dwelling place of foreigners and the property of strangers. At the present time there is no Englishman who is either earl, bishop, or abbot. Strangers prey upon the riches and vitals of England, nor is there any hope of an end to this misery.[2]]

—William of Malmesbury

Writing in Latin, speaking as an Englishman, growing up aftei the Norman Conquest, and writing in his history *Gesta Regnum Anglorum*, a history of the deeds of English, as opposed to Norman, kings, William of Malmesbury illustrates just how complicated cultural interaction between conqueror and conquered could be in medieval Europe. William's complaint about lack of Englishmen in positions of both political and religious authority, and his emphatic language on the alien nature of the kingdom's dominators and the resulting misery, demonstrate with unintentional poignancy how inappropriate it is to view any cultural interaction in the Middle Ages as a monolithic struggle between binary opposites. In this passage of the *Gesta Regnum Anglorum*, the problems of England do not stem simply from a conflict between Norman lords and Anglo-Saxon commoners; they instead arise from how the conquest has affected the Church. As Brehe makes clear after he translates William, "The kind of leadership that English bishops had provided before the conquest was badly missed under the Norman regime."[3] The mere presence of the Church, and the language of those who run it, creates another axis of cultural friction that goes beyond distribution of wealth, political power, or considerations of ethnicity. To blindly characterize the conquest of Anglo-Saxon England as imperialism of the kind that the contemporary world is acquainted is problematic. Susan Crane summarizes it well:

> The interactions of William the Conqueror's followers and peoples native to Britain were not simply adversarial, nor were the ethnic conceptions and political ambitions of the time equivalent to those inspiring

Britain's modern attempts at empire. The conquerors and their followers were unquestionably bent on dominating the inhabitants of Britain,
but this process was not entirely a matter of force, nor should the inhabitants' responding manoeuvres and successes be elided into a model of
hopeless subjection. The extent to which intermarriage, bilingualism
and cultural adoptions came to characterize Norman rule sharply contrasts with the later British program of empire-building and testifies
both to the Norman's desire to make Britain their permanent home and
to the conquered inhabitants' success at imposing themselves and their
ways on the new arrivals.[4]

For medieval England, much as for the rest of the medieval world, culture was not a monolithic and static structure, nor was conquest a one-way
ticket to cultural change. Imperialism in the Middle Ages could impact the
conqueror culturally just as much as it could impact the conquered.

However, when examining strategy-based video games that indulge in
medievalism, it is clearly evident that the industry norm represents imperialism as containing none of the elements of cultural interaction and
interchange described by Brehe, Crane, and William. Popular and bestselling games such as *Age of Empires II* (1999) may depict historical events
such as the Third Crusade, but they almost invariably depict the Middle
Ages in grossly anachronistic ways. Feudal political entities, such as Crusader states and Western European kingdoms, are depicted as unified nation
states with absolute power invested in the authority of a monarch. Culture is
depicted as uniform and unchanging. If a player begins a game as the faction
referred to as the Britons, this decision is permanent; no amount of conquest
or territorial loss will ever result in any kind of cultural change. And when
it comes to determining victory in a medievalism such as *Age of Empires II*,
there are only two options: completely annihilating all people in the opposing culture or accepting the surrender of the opposing player, which removes
the population from the game. In other titles, such as *Warlock: Master of
the Arcane* (2012), it is possible to conquer neighboring cultures without
annihilating them, but culture does not change. This leaves players with multi-
ethnic empires where different cultures exist, but never interact. Although
the Middle Ages were thoroughly familiar with the slaughter of noncombatants, games such as *Age of Empires II* and *Warlock: Master of the Arcane*
are anachronistic in the sense that they depict the relationship between the
conqueror and the conquered in binary, monolithic, and ultimately destructive terms. They do not depict a world where William of Malmesbury can
complain about strangers in the Church hierarchy or where the conquered
people have the ability to interact culturally with their conquerors.

However, one particular game stands out as a medievalism in stark
contrast to the popular norm in the video game industry: *Crusader Kings:
Deus Vult*. Originally published in 2004, with the *Deus Vult* expansion
pack published in 2007, *Crusader Kings* presents a game system that gives

cultural power to both the ruling class and the people they rule. It does this with cultural mechanics that attach culture and religion to characters and provinces alike while providing for interaction between them. Although the vast majority of strategy-oriented video games depict culture in the Middle Ages in monolithic and unchanging terms, *Crusader Kings* depicts culture as mutable. Members of the ruling class or the people they rule can change culturally, mimicking to some extent the kinds of cultural change found in England and elsewhere in the period. As digital medievalism, *Crusader Kings* models systems of cultural change in the Middle Ages rather than merely assigning cultural labels to people and geographic areas of Europe at specific chronological dates. The game attempts to avoid anachronism through historically based systems of gameplay, rather than through rote inclusion of historical facts.

FEUDAL OBLIGATIONS, CULTURE, AND VIRTUAL DNA

Due to the complexities in the game's mechanics, some definitions are in order. There are two classes of objects in the game that have culture and religion attached to them: characters and provinces. Characters in *Crusader Kings* represent people of the same social rank as John of Gaunt and Pope Innocent VI. They are earls, counts, dukes, kings, emperors, bishops, and popes. They may be historical or fictional figures. For example, if you start the game with the post-Hastings (1066) scenario, William the Conqueror is alive and well, having just undergone his coronation; after a hundred years of gameplay, thanks to dynastic intermarriage and infant mortality, a completely fictional set of characters may form the ruling elite of Europe's feudal and ecclesiastical lands. Characters hold various titles in the game, which, in turn, gives them ownership of certain provinces. They are also bound to each other by dynastic and feudal ties. William the Conqueror might own the province of Essex and be King of England, but a trusted vassal might own the province of York and have been given the title Duke of York as a reward. Provinces in *Crusader Kings* represent both geographic areas and the people who live there, such as Essex or Alexandria. As geographic entities, provinces possess terrain and borders, but they also possess the attributes of their people. These people are closer in social rank to Chaucer's pilgrims than they are to John of Gaunt; they are the knights, prioresses, and millers of the world. Both characters and provinces possess culture and religion. Culture, as defined in the context of *Crusader Kings*, is a label placed on a shared language and customs, excluding religion. Religion comprises a character or province's theological beliefs, excluding shared language and social customs. Characters, but not provinces, also possess DNA, which is not a mapping of their genome so much as it is a sequence of numbers assigned to the various permutations of the game's character portraits. When children are born in the game, they borrow DNA from both their mother and father, producing character portraits that give members of the same family similar appearances. It also means that culture does not impact the shape of cheeks or noses. In *Crusader Kings*, descendants of William the Conqueror may retain his facial characteristics over time even if they embrace a culture far removed from their famous ancestor. Provinces, unlike characters, possess technology, which includes farming techniques, architecture, and classical manuscripts and learning. Islamic scholars in Baghdad might have access to Aristotle's writings, while monks in Vestisland may not have copies of those manuscripts. Because technology can be transferred between provinces, this ensures that learning and technology can spread throughout Europe as it did historically and that contact between cultures occurs not only through warfare.

This system of culture, religion, provinces, and characters creates multiple sites of conflict as well as interaction. The most obvious site of conflict is religion. Rulers who do not share the same faith find it easier to initiate wars against one another. When fighting fellow Christians, rulers require some kind of justification for the war, such as a dynastic claim to titles or the pope's blessing upon the conflict. But when choosing to fight non-Christians, the difference in religion is justification enough for war. Even without the pope calling for a crusade, Christian rulers may attack their non-Christian neighbors without penalty or censure. Thus, places like Iberia remain hotbeds of conflict no matter what progress crusaders have made in the Holy Land. But the key here is not in the religion of provinces; it is in the religion possessed by the rulers of those lands. Characters declare war on one another over the ownership of provinces or other titles, but the culture and religion of the provinces being fought over is largely irrelevant. If the King of Castile wishes to invade Granada under the guise of religious differences, the ruler of Granada must not be a Christian, no matter what the religious beliefs of the people living there may be. After the conquest, the new rulers must then decide how to interact with their new subjects, creating another site of conflict and interaction; if the province does not share its ruler's religion, their relationship will be far different than if they share a common faith.

CULTURE AND RELIGION FROM THE CRADLE

The above example shows just one way in which *Crusader Kings* entwines culture, religion, characters, and provinces with imperialism. But the most interesting interaction among religion, culture, and provinces occurs after conquest. It is these scenarios of successful imperialism in the game that showcase the historical interplay between conquerors and conquered peoples outlined by Susan Crane. To begin with, all characters are assigned a culture when they are born. This process is not completely randomized and is weighted according to the culture of the character's father, mother, and the province in which they reside. The father's culture is 80 percent likely to be inherited by the child, the mother's culture is 10 percent likely to be inherited, and the province's culture is 10 percent likely to be inherited.[5] This means that it is possible for the ruling class to assimilate into the culture of their conquered peoples; however, because the process affects children of characters individually, this assimilation of the ruling class is not uniform, can alternate between generations, and can cause dynasties to split along cultural lines over time. Furthermore, while the ruling class may take on the culture of their people, it is entirely possible that cultural influences foreign both to the ruler and his people affect the dynasty's children via their mothers. Depending on inheritance, marriage, and the provinces ruled by a family of characters, it is entirely possible that the fashions of Paris might take London by storm in 1125 CE, while a Norman family that rules York might find themselves with children who have embraced Saxon culture the same year. Note that there are no real mechanics for changing the culture of characters after they are born; counterintuitively, characters are usually stuck with the culture they are assigned at birth.

Religion is also passed on to children, but the rules are very different. At birth, all children are assigned the religion of their father. This prevents odd scenarios in which children of crusaders embrace the religion of their enemies by virtue of proximity to another faith. It also means that if a ruler marries outside his or her religion for diplomatic purposes (a rare event in *Crusader Kings*), this cannot result in a generation of children who spurn the religion of their father and pointlessly plunge the realm into religious chaos.[6] However, unlike culture, religion is more changeable for characters. Characters at court might find their ruler or liege demanding that they convert their religion. Furthermore, children that receive an ecclesiastical education have their religion converted to their ruler's religion once they come of age, allowing for religious assimilation of children at the hands of the Church.[7] The game even supports the possibility of using force to attempt the conversion of characters; non-Christian characters who find themselves at the court of a zealous ruler might find themselves tortured or threatened with death if they do not renounce their faith. And, if a ruler appoints non-Christians to advisory positions at court, they can expect the pope to complain about the situation. Religious intolerance intersects with political life in *Crusader Kings*.

The examples I have shown so far all involve characters and their cultural and religious changes, but provinces also feel the impact of cultural and religious conflict and interaction. The rules for cultural changes in provinces are far more complicated than the cultural rules regarding characters, partly because each province represents a large number of people, but also because the developers of *Crusader Kings* understand how complex this process was historically. A number of conditions must first be satisfied before cultural conversion is even possible. The ruler must not be a heretic or excommunicated. The province must not be affected by heresy. The ruler must not currently be in a war. The ruler must own a province with his or her own culture and that province must have some kind of significant contact via harbors, roads, or geographic proximity to the province whose culture needs to be converted.[8]

Once these conditions are satisfied, it becomes possible for the ruler to convert the culture of the province. This process is randomized according to a weighted probability. With no modifiers, the Mean Time to Happen, or MTTH, for cultural conversion is 2,000 months.[9] This means that, on average, and assuming no mitigating conditions at all, it takes 166.66 years for the ruling class to assimilate their conquered subjects to their own culture. Bear in mind that this is the average of a randomized factor; sometimes conquerors might succeed in months, in other cases it may never happen at all. But *Crusader Kings* accounts for so many modifiers to this value that every case of cultural difference between the ruling class and the people of a province can produce unique situations that speed up or slow down this process of cultural conversion. The sheer number of factors at play are too many to list here, but some of the more interesting ones provide insight into how the game's developers view the Middle Ages.[10] If any kind of disease is affecting the province, and especially if the Black Death is present, the speed of cultural change is reduced by a flat 50 percent while the disease persists. If a province has international fairs active, the speed increases by 10 percent. If the target province has extensive roads and a grand harbor, the speed of cultural conversion increases by 10 percent for each one. But as important as these effects are, it is the ruler who has the most impact on the speed of cultural change. If a ruler is lazy or arbitrary, then the speed is reduced 10 percent.[11] If the ruler is highly skilled at stewardship, the speed is increased by 10 or even 20 percent. If the ruler has substantial prestige, this may increase the speed by 10, 20, or even 30 percent. Rulers who have built grand palaces find that cultural conversion is 10 percent faster. Furthermore, rulers who currently have the power of investiture in their realms find that cultural conversion accelerates by 10 percent. Perhaps the biggest impact on cultural conversion is religion; if the ruler shares the same religion as the province, the process is accelerated by almost 70 percent. These modifiers create situations where cultural conversion is heavily dependent on very specific and local circumstances. Crusaders find themselves having great difficulty in converting non-Christians in faraway lands, whereas rulers in areas of great conflict may never hold on to a particular province long enough to succeed in cultural conversion. And because the dynasty's children may embrace provincial culture, there is no way to predict whether the ruling class or the ruled will end up being changed culturally. The game's developers demonstrate a view of the Middle Ages that discards tropes of medieval uniformity, monolithic hierarchies, or a culturally static Middle Ages; instead, they embrace a view of the period as one of vibrant cultural change.

Religious conversion operates according to very different parameters. As explained earlier, the ruler and his family cannot embrace the faith of their provinces; therefore, religious conversion is only one-way. However, religious conversion is much more dependent on the education and skills of the clergy employed by the ruler than the ruler's personal ability. Without the direct support of the clergy employed by the ruler, the MTTH for religious conversion may be as high as 6,000 months. A ruler who shares the same culture as the province accelerates religious conversion by 50 percent. If the ruler is virtuous, the speed may be increased by 10 percent or more; if the ruler has an ecclesiastical education, it will increase the speed by as much as 10 percent if the ruler is a scholarly theologian. If the ruler is excommunicated or skeptical in religious matters, the speed of religious conversion is reduced by as much as 60 percent. However, rulers who are in the good graces of the Church and who cultivate competent clergy find that the MTTH of religious conversion becomes only 900 months, with the speed of conversion substantially increased if members of the clergy possess high values in piety, are modest and temperate, and if they possess strong educational backgrounds. Theologians with the intelligence and virtue of Thomas Aquinas find it much easier to convince provinces to convert to Christianity than corrupt pardoners and slothful priests who only know their "rhymes of Robin Hood."[12]

GAME MECHANICS AND AVOIDING ANACHRONISM

The ultimate goal of these mechanics for religious and cultural change is to create a dynamic system where anachronism is avoided via game rules. This is very important because of how the game's other rules work. The gameplay of *Crusader Kings* involves controlling one of these characters and guiding him or her and the dynasty through 400 years of history. Players have the freedom to contract their own marriages, engage in their own wars, and to wrangle with the Church over issues such as investiture. This means that over the course of 400 years it is impossible to predict which characters will rule which provinces. Players might be more successful than their historical counterparts in the Crusades, the kingdoms south of France might find themselves crushed, and the Byzantine Empire might avoid its historical defeats at the hands of Alp Arslan and his descendants. The game depicts infant mortality, so the number and quality of heirs over various generations may differ dramatically. And because disease and warfare are important facets of the game, there is no guarantee that anyone will live to enjoy his or her titles and lands for more than a few years even if he or she survives into adulthood. Inheritances, succession crises, and war create a dynamic world where the ruling characters of a particular set of provinces might be of any culture and religion. Assigning a new culture to a province on a certain date because of historical events would be arbitrary in a setting where the ruling class does not match the historical personages. William of Malmesbury would end up complaining about the lack of Englishmen in important Church positions in 1125 CE even if the Saxons had managed to end Norman domination of England. Instead, the dynamic system of cultural interaction means that no matter who rules the provinces of Europe and the Holy Land, culture remains an important and dynamic issue.

Clearly, there are limits to the nuances of the game's cultural mechanics. Although *Crusader Kings* provides for cultural shifts in characters and provinces, these mechanics are still adversarial and binary even if they do not portray culture as static and unchanging. Although games such as *Age of Empires II* and their ilk represent culture and religion in monolithic terms, it might appear that *Crusader Kings* does not really provide a better medieval experience for its players because, although culture can transfer between rulers and the provinces they rule, culture remains unchanging and static. Either the culture of the ruler or the province wins out, with the possibility of foreign cultures being imported with spouses. However, the game's designers include one exception to their own rules that indicates that they understand the limits of their own work. In recognition that cultural change need not simply shift from one culture to another, the game comes with an "English melting pot" cultural change event. This cultural conversion event bypasses the mechanics I outlined above, which are applied universally to all provinces and characters in the game. It only applies to provinces in northern and southern England. If the provinces are currently Saxon, Norman, Norwegian, or Danish, and the rulers are either Saxon or Norman, there is a chance that the province will spontaneously convert to English culture. The MTTH for it to occur is only 400 months, and the speed is increased by 20 percent if a province has a Norman ruler. If the provinces have a ruler who has already embraced English as culture (via the usual methods of generating culture in children outlined above), then the speed of conversion to English culture is increased by 60 percent. This makes it much easier for English culture to gain a foothold once someone of the ruling class accepts that culture. This event runs concurrently with the normal cultural conversion mechanics, so there is no guarantee that anyone in England will be English during any particular game. Sometimes Norman culture will triumph, and at other times Saxon culture will endure without change. The inclusion of this special exception to the normal rules demonstrates a recognition of the complexity of cultural interaction in the period.

Crusader Kings creates medievalism using a design philosophy centered around working medieval systems rather than historical tidbits or fantastic elements. We have seen how complicated these systems can be within the context of the game, but why would these mechanics be of interest beyond their novelty? The answer lies in how these mechanics present the Middle Ages to the game's players. Instead of trying homogenize the Middle Ages with modern and postmodern ideas of culture, nationalism, and race, these mechanics of culture highlight difference. Scholars know that the titles held by a particular ruler on a particular date in history may not tell us very much about the language or social customs of that person, but the average consumer of popular culture may not even know that there were cultural differences between the Normans and Saxons in 1066, to say nothing of how those differences were negotiated over the intervening centuries. But because players have the freedom to shape the politics of medieval Europe over the course of four centuries in the game, simple historical factoids do not give players a medieval experience. It is the system of cultural change that presents players with the complexities of the medieval world. Religion, too, gets a more nuanced presentation via these mechanics. Instead of just being told when certain areas change religion, the player experiences the process of that change. The game does not simply tell players that the Kingdom of Jerusalem had a ruling elite with cultural and religious differences between them and their subjects, but instead has the player experience first-hand the cultural and religious diversity of Crusader states. These attributes do not make *Crusader Kings* a tool for education; because players have the freedom to do so much, any player cannot get accurate historical data from playing the game for even a few game years, let alone a full game spanning four centuries of in-game politics, intrigue, and imperialism. Yet, with the game mechanics employed in *Crusader Kings*, players are invited to see the Middle Ages not as just a different historical period subject to nostalgia, but they are invited to avoid anachronism by participating in the kinds of cultural and religious shifts that occurred. This game, unlike the industry norm, depicts the Middle Ages as culturally diverse and capable of substantial change; the fact that it accomplishes this without using narratives of renaissance or progress to modernity makes it far more medieval than even its name suggests.

NOTES

1. William of Malmesbury, *Willelmi Malmesbiriensis Monachi De Gestis Regum Anglorum Libri Quinque: Historiae Novellae Libri Tres,* trans. William Stubbs (London: H. M. Stationery Office, 1887), 278.
2. S. K. Brehe, "Reassembling the First Worcester Fragment," *Speculum* 65 (1990): 535.
3. Brehe, "Reassembling," 535.
4. Susan Crane, "Anglo-Norman Cultures in England 1066–1460," in *The Cambridge History of Medieval English Literature,* ed. David Wallace (Cambridge, UK: Cambridge University Press, 1999), 35.
5. This weighted ratio has changed with various iterations of the game. In some versions, the ratio has been 70 percent/15 percent/15 percent, and in others it has had very different values. For an exhaustive discussion of this mechanic and its various iterations, see the following *Crusader Kings* forum and the wiki: "Crusader Kings Wiki," http://crusaderkings.wikia.com/wiki/Crusader_Kings_Wiki (accessed August 1, 2012). Paradox Interactive, "Forum: Crusader Kings," http://forum.paradoxplaza.com/forum/ forumdisplay.php?81-Crusader-Kings (accessed August 1, 2012).

6. This mechanic is important because if religious conversion to the provincial religion were allowed by the game's rules, then one might end up with Kings of Jerusalem who embrace Islam from the cradle or bastard children of Teutonic Knights growing up with the order and still worshipping Odin or other pagan deities.
7. All children in *Crusader Kings* are given one of three kinds of education: ecclesiastical, martial, or courtly education. These educations impact their abilities once they come of age and are substantially modified by the technologies available in the province where the children are educated. Provinces leave their mark on children in this way as well.
8. These conditions are not listed within the game's interface. To see them in detail, examine the game file labeled provincial_conversion_events.txt, which also houses the religious conversion conditions as well.
9. Mean Time to Happen, or MTTH, is the standard unit of weighted randomization in *Crusader Kings*. All event files in the game use this as part of their scripting, and the scripts are visible in plain-text files for anyone to read. They are located in the game's installation folder.
10. These modifiers can also be found in the provincial_conversion_events.txt file located in the game's installation folder.
11. All characters in *Crusader Kings* have character traits that represent medieval virtues and vices.
12. William Langland, *Piers Plowman*, ed. Elizabeth Robertson and Stephen H. A. Shepherd (New York: W. W. Norton, 2006), passus V, line 395. Note that the Norton Critical Edition uses the B-text as a base text.

4 The Portrayal of Medieval Warfare in *Medieval Total War* and *Medieval 2: Total War*

Gregory Fedorenko

Medieval: Total War (2002) and *Medieval 2: Total War* (2006) are strategy games that allow players to take control of one of a variety of medieval factions over an extended period of European history (1087–1453 in the original, 1080–1530 in *Medieval 2*). The games both combine a turn-based 'strategic' element, which involves players moving armies, navies, and agents (such as spies and diplomats) on a map of Europe, North Africa, and the Near East, with a real-time 'tactical' aspect where battles and sieges are fought either against the computer or against rival players. The results of these battles, once decided, are reflected on the main, strategic map, allowing players to manage the affairs of their faction from deciding on the construction of buildings and the forging of diplomatic alliances to micromanaging the positioning of military units on the battlefield. A successful player, therefore, will need not only to manage the finances and infrastructure of his or her emergent pan-European empire, but also to demonstrate skill in commanding troops in combat. Both games were well received by reviewers and the general public, with *Medieval: Total War* in particular praised for integrating a "nuanced and complex" turn-based game that touched on many of the key elements of medieval government (such as ensuring territories' religious compliance and maintaining the loyalty of subordinate generals) with "epic" battle sequences.[1] For the most part, the portrayal of medieval battlefield warfare is reasonably accurate, although the 400-year time span of each game inevitably introduces some anachronisms (such as army commanders in 1080 being portrayed on the battle map in sixteenth-century plate armor in *Medieval 2*). As in the Middle Ages, winning battles largely depends on generals' successful coordination of their infantry, cavalry, and archers to best effect, making use of terrain and weather effects and employing relevant tactical ploys (such as English longbowmens' planting of stakes) where necessary.

The present discussion, therefore, will not attempt to pick holes in the 'factual accuracy' of the portrayal of medieval warfare found in two games that are, ultimately, designed as works of entertainment rather than as of instruction. Moreover, such an exercise would arguably oversimplify a continuing and vibrant debate about what, precisely, the 'factual accuracy' of medieval warfare consisted of, given the voluminous and still-growing historiography of the subject.[2] Nonetheless, analysis of the 'total warfare' the games' developers have attributed to the period highlights certain revealing discrepancies between the idea as commonly understood by modern audiences on the one hand and 'total warfare' as evident in contemporaneous, medieval descriptions of conflicts on the other.

BATTLES

As is evident from a cursory examination of the marketing materials produced by The Creative Assembly in the case of both games, *Medieval: Total War* is above all concerned with battles. Although armies stationed in hostile territory on the campaign map automatically 'devastate' the land (thereby reducing the amount of revenue its owner receives in taxes), the main focus of both games is on the production of ever-more sophisticated units via the development of military infrastructure on the campaign map—units that are then banded together into armies and led against the armies of neighboring factions. Part of the reason for this is clearly practical. While the main campaign element of the game can only be played out to completion over a period of days (if not weeks), battles can each be completed in minutes and thereby afford the ideal forum for multiplayer encounters over the Internet. However, the concept of medieval warfare provided in the two games privileges land battles over both static engagements (i.e., sieges) and the plundering and devastation of armies' surrounding environments, with evidence from the game's developers suggesting that this was, in part, a deliberate decision. In planning *Medieval 2* after the completion of *Medieval,* the designers apparently approached the idea of allowing armies to construct castles or temporary field fortifications with some caution, seeking to avoid "too many repetitive sieges of small garrisons," and instead highlighted the fact that "Medieval 2's battles are the most spectacular and brutal we've ever created."[3] Although sieges occur both in the original *Medieval* and in *Medieval 2,* they are limited, for the most part, to sieges of the capital of each particular province the strategic map is divided into, with armies in *Medieval* unable to lay siege to each central settlement until any enemy troops occupying the same geographical region have been defeated in open combat. In winning the total war, therefore, players will typically fight a greater proportion of pitched battles than sieges, particularly given the relative paucity of settlements on the main campaign map (the Kingdom of England only featuring London, Nottingham, and York as towns in *Medieval 2*).

The games' privileging of battles, however, might plausibly be considered one of the points at which it most closely approaches its designers' intended Hollywood feel rather than the reality of medieval combat.[4] As is well-known to medieval scholars, but contrary to popular perception, battles were in fact relatively rare during the period. The reason for this was not difficult to understand. Battles carried with them great potential risk—particularly as the surest way for one side to achieve victory was to capture or kill the opposing commander in chief. Charles of Anjou (1226–1285) was able to cement his hold on the thirteenth-century Kingdom of Sicily by the expedient of defeating and killing one rival claimant at the Battle of Benevento (1266) and defeating, capturing, and executing another after the Battle of Tagliacozzo (1268).[5] Harold Godwinson lost his throne and his life after being defeated at Hastings, while the Bayeux Tapestry attests to the fact that his opponent, Duke William of Normandy, had to quell a potentially dangerous panic within his army caused by the news that he had been killed.[6] Moreover, it is important to note that we have no record of either leader at Hastings ever having commanded troops in pitched battle prior to 1066. William's victory at Val-ès-Dunes in 1047 is seemingly attributable with a greater degree of certainty to the overall command of King Henry I of France.[7] Even the most well-known and respected medieval 'generals' had far less experience of commanding battles than their twentieth-century descendants. Richard I ('the Lionheart') of England (1189–99), for example, never fought a single pitched battle in Europe.[8] The French King Philip Augustus (1180–1223), Richard's counterpart on the Third Crusade, fought his first at Bouvines in 1214 and was specifically targeted and nearly killed by enemy troops.[9] Henry V of England's experience at the Battle of Shrewsbury in 1403 distinguished him from the other principal English leaders at the Battle of Agincourt in 1415—Edward, Duke of York (1373–1415) and Thomas, Lord Camoys (1350–1420/21)—neither of whom had any significant experience of deploying troops for open combat.[10] In an age where royal or princely government was frequently itinerant, and in which great lords often went around accompanied by considerable retinues, the use of large bodies of armed soldiers more often proved useful primarily as a means to intimidate potential opponents rather than as part of a premeditated plan to engage and destroy their forces.[11] In 1069, for example, William the Conqueror marched north with an army in order to suppress a rebellion and counter an invading force of Danes. Cowed by William's show of force, the Danes agreed to leave the kingdom, with William thereafter defeating the English rebels not in open battle but with a campaign of systematic wasting of their lands and destruction of their property.

Battles, therefore, were both rare and risky, most often fought by commanders when there was no possible alternative, or when a conscious decision had been taken to gamble all on a single throw of the dice. This unpredictability was well-known to medieval monarchs, with so seasoned a medieval politician as Henry II of England (r. 1154–89) described as "dreading the doubtful arbitrament of war."[12] Amongst modern historians, Georges Duby has characterized battles as procedures of *peace* rather than of war—relatively rare events that were designed to conclusively resolve interminable, low-level conflicts in a climactic trial by combat, an attribute suggested by army commanders' committing of their causes to God and calling on him to arbitrate fairly on the coming fighting.[13] Indeed, the idea of the outcome of battles being in the gift of a higher power might have been especially appealing to medieval generals, given that contemporary armies—generally made up of a composite of the retinues of individual lords—did not usually train together as a single unit, making controlling forces that usually lacked knowledge of drill or battle formations a difficult task.[14] Stephen Morillo's observation that the command control of the armies of the Anglo-Norman kings "did not approach that of classical Macedonian or Roman armies" could plausibly be extended to all armies prior to the sixteenth century and means that the portrayal of battle tactics found in *Medieval 2* in particular (which is inherited from the game's immediate predecessor, *Rome: Total War*) is somewhat anachronistic.[15] Units appear in compact and relatively well-ordered blocks of ranks, with players able to order changes in the formation and facing of their troops with ease—a capacity that, though probably necessary for modern players' convenience, would have been the envy of many medieval commanders.

RAVAGING

The total warfare of the Middle Ages was an activity that primarily involved the destruction and laying waste of an enemy's property, rather than the confrontation of his or her armies in the open field. The chronicler Jordan Fantosme, for example, pictures Count Philip I of Flanders advising William I of Scotland in 1174 that the proper way to wage war was to "first destroy the land and then one's foe."[16] This strategy was in keeping with the advice offered in the military manual *De re militari*, written c. 400 by the late-Roman author Vegetius but widely copied in medieval Europe, which held that "on any expedition the single most effective weapon is that food should be sufficient for you while dearth should break the enemy."[17] Burning and pillaging had the effect not only of damaging an enemy's capacity to make war via the destruction of economic and human resources, but also of decreasing the will to fight of his subordinates whose lands were under imminent threat of devastation. Needless to say, given the fact that such acts were waged primarily against soft targets rather than an opponent's main army, they also approach much more closely in spirit to the kinds of atrocities associated with the total warfare of the modern era. Such a characteristic is evident from medieval fictional texts, with the epic poem *Raoul de Cambrai* (described by its most recent editor as offering a "nightmarish" vision of thirteenth-century France) featuring a protagonist, thirsting for vengeance against his enemies, commanding that "such war be unleashed on the Vermandois that countless churches will be burned and destroyed."[18] Rather than being merely acts of random violence or 'medieval savagery,' however, such ravaging was often enacted according to a predefined plan and with specific strategic objectives in mind. William the Conqueror's devastation of the neighborhood of Hastings after disembarkation in England shows, for example, that ravaging was used in order to draw enemies into confrontation when medieval commanders viewed this as desirable. It was also used in order to assault enemy strongholds indirectly, given the fact that their garrisons were usually dependent on surrounding regions providing them with sufficient supplies to withstand sieges. As King Stephen's advisors put it to him in 1149, following prolonged devastation, "reduced to the extremity of want, [your enemies] might at last be compelled to surrender."[19]

In cases where enemies did not surrender, however, then medieval campaigns shifted from mobile ravaging to static siege warfare, as attacking forces frequently found that they were unable to control a particular geographical area until they had successfully reduced its strong points. In contrast to the fluid impression of medieval warfare offered by the two games, armies of the period typically spent far more time moving to and from sieges of enemy settlements than maneuvering to gain an advantage against an enemy in a pitched battle, with a large number of the most famous battles of the period (such as Tinchebrai [1106], Lincoln [1141] and Formigny [1450]) themselves arising as a result of sieges.[20] The Fifth Crusade (1213–21), an expedition that included armed contingents from all over Europe, focused almost entirely on the siege of the Egyptian port of Damietta, which lasted well over a year.[21] Even in the 'Age of Gunpowder'—an invention *Medieval 2*'s battle system credits with the ability to reduce stone walls in a matter of seconds—sieges could still last a relatively long time. Henry V spent a month besieging Harfleur in 1415, for example, while Henry VIII's army took two months to gain control of Boulogne in 1544.

Fixed fortifications could also be used offensively rather than defensively, because they allowed a relatively small number of troops to operate from a secure base in attempting to assert control over a wide area. A medieval commander's campaign map would therefore have been pockmarked with a much larger number of small, problematic fortresses demanding assault than in either total war game, both of which feature wide, sweeping expanses of rolling landscape punctuated only by large and formidable fortified capital cities. Castle-based warfare favored ongoing local conflicts and political atomization—a world of the local 'knightly' gangster rather than the pan-European grand strategist. During the prolonged disturbances (generally referred to as the 'Anarchy') that occupied most of the reign of Stephen of England (1135–54), the *Anglo-Saxon Chronicle* famously refers to bands of marauders operating from castles violently oppressing the local population, whom they "tortured with indescribable torture to extort gold and silver."[22] Although several of these castles may have more closely approximated to temporary field fortifications rather than the substantial stone constructions of modern imagination, the comparatively primitive state of contemporary siege technology meant that ejecting their occupiers was often a difficult task. In bringing the period of turbulence to a close, one of Henry II's key objectives was the dismantling of all castles that had been built without royal authorization.[23]

WARFARE AND THE EUROPEAN STATE

If *Medieval*'s battles are large and decisive, and its armies large and professional, the entities in whose name 'total war' is waged bear, in certain cases, little resemblance to identifiable medieval polities. Instead of the complex, ever-shifting web of feudal allegiances depicted in titles such as *Crusader Kings*, the *Total War* games present an image of warfare between a relatively small number of participants, each roughly analogous to a modern European nation.[24] The most striking example is probably *Medieval*'s 'Italy' as a playable faction, a decision that serves to dramatically reduce the endemic warfare between peninsular city-states that marked much of the medieval period and that is partially remedied by the distinction between 'Milan' and 'Venice' introduced in *Medieval 2*. Although it might be argued that such amalgamations are necessary for reasons of balance and playability, it is also the case that *Medieval 2*, in particular, apparently revels in presenting an image of conflict during the Middle Ages that puts national distinctions at its heart. The game's sound effects include a series of prerecorded speeches that a player's general uses to address his men prior to a battle being joined. Each speech, delivered in heavily accented English according to the player's chosen faction, includes a passage highlighting the negative characteristics of the enemy in order to inspire troops for the coming fight. Examples include references to "arrogant and wine-sodden" Frenchmen, "sausage-eating, beer-swilling pudding heads" from the Holy Roman Empire (identified exclusively with Germany), and French criticism of English troops with "no sense of style, no élan, no manly virtue, no reason to live [and] no decent food." At the strategic map level, while the relative lack of urban settlements has already been remarked upon, it is nonetheless the case that the frontiers between various provinces are delineated clearly and along linear boundaries. Again, such boundaries are arguably more reminiscent of modern nation states than medieval polities, whose frontiers were frequently relatively ill-defined border zones themselves possessed of their own unique identities.[25]

The idea of warfare expressed in these *Total War* games, therefore, is arguably more at home in the European nineteenth century (an epoch which saw more and bigger set piece battles than any previous period of military history) than in either the medieval period or—given the recurrence of economic ravaging by carpet bombing and the normalization of massacres of noncombatants—the era of the World Wars. Even in the eighteenth century, we find such a distinguished commander as Maurice de Saxe stating the opinion that, when it came to battles, "a skillful general can go all his life without being forced to fight one."[26] A central reason behind such reluctance to fight was the cost of training and equipping armies, which, now assumed wholly by the state, made the replacement of the fallen an expensive procedure.[27] The size and intensity of the battles of the French Revolutionary and Napoleonic Wars, however, followed on from arguably the first ever declaration of total war as commonly understood today: the decree of the French National Assembly on August 23, 1793, that is now usually referred to as instituting the *Levée en Masse*:

> From this moment until that in which our enemies shall have been driven from the territory of the Republic, all Frenchmen are permanently requisitioned for service in the armies. The young men shall fight; the married men shall forge weapons and transport supplies; the women will make tents and clothes and will serve in the hospitals; the children will make up old linen into lint; the old men will have themselves carried into the public squares to rouse the courage of fighting men, to preach the unity of the Republic and hatred of Kings.[28]

The resulting army, which has been estimated at around 800,000 strong, was the largest ever seen in Europe up to that point.[29] Moreover, now that the revolutionary state was able simply to requisition its citizens for military service, preserving the lives of its soldiers by avoidance of battle became commensurately less important.[30] Emphasizing the irreconcilable ideological gulf between it and its enemies, the Republic had little use for restraint in the conduct of warfare. Rather, given the fact that allowing its soldiers to 'live off the land' (i.e., ravage) removed the need to find money to supply them, it had an active interest in escalating the conflict to include attacks on the property of noncombatants at the very least.[31] As Lazare Carnot, the principal organizer of the Revolutionary war effort, wrote, "one should wage war *à l'outrance* or go home."[32] The effects of this change can be seen in Table 4.1, which sets out the frequency and intensity of battles fought during the wars of the late eighteenth and early nineteenth centuries compared with both their predecessors and certain of their successors.[33]

Table 4.1   Army Size and Frequency of Battles in Wars of the Seventeenth to the Twentieth Centuries

	Average size of an army in battle, computed where possible from 30 battles in each war.	Number of battles in which opposing armies together numbered over 100,000.	Average number of battles per month.
Thirty Years' War	19,000	1	0.24
Wars of Louis XIV	40,000	7	
Spanish Succession			0.77
Wars of Frederick II	47,000	12	
Austrian Succession			0.82
Seven Years' War			1.40
French Revolutionary Wars	45,000	12	
First Coalition			3.0
Second Coalition			4.4
Napoleonic Wars	84,000	37	
Third Coalition			7.0
War of 1809			11.0
War of 1812			5.2
American Civil War	54,000	18	1.0
War of 1870	70,000	12	9.0
Russo-Japanese War	110,000	3	1.0

MEDIEVAL: TOTAL NATIONALISM

There was of course, however, plenty of 'patriotic' sentiment around in medieval Europe, and this patriotic sentiment often found itself intimately tied up with warfare. A study of prebattle rhetoric as recorded in medieval chronicles, for example, shows that it frequently shares certain common features with the speeches included in *Medieval 2*. Henry of Huntingdon (c.1088–c.1157), in imagining William the Conqueror's speech prior to the Battle of Hastings, has the Duke remind his soldiers that they are about to face "a people accustomed to defeat [and] devoid of military knowledge," while recalling to them the glorious achievements of their own ancestors— such as forcing the King of France to come unarmed to conferences while the Duke of Normandy was allowed to keep his sword.[34] Conversely, medieval generals in charge of armies made up of contingents from different realms frequently encountered difficulties in keeping them together and united in pursuit of a common end—a problem encountered in particular by the leaders of crusading forces. John of Brienne, who became the ruler of the Kingdom of Jerusalem (1210–25) after having been nominated to marry the realm's heiress by Philip Augustus, found controlling his multilingual, multinational armies a highly difficult task.[35] Richard the Lionheart, too, had difficulties with the French contingent within his army after their king, Philip Augustus, had departed for home in 1191, with commentators rationalizing a lack of French support for a march to Jerusalem on the grounds that the glory for such an endeavor would accrue to the English and not to their own nation.[36] Moreover, as Sean McGlynn has argued, medieval awareness of such 'national' differences led to the advocacy of brutal measures akin to those found in modern total wars, with war aims being extended to the eradication of all members of an opposing nation rather than merely its professional soldiers.[37] As a Scottish commander advised on the eve of the Battle of Flodden in 1513: "Leave no Englishman alive after you nor Englishwoman there to tell the tale. Burn their bad coarse women, burn their uncouth offspring, and burn their sooty houses, and rid us of the reproach of them. Let their ashes float downstream after burning their remains, show no mercy to a living Englishman."[38]

However, it is nonetheless important to note that the identification of medieval polities as proto-nation states— prominent in the *Medieval* games— is largely a product of the nineteenth century, the wars of which followed on from those of the French Revolution and of Napoleon in scale and intensity. For German historians, the wars of Napoleon stimulated a renewed interest in the medieval history of the Holy Roman Empire, with precedents from the Middle Ages advanced in defense of German historical uniqueness even as intellectuals differed markedly on what such 'uniqueness' might consist in.[39] As the nineteenth century progressed, a principal means by which historians sought to underscore the historical uniqueness of their particular nation was by the production of scholarly editions of the sources for its medieval past. The largest and arguably most distinguished of these projects, the *Monumenta Germaniae Historica* (established in 1819) had as its seal an oak wreath with the motto *Sanctus amor patriae dat animum*—"the sacred love of the fatherland inspires."[40] Moreover, the *Monumenta*'s conception of the extent of the 'fatherland' defined 'German-ness' in a markedly sweeping manner, encompassing all regions in which Germanic-speaking peoples had lived or over which they had exercised control. This schema included not only all those regions that had been part of the Holy Roman Empire (such as Italy) but also all of Frankish history (i.e., France and Belgium), Flanders and the Netherlands east of the river Scheldt, and the legal history of the Visigoths, Burgundians, and Lombards.[41]

The French state had paralleled the *Monumenta* by the foundation of the *Ecole des Chartes* in 1821 as an institute for training in the techniques of document editing, but it was in the years after the disastrous Franco-Prussian war of 1870–71 that study of the medieval past as a remedy for present-day national humiliations began to be advocated in earnest.[42] Jules Lair, for example, commenting on a study of a French manuscript by the German historian Georg Pertz, rejoiced that Pertz's analysis had remained in a half-finished, deficient state rather than "further advancing its invasion of a territory which is ours, and which we must defend and re-conquer."[43] His compatriot Léopold Delisle, whose bibliography of 2,102 items remains of key importance for historians of medieval France, introduced a lecture in 1875 by congratulating his audience for their scholarly endeavors at a time when "the misfortunes of the fatherland have made the memories of an often glorious, ever-interesting past even dearer to us."[44] 'National' medieval epics, such as the *Chanson de Roland,* were held up as suitable material for inspiring new generations of schoolchildren to emulate the deeds of their illustrious forefathers, while popular periodicals stressed the correct understanding of the medieval past as an essential step on the way to national reconciliation and rebirth.[45] British writers, too, saw in events such as the signing of the Magna Carta the essential precursors for their country's progress towards a modern parliamentary democracy, with no less a luminary as Bishop William Stubbs—author of a renowned *Constitutional History*—having begun his academic career as an editor of medieval manuscripts.[46]

The long-term effects of nineteenth-century medievalists' emphasis of national modes of thought have recently been decried by the historian Patrick Geary, who, in claiming that "modern history was born in the nineteenth century, conceived and developed as an instrument of European nationalism," has characterized the long-term effects of the era's historical scholarship as turning modern understanding of the medieval period into a "toxic waste dump"—video games presumably included.[47] The problem, however, is that today's historians remain reliant on the 'toxic waste' produced by their nineteenth-century antecessors to provide the raw materials for much of their own work, particularly with regard to editions and interpretations of primary source material. As modern medieval scholars will no doubt be aware, the versions of the works of authors provided in the *Monumenta Germaniae Historica* are, in a large number of cases, yet to be superseded. Indeed, it is perhaps because of the quality of this academic tradition, and modern reluctance to leave it behind, that a good deal of academic research continues to proceed along national lines. As Frits van Oostrom has highlighted, medieval polities that do not now correspond to a modern European state (such as the County of Hainaut) remain comparatively neglected—in part owing to a lack of philological groundwork in preparing editions of the source materials necessary for historians to access their past.[48] It is also important to note that the idea that the Europe of the Middle Ages predated genuine nation states itself remains open to debate, with Adrian Hastings extremely wide-ranging study of the history of nationalism taking medieval England as the archetype of this modern form

of political organization.[49] Continuity in awareness of 'national' classifications between medieval and modern Europe is one thing, however, while
objective continuities of 'national' characteristics—or indeed of 'national'
rivalries—are another. Today, after the destructive struggles of the last two
centuries, 'total war' now seems inextricably linked to 'total nationalism'—a
connection that hardened decisively in nineteenth-century Europe and one
which was itself nourished by the work of medieval scholars. The battles of
Medieval: Total War, for their part, derive far more directly from the works
of such thinkers than they do from any recent analysis of the conduct of
warfare in the Middle Ages.

NOTES

1. Elliott Chin, "Medieval: Total War Review," *Gamespot UK*, August 27,
   2002, http://uk.gamespot.com/medieval-total-war/reviews/medieval-total-war-
   review-2878535/ (accessed July 23, 2012).
2. A sample of which includes Charles Oman, *A History of the Art of War in
   the Middle Ages,* 2nd ed. (London: Methuen, 1924); R. C. Smail, *Crusading Warfare,* 2nd ed. (Cambridge, UK: Cambridge University Press, 1995);
   J. F. Verbruggen, *The Art of Warfare in Western Europe During the Middle
   Ages,* 2nd ed., trans. Sumner Willard and R. W. Southern (Woodbridge, UK:
   Boydell, 1997); Philippe Contamine, *War in the Middle Ages,* trans. Michael
   Jones (Oxford: Blackwell, 1984); Jim Bradbury, *The Medieval Siege* (Woodbridge, Suffolk: Boydell, 1992); John France, *Western Warfare in the Age of
   the Crusades* (London: University College London Press, 1999); Matthew
   Strickland, *War and Chivalry: The Conduct and Perception of War in England and Normandy, 1066–1217* (Cambridge, UK: Cambridge University
   Press, 1996). See also the summary given by Bernard S. Bachrach, "Medieval Military Historiography," in *Companion to Historiography,* ed. Michael
   Bentley (London: Routledge, 1997).
3. "Medieval 2: Total War Interview," *IGN PC*, March 31, 2006, http://uk.pc.
   ign.com/articles/699/699515p2.html (accessed July 23, 2012).
4. "Looking Back: Medieval II: Total War," *Computer and Video Games*, June
   24, 2007, http://www.computerandvideogames.com/166477/interviews/
   looking-back-medieval-ii-total-war/ (accessed July 23, 2012).
5. Norman Housley, "European Warfare: c. 1200–1320," in *Medieval Warfare: A History,* ed. Maurice Keen (Oxford: Oxford University Press, 1999),
   121–22.
6. David M. Wilson, ed., *The Bayeux Tapestry* (London: Thames and Hudson,
   2004), pl. 68. See also the account of this incident in William of Poitiers, *The
   Gesta Guillelmi of William of Poitiers,* ed. and trans. R. H. C. Davis and
   Marjorie Chibnall (Oxford: Clarendon Press, 1998), 128–31.
7. John Gillingham, "William the Bastard at War," in *Anglo-Norman Warfare:
   Studies in Late Anglo-Saxon and Anglo-Norman Military Organisation and
   Warfare,* ed. Matthew Strickland (Woodbridge, UK: Boydell, 1992), 145–46.
8. John Gillingham, *Richard I* (New Haven, CT: Yale University Press, 1999), 83.
9. John W. Baldwin, *The Government of Philip Augustus: Foundations of
   French Royal Power in the Middle Ages* (Berkeley: University of California Press, 1986), 217; Rigord, in Henri-François Delaborde, ed., *Œuvres
   de Rigord et de Guillaume le Breton* (Paris: Société de l'histoire de France,
   1882–85) 1:282–83, 286.

10. Anne Curry, *Agincourt: A New History* (Stroud: Tempus, 2005), 15, 187–88.
11. Stephen Morillo, *Warfare under the Anglo-Norman Kings, 1066–1135* (Woodbridge, UK: Boydell, 1994), 104–5.
12. W. L. Warren, *Henry II,* 2nd ed. (New Haven, CT: Yale University Press, 2000), 139; Gerald of Wales, *Giraldi Cambrensis Opera,* ed. J. S. Brewer, J. F. Dimock, and G. F. Warner, Rolls Series 21 (London: Longman, 1861–91), 5:303. It should, however, be noted that the idea that Henry sought always to avoid battle has recently been critically discussed by John D. Hosler, *Henry II: A Medieval Soldier at War* (Leiden: Brill, 2007).
13. Georges Duby, *The Legend of Bouvines: War, Religion and Culture in the Middle Ages,* trans. Catherine Tihanyi (Berkeley: University of California Press, 1990), 110. For analysis of medieval prebattle speeches, see John R. E. Bliese, "Rhetoric and Morale: A Study of Battle Orations from the Central Middle Ages," *Journal of Medieval History* 15 (1989): 201–26.
14. Morillo, *Warfare,* 146, 148.
15. Morillo, *Warfare,* 146.
16. Warren, *Henry II,* 231; Jordan Fantosme, *Chronique,* in *Chronicles of the Reigns of Stephen, Henry II and Richard I,* ed. Richard Howlett, Rolls Series 82 (London: Longman, 1884–89), 242–43.
17. Vegetius, *Epitome of Military Science,* trans. N. P. Milner (Liverpool: Liverpool University Press, 1993), 65. On the wide-ranging influence of this text, see Christopher Allmand, *The De Re Militari of Vegetius: The Reception, Transmission and Legacy of a Roman Text in the Middle Ages* (to Cambridge, UK: Cambridge University Press, 2011); John Gillingham, "Up with Orthodoxy! In Defense of Vegetian Warfare," *Journal of Medieval Military History* 2 (2003): 149–58; Bernard S. Bachrach, "The Practical Use of Vegetius' *De Re Militari* During the Early Middle Ages," *The Historian* 47 (1985): 239–55; Bernard S. Bachrach, "L'Art de la guerre angevin," in *Plantagenêts et Capétiens: confrontations et héritages,* ed. Martin Aurell and Noël-Yves Tonnerre (Turnhout: Brepols, 2006), 267–84; J. A. Wisman, "*L'Epitoma rei militaris* de Végèce et sa fortune au Moyen Âge," *Le Moyen Âge* 85 (1979): 13–31.
18. Sarah Kay, ed. and trans., *Raoul de Cambrai* (Oxford: Clarendon Press, 1991), 76–77.
19. Quoted in David Carpenter, *The Struggle for Mastery: Britain, 1066–1284* (London: Penguin, 2004), 177.
20. Sean McGlynn, "The Myths of Medieval Warfare," *History Today* 44, no. 1 (1994): 34.
21. For the history of this expedition, see James M. Powell, *Anatomy of a Crusade, 1213–1221* (Philadelphia: University of Pennsylvania Press, 1986), 137–62.
22. Dorothy Whitelock, David C. Douglas, and Susie I. Tucker, eds. and trans., *The Anglo-Saxon Chronicle: A Revised Translation* (London: Eyre and Spottiswoode, 1961), 199. Thomas N. Bisson has recently argued that the "disturbances" experienced in Stephen's reign in fact brought England more closely into line with what passed for government in most European realms. See *The Crisis of the Twelfth Century: Power, Lordship and the Origins of European Government* (Princeton, NJ: Princeton University Press, 2009), 269–78.
23. Warren, *Henry II,* 59–60, 140–42.
24. *Crusader Kings,* Paradox Interactive (Paradox Interactive, 2004).
25. For an overview of the historiography of medieval frontier societies, see Nora Berend, "Medievalists and the Notion of the Frontier," *The Medieval History Journal* 2 (1999): 55–72. See also Robert Bartlett and Angus MacKay, eds., *Medieval Frontier Societies* (Oxford: Oxford University Press, 1989); Daniel

Power and Naomi Standen, eds., *Frontiers in Question: Eurasian Border-lands, 700–1700* (Basingstoke: Macmillan, 1999); David Abulafia and Nora Berend, eds., *Medieval Frontiers: Concepts and Practices* (Aldershot, UK: Ashgate, 2002).
26. Quoted in D. A. Bell, *The First Total War: Napoleon's Europe and the Birth of Modern Warfare* (London: Bloomsbury, 2007), 45. The "limited" nature of the wars of the eighteenth century is disputed by John Childs, *Armies and Warfare in Europe, 1648–1789* (New York: Holmes and Meier, 1982).
27. Tim Blanning, *The French Revolutionary Wars, 1787–1802* (London: Arnold, 1996), 14.
28. Text as given in Tim Blanning, *The Pursuit of Glory: Europe, 1648–1815* (London: Allen Lane, 2007), 628.
29. John A. Lynn, "Towards an Army of Honour: The Moral Evolution of the French Army, 1789–1815," *French Historical Studies*16 (1989): 177.
30. Bell, *The First Total War*, 150.
31. Blanning, *The French Revolutionary Wars*, 158–63.
32. Quoted in Gunter Rothenberg, "The Age of Napoleon," in *The Laws of War: Constraints on Warfare in the Western World*, ed. Michael Howard, George J. Andreopoulos, and Mark R. Shulman (New Haven, CT: Yale University Press, 1994), 88.
33. Table source: R. R. Palmer, "Frederick the Great, Guibert, Bülow: From Dynastic to National War," in *Makers of Modern Strategy from Machiavelli to the Nuclear Age*, ed. Peter Paret (Oxford: Clarendon Press, 1986), 100; partially reproduced in Blanning, *The Pursuit of Glory*, 604.
34. Henry of Huntingdon, *Historia Anglorum: The History of the English People*, ed. Diana Greenway (Oxford: Clarendon Press, 1996), 389–93.
35. Gregory Fedorenko, "The Crusading Career of John of Brienne, c.1210–1237," *Nottingham Medieval Studies* 52 (2008): 62–63.
36. Ralph of Coggeshall, *Chronicon anglicanum*, ed. Joseph Stevenson, Rolls Series 66 (London: Longman, 1875), 39; Louis de Mas-Latrie, ed., *Chronique d'Ernoul et de Bernard le Trésorier* (Paris: Société de l'histoire de France, 1871), 278–79. As Christopher Tyerman has argued, "the most consistent hijack of the crusade for national objectives came from the French." See Tyerman, *God's War: A New History of the Crusades* (London: Allen Lane, 2006), 909.
37. Sean McGlynn, *By Sword and Fire: Cruelty and Atrocity in Medieval Warfare* (London: Weidenfeld and Nicolson, 2009), 218. A survey of medieval "laws of war" is given in Robert C. Stacey, "The Age of Chivalry," in Howard et al., *The Laws of War*.
38. McGlynn, *By Sword and Fire*, 218; K. H. Jackson, ed., *A Celtic Miscellany* (Harmondsworth: Penguin, 1971), 239–41.
39. James J. Sheehan, *German History, 1770–1866* (Oxford: Clarendon Press, 1989), 371–74; David E. Barclay, "Medievalism and Nationalism in Nineteenth-Century Germany," *Studies in Medievalism* 5 (1993): 5–22.
40. Joep Leerssen, *National Thought in Europe: A Cultural History* (Amsterdam: Amsterdam University Press, 2006), 143. See also the account of the genesis of the *Monumenta* in David Knowles, *Great Historical Enterprises: Problems in Monastic History* (London: Nelson, 1963), 63–97.
41. Patrick J. Geary, *The Myth of Nations: The Medieval Origins of Europe* (Princeton, NJ: Princeton University Press, 2002), 28.
42. Charles Ridoux, *Évolution des études médiévales en France de 1860 à 1914* (Paris: Champion, 2001).
43. Jules Lair, "Mémoire sur deux chroniques latines composées au XIIe siècle à l'abbaye de Saint-Denis," *Bibliothèque de l'école des chartes* 35 (1874): 545.

44. Léopold Delisle, "Procès-verbaux, séance du conseil d'administration," *Bulletin de la Société de l'histoire de Normandie* 2 (1875–80): 2.
45. John F. Benton, "'Nostre franceis n'unt talent de fuïr,' the *Song of Roland* and the Enculturation of a Warrior Class," in *Culture, Power and Personality in Medieval France,* ed. Thomas N. Bisson (London: Hambledon, 1991); Elizabeth Emery, "The 'Truth' About the Middle Ages: *La Revue des Deux Mondes* and Late Nineteenth-Century French Medievalism," *Prose Studies* 23 (2000): 99–114.
46. J. Campbell, "Stubbs, William (1825–1901)," in *Oxford Dictionary of National Biography,* ed. H. C. G. Matthew and Brian Harrison (Oxford: Oxford University Press, 2004); online ed., ed. Lawrence Goldman, http://www.oxforddnb.com/view/article/36362 (accessed August 27, 2012).
47. Geary, *The Myth of Nations,* 15.
48. Frits van Oostrom, "Spatial Struggles: Medieval Studies between Nationalism and Globalisation," *Journal of English and Germanic Philology* 105 (2006): 12.
49. Adrian Hastings, *The Construction of Nationhood: Ethnicity, Religion and Nationalism* (Cambridge, UK: Cambridge University Press, 2007), 35–65.

5 Gabriel Knight
A Twentieth-Century Chivalric Romance Hero

Angela Tenga

Long before Tom Hanks played the role of Harvard professor Robert Lang-
don in the screen adaptation of Dan Brown's *The Da Vinci Code*—indeed,
well before Brown's novel was even published—the hero of a critically
acclaimed video game series had already stumbled upon the secret bloodline
of Jesus. In the 1990s, Sierra On-Line game designer Jane Jensen forged
a path for new-millennium fiction with a trilogy of paranormal detective
mysteries that incorporated the theory, popularized in the 1980s by Baigent,
Leigh, and Lincoln, that the Holy Grail (*Sangreal*) is Mary Magdalene,
who, as the wife of Jesus, became the vessel that carried the 'Sang Réal,' or
royal blood—a holy bloodline that includes the Merovingian kings and their
modern day descendants.[1] Sierra's *Gabriel Knight* series reinterpreted the
Grail legend and revived the figure of the Arthurian knight in the guise of its
unlikely hero—a lowbrow rogue, inveterate womanizer, third-rate novelist,
and amateur sleuth. Although it is not advertised as such, Gabriel's story is
a profoundly medieval narrative, yet at the same time it adapts tradition and
legend in a way that is particularly suited to its cultural moment. Indeed, the
Gabriel Knight series is best understood as a late-twentieth-century chivalric
romance about a knight who becomes worthy—through ritual, battle, and
illumination—of completing the Grail quest.

Unlike openly Arthurian- or chivalric-themed fiction, the *Gabriel Knight*
series does not loudly proclaim, apart from Gabriel's surname, its link to
knightly traditions. Nor does it appropriate Arthurian material in a super-
ficial, Disneyesque manner; Gabriel does not live on Avalon Way, have
a brawny pal called Lance, or work for Camelot Industries. Instead, the
themes and motifs are woven into the fabric of the series, which traces
Gabriel's evolution from ordinary bookshop proprietor to full-fledged hero.
In this respect, the series echoes what some commentators see as the essence
of the Grail quest: not a search for a physical object, but rather a personal
initiation or "occult investigation," a path along which "one is led gradually, step by step" toward spiritual enlightenment.[2] As Roberta Sabbath has
noted, "Gabriel's quest is the discovery of his true nature. An anti-hero . . .
[t]ied to ghosts and myths and a past he cannot remember, he has no identity."[3] Indeed, as the series opens, Gabriel is haunted by nightmares that

hint at this hidden past. His dreams function in much the same way as the Grail procession witnessed by the knightly hero at the Grail castle, offering what folklorist Juliette Wood has called a "kind of evocative but unspecified significance which was the stock-in-trade of medieval romances."[4] Gabriel's dreams reveal scenes and objects—including a bloody medallion, reminiscent of the bleeding lance seen by Perceval—whose roles he must discover. In doing so, Gabriel learns that he is fated to be a *Schattenjäger*—a warrior whose name means "shadow hunter" and whose mission is to fight the forces of evil—and meets the challenges that come with that destiny.

MONSTROUS IDENTITIES

In each game, Gabriel faces a supernatural menace that challenges him to come to terms with a specific aspect of himself. His monstrous adversaries function as "identity machines," as described by Jeffrey J. Cohen, insisting "that human identity is—despite the best efforts of those who possess it to assert otherwise—unstable, contingent, hybrid, discontinuous."[5] Gabriel's foes dismantle his identity as he knows it so that he can (re)learn and (re)construct who he is. To do so, they force him to learn who he is not, or does not wish to be. David Williams has argued that the medieval theoretical precept that God "can only be known by what He is not" ultimately formed the foundation of "a more generalized medieval habit of thought."[6] This notion is an important heuristic underpinning of Gabriel's adversaries. His monstrous foes lead him to personal illumination largely by negation; by showing him a vision of what he *could* be, they force him to choose what he will *not* be so that he ultimately reveals what he truly *is*. In confronting these enemies, Gabriel embarks on a journey of self-discovery and spiritual refinement that demands recognition and acceptance of his knightly destiny.

THE PATH OF A ROMANCE HERO

From his ritual Schattenjäger initiation to his recovery of the stolen Grail, Gabriel's experience follows the model of chivalric romance. K. S. Whetter identifies several defining features of medieval romance: "the role and prominence of ladies; the role and prominence of love; and the role and prominence of adventure . . . culminating in a happy ending."[7] These are also fundamental building blocks of the games of the *Gabriel Knight* series, both on an individual basis and in aggregate as a cohesive narrative. The first adventure, *Sins of the Fathers,* is set in Gabriel's home town of New Orleans, where his small bookshop takes in barely enough to provide for his needs and compensate his one employee—Grace Nakimura, a graduate student who handles the shop's day-to-day affairs and helps Gabriel with his unofficial investigation of a series of murders that are linked to a voodoo cult. Gabriel's inquiries lead him to Malia Gedde, a wealthy and prominent woman with whom he becomes romantically involved. She is also a voodoo priestess and leader of the powerful underground cartel that is responsible for the murders. In the course of his investigation, Gabriel must seek his Uncle Wolfgang in Germany, where he connects with his ancestry. He learns that Wolfgang is the current Schattenjäger, they work together to defeat the cult, and Wolfgang gives his life in the process. After solving the voodoo murders, Gabriel returns to Germany to take up residence in Schloss Ritter, his ancestral home, and begins his second adventure, *The Beast Within*. When a child is killed by a wolf, the townspeople call upon Gabriel, who is recognized as the new Schattenjäger, to fight the menace that they believe is a werewolf. His investigation leads him to join a local hunt club, led by the charismatic Baron Von Glower, who welcomes Gabriel warmly. Von Glower turns out to be not just a werewolf, but the so-called "Black Wolf" who caused (in the game's fictive history) the downfall of King Ludwig II of Bavaria, the most romantic and romanticized of German kings.[8] Often called the *Märchenkönig*, or fairy-tale king, Ludwig was declared insane and deposed before dying under mysterious circumstances; the game suggests that he was not insane, but a werewolf transformed by Von Glower. On a hunting trip with the other club members, Gabriel is bitten and becomes a werewolf but is later saved, with much help from Grace, through the destruction of Von Glower. In his final adventure, *Blood of the Sacred, Blood of the Damned*, Gabriel travels to the French town of Rennes-le-Chateau to find the kidnapped son of Prince James of Scotland. With Grace's help, Gabriel rescues the infant, a descendant of Jesus, and thereby thwarts the attempt of a vampire cult to steal the Holy Grail—that is, the vessel that carries the sacred blood in the current generation. In doing so, Gabriel learns the secret of his lineage, an atonement two millennia in the making: Gabriel's ancestor, a penitent Roman soldier who had nailed Jesus to the cross, promised that his descendants would serve the family of Jesus. Jesus forgave him, kissed his sword, confirmed him as a "servant to the light," and established his sacred knighthood. With the Grail restored, the hidden origins of the Schattenjäger disclosed, and his ancestral duty fulfilled, Gabriel is fully realized not just as a romance hero, but also as an ordained Christian knight.

Gabriel knows nothing of his ancestry and this ancient debt when he formally accepts his Schattenjäger duty in the first game of the series. Having failed to find Wolfgang at his Bavarian home, Gabriel goes to the chapel at Schloss Ritter and 'reads' a series of tapestry panels that depict the Schattenjäger initiation rite, which mirrors features of historical accounts of the ceremonial induction into knighthood. Gabriel's initiation begins with a cleansing of hands, a parallel to the ritual bath taken by medieval knights on the eve of their induction to signify "the need to cleanse their bodies henceforth from all impurities of sin and dishonorable ways of life."[9] Gabriel mixes blood and salt in a chalice; this seems to serve as a (more literal) substitute for medieval knights' donning of red tunics to symbolize that they were "pledged to shed their blood to defend and maintain the faith of Our Lord."[10] In the final step, Gabriel kneels at an altar and recites an oath dedicated to St. George (for whom his French Quarter bookshop is also named), echoing the knightly oaths and "sworn obligations" described in medieval sources.[11] In this ceremony, Gabriel yields to the instability and discontinuity of his identity to establish a new relationship with history; he indicates his willingness to leave his accustomed life behind to find his rightful place in an ancestral time line. This rite of passage—an important prelude to the Schattenjäger battles that he will face—is rooted in the medieval knighthood upon which romance heroes were modeled.

KNIGHTLY BATTLES

As a thematic and structural motif, the battle, trial, or test is as integral to the *Gabriel Knight* series as it is to chivalric romance. "Chivalric prowess is represented as something like a bloodright," notes Peggy McCracken, "and the importance of lineage is particularly evident in romances about unknown knights who reveal their noble identity through their extraordinary prowess."[12] Similarly, Gabriel demonstrates his prowess, battle by battle, to reveal ever-deepening layers of his hidden identity throughout the series. His first challenge is overcoming the beautiful, seductive Malia Gedde, despite his powerful attraction to her. Malia is controlled by the spirit of her ancestor, Tetelo, who was wronged by one of Gabriel's ancestors and is thus an enemy of the Schattenjäger. As Malory's Morgan le Fay deprived Arthur of the legendary Excalibur and its magical scabbard, Tetelo has stolen the protective Schattenjäger talisman belonging to Gabriel's ancestor. Reclaiming the talisman is one of Gabriel's first tasks on his journey to becoming a Schattenjäger, and doing so establishes his claim to that title as pulling a mystical sword from a stone establishes Arthur's kingship in medieval sources. Moreover, Tetelo's enslavement of a descendant's will is a neat metaphor for familial duty: as Malia serves her family, so Gabriel—as he learns in the course of the game—is bound by duties that come with his own heritage, a heritage of which he, like young Perceval, is ignorant. Malia teaches Gabriel by negation, offering a vision of ancestry that should *not* be honored; she is a fitting teacher because her monstrosity is a function of her lineage, and Gabriel's task here is to discover how his lineage has shaped him.

In *The Beast Within*, the Arthurian fellowship is reconstituted as an all-male hunt club led by an alluring, well-bred werewolf who invites Gabriel to become his eternal companion. When Gabriel is bitten, he must choose whether to accept a life of physical pleasure as a werewolf or fight for his humanity. Baron Von Glower is a fitting teacher not only because his monstrosity, too, has been shaped by his lineage—an inherited curse—but also because he reflects Gabriel's primal drives, especially his notorious libidinous and predatory instincts. Von Glower, like monsters and giants faced by some Arthurian heroes, is a figure of a threatening "hyper-masculinity" that operates outside social rules: "uncivilized and ungoverned," they are man "let loose to express his basest nature."[13] However, while Von Glower has formed a werewolf pack that threatens the civilized order, he also embodies the order itself—a perfect image of the medieval monster, whose "proper function is to negate the very order of which [it] is a part."[14] An aristocrat whose life is based on hereditary privilege, Baron Von Glower is a gracious, well-read, refined, and courteous monster.[15] Thus, although the narrative presents a dualistic reality in which light and dark, civilized and savage, Schattenjäger and werewolf oppose each other, it also presents a world that resists such easy binary division, a world whose borders are no longer fixed and stable. Even Von Glower's invitation to Gabriel is ambiguous; although he and Gabriel trade anecdotes about their dealings with women, and Von Glower 'lends' Gabriel his own curvaceous female companion one night, there are strong hints that his interest in Gabriel is, on some level, romantic. Indeed, although the narrative 'clarifies' that King Ludwig's alleged suicide was motivated not by guilt for his homosexual desires, but by hate of his werewolfism, the parallels between Gabriel's friendship with Von Glower and Ludwig's friendships with his male companions—Von Glower among them—highlight the duplication of tensions from the game's imagined history in the present narrative. Von Glower's otherness unites a disorienting assortment of apparent contraries, forcing Gabriel to confront his own hybridity and examine the beastly, ungovernable, unmapped territories within himself. Through Von Glower, Gabriel ultimately commits to a more spiritual vision; rejecting his wolf-self, he decides what he is *not* and chooses his humanity, thus preparing for his final test.

In the last game of the series, *Blood of the Sacred, Blood of the Damned*, Gabriel pursues a vampire coven that wants to drink the powerful blood of the modern-day descendants of Jesus. His adversary, Excelsior Montreaux,[16] is the coven leader and also a vintner. His consumption of human blood behind the facade of his vineyard highlights the traditional vampiric inversion of the Christian sacrament of communion: he unites in himself the wine both before and after transubstantiation. It is here that Gabriel's life mission is most explicitly linked to Arthurian legend as he discovers that the secret of Rennes-le-Chateau is nothing less than the truth of the Holy Grail— the well-hidden bloodline of Jesus and Mary Magdalene. As a monstrous teacher, Montreaux is an inverse Gabriel who reflects the dark potential of his supernatural blood. As leader of the Adepts of the Holy Blood, Montreaux seeks to usurp the power of the sacred blood; Gabriel, in contrast, honors the duty that was conferred upon him because of his ancestral role in shedding that blood. The name of Montreaux's vineyard, Chateau de Serres, echoes that of one of the legendary Grail sites, Sarras, suggesting that vampiric Montreaux is an anti-Grail king; nourished by blood and steeped in the occult, he is sustained in a magical, but unholy, way. In vanquishing Montreaux, Gabriel not only completes his knightly mission by recovering the Grail, but also, by repaying his ancestral debt, becomes worthy of the revelation of his familial calling; in that moment, he is literally struck by light and, through this spiritual illumination, finds his personal grail as well.

LADIES, LOVE, AND LIGHT

Just as Gabriel's adversaries are monstrous Others who help him renegotiate his identity, gendered Others also play an important role in the illumination that reveals his true self. Game designer Jane Jensen has stated that she wanted to "reach a demographic—older people and more women—who would like story-based gaming."[17] Although measuring Jensen's success at reaching this audience is not an objective of this study, the role of women in her narrative deserves attention; women occupy an important imaginative space in the *Gabriel Knight* series, as they do in chivalric romance, and their roles both recall and revise that tradition.

The construction of the feminine in the series relies heavily on its central female figure, Grace Nakimura.[18] Although Grace's character varies throughout the series, her contribution is always essential; her research supports Gabriel's investigation, field work, and direct confrontations with suspects. However, although Grace is rightly considered Gabriel's costar, she is not his equal. Her role is primarily a response to Gabriel's decisions and directives, and in a hypothetical organizational chart of the series her place would lie beneath Gabriel's executive-level position in what would be classified as a support function. In *Sins of the Fathers,* only Gabriel is seen outside the confines of the bookshop; although Grace works independently within the shop, she does not even exist outside of it until she is kidnapped by members of the voodoo cult—a development that emphasizes female vulnerability by making her a damsel in distress who must be rescued. Further, despite her barbed comments about Gabriel's womanizing, Grace exhibits few interests that are not firmly rooted in him and his work. Moreover, in *The Beast Within* a new Grace emerges. This Grace, though intelligent, capable, and resourceful—and now even endowed with an autonomous existence through the device of alternating gameplay as Gabriel and Grace—is also aggressive and volatile, and her belligerence toward a perceived rival draws on the stereotype of the jealous, territorial woman. Her research uncovers essential insights, though, and she is instrumental in destroying Von Glower. Finally, at the end of *Blood of the Sacred, Blood of the Damned,* Grace leaves secretly after Gabriel not only fails to acknowledge a passionate night that they spent together, but also continues to show interest in Madeline Buthane, the leader of a tour group staying at their hotel. Her disappearance is ambiguous; players are not permitted to read the note that she leaves for Gabriel, but it is strongly suggested that she plans to seek enlightenment by studying with a spiritual mentor. It is not clear, however, if this decision is prompted by Gabriel's response or by her own initiative. The former conclusion is invited by the parting comment made to Grace by Emilio Baza, another figure in the cosmic drama; his advice—"When one path to your destiny is blocked, another will appear"[19]—suggests that the blocked path is a future with Gabriel, with the alternate path as second choice. Indeed, it is not clear that Grace would seek another path at all if she had confidence in Gabriel's feelings for her. Her decision to leave is thus presented more as a reaction to Gabriel than as a manifestation of an independent, preexisting desire for self-actualization. Overall, the series does not, through its depiction of Grace, clearly and consistently transform traditional views of women as helpers, subordinates, objects, and secondary beings. Although the series hints at the potential for a more fully realized woman, its construction of the feminine owes much to medieval predecessors, which characterized women as "reactive, defensive" and focused on "damage limitation" for the more central male figure.[20]

If women in the *Gabriel Knight* series do not fully transcend medieval romance limitations, they at least retain the prominence of romance heroines, even as the narrative questions the stability of heteronormative constructs. In particular, the courtly ideal of an ennobling femininity finds voice in the series as numerous women help Gabriel fulfill his destiny. This is first suggested on the night after Gabriel performs the Schattenjäger initiation rite, when a dream-vision informs him that he will be allowed to tread the Schattenjäger path because three women have loved him purely, proving his worthiness.[21] In *Sins of the Fathers*, Gabriel is helped by Magentia Moonbeam, a voodoo priestess; Madame Lorelei, a fortune teller; and Madame Cazaunoux, a voodoo adherent. Even Malia Gedde, at times his adversary, ultimately suggests a redemptive femininity as she falls willingly to her death to destroy Tetelo and thereby save Gabriel. However, in the second game of the series, the prominence of femininity is challenged by Gabriel's deepening relationship with Baron Von Glower. Not only is Gabriel's humanity compromised, but his gender role is, too, as *The Beast Within* demands reconsideration of the hypermasculine protagonist of *Sins of the Fathers*. Knighthood, however, is at odds with the homoerotic, which is linked to aggression, violence, and degraded humanity. The destruction of Baron Von Glower—along with Grace's role in exposing and eliminating him—signals a 'safe' return to a heteronormative reality; Gabriel's reclaiming of his traditional heterosexual identity despite his (symbolically sexual) blood bond with Baron Von Glower is a step toward revealing his illuminated self. On the prowl again in *Blood of the Sacred, Blood of the Damned*, Gabriel resumes his flirtation with Madeline Buthane until his eventual realization (long anticipated by many players) that he belongs with Grace. His rejection of Madeline, coupled with Grace's decision to leave, confirms Gabriel's role as a courtly lover. As the series closes, Gabriel and Grace are parted, but she has fostered his heroic evolution by supporting his work, conducting life-saving research, standing by him through his trials, and offering him the possibility of genuine love. Thus, upon completing his mission, Gabriel attains grace, but loses Grace. The series denies Gabriel one of the traditional features of a happy ending—marriage—but in a way, it leaves him at an appropriate ending: single, mission-oriented, in service to Christ, and devoted to a lady whom he cannot have.

A HERO FOR HIS TIME

Like its medieval predecessors, the *Gabriel Knight* series is also a class-conscious artifact that associates moral understanding with social status. Becoming the new Schattenjäger propels Gabriel upward socially as he advances into the ranks of privilege. Initially, Gabriel lives at society's margins and casually exploits the disenfranchised, including hungry street performers and hapless drug addicts. As the series progresses, Gabriel moves from his one-room dwelling in the back of his bookshop to his hereditary castle in Rittersberg; his work on the voodoo murders becomes the basis of a novel that transforms his unsuccessful literary career; he starts socializing with German aristocrats; and, ultimately, he undertakes a critical mission for a European prince. Gabriel's progression nicely fits the model of knights like Parzival, who is raised without knowledge of chivalry and must discover his knightly destiny. As Constance Bouchard notes, "Noble birth, with its glorious attributes, always emerged . . . no matter how much someone tried to hide it . . . [yet] there was always a tension between nobility of blood and nobility of spirit."[22] Unlike chivalric romance, though, the *Gabriel Knight* series was not designed for a social elite; a democratized hero suits the tastes of late-millennium Western players. Thus, even as Gabriel evolves spiritually and climbs socially, his manners remain rough and his exterior coarse, suggesting that inner nobility will indeed come out—but it might come out perpetually clad in jeans and a T-shirt.

Gabriel is thus best understood in terms of both contemporary values and his chivalric roots; because the medieval knight remains embedded in Gabriel Knight, his heroic status cannot be measured by the yardstick of our own era alone. Ray B. Browne has argued that today's hero, "perhaps best stereotypically and formulaically exemplified by soap operas," is, like heroes of old, a mirror for our ideals; however, because of shifting ideals, today's heroism is based on "wealth, power, beauty, self-indulgence," reflecting "the new materialistic bent."[23] Gabriel Knight does not fit neatly into this mold. However, he follows the model of medieval romance heroes in important ways: although his parentage is not obscure in the traditional sense, he knows little of his parents, who died when he was eight years old; the basic facts of his identity are known, but larger truths about who he is are hidden; he overcomes extraordinary challenges in a series of adventures; and his success contributes to the safety of those whom he serves and to the stability of his community. Moreover, his duality—as both knight and rogue, man and beast, savior and sinner—aligns him with many heroes of medieval romance, who can be, as Neil Cartlidge has noted, "morally ambiguous, antisocial or even downright sinister."[24] Gabriel, in his most highly evolved state, also reflects human values that are not bounded by cultural milieu, values that have long persisted in Arthurian cultural productions—the drive to defeat the dark powers in the ongoing battle of life and the quest for self, enlightenment, and transcendence.

The relevance of such values was renewed in the years during which Gabriel Knight was undertaking his quests. As the Great Famine, the Black Death, the Hundred Years' War, the Western Schism, and other crises undermined belief in late medieval society, so late-millennium Western society had lost its faith. Writing in 1989, James Combs describes the contemporary era as a "historical vacuum" that was "reminiscent of the waning of the Middle Ages" in that both suffered from a profound and widespread disenchantment that led many to seek new sources of meaning and, on some level, magic: "If the world is being emptied of miracle, mystery, and authority, we seek it all the more in experiences that substitute for the institutions . . . that used to be the agencies of sacral values, but have been eclipsed by their slow but sure delegitimation."[25] In the United States in particular, a climate that Haynes Johnson has described as one of alienation, distrust, and disbelief prevailed, in an age of "opportunities missed" when a nation that had "arrived at a moment of peak power and influence . . . permitted those opportunities to be squandered."[26] At the center of this drama, Johnson places William Jefferson Clinton, "a leader of such talents and complexities, such strengths and weaknesses, that his very successes and failures typify America."[27] This is not to say that President Clinton should be viewed as the model for Gabriel or that Gabriel's adventures were modeled after Clinton's presidency, which spans the period during which the *Gabriel Knight* games were released. Instead, the series can be studied as an artifact that responds to its cultural climate. Gabriel's own ambivalent duality mirrors that of 1990s America and its leader for most of that decade. Perhaps Gabriel is not unlike the troubled nation in which he was born (or its leader), a hero whose adventures are fraught with unsteady progress and inglorious moments—yet in the fantasy world of the video game, also a hero who manages, despite internal contradictions and persistently rough edges, to overcome all the obstacles and save the day. Like the hero figures described by Susan Butvin Sainato, Gabriel is "not necessarily perfect" but "strive[s] to make the world a better place, battle by battle."[28] He is, perhaps, the gestalt of a knight in shining armor to a 1990s American. To connect that knight with Arthurian legend is a small step in a culture that was haunted by its own unrealized potential, a culture that had, as it were, glimpsed the Grail procession but failed to ask the Grail questions.

Posing the right questions is also a key task in the series as players must interview non-player characters (NPCs) to obtain essential information. Omitting an important question can impede or prevent progress in the game. Through interaction with NPCs and application of the information received from them to complete tasks, players simulate the experience of undertaking a hero's quest and sharing a hero's risks. In the course of the game, players die repeatedly and are reborn, but the hero's true death is so inconceivable that the risk is not loss of life but lack of closure. The games thus pose primarily a narrative danger: the player has confidence in his character's survival but lacks the certainty of completion. In this way, the player's position with respect to the interactive romance nearly parallels literary antecedents: "In Chrétien's finely-constructed Arthurian world, there is no risk at all; the court, the testing-ground . . . and all obstacles and opponents exist solely to permit the development of the knight-protagonist; the threat of death . . . is understood to be an illusion, no more than a function of narrative drama."[29] The success of the player-hero also rests in the ability to close the tale and fulfill the hero's narrative potential.

CONCLUSION

By crafting an imaginative space where knighthood is renewed and revised, the *Gabriel Knight* series explores the relationship of identity and lineage in terms that are meaningful to a late-millennium audience. Juliette Wood has explored how the concern with the corruption of secular chivalry found in some later Arthurian romances led to a contrast between "the courtly world of Arthur, typified by Gawain, and the grail world to which only knights like Parzival can aspire."[30] As a late-millennium knight, Gabriel is both Gawain and Parzival, uniting the secular chivalry of the former with the Grail knighthood of the latter. Roberta Sabbath has proposed that the Gabriel of *Sins of the Fathers* "represents a dominant culture that has lost its values and soul."[31] If this is true, perhaps Gabriel's redemption in *Blood of the Sacred, Blood of the Damned* suggests hope for a redeemable world. By suggesting that his current trials are rooted in an ancestral debt incurred at the crucifixion of Jesus, the series constructs Gabriel's present as a response to and culmination of history. The centrality of history and mystery in the series infuses the human quest for meaning with a magical flavor, revealing the connection of an inscrutable present with the past that has shaped it, while the revelation of the true nature of Gabriel's calling at the end of the series spiritualizes his quest, transforming adventure into mission and returning the series to the medieval roots of mystery: dramatic depictions of biblical themes. An interactive, digitized chivalric romance, the *Gabriel Knight* series invites game players to seek the 'Knight' within and recover Camelot in the postmodern city.

NOTES

1. Michael Baigent, Richard Leigh, and Henry Lincoln, *Holy Blood, Holy Grail* (New York: Dell, 1983). Gabriel actually sees an advertisement for this book in a bookshop window in Rennes-le-Chateau in the third game of the series.

2. Rudolf Steiner, *Christ and the Spiritual World and the Search for the Holy Grail*, trans. C. Davy and D. Osmond (London: Rudolf Steiner Press, 1963), 99.
3. Roberta Sabbath, "Jane Jensen's *Gabriel Knight: Sins of the Fathers*/The Numinous Woman and the Millennium Woman," *Journal of Popular Culture* 31, no. 1 (1997): 142.
4. Juliette Wood, "Holy Grail: From Romance Motif to Modern Genre," *Folklore* 111, no. 2 (2000): 176.
5. Jeffrey J. Cohen, *Medieval Identity Machines* (Kindle edition), Kindle Location 190.
6. David Williams, *Deformed Discourse: The Function of the Monster in Mediaeval Thought and Literature* (Montreal: McGill-Queen's University Press, 1996), 5.
7. K. S. Whetter, *Understanding Genre and Medieval Romance* (Burlington, VT: Ashgate, 2008), 64.
8. In its construction of an alternate, supernatural history, Jensen's storyline is perhaps ahead of its time, anticipating a wave of popular works, such as *Abraham Lincoln, Vampire Hunter*, that would do the same.
9. Geoffroi de Charny, *A Knight's Own Book of Chivalry*, trans. Elspeth Kennedy (Philadelphia: University of Pennsylvania Press, 2005), 91.
10. de Charny, *A Knight's Own Book*, 91.
11. Maurice Keen, *Chivalry* (New Haven: Yale University Press, 1984), 71.
12. Peggy McCracken, "The Poetics of Sacrifice: Allegory and Myth in the Grail Quest," *Yale French Studies* 95 (1999): 162.
13. Kathleen L. Nichols, "Many Monsters to Destroy," *Arthurian Legend*, http://www.uiweb.uidaho.edu/student_orgs/arthurian_legend/quests/monsters/agiants.html (accessed June 25, 2010).
14. Williams, *Deformed Discourse*, 14.
15. Reading the hunt club's predation upon the townsfolk as a general comment on the relationship between the privileged and the common is attractive, but such a reading falls outside the scope of this study.
16. This name is given variously as "Montreux" and "Montreaux" within the game.
17. Alistair Wallis, "Playing Catch Up: *Gabriel Knight*'s Jane Jensen," *Gamasutra News*, http://www.gamasutra.com/phpbin/news_index.php?story=13978 (accessed July 7, 2012).
18. Like Gabriel's foes, Grace also teaches by negation; a Japanese-American who resists her parents' traditional ways, she shows what Gabriel must *not* do if he is to fulfill his heroic potential.
19. *Blood of the Sacred, Blood of the Damned*, Sierra On-Line (Sierra On-Line, 1999).
20. Amanda Hopkins, "Female Vulnerability as Catalyst in the Middle English Breton Lays," in *The Matter of Identity in Medieval Romance*, ed. Phillipa Hardman (Cambridge, UK: D. S. Brewer, 2002), 44. For an interesting view that counters the traditional notion of women as passive objects in the world of medieval literature, see Amy N. Vines, *Women's Power in Late Medieval Romance* (Cambridge, UK: D. S. Brewer, 2011).
21. These three women are not named, but players may reasonably guess that they are Gabriel's grandmother, who raised him after his parents' death; Grace; and Malia, who acts as an enemy only when controlled by Tetelo's spirit.
22. Constance Bouchard, *Strong of Body, Brave and Noble: Chivalry and Society in Medieval France* (Ithaca, NY: Cornell University Press, 1998), 3–4.
23. Ray B. Browne, "Hero with 2000 Faces," in *Profiles of Popular Culture, A Reader*, ed. Ray B. Browne (Madison: University of Wisconsin Popular Press, 2005), 21.

24. Neil Cartlidge, introduction to *Heroes and Anti-Heroes in Medieval Romance,* ed. Neil Cartlidge (Cambridge, UK: D. S. Brewer, 2012), 1.
25. James Combs, "Celebrations: Rituals of Popular Veneration," in *Profiles of Popular Culture: A Reader,* ed. Ray B. Browne (Madison: University of Wisconsin Popular Press, 2005), 279.
26. Haynes Johnson, *The Best of Times: The Boom and Bust Years of America Before and After Everything Changed* (New York: Harcourt, 2001), 6.
27. Johnson, *The Best of Times,* 7.
28. Susan Butvin Sainato, "Not Your Typical Knight: The Emerging On-Screen Defender," in *The Medieval Hero on Screen: Representations from Beowulf to Buffy,* ed. Martha W. Driver and Sid Ray (Jefferson, NC: McFarland, 2004), 134.
29. Laura Ashe, "*Sir Gawain and the Green Knight* and the Limits of Chivalry," in *The Exploitations of Medieval Romance,* ed. Laura Ashe, Ivana Djordjević, and Judith Weiss (Cambridge, UK: D. S. Brewer, 2010), 164.
30. Wood, "Holy Grail," 178.
31. Sabbath, "Jensen's *Gabriel Knight*," 136.

Part III
Case Study 1: *World of Warcraft*

6 Coloring Tension

Medieval and Contemporary Concepts in Classifying and Using Digital Objects in *World of Warcraft*

Elysse T. Meredith

In *World of Warcraft*, digital objects function as both necessity and reward. Each of these pseudomedieval articles is automatically ordered within a color-based classification system that blends late-medieval color values with modern color symbolism. Although the most useful or prestigious items are only gained through long hours of play, items are also bought or received from non-player characters (NPCs) and traded with Player-Characters (PCs) through several methods. By examining the color classification system in *World of Warcraft*, this essay addresses how in-game treatment of pixel-based artifacts mediates between certain capitalistic game structures and the nominally feudal and manorial setting to alter the overall gaming experience. After establishing the relationship between medieval and modern color conceptions, this study examines how color-based classifiers are employed in-game before analyzing the relationship between the game's classification structures and economic systems.

Within video games, the relationship between person and object is particularly interesting because the object is not physically real. Although these objects blend digital art and text (via item descriptions and statistics), continuously pointing towards real objects, they are intangible. Existing solely as projected renderings, they are only relative to physical objects.[1] Yet the items presented in *World of Warcraft* are not even facsimiles of real armor and weaponry; rather, they are filtered through the limitations of video game modeling and *World of Warcraft*'s quasi-cartoonish aesthetic and high-fantasy lens. Indeed, these objects reflect Merleau-Ponty's description of language: they are outside reality, acting as that which "speaks *of* being and *of* the world" but that can never be physically experienced.[2] These items are truly ethereal.

The items in *World of Warcraft* are part of a legacy. *World of Warcraft* is Blizzard Entertainment's most recent addition to its successful *Warcraft* franchise, begun in 1994 with *Warcraft: Orcs and Humans*. *World of Warcraft* was released in 2004 in celebration of the tenth anniversary of the original *Warcraft* and is the only game within the franchise to not be a real-time strategy (RTS) game. Instead, *World of Warcraft* is a massively multiplayer online role-playing game (MMORPG), and it necessarily emphasizes individual character and personal interaction within the world and its wider storyline (its 'mythology' or 'lore'). The game itself is part of the high-fantasy genre inspired by medieval literature (and nominally created by J. R. R. Tolkien's *Lord of the Rings*). This essay is based upon *World of Warcraft* version 4.3.4, which includes three expansions: *The Burning Crusade* (2007), *Wrath of the Lich King* (2008), and *Cataclysm* (2010).[3] In addition, this examination utilized the official U.S. *World of Warcraft* website, particularly the official "Game Guide" and "Forums"; two user-edited fan-built databases endorsed by Blizzard, *Wowpedia* and *Wowhead*; and *WoW_Ladies*, an independent group blog organized as a safe space for female players.[4]

Though individual players may approach the game through different lenses, to adequately examine such broad subject matter this essay approaches *World of Warcraft* as a type of interactive visual literature that is somewhat malleable, sequential, and unrepeatable. Although quests (storylines involving various tasks) may be repeated using a different PC, most quests once completed cannot be repeated by the same PC, therefore making that PC's experience of the narrative unique. Furthermore, expansions advance the game's overall story arc; although previous quests and in-game events may be referenced, PCs are no longer able to experience these earlier narratives. This quasi-literary approach is justified through *World of Warcraft*'s heavy reliance on text. All player interaction takes place via a text-based chat room, and all quests are given to the PC through a written text (nominally spoken by an NPC) divided into task, description, and reward (whereby the description is a small story that may connect with other quests or the larger mythology).[5]

The false primacy of the image in *World of Warcraft* is evidenced particularly by objects. When offered in transaction, items are represented not by their three-dimensional model but through a two-dimensional icon that, when touched with a mouse, presents a box with the item's statistics. These icons are limited in number and do not accurately represent the item's three-dimensional appearance. Instead, this structure allows for and emphasizes instant analysis of the quality of the item offered. Specifically, it is the color of the name of these objects that indicates in which level of the color-based quality-classification system it belongs. Therefore, this discussion focuses primarily on the colors given to the labels of these objects.

MEDIEVAL AND MODERN COLOR CONCEPTIONS

The perception of colors and their associated attributes are both specific and plural, differing depending on historical period and culture; perception and interpretation are heavily reliant on context.[6] In many ways the cultural color associations concerned here, from the fourteenth and fifteenth centuries and the twenty-first century, differ drastically from one another.

Indeed, to suggest that the spectrum of classification colors used in *World of Warcraft* is directly inspired by any medieval conception of colors would be a misstep. However, as close examination shall demonstrate, the spectrum employed in *World of Warcraft* bears close similarities to valuation of colors in the late Middle Ages, a period that in visual aesthetics and social norms has strongly influenced the high-fantasy genre. This suggests a strong correlation, if not causation. At minimum, there is a cultural comprehension that certain colors are appropriate and/or prestigious within a high-fantasy, quasi-medieval setting.

The modern spectrum is arguably the rainbow—red, orange, yellow, green, blue, indigo, violet. Red, yellow, and blue are primary colors that when combined create secondary colors (orange, green, purple). Within this system, black and white are not colors but shades. However, this spectrum was only developed after Newtonian optics were introduced. Although aspects of the modern spectrum may be scientific fact, human perception of colors is by no means consistent. Indeed, when Woolgar discussed in *The Senses in Late Medieval England* an argument that all languages will, at minimum, contain seven basic colors (red, yellow, green, blue, black, white, and brown), he noted that twelfth- and thirteenth-century French regularly only used six colors (combining brown-black).[7] Recent linguistic work by Daniel L. Everett has challenged this further with claims that the Pirahã language of the Brazilian Amazon only distinguishes 'light' and 'dark'; there are no colors in Pirahã.[8] This rejection of the concept of a 'natural' spectrum of colors is also supported by Michel Pastoureau's study of colors, which notes that the primary spectrum used in antiquity was red, white, and black.[9]

Modern color theory further complicates discussion by distinguishing between pigment-based and light-based colors.[10] To simply label colors in language is difficult, for color names may be simple, conceptual, specific, complex, referential, or descriptive of value; their symbolic associations are equally complex.[11] Because of such issues, modern industries dealing with color forgo names (outside of those given to entice consumers) and instead use numbers that are either pigment- or light-based. For example, computer monitors, being light-based, generally use RGB (red, green, blue) light values, while HTML uses hexadecimal codes (for example, #000000 is pure black) that are then interpreted into RGB values.

Naturally, medieval color conceptions predate Newtonian optics. Instead, medieval color theory was descended from Aristotelian theory (which included the red–white–black triad of antiquity) and was developed by medieval theorists such as Robert Grosseteste, his student Roger Bacon, and Bartholomew the Englishman.[12] However, recorded color associations were as varied, opaque, and potentially contradictory as in the modern spectrum and were associated with things as disparate as the seasons, the liturgical year, the humors, gender, and morality.[13] Nonetheless, medieval color theories differ strongly from contemporary concepts in that color value was divided into three categories: hue, depth, and luster, the latter being arguably the most important.[14] As modern conceptions of color focus primarily on hue, the other two concepts must be excluded in this discussion. Indeed, luster is almost impossible to quantify in a discussion of light-based color values, as luster relies upon reflection, not emanation, of light.

Thus, it seems most sensible to compare the categories in *World of Warcraft* to heraldic blazon. Heraldry is also a classification system that serves to order what is otherwise an abstract identificatory art form.[15] Overall, its colors are minimal, limited to *argent* (silver), *azur* (blue), *gules* (red), *or* (gold), *sable* (black), and *vert* (green) in the fourteenth century, with the fifteenth century adding *purpure* (purple).[16] These terms themselves are categories, organizing multiple hues under one monochromatic conceptual term. Thus lemon yellow, neon yellow, and pure gold are all *or*, baby blue and indigo are both *azur*. Hue, depth, and luster are superfluous in heraldry. Heraldic colors are both concept and category.

IMPLEMENTATION OF COLOR IN *WORLD OF WARCRAFT*

World of Warcraft introduces the conceptual aspect of colors to its classification system through naming each item-quality category with a prestige-value descriptor: poor, common, uncommon, rare, epic, legendary, and heirloom/ artifact. However, these descriptors are not used on in-game item statistics bubbles. Instead, the title of the item is colored with the color that corresponds with the category: grey (poor), white (common), green (uncommon), blue (rare), purple (epic), orange (legendary), and pale gold (heirloom/ artifact). The player is expected to identify the quality of these items based on a combination of its statistics and its title color. Indeed, it is not uncommon for players to refer to categories by their colors (thus uncommon items are 'greens,' epic items are 'purples').

Labeling common items with white is particularly intriguing because medieval white was often seen as a positive, even heavenly, color, and was used to represent precious silver or *argent* in heraldry; even today white is often given positive moral values.[17] Rather, white seems to be drawn correlatively from the use of gray, which is not part of medieval heraldry. In this system, the colors of the poor and common items are drawn from modern symbolisms: gray is a noncolor, median of the shades black and white, with no greater value (like poor-quality items). White is therefore an improvement from worthless gray: it is unstained and purified. The purity of white is exactly why it was (and can still be) viewed as a heavenly or positive color; it was devoid of impurity and therefore demonstrated sinlessness. However, although *World of Warcraft* contains fictional religions, these do not have a strong moral bent; therefore, white only functions as 'blank,' basic, and undyed. It is without the prestige of rich colors and higher-ranked items.

Notably, the valuation names of 'common' (white) and 'uncommon' (green) are not actually entirely accurate. Common items are primarily used at the lowest levels of the game, and some poor-quality items may be of better use at this level (e.g., offering greater armor protection, though not worth more in-game currency). For example, there are four two-handed swords of poor quality available to players that outrank all two-handed swords of common quality, while the lowest level of poor-quality trousers, 'Unkempt Pants,' are minutely better than the common trousers that a PC begins with.[18] Furthermore, uncommon (green) items are in fact roughly equal in number to common items: uncommon and common items are equally common.[19]

Green (uncommon) items' widespread availability and equivalent middling status roughly corresponds with late-medieval color valuation of green: although a common color it was never popular, and *vert* was the least-used color in heraldry.[20] Conversely, rare (blue) items are much more limited and therefore prestigious in *World of Warcraft*. Indeed, no uncommon daggers outrank the rare dagger Barim's Main Gauche, which can only be received from two specific *mobs* (short for *mobile objects*—monsters or NPC opponents) in the same dungeon (a repeatable multiplayer quest requiring five to forty people with several linked phases).[21] Because of this, only one PC per group per dungeon experience might receive Barim's Main Gauche. The prestige of these rare items corresponds with the popularity of blue in the late medieval period. Thanks to technological advances, blue pigment became available in the twelfth century and cloth dye by the fourteenth.[22] Blue became strongly tied to significant figures in religion, politics, and culture, such as the Virgin Mary, French royalty, and King Arthur.[23] By 1400, *azur* was the most popular color in heraldry, appearing on 30 percent of arms and rivaled only by *sable*.[24] This color's prestige translates to the rare items of *World of Warcraft*, which give multiple statistical plusses and, as with Barim's Main Gauche, are often rewards from special *mobs*.

Although epic (purple) items actually outnumber rare items in-game, they are primarily available from difficult and high-level *mobs*, many of which are only found in multiplayer dungeons. Combined with the greater statistical bonuses of epic items, the greater prestige of receiving a purple increases its value. Notably, although purple only appeared in heraldry in the early fifteenth century as *purpure*, the concept of 'royal purple' is first recorded in late antiquity, when it was a cloth dye produced from the *Murex* species of sea snail.[25] This dye yielded a range of colors that included blues and greens as well as royal purple. The popular medieval dye *kermes*, from the *Kermes* insect, was used similarly as it yielded comparable colors (including purples), but *kermes* was more prized for the rich red it produced.[26] The royal purple produced by these dyes was not a true intermediary between red and blue, but rather less blue, appearing red or even pink to a modern eye. Yet the concept of royal purple is a powerful and historically lengthy one, and the prestige of *World of Warcraft*'s epic items seems to connect to this concept, if not the exact color.

Uncommon (green), rare (blue), and epic (purple) items are the most commonly used items within *World of Warcraft*. Indeed, *Wowpedia* notes that "epic [items] may often be considered the best in the game" due to the rarity of legendary items and the usefulness of epics.[27] These three brackets contain colors that are appropriate in a medieval sense: the common uncommons are common green, rares are popular prestigious blue, and epics are royal purple. Unsurprisingly, these colors remain popular today under the title of 'jewel tones.'

In contrast to uncommon, rare, and epic items, only forty-eight distinct legendary (orange) items are available in *World of Warcraft*, and "it usually takes multiple end-game raid instance runs to acquire or craft these items."[28] Indeed, before *The Burning Crusade* expansion, to achieve a legendary item necessitated following "a complicated and arduous quest line."[29] This was particularly true of the one-handed sword Thunderfury, Blessed Blade of the Windseeker, one of the first legendary items (introduced in patch 1.11.1 of the original game). Although this sword increased four of the PC's five statistics, in addition to providing combat bonuses, its attainment required significant expenditure of time and in-game currency, arduous gameplay, and the help of multiple players to defeat a particularly dangerous *mob* (despite the *mob* not being within a dungeon).[30] It seems peculiar to color such prestigious and rare items orange, because orange is neither a popular contemporary color nor heraldic; indeed, orange was starkly unpopular in the Middle Ages.[31] However, it should be considered that heirloom (pale gold) items were not introduced until the second expansion, *Wrath of the Lich King*, and that Blizzard Entertainment does not use official color names for the quality levels. Indeed, Blizzard Entertainment only visually presented color categories from the beginning of *World of Warcraft*, and the color names used in this essay are derived from the game's community consensus attested to on *Wowpedia*.[32] Therefore, it seems likely that the color of the legendary category may not have been intended to represent orange but rather a rich gold. Indeed, the most precious gold throughout much of antiquity and the Middle Ages was red-gold, which would most easily be interpreted on a computer monitor as orange.[33] When viewed as gold instead of orange, the color of the legendary category becomes equivalent to the prestige of the items it labels.

This prestige is not eliminated by the introduction of heirloom items, whose color is specifically referenced as 'light gold' in *Wowpedia*; this supports the interpretation of legendary items' orange as red-gold. This 'light' quality suggests something diluted or lesser, which is appropriate to heirloom items: they offer fewer statistical advantages than epics, instead acting like rare items. However, heirloom items do not need in-game repairs and scale with the PC's level, thereby never requiring an upgrade. For example, the Dignified Headmaster's Charge, a two-handed staff, can be used by a first-level PC, but will only give eighteen to twenty-seven points of damage when used against *mobs*. However, once the PC reaches level eighty the staff will have increased to create maximum damage of 361 points.[34] Furthermore, heirloom items are particularly prestigious to players who have played the other *Warcraft* games or particularly enjoy the game's lore, as heirlooms often resemble items from earlier *Warcraft* games in both name and design.[35] Therefore, although it is appropriate to assign heirlooms the prestige of gold, it must be quantified by 'light,' because they are technically less useful than certain epic items. Their prestige instead comes from the lengthiness of their employability and their interest to a subset of players.

The final section of the classification system is artifact. Because artifacts have never been available to PCs, *Wowpedia* and *Wowhead* combine them with heirlooms and light gold. Previously, the official *World of Warcraft* website colored artifacts red, with the quantifier that red-colored items cannot be used by one's PC.[36] As of July 7, 2007, artifacts were removed from the page, which still noted that red indicated unusable items. This use of red also appears in-game, with items' icons being shaded in red and black when they are not of use to the player. The official status of artifacts is unknown; the current *World of Warcraft* website has removed this list and simply points readers to *Wowpedia* and *Wowhead*. However, another classification system within *World of Warcraft*, separate from the items' color categories, suggests that the color of artifacts was adhering to a simpler, more modern system.

This is a basic classification system that is best described as using 'stoplight' colors: red means stop/danger, yellow is caution, green is go/safe. In a player's quest log, this is used for active quests, which are coded green (easy), yellow (challenging, possibility of PC death), and orange-red (too difficult and highly likely to result in PC death). Quests that are significantly beneath a PC's level are colored grey (like poor items, without value). This stoplight symbolism is also used for the names of *mobs:* green targets are friendly (cannot be attacked), yellow targets attack only when provoked, and red targets trigger an attack if a PC is sufficiently close. When attacking, a *mob's* name then cycles between orange and red. Red is used elsewhere to indicate urgency and danger; for example, if players use the full-screen game map when attacked, their screen will gain a red mist. A blended color symbolism is employed elsewhere, such as in the chat client where 'say' actions are rendered in white (neutral or positive), whereas 'yell' actions are red; other colors in chat seem to be arbitrarily assigned, presented more for color-contrast than meaning.

These two color classification systems are used quite differently in-game. Although the contemporary stoplight symbolism is used to convey simple information about the environment, the item-quality spectrum is specifically constructed to indicate value and prestige. This prestige system employs color valuations that are consistent with modern perceptions of medieval color significance. Although the termini of this spectrum (grey and red) allow it to align with the contemporary stoplight symbolism, the use of the inner spectrum of green, blue, purple, orange/gold, and light gold is strongly related to medieval concepts.

COLOR CATEGORIES AND IN-GAME ECONOMICS

It is the application of these medievalisms in the economic structures of the game that alter the overall experience. The primary means of receiving items in-game are as rewards for quests assigned by NPCs or from the corpses of *mobs*. In addition to in-game currency, the most common rewards are items that serve as armor, weapons, or magical trinkets (jewelry). Both expensive clothing and fine jewelry were commonly employed as gifts and rewards between nobility in the thirteenth, fourteenth, and fifteenth centuries, and using such items for rewards in a pseudomedieval setting echoes such a culture of knightly deed and reward.[37] Although this highlights that the game's setting is intended to be nominally feudal and manorial, it also contrasts with the capitalistic structures of *World of Warcraft*'s NPC vendors and the Auction House.

As a generalization, item exchanges outside straightforward barter/buy/sell situations reinforce social bonds and are often extended from a sense of obligation or desire.[38] Both rewards and gifts are drawn from a subset of exchangeable goods (primarily luxury or prestigious objects) that are considered suitable for such purposes.[39] However, as quest rewards (and their statistics) are viewable as part of the quest assignment, *World of Warcraft*'s structure encourages an interpretation where rewards act more like payment. As item statistics include an item's worth when sold to an NPC, the exchange is not one to create or reinforce social bonds with an NPC but rather simply for the PC's financial gain. This shifts the PCs from heroes and altruists (as the narrative initially frames them) to mercenaries and opportunists. Intriguingly, the game's overarching mythology employs a pluralistic morality, refusing to paint any faction as entirely good or evil. Indeed, the game mechanics of quest rewards may intentionally encourage the moral ambiguity that the game's lore portrays.

At its simplest, the trade path of an item would involve two exchanges: received from an NPC or *mob* and then sold to an NPC. This relationship between intangible object and player imitates contemporary globalizations of production, which "do not so much knit together the various inhabitants of the world in tighter, more productively and mutually supportive communicative networks, as they simply make more entrenched our isolation from each other."[40] However, although quest rewards and items from *mobs* are the most common methods of receiving items in *World of Warcraft*, PCs may also modify and create items through the employment of 'professions.'[41] Production therefore ranges from fully automated, with items received from and sold to NPCs, to extremely personal, with items crafted or improved by a PC.[42] *World of Warcraft* supports further interpersonal interactions involving items via the 'trade' chat channel, wherein players can barter for gear and improvements (either via help in questing or others' professions). By providing professions and trade chat, *World of Warcraft* instigates a casual barter society for PCs.

World of Warcraft also encourages interpersonal interaction through the creation of guilds. Ostensibly inspired by medieval craft and professional organizations, guilds are a common feature of the high-fantasy genre. Within *World of Warcraft*, they serve as optional social groups that may fulfill multiple functions and have several goals. Many guilds focus on creating groups that can tackle dungeons, whereas others provide social connections, support role-playing, or encourage raising PCs to the top levels; these goals often overlap. Guilds also serve as centers for the redistribution of goods via their 'guild bank,' where members can deposit unwanted or unneeded items for other members' usage. Furthermore, guilds often help their members in attaining gear of rare or higher levels, and members will advise one another on what is best for an individual PC. Some guilds embrace this gaming camaraderie to the extent that they engage in random acts of kindness towards new players.[43] Indeed, *World of Warcraft* encourages positive interactions by including an ethical element in its dungeons through the 'need before greed' system.[44] Although this can force distribution of items to the PC who needs it most, certain gaming options also allow players to choose whether they need an item (as opposed to the system automatically evaluating a PC's statistics). As a primarily honor-based system, need before greed can create conflict and foster jealousy when it is violated.

To conclude, *World of Warcraft* employs several pluralistic systems that combine medievalism and contemporary conceptions to affect players' comprehension of items of prestige. In functional gameplay, these can combine in intriguing ways. For example, the Formal Dangui is a common-level item that has no attributes beyond resembling a dress (primarily worthwhile for role-players, who value a distinguishable character). Yet because the Formal Dangui is rarely available from the NPC who sells it, it can be resold to other players for thousands of times its initial cost.[45] This contradiction of item rank and player value is one that *World of Warcraft* embraces elsewhere, as in the combination of contemporary stoplight symbolism and medievally inspired item quality categories. By combining medieval processes in its classifications and trade systems, *World of Warcraft* allows players to experience medievalism within familiar contemporary systems. However, when combined with the ambiguous morality of the overarching mythology, the complex use of color and economic strategies suggests that the game is intentionally contradictory and conflicted. It opposes itself. This, of course, reflects the in-game world. It is inherently unstable, discordant, and conflicted, for it is the *World of Warcraft*.

NOTES

1. Roland Barthes, *The Fashion System*, trans. M. Word and D. Howard (New York: Hill and Wang), 4–5, 41.
2. Maurice Merleau-Ponty, *The Visible and the Invisible*, trans. A. Lingis (Evanston, IL: Northwestern University Press, 1968).

3. This necessarily excludes the fourth expansion, *Mists of Pandaria*, which was primarily in beta testing during the writing of this essay. *Mists* beta testing began in March 2012, and it was released to the public on September 25, 2012. Its release does not alter the argument of this essay.

4. *Wowpedia* and *Wowhead* fulfill a much-needed function by recording both the in-game worth of items and their value to the player community.

5. Although some players use headsets and voice-conferencing programs to communicate with one another, these use separate programs that are not supported by *World of Warcraft*.

6. Roland Barthes, "The Imagination of Signs," in *Critical Essays*, by Roland Barthes, trans. Richard Howard (Evanston, IL: Northwestern University Press, 1972), 205–6; Jean Baudrillard, *The System of Objects in Jean Baudrillard: Selected Writings*, trans. James Benedict (London: Verso, 1996), 30; John Gage, *Colour and Culture: Practice and Meaning from Antiquity to Abstraction* (London: Thames and Hudson, 1993), 79; John Gage, *Colour and Meaning: Art, Science and Symbolism* (London: Thames and Hudson, 1999), 43; Michel Pastoureau, *Blue: The History of a Color*, trans. Markus I. Cruse (Princeton: Princeton University Press, 2001), 7.

7. C. M. Woolgar, *The Senses in Late Medieval England* (London: Yale University Press, 2006), 157–58.

8. Daniel L. Everett, "Cultural Constrains on Grammar and Cognition in Pirahã: Another Look at the Design Features of Human Language," *Current Anthropology* 46 (2005): 621–46. Everett's claims have been controversial.

9. Pastoureau, *Blue*, 81.

10. For literary theory discussions of color, see cited works by Barthes and Baudrillard.

11. Barthes, *Fashion*, 106.

12. Pastoureau, *Blue*, 74, 81; Woolgar, *Senses*, 156. For further information on medieval colors, see cited works by Gage, Pastoureau, and Herman Pleij, *Colors Demonic and Divine: Shades of Meaning in the Middle Ages and After*, trans. Diane Webb (New York: Columbia University Press, 2004).

13. C. P. Biggam, "Aspects of Chaucer's Adjectives of Hue," *The Chaucer Review* 28 (1993): 41–53; Michel Pastoureau, *Noir: Histoire d'une couleur* (Paris: Seuil, 2008), 50; Pleij, *Colors Demonic and Divine*, 14–15.

14. Désirée G. Koslin, "Value-Added Stuffs and Shifts in Meaning: An Overview and Case Study of Medieval Textile Paradigms," in *Encountering Medieval Textiles and Dress: Objects, Texts, Images*, ed. Désirée G. Koslin and Janet E. Snyder (New York: Palgrave MacMillan, 2002): 235; Pastoureau, *Noir*, 28–29; Woolgar, *Senses*, 1, 150, 157, 159.

15. Gage, *Colour and Culture*, 80; Pastoureau, *Blue*, 55–56, and *The Devil's Cloth: A History of Stripes and Striped Fabric*, trans. Jody Gladding (New York: Columbia University Press, 2001), 26.

16. For further information on color terms between the thirteenth and fifteenth century, see Pastoureau, *L'Hermine et le sinople: Études d'héraldique médiévale* (Paris: Le Léopard d'or, 1982), 138–39, 144–47.

17. Woolgar, *Senses*, 162.

18. "Items Database," *Wowhead*, http://www.wowhead.com/items (accessed July 29, 2012); "Unkempt Pants," *Wowhead*, http://www.wowhead.com/item=21006 (accessed October 12, 2012).

19. "Items Database."

20. Gage, *Colour and Meaning*, 71; Pleij, *Colors Demonic and Divine*, 85; Woolgar, *Senses*, 156–57; Pastoureau, *Heraldry: An Introduction to a Noble Tradition* (New York: Harry N. Abrams, 1997), 45, and *Noir*, 69.

21. "Barim's Main Gauche," *Wowhead,* http://www.wowhead.com/item=56390 (accessed October 12, 2012); "Items Database." Although *Mists of Pandaria* introduces several uncommon items that outrank Barim's Main Gauche, it also added several rare daggers that outrank these uncommon items, retaining the relationship between rare and uncommon items that Barim's Main Gauche demonstrates in the game pre-*Pandaria.*
22. Pastoureau, *Blue,* 41, 49, 52, 62.
23. Pastoureau, *Blue,* 80
24. Gage, *Colour and Culture,* 82; Pastoureau, *Blue,* 56–57, 96–97; *L'Hermine,* 134; and *Noir,* 69.
25. John H. Munro, "The Medieval Scarlet and the Economics of Sartorial Splendour," in *Cloth and Clothing in Medieval Europe: Essays in Memory of Professor E. M. Carus-Wilson,* ed. N. B. Harte and K. G. Ponting (London: Heinemann, 1983), 14.
26. Gage, *Colour and Culture,* 80; Margaret Scott, *Medieval Dress and Fashion* (London: British Library, 2007), 85; Kay Staniland, "Medieval Courtly Splendour," *Costume* 14 (1980): 8–9; Monica L. Wright, "Dress for Success: Béroul's *Tristan* and the Restoration of Status through Clothes," *Arthuriana* 18 (2008): 8.
27. "Epic," *Wowpedia,* http://www.wowpedia.org/Epic (accessed July 29, 2012).
28. "Legendary," *Wowpedia,* http://www.wowpedia.org/Legendary (accessed July 29, 2012).
29. "Legendary."
30. "Thunderfury, Blessed Blade of the Windseeker," *Wowhead,* http://www.wowhead.com/item=19019 (accessed October 13, 2012); "Thunderfury, Blessed Blade of the Windseeker," *Wowpedia,* http://www.wowpedia.org/Thunderfury (accessed October 13, 2012).
31. Ruth Mellinkoff, *Outcasts: Signs of Otherness in Northern European Art of the Late Middle Ages* (Berkeley: University of California Press, 1994), 55; Pleij, *Colors Demonic and Divine,* 78.
32. "Item Basics," World of Warcraft Community Site, archived from November 5, 2004, to May 7, 2011, http://wayback.archive.org/web/*/http://www.worldofwarcraft.com/info/items/basics.html (accessed July 29, 2012); "Quality," *Wowpedia,* http://www.wowpedia.org/Quality (accessed July 29, 2012).
33. Gage, *Colour and Meaning,* 71.
34. "Dignified Headmaster's Charge," *Wowpedia,* http://www.wowpedia.org/Dignified_Headmaster's_Charge (accessed October 13, 2012).
35. "Heirloom," *Wowpedia,* http://www.wowpedia.org/Heirloom (accessed July 29, 2012).
36. "Item Basics."
37. Kathleen Ashley, "Material and Symbolic Gift-Giving: Clothes in English and French Wills," in *Medieval Fabrications: Dress, Textiles, Clothwork, and Other Cultural Imaginings,* ed. E. Jane Burns (New York: Palgrave Macmillan, 2004), 142; Brigitte Buettner, "Past Presents: New Year's Gifts at the Valois Courts, ca. 1400," *The Art Bulletin* 83 (2001): 604, 615; Laura F. Hodges, "Sartorial Signs in *Troilus and Criseyde,*" *Chaucer Review* 35 (2001): 250.
38. Arjun Appadurai, *The Social Life of Things: Commodities in Cultural Perspective* (Cambridge, UK: Cambridge University Press, 1980), 38; Buettner, "Past Presents," 600, 615; Ad Putter, "Gifts and Commodities in *Sir Amadace,*" *Review of English Studies* 51 (2000): 377. For various attempts to define gifts and exchanges, see Appadurai, *Social Life,* 3; Michael Camille,

The Medieval Art of Love (London: Harry N. Abrams, 1998), 52; Sarah-Grace Heller, *Fashion in Medieval France* (Cambridge, UK: D. S. Brewer, 2007), 142; Putter, "Gifts," 378; and Sarah Kay, *The* Chansons de Geste *in the Age of Romance: Political Fictions* (Oxford: Clarendon, 1995), 39, 223. Most convincing are Kay and Camille, who assert that gift exchanges focus on the person, whereas commodity exchanges focus upon the item.

39. Appadurai, *Social Life*, 38; Britton J. Harwood, "Gawain and the Gift," *PMLA* 106 (1991): 483; Marcel Mauss, *The Gift: Forms and Functions of Exchange in Archaic Societies*, trans. Ian Cunnison (London: Cohen and West, 1954), 42.

40. Eileen A. Joy and Craig Dionne, "Before the Trains of Thought Have Been Laid Down So Firmly: The Premodern Post/Human," *Postmedieval* 1 (2010): 2.

41. Of eleven primary professions available, seven are specifically related to creating or altering items.

42. Items made by PCs will bear their name in the statistics box.

43. For example, the post "Silly Question" by Rayce on the *WoW_Ladies* blog on July 13, 2012, concerned organizing a help-session for new players, wherein her guild will also give useful gifts. This event was inspired by another contributor to the blog.

44. "Need Before Greed," *Wowpedia*, http://www.wowpedia.org/Need_Before_Greed (accessed July 29, 2012).

45. "Formal Dangui," http://us.battle.net/wow/en/item/13895 (accessed July 29, 2012); "Formal Dangui," *Wowhead*, http://www.wowhead.com/item=13895/formal-dangui (accessed July 29, 2012); "Formal Dangui," *WoW_Ladies*, http://wow-ladies.livejournal.com/16155719.html (accessed July 29, 2012).

7 Sir Thomas Malory and the Death Knights of New Avalon

Imagining Medieval Identities in *World of Warcraft*

Kristin Noone and Jennifer Kavetsky

"The marketplace," Elizabeth S. Sklar once declared, "contributes more vitally to the survival and perpetuation of the Arthurian narrative than does the academy, for it reaches an infinitely larger and more complicitous audience."[1] Although academic medievalists may wish to debate the vitality of their contributions, Sklar's statement provokes a multitude of questions: Who constitutes that audience? In what ways are they complicit in the Arthurian narrative? And to what extent is the marketplace involved?

In his introduction to *Mass Market Medieval*, David Marshall begins to answer some of these questions, commenting that the study of popular-culture medievalism "becomes a means of locating the ways in which the Middle Ages continue to be used to justify or naturalize socio-political agendas."[2] The video game *Age of Empires* (1997), for example, reflects a continuing interest in medieval social structures, especially the so-called 'third estate' and the methods of crop production. Marshall refers to the process of packaging and commodifying the Middle Ages as "shrink-wrapping time," turning 'the medieval' into an object for consumer purchase. Although Marshall's argument is certainly sound—and has fascinating implications for reading consumer responses to political media in terms of medievalism—this analysis could be extended productively beyond "socio-political agendas" and examined in terms of gameplay and pleasure. In their preface to *King Arthur in Popular Culture*, Elizabeth S. Sklar and Donald L. Hoffman argue that "more than a handy vehicle for official ideologies and cultural credos . . . the Matter of Arthur [sic] speaks with equal eloquence to the less codifiable facets of human nature: to our wishes, anxieties, desires, and above all to our innate sense of play."[3] Here, we suggest that the medievalism of *World of Warcraft* is a conscious construction by its creators, relying on the game's ability to imaginatively embody both continuity with the past and a form of playful, postmodernist discontinuity, taking joy in its own additions to and alterations of the Arthurian legendarium.

WORLD OF WARCRAFT AND THE SUBVERSION OF HEROIC FANTASIES

Since its initial release in November 2004, Blizzard Entertainment's *World of Warcraft* has become one the most popular video games of its kind. Set in the fictional world of Azeroth, *World of Warcraft* features many quasi-medieval elements common to Tolkienesque high fantasy: powerful magic-users; enchanted jewelry; swords with heroic-sounding names; and nonhuman races such as elves, dwarves, and orcs. Players can choose to play as characters from a variety of human and nonhuman races. Players must also choose a class for their character, which determines whether the character will be a close-combat warrior, a healer, or a ranged fighter;[4] one player can create several characters and pursue different goals with each one. Players attempt to improve their characters by earning in-game experience points, obtaining items, and learning in-game skills. Experience points can be earned by defeating in-game opponents, exploring the game world, and completing quests.[5] When a player earns enough experience points, his or her character reaches the next level. In *World of Warcraft,* levels can be thought of as a way of measuring a character's strength and abilities. A higher-level character will be able to defeat stronger opponents and have access to more powerful abilities than a lower-level character. Players are also able to interact with each other in real time and can trade items, compete against each other in battle, or work together towards common goals. Unlike many computer games in which time effectively stops when the player logs off, the *World of Warcraft* environment is constantly changing regardless of whether a particular player is currently connected to the game. In *A Short History of Fantasy*, Farah Mendlesohn and Edward James suggest that *World of Warcraft* may be considered part of the sword-and-sorcery genre, but also what they term a "theatre world," one in which the ground rules are established but each individual act is part of a collaborative performance of fantasy.[6] Sword-and-sorcery, in turn, they call barely distinguishable from high fantasy or heroic fantasy, which, importantly, consists of "fantasy set in a world which often resembles the ancient or medieval past, drawing on their epic traditions of heroes."[7] In both the construction of the game world and in the game's overall narrative, *World of Warcraft* draws explicitly on the players' shared ideas about the nature of heroic medieval fantasy.

One of the game's most obvious parallels to medieval tradition can be seen in the storylines surrounding the once-noble Prince Arthas, who has fallen from grace and become the evil Lich King. He is joined by his Death Knights, former heroes of Azeroth who had previously died in battle only to be raised from the dead and enslaved to the will of the Lich King. *The Wrath of the Lich King,* the 2008 expansion that features Arthas, also made Death Knights available as player-characters.[8] Death Knights are not simply *World of Warcraft* versions of the Knights of the Round Table, however. These knights do not rescue damsels in distress or fight in just causes. Instead, they engage in the wholesale slaughter of civilians and burn the town of New Avalon to the ground.

Although it is tempting to view the Death Knights as simply inversions of Malory's Knights of the Round Table, the Death Knight story is far more complicated. Betrayed by the Lich King during battle, the Death Knights and their field commander rebel against him and join the rest of Azeroth in the fight against the Lich King's forces. Officially pardoned by Azeroth's leaders, the rebel Death Knights are welcomed as 'Champions of the Light.' Although the Death Knights have been reincorporated into the game's fictional society, they remain marked as Others. Even after they have been welcomed back into the fold, the Death Knights still use their preconversion abilities. They may complete the same quests as the other players do, but they do so by raising ghouls from the bodies of the slain and casting spells like 'Unholy Blight,' 'Pestilence,' and 'Desecration.' They also remain visibly marked as separate from other character classes. Although they have returned to their home countries, Death Knights are no longer the people they once were. They are the living dead, and their clothing, appearance, and even their mounts designate them as such. As we can see in Figure 7.1, the female Gnome and male Draenei Death Knight characters, despite substantial race and gender differences, bear more resemblance to each other than either does to the male human.

Figure 7.1 Male Draenei, Female Gnome, and Male Human player-characters (from left to right)

Class differences are usually denoted by differing armor and abilities. In the case of Death Knights, however, their eerily glowing eyes, visible even through a faceguard, serve as constant reminders that they are a class apart. These are not like the defeated knights sent back by Lancelot and Gareth to be seamlessly absorbed into the Round Table community, nor are they noble figures who are simply fighting for the wrong side like the Saracen defeated by Gawain during the Roman War. The Death Knights may have been redeemed, but it is unlikely that anyone will mistake them for Knights of the Round Table. As the story of Arthas and the Death Knights illustrates, the game's engagement with Arthurian legends is both playful and subversive, and we argue that part of the appeal of creating and playing a Death Knight is the opportunity to subvert the medieval knight-as-hero model. In *Medieval Identity Machines*, Jeffery Jerome Cohen has argued for an understanding of medieval selves and bodies as "identity machines," constructed and fluid assemblages that partake of both human and nonhuman components—a knight, for example, requiring a horse and a sword—and always in motion, continually built and rebuilt with the gain or loss of those constituent parts.[9] *World of Warcraft,* and the Death Knights, specifically, gives players a chance to assemble a new identity machine that emphasizes the perceived cultural value of the medieval past while also incorporating a digitally hybrid self and fostering a self-aware pleasure of participating in the processes of the destruction, imagination, and (re)construction of familiar narratives.

LE MORTE DARTHUR, CHIVALRY, AND THE WORK OF MOURNING

Malory's *Le Morte Darthur*,[10] although not the earliest or even the most complex of medieval Arthuriana, engages the Matter of Britain in ways that are explicitly paralleled in *World of Warcraft*. Like the various *Warcrafts*,[11] Malory's text is also in many ways a game, albeit a profoundly serious one that uses its playfulness to suggest a means of affective connection to an always-already vanished past. Patricia Clare Ingham observes in *Sovereign Fantasies: Arthurian Romance and the Making of Britain* that late Middle English Arthurian romance offers a fantasy of insular union, a "shared community" that carries within it the potential for multiple applications. The Arthurian tales, Ingham claims, "encode utopian hopes for communitarian wholeness, yet they also poignantly narrate the impossibilities, the aggressions, and the traumas of British insular community."[12] In other words, the Arthurian story is always a story of a kingdom doomed to fail—a kingdom that, in fact, has failed, by the time of Malory's writing and Caxton's printing. Ingham suggests that fantasies of centralization require a "sustained attention to loss and mourning," which helps the community analyze how and which sacrifices might serve it best; fictions of community, particularly those about nations, "must imagine a coherent identity that crosses both time and space despite the passings that constitute history."[13] Speaking specifically of Malory, she writes that his work "offers the mournful story of insular mutability, of an archaic sovereignty passing away . . . evocative of British territorial losses, both insular and continental, which ground a unified, insular future."[14] *Le Morte Darthur*, written against the turmoil of the fifteenth century, creates a vision of a potential English future by successfully engaging in a work of collective mourning for the past—a theme present in the language of Caxton's Preface, which urges readers to "see and learn the noble acts of chivalry, the gentle and virtuous deeds that some knights used in those days, by which they came to honor; and how they that were vicious were punished and oft put to shame."[15] The story of Arthur's death (already present, of course, embedded in the title of the work) is a story presented for the readers' "remembrance," in Caxton's word, in order to provoke action in the present day, a memory that nevertheless continues actively working to affect the future. Malory's own ending envoy, begging "gentlemen and gentlewomen that readeth this book of Arthur and his knights from beginning to end" to "pray for me while I am alive, that God send me good deliverance, and when I am dead, to pray for my soul,"[16] also suggests a fundamental optimism about the power of history: those who read the book (from beginning to end, as Malory makes clear, instructing his audience even as he asks mercy from them) have the ability to change its author's fate. Witnessing the fall of Arthur leads to compassion and connection: an act of successful mourning, in Freudian terms, and of recuperation.

This recuperation occurs within Malory's text as well, in a somewhat different but equally complex form, and which will be echoed in the gameplay of *World of Warcraft* centuries later. Players in the world that is *Warcraft* imagine and create their own identities, building their stories through digital performances. Swords, for example, become representations of identity and worth at both group and individual levels. This form of identification through physical enhancement is found throughout Malory's text, as arms and armor become the means by which figures are recognized (or not) and valorized (or not). Borrowing from Deleuze and Guattari, Jeffery Jerome Cohen suggests that the medieval body must always be read as an assemblage of identity, a site of possibilities that is always unstable, hybrid, contingent, and embodied: "because the trajectory of chivalric identity tended to scatter knightly identity across a proliferating array of objects, events, and fleshly forms, knighthood never precisely resided within the stable and timeless body that chivalric myth obsessively envisioned."[17] The identity of 'a knight' is always a mobile one, part of a transformative assemblage including, for example, the horse, the man, the armor, the sword, the spurs, the shield, the saddle, and the stirrups.[18] In Ramon Lull's *Libre del Ordre de Cauayleria* (translated into English in 1484 by William Caxton as *The Book of the Order of Chivalry*), each piece of the knight's armor becomes not merely an object, or indeed even a symbolic prop, but an extension of the specific character of the knight who wears or carries it: "unto the knight is given a sword, which is made in the semblance of a cross to signify [that] our lord God vanquished in the cross the death of human lineage . . . likewise a knight vows to vanquish and destroy the enemies of the cross by the sword, for chivalry is to maintain justice. And therefore the sword is made to cut both ways, to signify that the knight ought to with his sword maintain chivalry and justice."[19] The reflection on personal character becomes even more evident when Lull discusses the knightly hauberk: "the knight's hauberk signifies a castle and fortress against vices and flaws, for likewise as a castle or fortress is closed about, a hauberk is firm and gives significance that his courage ought not to enter into treason or vice."[20] As we will see with the characters of *World of Warcraft,* and with the Death Knights, specifically, swords, armor, and clothing function similarly as an extension and performance of identity; this performance, as read and understood in terms of gameplay by other players, creates a space for community formation through imaginative and playful (re)construction of variations on pseudo-Malorian attire and weaponry, productively incorporating the past into a digital and hybrid world.

WEAPONRY, POWER, AND TRANSFORMATION

Most new *World of Warcraft* player-characters begin at level one with only the most rudimentary of armor and weapons. The player is eventually able to obtain better equipment by completing quests or by purchasing it from in-game vendors. As it is for Malory's knights, a character's armor is a display of his or her fighting prowess. A particular piece of armor may only be available if a player completes a difficult quest or amasses enough in-game wealth to purchase it, and players frequently examine each other's equipment in order to gauge combat ability. Much like for Malory's knights, the armor becomes a representation of both the character's abilities and the player's skill. The Death Knight, however, does not follow the same path as other newly created characters. Unlike them, the Death Knight begins at level fifty-five and comes already equipped with level-appropriate armor. Reaching level fifty-five on a normal character is something of an achievement, and by starting at this level the Death Knights are set up as a class apart. Furthermore, players can only create a Death Knight character if they already have a character who has reached level fifty-five. Thus, the Death Knight character itself is a sign of the player's in-game achievements. Much like the Fair Unknowns of medieval romance, Death Knights, and their players, do not need training from their lord. Instead, they seek to demonstrate the superiority of their already acquired skills within the game community.

Soon after beginning the game, the Death Knight quickly obtains the remaining trappings of knighthood. The first quest that a new Death Knight must complete is the forging of a weapon unique to the Death Knights: a runeblade. He or she is told that that this sword "is an extension of your being. A death knight cannot battle without a runeblade."[21] If the player acquires a new weapon in the future, he or she can convert it into a runeblade, which, in addition to its other abilities, glows with an unholy light and is a visible reminder of the Death Knight's unique abilities and status. As Carl James Grindley notes in the "The Hagiography of Steel," the hero's weapon in narratives such as *The Iliad* and *Beowulf* often functions more symbolically than it does as an actual means of defeating opponents. Grindley argues that "the hero's item functions like a medal; it is the public recognition of perceived ability."[22] In the case of *World of Warcraft,* the presence of the game interface ensures that the Death Knight's runeblade can only function symbolically. It exists only as computer code and can only be used to slay in-game enemies. Its actual function, then, is as a representation of a player's (digital) fighting prowess that can be symbolically read by other players within the game world.

The Lich King's sword, Frostmourne, has its own complicated history, which further reflects the overdetermined significance of weapons in heroic narratives. Frostmourne was originally designed as a prison for the tortured spirit of the orc shaman Ner'zhul, who initially oversaw the invasion of Azeroth by the undead Scourge.[23] Thus, the sword's first function was not as a weapon but as a prison for and physical representation of the incorporeal Lich King. When his kingdom was attacked by the Scourge, Arthas became obsessed with defending his home by any means necessary. When the Scourge infected a city with a plague that would both kill its hosts and turn them into murderous zombies, Arthas had the city burned and the citizens killed. Arthas also sought out the legendary sword Frostmourne, believing himself strong enough to control its power and, in turn, to use it to control the Scourge. He located the blade and, despite warnings that it would mean his doom, drew the sword from a block of ice, swearing ". . . that he would pay any price to possess the blade."[24] Frostmourne did grant Arthas immense power, but much like Malory's Sword in the Stone, Arthas's attempt to claim that power had mixed results. By drawing Frostmourne, Arthas became a king, but his rule is challenged by his one-time allies. Instead of using his newly acquired power to protect his home, Arthas's soul was quickly corrupted by the spirit tied to the sword. Unlike the king-making Merlin, this magic user had carefully orchestrated events so that he could escape his prison by possessing the body of whoever claimed Frostmourne. Now embodied, the Lich King is able to use Frostmourne as a weapon, and it is one of the most powerful in the game. During the final battle with the Lich King, Arthas is able to kill an entire group of players, themselves accomplished in-game warriors, with a single blow of Frostmourne. Players are only able to defeat Arthas when the paladin, Trion Fordring, shatters Frostmourne and releases the sprits trapped within the blade. Arthas, incapacitated by the simultaneous loss of his weapon and the attacks of the vengeful spirits, can finally be defeated. Like Excalibur, Forstmourne is thus both a symbol of Arthas's power and the source of his downfall.

Arthas's transformation into the Lich King, while much more overtly fantastical than most of Malory's text, nonetheless draws its themes from *Le Morte Darthur* in more subtle references than the matter of similar character names. The young Arthur, for example, undergoes his own transformation—arguably not for the better—upon retrieving his own symbolic sword from the stone in London. The sword appears, Malory relates, via supernatural means; at a time when "stood the realm in great jeopardy long while, for every lord that was mighty of men made him strong, and many weened to have been king,"[25] the Archbishop of Canterbury (advised by Merlin), and all the gentlemen of arms gather in the greatest church of London to pray. When they emerge, they see the "fair sword" with its famous inscription embedded in the stone. This miracle, unsurprisingly, does not resolve the ongoing arms race, as everyone wishes to win the sword, though it does redirect the energies of the lords into great tournaments for the right to try. Once the boy Arthur achieves the sword, however, his kingship is by no means certain: "wherefore there were many lords wroth, and said it was great shame to them all, and to the realm, to be over-governed with a boy of no high blood born, and so they fell out at that time."[26] Arthur's first war, against King Lot, follows promptly thereafter; Arthur must defend his throne with blood, and Malory includes details such as these: "[his sword] was so bright in his enemy's eyes that it gave light like thirty torches. And therewith he put them back, and slew much people. And then the commoners of Caerleon arose with clubs and staves and slew many knights."[27] Arthur's rule from the beginning is a rule of warfare, and the bloodthirst extends to the commoners. This brutality is reflected, for example, in the May Day deaths of the lords' children, ordered to be put out to sea by Arthur for fear that one of them will—as prophesied—kill him; though Arthur does not execute the children directly, as Malory notes, some of them are "four weeks old, and some less," and their transport ship strikes a "castle" and all aboard except the infant Mordred are killed.[28] Even the later Round Table oath is designed to guard knightly behavior, its prescriptive nature suggesting the depth of this concern. Arthur, in fact, is warned by Merlin early on that the dream of Camelot will not last. The first warning comes when Arthur vows to wed Guenever ("Merlin warned the king covertly that Guenever was not wholesome for him to take to wife, for he warned him that Lancelot should love her, and she him; and he turned his tale to the adventures of the Sangrail"[29]); the second warning is uttered in reference to Sir Balin's striking of the Dolorous Stroke against King Pellam, as a result of which "three kingdoms shall be in great poverty, misery, and wretchedness."[30] The world of Camelot, in which Sir Balin can slay the Lady of the Lake and wound King Pellam with a spear, is never the ideal that it claims to stand for; violence is encoded in its existence, and Malory's text recognizes that fact, even while regretting the loss of that ideal.

In the case of *World of Warcraft,* violence is, quite literally, encoded in its nature. Unsurprisingly for a game that is centered on (digital) combat, weapons are of supreme importance within the game world. Although Frost-mourne remains the special possession of the Lich King, players can obtain their own powerful in-game weapons. Of particular interest in this context is the axe Shadowmourne. At the time of *The Wrath of the Lich King*'s release, it was one of the most powerful player-obtainable weapons in the game. Furthermore, only certain classes of characters, Death Knights among them, could possess it, giving it an aura of exclusivity. Shadowmourne is forged from Light's Vengeance, the weapon once wielded by Prince Arthas that he discarded to seize Frostmourne. Although Shadowmourne is not necessary to slay the Lich King, its presence marks an alternative narrative path. If Arthas had kept his weapon instead of claiming Frostmourne, the fate of an entire (game) world might have been different. Much as *Le Morte Darthur* mourns an always already lost time of peace and prosperity, a game whose name makes a craft out of waging war contains its own elegy for a peace that never existed.

To obtain Shadowmourne, a player must overcome numerous challenges. The player must complete a series of nine quests and gather a large number of rare and expensive items. All told, a player can easily spend four to six weeks acquiring the necessary materials and completing the required quests to obtain the weapon. Many of these materials can only be gathered during complex cooperative battles against specific in-game opponents, called 'instances.'[31] Thus, possession of Shadowmourne declares both the player's own fighting prowess and that of his or her guild.[32] Although questing is usually a solitary activity for *World of Warcraft* players, like the Knights of the Round Table they also belong to larger communities. Arthur's knights are not just known as skilled warriors; their reputations are enhanced by their association with the Round Table community. There are a limited number of seats at the Round Table, certainly not enough for every knight in Britain. Much like any organization that has more applicants than openings, being accepted not only confirms individual ability, it also clearly demonstrates one's superiority over those who were not accepted. This key aspect of Arthurian legend was not overlooked by *World of Warcraft*'s designers. Although it is possible to learn details about another player-character by clicking on his or her avatar, two vital pieces of information are always displayed above the character's head: his or her name and guild (see Figure 7.2).

Much like a knight who declares that he is a member of the Round Table, a character who has the name of a well-known guild floating above his or her head is treated with a certain measure of respect. The guild's reputation exists in a reciprocal relationship with that of its members. The most sought-after equipment in the game can only be obtained by defeating difficult opponents that require a coordinated effort by multiple players. Guilds that routinely complete the toughest instances in the game quickly gain prestigious reputations, which, in turn, attract the best players, and so the guild can be choosy about whom it admits. Membership in a highly esteemed

Figure 7.2   A player who belongs to the Heaven and Earth guild

fighting organization, be it the Round Table or a *World of Warcraft* guild, gives players an additional confirmation of their status as fighters.

World of Warcraft's Shadowmourne, in fact, consolidates the functions of three Malorian swords: the Sword in the Stone (as previously discussed); Excalibur itself; and Sir Balin's (later Galahad's) sword, which at once encompasses acts of destruction and reconstitution—in other words, performing the medievalism of the game in microcosm. Like both Frostmourne and Shadowmourne, the sword Excalibur becomes a site of conflicting possibilities, at once hope for communal continuity and an acknowledgment that for something new to be forged something else must pass away. Excalibur is given to Arthur by the Lady of the Lake only after the Sword in the Stone—the original symbol of his worthiness—breaks in battle; it becomes a site of contention between Arthur and one of his knights, a point to be returned to shortly; and it is the locus of the final failure of the Round Table, when the dying Arthur requests repeatedly that Sir Bedevere return the sword to the lake, and Sir Bedevere—in a moment that might have been an act of loyalty—instead disobeys his liege lord twice. In Arthur's words, "Who would have deemed that thou that hast been to me so leve and so dear . . . would betray me for the riches of my sword? But now go again, for thy long tarrying putteth me in great jeopardy of my life, for I have taken cold . . . if ever I see thee, I shall slay thee with mine own hands, for thou wouldst for my rich sword see me dead."[33] Sir Bedevere, despite the obligations and loyalty he has toward Arthur, as his lord and king, has, in Arthur's mind, assisted his death: there is no successful peace at the end of this story, only Arthur's mournful departure with the Ladies of the Lake. Malory observes that "men say he shall come again" and refuses to proclaim that Arthur is dead, opting instead for "here in this world he changed his life," and quoting the tombstone inscription: *Hic Iacet Arthurus, Rex Quondam Rexque Futurus.*[34] Arthur may be a future king, but before that time can come, he must always pass away.

Balin's sword and Excalibur are inextricably entangled even in Malory's text; the Lady of the Lake, after presenting Arthur with his symbol of kingship, requests only one favor: the head of Balin, who has killed her brother. Arthur refuses—a practical move that keeps a valiant knight in his service, but a technical breach of his promise that "ask what ye will, and I shall give it."[35] Balin, for his part, recognizes the Lady of the Lake as the woman who slew his mother, and "with his sword lightly he smote off her head before King Arthur."[36] Balin's punishment is simply banishment, for an unspecified time, in physical terms; the shame of being denied access to his liege lord, however, makes this type of punishment a weighty one for any medieval knight. Balin's sword here becomes a symbol of the failure of Camelot to contain violence and blood feuds, despite all oaths. Though this sword breaks in the encounter with King Pellam, Balin's second sword (and he is known as the 'Knight With Two Swords') returns, floating in a river, stuck into a stone, at the coming of Galahad. Galahad, the only knight of Arthur's court worthy of drawing the sword—both a reflection of the young Arthur, and a perceptive comment on Arthur's failures to live up to his promises— claims it as his own, and, when asked if he knows its history, offers this succinct summary: "now have I that sword that sometime was the good knight's, Balin le Savage, and he was a passing good man of his hands; and with this sword he slew his brother Balan, and that was a great pity, for he was a good knight; and either slew the other through a dolorous stroke that Balin gave unto my grandfather King Pelles, the which is not yet whole, nor shall be until I heal him."[37] Here, Galahad demonstrates a knowledge of history—both personal and social—that is embodied in the sword, an object that is read in terms of the characters who have wielded it. The sword's own history is the history of persons; Galahad's speech at once signifies the importance of this knowledge—he is aware of whose sword he holds—and his ability to imagine a future of healing. Galahad proclaims his intentions to heal straightforwardly, with confidence. His identity includes the wounds of the past to which he is responding, as well as his own convictions; in this way, through the physicality of Balin's/Galahad's sword, Malory suggests a more complex assemblage of identity, one that encompasses disparate times and spaces, and flesh and steel. This self-aware and even joyful act of salvage and transformation has been, as we have seen, a powerful one, echoed as it is in the spaces and swords of the *World of Warcraft*.

David Marshall concludes his introduction to *Mass Market Medieval* by calling for a return to the consideration of enjoyment of the medieval: "examinations of the medievalism of popular culture offer inroads into studying appropriations of the medieval into mainstream culture—and perhaps into enjoying those appropriations as well."[38] *World of Warcraft*, in particular via its appropriated symbols of Arthurian culture—swords, armor, character and place names—can be read as one especially diverse and successful reclamation of that enjoyment: the Middle Ages are both reenacted and transformed in players' quests, arms, and achievements. The paradoxically episodic and yet continuous nature of the game reflects the continuous yet episodic adventures of Malory's knights; Arthur's name may have been transmuted to Arthas's, but this, in Malory's terms, is only another change of life, a newly assembled identity that remains relevant in a digital future world.

NOTES

1. Elizabeth S. Sklar, "Marketing Arthur: The Commodification of Arthurian Legend," in *King Arthur in Popular Culture*, ed. Elizabeth S. Sklar and Donald L. Hoffman (Jefferson, NC: McFarland, 2002), 21.
2. David W. Marshall, "Introduction: The Medievalism of Popular Culture," in *Mass Market Medieval*, ed. David W. Marshall (Jefferson, NC: McFarland, 2007), 2.
3. Elizabeth S. Sklar and Donald L. Hoffman, "Preface," in *King Arthur in Popular Culture*, ed. Elizabeth S. Sklar and Donald L. Hoffman (Jefferson, NC: McFarland, 2002), 6.

4. Races: Draenei, Dwarf, Gnome, Human, and Night Elf (Alliance); Blood Elf, Orc, Tauren, Troll, and Undead (Horde). Classes: Death Knight, Druid, Hunter, Mage, Paladin, Priest, Rogue, Shaman, Warlock, and Warrior.

5. Quests are the driving force behind much of the game. A player may need to kill a certain number of opponents, gather supplies, or deliver a message in order to complete a particular quest. The number of experience points awarded depends on the level of the character and the difficulty of a particular quest.

6. Farah Mendlesohn and Edward James, *A Short History of Fantasy* (London: Middlesex University Press, 2009), 107–8.

7. Mendlesohn and James, *Short History*, 253.

8. Expansions add new content to the existing game world for players to explore.

9. Jeffrey Jerome Cohen, *Medieval Identity Machines* (Minneapolis: University of Minnesota Press, 2003).

10. For the purposes of this essay, we are using the Penguin Classics rendition of *Le Morte Darthur*; the massively informative and scholarly editions by, for example, Vinaver, are extraordinarily useful for medievalists, but as we hope to show that the popular-culture medievalism of *World of Warcraft* is both deliberate and enjoyed by players, we have opted to reference a widely recognized and generally accessible edition of the text.

11. *World of Warcraft* is the most recent, and the most successful, entry in Blizzard Entertainment's line of *Warcraft* games. Although our focus here is on *World of Warcraft*, the game frequently references its own internal history, which includes *Warcraft: Orcs &Humans* (1994), *Warcraft II: Tides of Darkness* (1995), *Warcraft III: Reign of Chaos* (2002), and *World of Warcraft* (2004).

12. Patricia Clare Ingham, *Sovereign Fantasies: Arthurian Romance and the Making of Britain* (Philadelphia: University of Pennsylvania Press, 2001), 2.

13. Ingham, *Sovereign Fantasies*, 8.

14. Ingham, *Sovereign Fantasies*, 193.

15. Thomas Malory, *Le Morte Darthur*, 2 vols. (New York: Penguin, 2004), 1, 5.

16. Malory, *Le Morte*, 531.

17. Cohen, *Medieval Identity Machines*, 47.

18. Cohen, *Medieval Identity Machines*, 50.

19. Ramon Lull, *The Book of Knighthood and Chivalry*, trans. William Caxton, modern English edition by Brian R. Price (Union City, CA: Chivalry Bookshelf, 2001), 64.

20. Lull, *Book of Knighthood*, 65.

21. "The Emblazoned Runeblade," *World of Warcraft: The Wrath of the Lich King*. Blizzard Entertainment (Blizzard Entertainment, 2008).

22. Carl James Grindley, "The Hagiography of Steel: The Hero's Weapon and Its Place in Pop Culture," in *The Medieval Hero on Screen: Representations from* Beowulf *to* Buffy, ed. Martha W. Driver and Sid Ray (Jefferson, NC: McFarland, 2004), 152.

23. The history of the Scourge spans several of the *Warcraft* games. The Scourge are undead creatures sent by demons to weaken the world of Azeroth and thereby make it easier to conquer. Scourge can take many forms, including reanimated corpses/skeletons, ghouls, and Frankenstein monster-like constructs.

24. Quoted in "Rise of the Lich King," *WoWWiki*, http://www.wowwiki.com/Rise_of_the_Lich_King (accessed July 30, 2012).

25. Malory, *Le Morte*, 15.

26. Malory, *Le Morte*, 19.

27. Malory, *Le Morte*, 23–24.
28. Malory, *Le Morte*, 58.
29. Malory, *Le Morte*, 91–93.
30. Malory, *Le Morte*, 71–72.
31. 'Instances' are group-specific versions of a particular game area. Several groups can be in the same instance at the same time, but they would be unaware of each others' presence because each group is effectively in its own parallel version of the game. Each group (and the players within that group) are 'saved' to a particular version of the instance. If groups/players leave the instance and then return, they come back to 'their' version. An individual player can be saved to more than one instance but cannot be saved to more than one version of the same instance at the same time. Instances are reset on a regular basis; all players and groups are unsaved and must begin the instance anew.
32. Guilds are player-created, in-game associations. Members of the same guild often become friends, but the functional purpose of guilds is to provide a player with a network of other players who can help him or her complete difficult tasks.
33. Malory, *Le Morte*, 516–17.
34. Malory, *Le Morte*, 519.
35. Malory, *Le Morte*, 64.
36. Malory, *Le Morte*, 65.
37. Malory, *Le Morte*, 245.
38. Marshall, *Mass Market Medieval*, 10.

8 Accumulating Histories
A Social Practice Approach to Medievalism in High-Fantasy MMORPGs

Jennifer C. Stone, Peter Kudenov, and Teresa Combs

Far from the major cities, in a sparsely traveled area of Arathi Highlands, a powerful druid named Sage hunts elemental fires at the Circle of West Binding. An experienced player would know from her armor that she has spent many hours battling in end-game dungeons and that few monsters in the area could hurt her. High-level players regard her as one of the most accomplished druids on the server, who leads one of the most accomplished guilds and raid groups. She gathers several creatures at a time, killing them systematically. After an hour, she has gathered twenty elemental fires—half of what she needs to restock her guild's supply of Greater Fire Protection Potions for this weekend's raid on Blackwing Lair. She just pulled about five creatures; her health is untouched, but even so, a level thirty-two dwarf joins the fight shouting, "I will save ye, lass!" Sage finishes the fight with the dwarf's 'help' and curtsies politely to him in greeting. He kneels, taking her hand and kissing it before running off to continue his adventures.

This scene was a common occurrence for Sage, Jennifer's primary character in *World of Warcraft*. *World of Warcraft* is a massively multiplayer online role-playing game (MMORPG), a game genre in which people from around the world play together in a fantasy realm. Players complete quests that earn experience points (XP). Over time, they gain levels, acquire in-game currency, and earn better gear. As these games progress, the quests become harder and the rewards become greater. Over time, players learn that to advance they must join other players in larger groups that require specialized roles and strategies. Ultimately, they reach a maximum level and can engage in more complex content, such as the forty-person Blackwing Lair raid for which Sage was preparing.

High-fantasy MMORPGs like *World of Warcraft* engage players in contemporary versions of medieval worlds, complete with identities, settings, and activities. Players start by selecting the faction, race, class, and gender for their characters, which allow them to develop certain abilities and explore certain areas. For instance, choosing to play a healer archetype, which specializes in healing others, will lead to different opportunities than choosing to play a tank archetype, which specializes in absorbing damage and holding the enemy's attention. Likewise, choosing to play an elf will lead to different opportunities than choosing to play a goblin. Such choices frame the identities available to players while in the game world as that character. The game settings are filled with places and objects that are common in contemporary visions of the medieval. Castles serve as hubs; dragons and other fantastical creatures roam the landscape; characters dress in armor, travel by horseback or ship, and exchange gold-based currency. Common events include crafting, role-playing, and fighting against monsters or other players.

Together, these characters, settings, and activities create a backdrop for players to engage in contemporary medievalist gender practices. In particular, we examine how high-fantasy MMORPGs provide contexts that hail players into longstanding motifs of neomedievalist gender practices, such as expectations for masculinity and femininity, chivalry, courtly love, and warfare. Although these motifs have strong influence over players' actions, we also investigate moments of transgression, where medievalist historical structures of gender are exposed or questioned.

Collectively, the authors of this chapter have played high-fantasy MMORPGs for thousands of hours, including games such as *World of Warcraft*, *Everquest II* (2004), *Vanguard* (2007), and *Warhammer Online* (2008). We have participated in more 'casual' and more 'hardcore' player groups. We also have played on a range of servers, including those emphasizing player versus environment (PvE), player versus player (PvP), and role playing (RP). As such, we bring a wide range of experiences to this project. We use our experiences to illustrate how medievalist game contexts shape gender practices in relation to history and identity.

In a sense, the recasting of the medieval into the present is common in contemporary popular culture. As explored by Marshall's *Mass Market Medieval*, contemporary media often invoke popular nostalgic conceptions of the medieval—referred to variously as 'medievalism,' 'neomedieval,' and 'pseudomedieval'—which provide a rich set of characters, settings, and storylines.[1] We use the concept of medievalism to highlight the continuing historical impact of the Middle Ages on the present. Rather than dismissing these contemporary versions of the medieval as mere distortions, simplifications, or historical inaccuracies, scholars of medievalism critically engage with contemporary reformulations of the medieval. In MMORPGs, medievalism helps us to explain how aesthetic and narrative decisions made by designers and players shape gendered social practices.

Such medievalist media create contexts that are imbued with medieval (or at least medieval-like) images, values, objects, contexts, and activities, alongside contemporary concerns. In high-fantasy MMORPGs, players interact within fully developed medieval settings. Inevitably, gender plays an important role in such settings, shaping players' talk, actions, and bodies. Indeed, such games create opportunities to participate in or challenge longstanding storylines of gender.

We extend work on medievalism and gender in games by drawing on social practice theory. In particular, we use Holland and Lave's theory of "history in person," which argues for a dialogic theory of identity as historically and socially situated.[2] In the context of high-fantasy MMORPGs, "history in person" helps us to see how players shape and are shaped by the neomedieval. MMORPGs allow players to refashion history—and themselves in relation to history—in contemporary, virtual spaces.

At the center of Holland and Lave's theory is what they call "local contentious practice," which emphasizes the situated and productive nature of history and identity.[3] From this standpoint, history and identity are not stable and fixed; they are not completely imposed, nor are they completely liberatory and unrelated to structural power relations. Rather, history and identity are realized—often in unpredictable ways—in the context of situated practice.

Therefore, history—and in particular, the enduring struggles that continue to shape history—are, "appropriated and lived in practice."[4] In other words, historical struggles, such as those surrounding gender, are lived in the present and are shaped by longstanding power relationships. In high-fantasy MMORPGs, this results in an accumulation of histories, where medievalist conceptions of gender, which have been recast into new settings, pile up in a sense, so that at once we can observe medievalist genders in practice that are imbued with medievalisms of different eras (Middle Ages, Victorian, post–World War II, and contemporary). At the same time that history perpetuates enduring struggles, Holland and Lave argue that history interacts generatively with local practices, which creates possibilities for transformation. In high-fantasy MMORPGs, this creates a potentially productive tension between medievalist and competing contemporary versions of gender.

Through local contentious practice, not only are historical struggles continued and transformed, but identities are also generated. Identities, according to Holland and Lave, "live through practices of identification. Subjectivities are neither simple reflexes of social position . . . nor simply the meaning that individuals give to these positions. Subjectivities, and their more objectified components, identities, are formed in practice through the often collective work of evoking, improvising, appropriating, and refusing participation in practices that position self and other."[5] In other words, identities are realized in the context of local contentious practice and are shaped, at least in part, by enduring historical struggles. In games, identities are particularly complex. As Gee describes, we must account for virtual identities of avatars, real-world identities of players, and projective identities of player-characters.[6] Projective identities, according to Gee, are formed in the liminal space between a players' real-world and virtual identities. They incorporate 'project' in two senses: "to project one's values and desires onto the virtual character" and "seeing the virtual character as one's own project in the making."[7] In high-fantasy MMORPGs, such identities are complicated further because they are not just shaped through interaction with the game, but also with other avatar–player–projective constellations.

From this perspective, high-fantasy MMORPGs provide mediating environments for players to engage in medievalist gendered identities. These environments engage players in medievalist contexts, complete with story-lines (both coded into the game and improvised by players), props, and places related to gender. Gender, then, is shaped within local contentious practice, located at the intersection of accumulated medieval histories along with layered interactions among 'real,' virtual, and projective identities.

If we return to the vignette of Sage's interaction with the dwarf, a social practice perspective helps us understand the interaction. Sage's identity is shaped in relation to her avatar—she is a female night elf, so visually she is a hyperfeminized being. She wears a dress, yields a staff, and is being attacked by a number of creatures. The dwarf does not see her as a power-ful high-level player, but as a damsel in distress who needs his assistance. In a medieval-inspired world, his actions are already scripted—he is com-pelled to jump into the fight and 'save' her. This scene shows how, even in a mundane chance interaction in a remote virtual space, players engage in gendered practices of medievalism.

MASCULINITY AND FEMININITY

In high-fantasy MMORPGs, gender is performed and dependent on con-text. As Mayer asserts, gender in MMORPGs is "performative *within* [a] *context*," and medievalism provides that context with an endlessly revisable canvas on which to explore "gender boundaries."[8] With avatars that are framed within gendered binary oppositions, gender becomes a manipulable variable in games. As a performative type of embodiment, gender becomes a guise to assume as circumstances warrant. Game designers continuously adjust medieval motifs, and players respond by both following and defying medievalist definitions of masculinity and femininity.

The medievalist contexts of MMORPGs help to define gender roles for players. Players come to fantasy MMORPGs with a "body of received knowl-edge and information" about medievalism, including what people look like, act like, and the roles they play.[9] According to Henthorne, fantasy media can be understood as a conservative social response "to the social transforma-tions that followed World War II, particularly those related to gender."[10] Simply put, fantasy media was (and still is) used to reinforce gender ideals. As Schut argues, fantasy games actively define manhood and womanhood for players. Multiple versions of masculinity exist, including what Schut describes as "respectable manliness," which values responsibility, restraint, intelligence, and hard work; "rough masculinity," which values physical power and dominance; and "eternal boy," which values playfulness, humor, and escape from responsibility.[11] These versions of masculinity define trajec-tories available to players in enacting masculinity.

Parallel femininities are available to female avatars. Millar-Heggie notes that, "the performative nature of gender identities has often been highlighted" within medieval contexts.[12] Because fantasy MMORPGs are constructed upon the foundation of medievalism, female characters are unable to escape the expectation of being submissively feminine, even if they are as powerful as their male counterparts. Although there are no performance penalties based on gender (such as programming male characters to be stronger than females), female avatars often are designed as svelte and voluptuous, emphasized by revealing armor and feminized actions. Animations for actions, such as laughing, are highly feminized, with the avatar's actions depicted as shy or submissive compared to males. Because animations are preprogrammed, players must work within predetermined performances of gender. These performances further delineate differences between masculinity and femininity, which frame the identities that players must negotiate through their avatars.[13] Even if a female character possesses equivalent armor, power, and ability as a male character, she is typically smaller and sexier. With her form-fitting outfits and flirtatious voice, her avatar makes others "aware of her attractiveness and desirability."[14]

When creating characters in high-fantasy MMORPGs, players make fundamental choices about their avatars' gendered identities. Games vary significantly in the choices they afford players, from the minimal choices of *World of Warcraft*, to the significant customization of *Vanguard*. With few exceptions, players first choose their character's gender, along with race and class, which further define the body shape and appearance of armor. Hypersexualized body types are available in most games (often elves, humans, and similar creatures). Most games also provide a range of other body types, such as the Rubenesque dwarves of *World of Warcraft*; petite halflings of *Everquest II*; huge orcs and lesser giants of *Vanguard*; and even a handful of animal races, such as the lizardmen of *Warhammer Online*. Some games, such as *Everquest II*, also include athletic body types for female avatars. Uniquely, *Warhammer Online* includes two gender-neutral races. Armor is also visually marked for gender, revealing more of the neck, breasts, and stomach of female avatars. Even though gender makes no difference to gameplay and interactions with non-player characters (NPCs), the aesthetic range afforded by games, along with player preferences, tend to support more traditional gender forms. For instance, a population study of *World of Warcraft* showed that the most common races were humans, blood elves, and night elves, all of which conform to highly feminized and masculinized body types.[15]

In our years of play, we have observed an array of reasons that players choose to play specific genders in relation to their real-life gender identities. Many real-life men and women simply prefer to play their own genders. Among female players who prefer female characters, many described the power of being a 'real' female; others prefer the aesthetics; some cite the desire to feel pretty; yet others feel uncomfortable being in a projected male body. Among males who prefer male avatars, many perceive males playing female characters as 'gay' or suspicious; many describe liking to feel powerful; and like their counterparts, some simply feel more comfortable playing in projected male bodies.

However, we have met many players who enjoy playing opposite gender avatars. Among men who prefer female characters, some say that they like the aesthetics of female avatars; some perceive an advantage because they receive more help and social opportunities; some want the experience of being in the game world as female; others enjoy the role-playing challenge or simply enjoy experimenting. Females who prefer playing male characters cite similar reasons along with avoiding unwanted attention, curiosity, and a desire to feel powerful.

We also have met players who prefer to play atypical depictions of gender. They describe the desire to feel unique; to be humorous; to be grotesque and intimidating; to explore role-playing different kinds of people; or to play characters that look like themselves. Some games also encourage players to choose nonstandard gender representations by giving them special abilities and statistical advantages. For example, Jennifer played a dwarf priestess in *World of Warcraft* because at the time dwarves had a special ability that made them valuable in certain end-game raid encounters. She also had friends who played gnome mages because they received a statistical boost to intellect, which made them the ideal race to play the mage class.

Not only do high-fantasy MMORPGs engage players with medievalist ideals of masculinity and femininity in character creation, but also through the roles that are encouraged for each gender. Even though gender does not affect strength or ability in high-fantasy MMORPGs, players often create characters that play masculine and feminine neomedievalist roles. Often, strong warriors tend to be enacted through male avatars, whereas healing roles are framed as feminine. Peter and a longtime male friend experienced this gendering of roles in *World of Warcraft* through their PvP gameplay. After the game expanded to include blood elves, the first 'beautiful' Horde race, Peter's friend decided to create a female blood elf paladin. Together, Peter's warrior and the paladin engaged in PvP battle, with Peter taking the brunt of attacks and his friend keeping him alive with his healing powers.

At the time Peter felt like they were fulfilling predetermined roles with the associated medievalist motif's preferred genders. Imagine a large, physically imposing cow-man with huge shoulders, a giant axe, and spiky armor followed around by a seductive, blonde elven woman in svelte armor with a glittering magical shield. The contrast in appearances and roles was accentuated by gender: the female healed; the male destroyed. Good players of PvP know to attack the healers first, and Peter knew that his role was to defend his healer. Peter would rush to his companion's defense, hamstringing and stunning the attackers so 'she' could make an escape. Often, Peter's rescue was sacrificial, a form of falling on a virtual axe in the hope his healer would escape to resurrect and heal Peter's character. The pair spent much time in these roles, and the medievalist backdrop of the game ensured they performed them accordingly.

CHIVALRY

In addition to creating characters and enacting gendered roles in high-fantasy MMORPGs, players also take up common medievalist motifs in their interactions with each other. Chivalric values, such as Peter's self-sacrifice described above, formed the basic storylines for many interactions between male and female avatars. Henthorne identifies key elements in contemporary medievalist media that illustrate an "expressed nostalgia for imaginary, simpler times when men were knights and warriors, and women were damsels and princesses."[16] These include calls for simplified chivalric values such as faith, loyalty, and courage, particularly for young male characters.[17] As Taylor points out, women play for the same reasons as men, seeking the same kinds of performative mastery and status men do.[18] Indeed, women can be chivalrous in the same ways men can.

Even so, chivalry is often acted out by male player-characters toward female avatars. As players, we witnessed and participated in numerous acts of chivalry. Such acts stem from a sense of duty to protect the weak, to provide assistance (whether needed or not), and to experience the pleasure of saving damsels in distress. The appearances and animations for female avatars "reinforc[e] the overarching norm of male chivalry."[19] As games are "decidedly masculine," high-fantasy MMORPGs usually are designed with typical gender performances aligned with what is traditionally accepted chivalrous behavior, perpetuating a "masculine culture."[20]

Like many players, Peter often felt a duty to protect the weak, especially in PvP settings. For example, Strangethorn Vale in *World of Warcraft* created a mix of mid- and high-level players by placing Horde and Alliance towns in close proximity. High-level players ventured to Zul'Gurub, a twenty-person raid instance. Simultaneously, mid-level players were in the zone to complete quests. The mix of players proved volatile, and the strong often preyed on the weak. With his warrior, Peter often became embroiled in others' fights by coming to their aid upon seeing that they were being unfairly attacked. Aiding others—especially in fights that were perceived as unfair based on level or numbers—was a matter of principle for Peter as part of his chivalric duty as a high-level player.

Chivalry also frames a drive to provide assistance to lower-level characters. In our experience, this is especially true of male player-characters toward female characters and is why some men see an advantage to playing female characters. As the opening vignette illustrates, such actions are often misplaced, where storylines of chivalry outweigh the real needs of the recipients of chivalric acts. Teresa had a similar experience of chivalry in action while playing *World of Warcraft*. Although there are many people who would gladly help a new player if asked, oftentimes unwanted or unwarranted aide is imposed upon others in the name of chivalry. Teresa's female undead rogue, Maru, was a recipient of such treatment by Logan, a higher-level character.

At the time, Maru was new and unfamiliar with Durotar, a desert wasteland in *World of Warcraft*. While perusing her quest log and standing outside the gates of the mighty orc city, Orgrimmar, Logan approached and immediately gifted her with his assistance. After openly flirting, Logan admonished Maru for her gear, telling her that it was 'crap.' He took her to the armory, where he purchased the best armor for her level and class. Feeling obligated to play the role of the grateful female, Maru gasped and thanked him for his gifts. Executing a few actions of thanks, such as curtsying and blowing a kiss, Maru's responses made the appearance of accepting Logan's role as her savior. Logan's behavior declared that he was acting as the strong man, swooping in to help the hapless damsel in need, and Maru validated his approach by playing the coquettish female. Whether his treatment was intentional, she felt obligated to react based on her own understanding of how a damsel 'ought' to act with males. She even saved the armor he bought for months, even though she had far out-leveled its usefulness, just in case she ran into Logan. As these tales of chivalry demonstrate, the storylines of protecting the weaker, providing assistance, and saving damsels in distress are pervasive in high-fantasy MMORPGs.

COURTLY LOVE

In addition to chivalry, high-fantasy MMORPGs also support romantic story-lines to fit the medieval-inspired universes. Even if a female is capable of handling her own battles, males often need to satisfy the desire of being the protector or 'winning' the spoils of the girl. As discussed in Dell's article about the relationship between the maiden Jocelyn and the faux-knight, William, in *A Knight's Tale,* Jocelyn is a "trophy to be gained," though she desires to be treated as an equal.[21] So although female avatars may perform just as well as males, they often are treated as something to protect and are seen as a potential love interests. Courtly love frames female avatars as the recipients of generous and heroic male actions.

High-fantasy MMORPGs are designed to support medievalist notions of courtly love and romance. All of the games include props for romance and marriage, such as flower bouquets, engagement rings, and wedding dresses. As Jennifer observed in many games, if she played hyperfeminized races males would almost always pursue her as a love interest, including behaviors such as flirting, hand-holding, acts of adoration, and chaste kisses. Inevi-tably, the males would propose marriage after several weeks of courtship (which is why Jennifer prefers to play goblin characters now!). In some games, game masters (GMs) would even officiate wedding ceremonies. In other games, players would create elaborate wedding ceremonies for each other. In *Vanguard,* Jennifer attended two wedding ceremonies. At one, a GM presided over the ceremony and even spawned ceremonial dragons to celebrate the event. On another occasion, a guildmate translated a couple's wedding vows into Elvish and conducted a bilingual wedding ceremony.

Females are not merely passive recipients of male attention, however. At times, we observed female player-characters using the storylines of courtly love to their advantage. For example, in Peter's guild in *World of Warcraft*, like many raiding guilds, both of the tanks were males and there were few female players. One of those females, Hesha, played the role of 'maiden in distress,' often using cute and flirty behaviors to extract favor from the males in the group. And from the position of guild-leader, Peter was amazed to see how often her wiles succeeded. At one point, she used her influence with the tanks to assert authority in the guild. She wanted to be a healing class-leader, but Peter's guild had had a lead healer already. As guild-leader he was faced with the decision to let her mini-coup succeed or fail. He removed her from the guild, and an exodus followed, with the tanks and many of her friends leaving. Hesha projected femininity within the game, reinforcing the performative nature of gender and benefiting from the successful mobilization of a medieval motif. Kicked from the guild, she became a true damsel in distress, her friends rushing to her rescue.

WARFARE

A final and central set of gendered activities in MMORPGs surrounds acts of warfare. Whether slaying an epic dragon like Onyxia in *World of Warcraft*, or engaging in siege-based realm-versus-realm warfare as in *Warhammer Online*, players must battle either game-generated creatures or each other. The values of such warfare inevitably connect to the values of "rough masculinity"[22] or "militarized masculinity."[23] Whether a male or female player, or a male or female avatar, players must at least partially accept the values of power, domination, and conquest to be successful in such warfare.

However, despite the gender of players and avatars, battle is in our experience almost always framed as a male activity. And in large part it is—by the end of the game, high-level dungeons and PvP play is overwhelmingly populated by male players, with only a handful of females making it that far into the game. Although the avatars are much more mixed, most players and raid leaders assume that most of the players are male even if they play female characters. This is not to say that females never make it to that level of play, but it is certainly less common than for their male counterparts.

The male-oriented nature of high-level battle is best captured by the language used in such contexts. In Jennifer's experience, raid leaders often lead groups into battle with shouts referring to the group members as 'lads,' 'men,' or 'boys.' They certainly never referred to the group as all female, except on occasions where the group failed at their mission. In such circumstances, raid leaders would sometimes refer to the group as 'ladies' or even derogatory words for females.

TRANSGRESSING GENDER

Even though motifs of masculinity and femininity, chivalry, courtly love, and warfare create compelling medievalist storylines for players, gender is still flexible in fantasy MMORPGs, particularly when juxtaposed with conflicting contemporary values and less traditional notions of gender. Understanding that gender is realized in local contentious practice reveals opportunities for transgression and the potential for critique of medievalist motifs. Although received knowledge of medievalism shapes players' performative roles, modernity, endowing players with medieval knowledge "much more readily than . . . previous generations," has destabilized "traditional hierarchies of knowledge and expertise."[24] This destabilization leads to new contexts in which medievalist concepts like chivalry, courtly love, and heroic warfare can be performed.

One example of a transgression of medievalist gender roles often happened in Jennifer's engagement in end-game raids. Although most of the players were male, Jennifer would often take the opportunity to assert her female player-character identity in the course of warfare. When raid leaders used male words to refer to the group, she would lightheartedly make moves like "*peeks under her armor* Nope, not a lad!" or "Some of us ain't men, ye know!" Such discursive moves would lead to responses ranging from apologies and restatements into more inclusive language to uncomfortable silence and outright hostility. These moments indicate that enduring struggles over gender are not resolved and illustrate how medievalist contexts such as high-fantasy MMORPGs engage players in conflicting notions of gender in the course of play.

Jennifer also played with gender on her female dwarf, Kyru, in *World of Warcraft*. On one occasion, Kyru was looking for help with a quest. None of her friends were available, so she posted a request in a public chat channel. After several minutes of no response, Kyru stuck out her leg and showed some ankle to get attention and made an impassioned plea for help in dwarven-accented language, hoping to trigger a sense of chivalry on the part of some of the male player-characters. Several players responded in shock and disgust, with the exception of a few dwarven men who responded with catcalls and excitement. Similar actions on a slender and buxom night elf would be met with very different responses.

A final set of circumstances that often created transgressions of medievalist gender practices, particularly chivalric values, surrounded PvP situations. In certain PvP situations, chivalry, including beneficent behavior toward female players and ethical warfare, ceased to influence player's actions. For example, while playing on Kil'Jaeden, an open-world PvP server in *World of Warcraft*, Peter and his friends sought out opportunities to attack and defeat Alliance members. "Red is dead," the saying went; red signifying the 'enemy.' On a typical day, high-level Alliance would sweep over Thousand Needles, killing lower-level Horde players. Peter and his friends would retaliate, logging into their high-level characters, riding with vengeance to find the perpetrators. Open-world PvP often came down to numerical superiority and was fueled by vendetta. During an attack, word would spread amongst friends, local chat channels, and guild chats until a group had assembled to find and defeat the offenders. And sometimes Peter and his friends would play the 'gankers,' indiscriminately attacking players until they called for help and retaliated. Gender at such times never seemed to matter; Peter and his friends took pleasure in killing female avatars just as much as males.

Jennifer, on Sage, learned the limits of chivalry in PvP the hard way. One day she decided to sneak into the Undercity, a large Horde city where she was not welcome as an Alliance player. She was a high-level druid, so she was able to become invisible and creep into the city undetected by guards. However, a high-level Horde rogue spotted and quickly killed her. Then, the player and friends ran to the graveyard where they repeatedly waited for Sage to respawn before killing her repeatedly. Sage tried blowing kisses, flirting, and apologizing to the Horde players, but her feminine wiles held no sway with her sworn enemies.

As these experiences demonstrate, medievalist notions of gender are central to local contentious practices of high-fantasy MMORPGs. As such, historical struggles over gender are lived in the present and shape identities available to player-characters. In many cases, common medievalist storylines of gender like chivalry and courtly love provide compelling motifs for players. All of us found ourselves complicit with such motifs at various times in our play. Whether Peter's sense of chivalry toward weaker players, Jennifer's passive acceptance of the dwarf's 'help' in the opening vignette, or Teresa's coquettish response toward gifts from a male player-character, medievalist values of masculinity, femininity, chivalry, courtly love, and warfare productively shape many interactions. Such storylines are safe and familiar for players, including ourselves, and frame social practice in ways that are supported by the neomedieval backdrops, props, character aesthetics, and activities of such games.

However, it is important to remember that medievalist gender practices do not determine local contentious practice. Indeed, we have observed and participated in many interactions where medievalist motifs of gender were questioned, ignored, or exposed. As conflicting representations of gender come into contact with medievalist motifs, enduring struggles over gender are highlighted in the flow of play. At times these moments are created through players actively questioning the status quo, as with Jennifer's persistence that not all end-game raid members are men; at other times, they are created in particular activities and constellations of players, such as the suspension of chivalrous values in the course of PvP battle.

Whether we are complicit or critical of medievalist notions of gender, our experiences illustrate the range of choices, roles, and storylines that players enact in the course of everyday interactions. This is important for players to recognize the force that these medievalist ideals exert on them. Likewise, it is important for game designers to be aware of the role that games play in shaping gendered interactions. We would like to see more players and games create opportunities for transgressions of gender—such possibilities enable critiques of longstanding medievalist gender norms to emerge and evolve.

NOTES

1. David W. Marshall, ed., *Mass Market Medieval: Essays on the Middle Ages in Popular Culture* (Jefferson, NC: McFarland, 2007).
2. Dorothy Holland and Jean Lave, "History in Person: An Introduction" in *History in Person: Enduring Struggles, Contentious Practice, Intimate Identities*, ed. Dorothy Holland and Jean Lave (Santa Fe, NM: School of American Research, 2001), 3–33.
3. Holland and Lave, "History," 7.
4. Holland and Lave, "History," 22.
5. Holland and Lave, "History," 29.
6. James Paul Gee, *What Video Games Have to Teach Us About Learning and Literacy* (New York: Palgrave Macmillan, 2004).
7. Gee, "Video Games," 55.
8. Lauryn Mayer, "Promises of Monsters: The Rethinking of Gender in MMORPGs," *Studies in Medievalism* 16 (2008): 198.
9. Jane Tolmie, "Medievalism and the Fantasy Heroine," *Journal of Gender Studies* 15 (2006): 149.
10. Tom Henthorne, "Boys to Men: Medievalism and Masculinity in *Star Wars* and *E.T.: The Extra-Terrestrial*," in *The Medieval Hero on Screen: Representations from Beowulf to Buffy*, ed. Martha W. Driver and Sid Ray (Jefferson, NC: McFarland, 2004), 73.
11. Kevin Schut, "Desktop Conquistadors: Negotiating American Manhood in the Digital Fantasy Role-Playing Game," in *Gaming as Culture: Essays on Reality, Identity, and Experience in Fantasy Games*, ed. J. Patrick Williams, Sean Q. Hendricks, and W. Keith Winkler (Jefferson, NC: McFarland, 2006), 102–103.
12. Bonnie Millar-Heggie, "The Performance of Masculinity and Femininity: Gender Transgression in *The Sowdone of Babylone*," *Mirator* 5 (2004): 1.
13. Millar-Heggie, "Performance," 1.
14. Millar-Heggie, "Performance," 7.
15. Census Data, http://www.warcraftrealms.com/census.php?guildid=-1 (accessed July 20, 2012).
16. Henthorne, "Boys to Men," 74.
17. Henthorne, "Boys to Men," 73.
18. T. L. Taylor, *Play Between Worlds: Exploring Online Game Culture* (Cambridge, MA: MIT Press, 2006), 102.
19. Clairellyn Rose Gregory, "Who Gender-Bends and Why? A Qualitative Study of *World of Warcraft*" (PhD diss., Portland State University, 2011), 15.
20. Gregory, "Who Gender-Bends and Why?" 11.
21. Helen Dell, "Past, Present, Future Perfect: Paradigms of History in Medievalism," *Parergon* 25 (2008): 62.
22. Schut, "Desktop Conquistadors," 113–15.
23. Stephen Kline, Nick Dyer-Witheford, and Greig De Peuter, *Digital Play: The Interaction of Technology, Culture, and Marketing* (Montreal: McGill-Queen's University Press, 2003), 194.
24. Stephanie Trigg, "Medievalism and Convergence Culture: Researching the Middle Ages for Fiction and Film," *Parergon* 25 (2008): 100.

9 "Awesome Cleavage"
The Genred Body in *World of Warcraft*

Kim Wilkins

In 2007, NCsoft released a free medievalist MMORPG (massively multi-player online role-playing game) called *Dungeon Runners*. The game was often parodic, as some of the names demonstrate: locations such as "Pwn-ston," loot such as the "Well Rounded Rusty Great Helm of the Freakish Liger," and acquirable weapon skills such as "Awesome Cleavage." It is this last name that I have adopted for the title of my chapter because it is so suggestive of the issues I want to raise about gender and genre in medievalist MMORPGs: it references the medieval violence ubiquitous in these games; it references the way the female body is often depicted within them; and, as parody, it plays on generic expectations, and so implicitly or explicitly acknowledges the audiences that respond to and shape genres. These ideas underpin the discussion that follows concerning genre, gender, and the medium-specific uses of the medieval in Blizzard Entertainment's medievalist MMORPG *World of Warcraft*.[1]

World of Warcraft is a highly successful game with enormous cultural reach. At its peak in 2009, it boasted nearly 12 million active subscribers, a number comparable to the population of Greece. Despite a recent dip in popularity, it still retains around 10 million active subscribers. *World of Warcraft* game designer Rob Pardo estimated in an interview that the actual figure of subscriptions that passed through the game in its first five years was in the vicinity of 25 million.[2] Given this large player base, its longevity (it was first released in 2004), and its ability to develop and change through expansions and patches, *World of Warcraft* can be seen as a key site for understanding what the medieval means and what uses are made of it in the twenty-first century, and it is certainly a key site for understanding the intersections between medievalism and gender.[3]

World of Warcraft, like many video games, is far more complex than it might first appear on the surface. Many different aspects of the game could underpin a variety of arguments. Indeed, it may seem almost fatal to make assertions about a game that offers so many choices of gameplay. When one creates an avatar, one must not simply consider gender. One must choose a faction (Horde or Alliance) and within that faction, a race. At the time of writing, there are twelve races, and each opens up a range of choices about appearance: dwarven women are stout and stocky, blood elf women are svelte and curvaceous, dranei men have hypermasculine torsos, undead men shuffle stoop-shouldered. Beyond avatar appearance, there are considerations of gameplay: which class and speciality trees (from warriors and paladins to hunters and mages), which environment (player versus player, player versus environment, role playing), and even the choices of what kind of activities the player will undertake—for example, solo questing, joining a guild, competing in arenas, or cooperating in raids. Time and again, though, my experience of gameplay aroused for me questions of gender and genre: how the fantasy-genre medievalist space of the game opens up nonconventional possibilities for the representation of feminine comportment and motility. My contention is that *World of Warcraft* neither rigidly enforces feminine stereotypes, nor is endlessly flexible about them. Rather, as a game that is as ongoing and mutable as its player demographic, its concept of what is 'feminine' is contingent, shifting, and continually shaped and reshaped within the game. The incongruity of a medievalist setting rendered with up-to-the-minute technological tools creates what Halberstam might call a "queer time,"[4] which is key in allowing, enabling, even insisting on dynamically contingent gendered performances.

GENDER, GENRE, AND MEDIEVAL VIOLENCE

MMORPGs such as *World of Warcraft* are evidently and eminently "prime loci" of contemporary medievalism.[5] A key reason the Middle Ages have continued to be adapted for games is the power of genre. These games overwhelmingly belong to the fantasy genre (*Eve Online* [2003], *Anarchy Online* [2001], and *DC Universe Online* [2011] are notable exceptions). The fantasy genre has a long and established association with medievalism across media, growing out of the popularity of J. R. R. Tolkien's *Lord of the Rings,* a text that has, itself, been adapted for a number of video games, including a recent MMORPG called *Lord of the Rings Online* (2007). Tolkien, himself a medievalist, popularized for common usage medieval mythological creatures such as orcs and trolls, creatures that have become standard inhabitants in MMORPGs. Across media, the medieval provides specific conflicts for the fantasy genre that build incrementally through series of quests and lead to large, definitive battles that must be won or lost for the resolution of a narrative or series of narratives. That is, the thrill of conflict in the medievalist fantasy narrative is nearly always linked with medieval violence.

Violence in the medieval period was intrinsic and omnipresent, saturating most social relationships and structures.[6] Social power was displayed through acts and symbols of aggression:[7] "violence was integral to the processes through which social status was contested and affirmed and economic resources allocated within communities"; that is, violence was a "normative" practice by which society reproduced itself.[8] Similarly, social and cultural power in a significant proportion of video games "cannot be unlinked from violence."[9] But it is not any kind of violence that provides pleasure and interest in MMORPGs; it is specifically medieval violence. There is a directness in our understanding of medieval violence: these are not battles fought at range with guns and missiles, but rather battles fought predominantly up close in melees. Although ranged attack by arrow exists in both medieval history and in medievalist MMORPGs, melee weapons such as swords and axes retain a privileged position in both our popular understanding of medieval violence and in MMORPGs. This kind of direct violence signifies a bodily and brutal domination of objects and bodies in the medieval world and in medievalist digital space.

Direct medieval violence, it must be noted, was not largely performed by women. The role of women was much more circumscribed: women inhabited the private realm of domestic life and child-raising and men the public realm of social power and war. In Old English, for example, we see the two words *wæpmenn* and *wifmenn* used for men and women: essentially "weapon people" and "wife people." Italian lawmakers of the seventh century observed that "it is clearly absurd that a woman . . . could commit a forceful act with arms as though she were a man."[10] However, it is from the Middle Ages that the fantasy genre derives the prototype of the martial woman: in medieval Germanic culture, there exists the "literary fantasy" of the shield maiden.[11] The possibility of her potentially transgressive presentation, motility, and comportment is evidenced across a number of nonliterary texts. An early thirteenth-century chronicle of the history of Denmark, for example, speaks of shield-maidens having to "take off the woman" to perform military deeds;[12] Danish legal codes forbade cross-dressing and the adoption of "male practices;"[13] and Norwegian and Icelandic medieval law held that cross dressing and "women who wear weapons as a man" were punishable.[14] Where martial women are written of in medieval culture, then, they are disguised as men. In chapter twenty of *Volsung Saga,* for example, Sigurd mistakes Brynhildr for a man the first time he sees her. In the medieval imagination, women did not look like women when committing violence. In *World of Warcraft,* they always do (and, as I shall discuss below, sometimes the men do, too).

I have laid out these 'facts' about women warriors in the medieval period and suggested what is different in contemporary gaming's adaptation of these facts, as though the medieval period is whole and replicable and all re-imaginings that follow have a moral responsibility to reproduce it faithfully. In fact, contemporary medievalism is at its most critically interesting when deviating from the facts because those little acts of faithlessness reveal that something culturally interesting is happening. Evidently, when contemporary culture continues to imagine medieval martial women, they mostly appear in unmistakably feminine forms, and MMORPGs are a key site for these re-imaginings. The power of genre is worth mentioning again here: *World of Warcraft* is not the first place we see women enacting medieval violence in costumes that emphasize their femininity. As early as the nine-teenth century, through Wagnerian opera—particularly the influence of designers Julius Noerr and Theodor Pixis and artist Arthur Rackham—Sigurd's Brynhildr became the bare-armed woman with long fair hair and armored breasts that is iconic (and sometimes lampooned) today.[15] This image of the armored medieval woman whose breasts are on display, usu-ally drawn from the Germanic medieval imagination, was built upon by the post-Tolkien medievalism of the 1960s, 1970s, and 1980s in the fantasy art of Boris Vallejo and Frank Frazetta and in Marvel Comics' representa-tion of Valkyrie/Brunhilda in the *Thor* series. Vallejo's famous poster art of valkyries is a notable example. Two women with horned and winged helmets and flowing blonde hair carry spears while riding gleaming, mus-cular horses across a setting of smoke and fire. They wear knee-high boots and armored, gold string-bikinis. Although their breasts and hips are full and womanly, their stomachs and arms are toned and muscular, echoing the 'ripped' look of the idealized masculine body. These figures are both feminine/sexual and masculine/powerful. The body we see in art like this is certainly a gendered body, but it is also, importantly, a *genred* body. That is, it is a body that has been shaped by the expectations and pleasures of the fantasy genre for specific audiences at specific times.

WORLD OF WARCRAFT AND THE ARMORED WOMAN

Genres are not restrictive taxonomical categories. They are shifting and con-tingent and agreed upon tacitly between those who participate in the genre, for example, game designers, game players, the industrial bodies that bring games to consumers, and so on. Because *World of Warcraft* has had a long life, especially for a video game (eight years at the time of writing), it has evolved over time. In the earlier years of the game, it was commonplace for a piece of armor to look radically different on a male avatar than a female avatar, appearing skimpy and body-revealing like the armor on Vallejo's valkyries. Magoulick criticizes the comparable "ridiculously impractical outfits" worn by Xena and Buffy, arguing that the female warrior figure's key role is "to fulfil male fantasies."[16] Body-revealing, sexualized armor on female avatars aroused recurring criticism in the earlier years of *World of Warcraft,* for example, in forum discussions: "the full vicious looking battle-gear on men, hot date on women [look] bothers me A LOT."[17] Criticism also appeared in entries to the comic contest; in fact, Blizzard Entertain-ment now excludes "references/depictions of disproportionate armor size as it may appear on female characters" due to the high volume received.[18] This backlash against skimpy armor on female avatars signaled a shift in generic expectations, perhaps borne of a shift in the game's player base. The "presumption of [male] heterosexual interests"[19] that Consalvo once argued pervaded gaming is shown here to be a presumption that no longer holds so tightly: since the *Lich King* expansion (2008), quests no longer reward success with revealing armor.

But whether or not armor is overtly revealing on female avatars, these avatars are still recognizably female. Even the heaviest armor is molded to outline hips, waists, and especially breasts. In fact, in some areas of the game, such as Stormwind, breasts allow us to distinguish between male and female guards, who wear full-faced helmets. The genred body of medievalist fantasy still stands with few concessions in *World of Warcraft,* and there is debate about what function it performs. On the one hand, Taylor argues that while hypermasculine, muscular men represent power as well as sexual attractiveness, breasts never function as a representation of power.[20] Yee argues that this emphatically womanly body "encourages players to think about women as token spectacles rather than actual players," and therefore female players are "constantly reminded of the intended male subject position they are trespassing upon."[21] On the other hand, the female body is very visible in this traditionally male space. Hilde Corneliussen points to the sheer number of female non-player characters (NPCs) in *World of Warcraft,*[22] and my own research indicates that roughly one-third of avatars in the game are also female. She argues that these numbers mean that *World of Warcraft* is "a perfect cultural playground for perceptions of gender," claiming it is a "true cross-gender game."[23] In *World of Warcraft,* being male or female is "a choice that makes no technical difference to the playable character's attributes"[24] compared with a game like *Resident Evil,* in which the female avatar is weaker and therefore must equip more powerful weapons.[25] Christian Schmieder also holds that "dissolution of gender categories is a side effect" of the high visibility of women in the game.[26]

I want to move away, however, from a position that argues that the genred body in *World of Warcraft* is a necessarily liberating or necessarily restricting phenomenon, taking my cue from Halberstam, who writes of moving beyond "claims of either uniqueness or unilateral oppression, and beyond the binary division of flexibility or rigidity."[27] I acknowledge that the genred body emphasizes aspects of the female body that are culturally linked to the private sphere (sexuality, fertility, nurture), quite possibly for reasons related to fulfilling the expectations of the heterosexual males who are often assumed to make up the bulk of the gaming player base. But the recurring figure of the martial woman *in a womanly body* is an interesting and potentially progressive way of imagining feminine physical presence. Two key aspects of the medievalist setting of *World of Warcraft* make this particular iteration of the genred body possible: first, its medium-specific qualities and, second, the incongruity of rendering "a pre-industrial world using the most advanced post-industrial tools."[28]

In her recently republished essay "Throwing like a Girl," Iris Marion Young writes of "modalities of feminine bodily comportment, motility, and spatiality" that have their source "in the particular situation of women as conditioned by their sexist oppression in contemporary society." Women, she argues, experience their bodies "as object as well as subject," which results in their tendency "not to move openly, keeping their limbs closed around themselves."[29] The video game medium, however, allows a particular and pleasurable infidelity to the facts of medieval history: women dominating the objects and bodies around them with direct and violent agency. The genred body in *World of Warcraft* can be seen as "object as well as subject" but, in a subversion of Young's findings, this never results in these female avatars being limited in movement. Digital bodies moving in digital spaces are not subject to the same limitations as nondigital bodies moving in nondigital spaces, medieval or otherwise. Consider that an Anglo-Saxon warrior would have gone into battle wearing approximately twenty kilograms of armor, with most of the weight distributed across the shoulders and upper body. Lifting weapons and fighting with this kind of weight would have been challenging for men, but almost impossible for most women. In *World of Warcraft,* though, women can not only wear plate and mail armor, they can lift and wield large axes and swords with ease (in some specialities, one in each hand).

Moreover, the digital medievalist game world can function as a time outside of time, not delimited by one temporality, opening the possibility that gender-based restrictions may also function without clear delineation. The MMORPG evidences an obvious incongruity of times and technologies. We understand the medieval as a period of direct and visible technology, superstition, and scientific ignorance, characterized by a life circumscribed by village and church. The technology that enables digital gaming is, by contrast, indirect and invisible, borne out of complex and ingenious science, and able to connect people globally with previously unimaginable speed and clarity: *World of Warcraft* is, after all, a multiplayer game, and it is not unusual to find oneself playing with gamers on the other side of the world. Stern argues for the historical and philosophical sympathies between technology and magic in order to understand why medievalism has "resurfaced now precisely at the apex of the 'digital revolution.'"[30] Rather than explaining, rationalizing, or trying to neaten up the incongruity between the medieval past and the digital present, however, I think it is more fruitful to let it stand and acknowledge the critically interesting disorientations that this incongruity represents. Much recent work in medievalism concerns itself with writing against the idea of sharply defined chronologies, in order to "undetermine" the medieval period and "supplant the predictability of history with philosophically complex notions of temporality."[31] Key ideas here can be drawn from queer theory: Dinshaw, for example, writes of moments of temporal disorientation as bearing "the touch of the queer"; that is, they are moments that reveal "something disjunctive within unities that are presumed unproblematic, even natural";[32] while Halberstam, too, writes of "queer time," found in spaces and times of non-normativity and often associated with "sexual identity, embodiment, and activity."[33] Temporal unease created by the medieval and the modern rubbing against one another marks the game environment of *World of Warcraft* as a potential "queer time." As such, *World of Warcraft* allows (by lifting restrictions), enables (by providing items), and sometimes even insists upon (through game rules) different kinds of feminine comportment and motility. In *World of Warcraft*, the genred body functions equally in masculine space and can take up a masculine relation to space.[34] I turn now to some examples of gameplay—both sandboxing and questing—that evidence the complex shifts of traditional and nontraditional gender in *World of Warcraft*.

"QUEER TIME"

The term *sandboxing* refers to a mode of gameplay in video games where a player ignores the linear quest narrative available and plays in the game world in an unrestricted way: leveling up secondary skills, exploring new areas, partaking in social activities such as impromptu cross-faction raids, or freeform occasional gatherings (e.g., guild meetings, dance-offs, weddings, drinking in inns, and so on). Most MMORPGs, including *World of Warcraft*, can be played in this way, and game designers support sandboxing with in-game items and areas that allow imaginative and open-ended play. Importantly for my argument, open-ended gender play is allowed and enabled in *World of Warcraft*. While sandboxing, female avatars are not restricted to traditional feminine activities, nor are male avatars restricted to traditional masculine activities: a battle-hardened male orc warrior may wander through meadows picking heartblossom flowers just as readily as a female gnome mage with pink pig-tails may kill and skin a crag boar. The game also provides materials and designs for making nonstandard attire for avatars, including evening gowns, wedding dresses, dinner suits, and tuxedos, which can then be sold and bought at auction houses and acquired by any player. All of these clothes can be worn by either male or female avatars, and they have been used in activities such as in-game weddings (including gay weddings). By making wedding dresses wearable by male avatars and tuxedos wearable by female avatars, *World of Warcraft* is not just acknowledging the possibility of desire for gender play, it is enabling it: options are opened up rather than closed down. The social nature of the game means this gender play is not something done behind closed doors, but in a public forum (indeed, the special attire seems purpose-designed for publicly visible occasions). By making a wedding dress available in game, the game doesn't just allow a wedding; it enables it and inspires the potential for it. Similarly, by making men's clothes available for female avatars to wear (and vice versa), it enables, perhaps even inspires, digital cross-dressing.

There is one particular quest chain and an associated geographic location, however, that does not just allow or enable digital cross-dressing; it insists upon it. The Hyldnir quest chain takes place in and around the villages of Sifreldar and Brunnhildar in Storm Peaks, in the land of Northrend, which features many geographical, social, architectural, and cultural aspects of Old Norse culture. The initial quest in the chain is called "They Took Our Men." An NPC named Gretchen tells of Vikings (called Vyrkul in *World of Warcraft*) who were "all female" abducting the local men and taking them to their mountain village. The quest leads the player underground to retrieve runes for a magical crone, and we learn that the name of the female Vikings is the Hyldnir. The player is now put under a spell that means his or her avatar adopts the appearance of a Hyldnir so that she or he may go undercover to complete tasks, and for male avatars this means a change in gender. The Hyldnir are tall, stocky, pale blue women in horned helms and leather-and-mail armor, wearing furs and wielding swords. The first we see of them, they are dominating male NPCs in a mine. As the quest-giver, Mildred the Cruel says, "the male Vyrkul that work the mines for us do so against their will . . . purely out of fear of our blades." The player's initial task is to discipline men in the mine without killing them and so blend in the with Hyldnir, though accidentally killing some of them is unavoidable.

The result of this harsh discipline is an insurrection plot among the men: "The bearded pig behind this rabble-rousing is called Garhal. Put an end to him . . . and make sure the other males see his demise. They must learn that insubordination will not be tolerated." After killing Garhal, the player is congratulated on his or her lack of mercy and asked to kill a female prisoner, but to "make it as painless as possible. She's a female after all, even if not one of us." The player then travels to Brunnhildar Village to receive the rest of the quest chain. The first task is to challenge the Hyldnir warrior Agnetta Tyrsdottir to single combat in a competition called the Hyldsmeet: "the great competition of Hyldnir against Hyldnir to determine who will rule by Thorim's side." Taking part in the Hyldsmeet means an increasingly difficult set of tasks, including training war bears, defeating frost giants in Dun Niffelem, and eventually besting a group of dragon-riding 'sisters' to get an audience with Thorim, who momentarily mistakes the player for his lost love, Sif. Throughout these quests, what it means to be a female warrior is constantly at issue: "Do you have the heart of a warrior queen? Or that of a sniveling seamstress?"

This genred body is central to the Hyldnir quest chain. The names Hyldnir and Brunnhildar reference Brynhildr and draw on the subversive figure of the *skjaldmeyjar* of Germanic heroic literature. The subversion within this quest chain is explicit but not complete. A topsy-turvy gender hierarchy is explicit in the idea that a group of women subjugate and dominate a group of men through physical violence, specifically through the use of swords: "our blades" (both phallic and medieval). Indeed, female violence is so forceful in this hierarchy that it can kill a man by accident. There are hints that this reversal of gendered power is revenge or punishment for an imagined male impulse to subjugate women: the head of the insurgents is a "bearded pig," and the word choice alludes to an abject animal as well as a chauvinist, marked by his facial hair as unquestionably male. By contrast, a female enemy needs to be treated well and offered a "painless" death. The Hyldnir's activities are explicitly nontraditional: they are encouraged in their roles as "warrior queens" in contrast to emotionally weak private-sphere roles as "sniveling seamstresses." However, these activities lead to a high point where the Hyldnir abandon the role of dominator and assume the more traditional role of consort to the god Thorim: indeed, it is the violent assertion of power that brings the Hyldnir to wifely status. This destiny is reflected in their physical appearance: the Hyldnir have large breasts and full lips, and they wear short skirts and bare their shoulders; but the lips are only visible under a horned helmet, and the skirts reveal strong mail-clad legs. The Hyldnir, then, function in dual roles as subversive and conventional. Rather than suggest that the Hyldnir's subversive nature is undermined by their ultimate recoupment into a traditional feminine role, I would argue that the game allows this duality to stand and meet the expectations of a range of audiences coming to fantasy genre gaming from a range of perspectives. I would also argue that the genred body of the Hyldnir is, in fact, a queer figure: she embodies "nonnormative logics and organisations of community."[35] This queerness is allowed, enabled, and insisted upon by the digital medium.

In this quest chain, the medium-specific queerness of the game environment and issues of gender and genre are all in evidence. The medievalism is apparent in references to Old Norse myth, including Thor and his wife Sif; Niflheim echoed in the place name Niffelem; the surname Tyrsdottir (daughter of Tyr, the Norse god of combat); and the nornlike crone. But the medievalism is generic. The names are borrowed and respelled in a way that suggests a desire to make them different, but not too different, from the original (the "im" in Thorim) or to suggest the fantasy genre's impulse to defamiliarize through obvious strangeness (the nornlike crone is named Lok'lira employing the meaningless apostrophe so common in the genre). The reference to Sif as Thor(im)'s partner nods to previous iterations of these characters in the fantasy genre. In Old Norse literature, Sif is not a shieldmaiden figure; she is a goddess without particular function, as Simek argues, whose name simply means "relation by marriage."[36] This quest chain's reference to Sif comes via Marvel's *Thor* comic series, where Sif is a shieldmaiden in Thor's retinue. Sif-via-*Thor* has the genred body that borrows from the Old Norse shieldmaiden and is reimagined across the fantasy genre, including *World of Warcraft*'s Hyldnir: a body so generic that Thorim mistakes the player in Hyldnir disguise as his dead wife.

The Viking past in this game is rendered with the most up-to-date technological tools, an incongruity that sets the tone for the gender incongruity that follows. All games have rules by which certain actions and outcomes are allowed or disallowed, and a critically interesting rule here is the spell that changes the player's avatar into a Hyldnir, that is, into the genred body of the female fantasy warrior. This bodily fluidity is not only enabled by the digital game space, which lifts all bodily limitations but also is enabled by the fact that the game space is already functioning in a 'queer' way. For any player, the change into the Hyldnir body requires a change of appearance, perhaps just a change of race or class. For male avatars it means a change of gender, an object lesson in equality of physical strength of the genred body. Nor are these effects confined to the quest chain: once the spell has been administered, it always applies in the Storm Peaks region of the game. Even if players are flying over the region on the way to somewhere else, they will change into Hyldnir and only change back once they have passed over.[37] Titles and honors from other quests are also affected: for example, players who have won the title 'patron' in Children's Week activities will see their title changed to 'matron' as they pass over Brunhildar Village. For male players, it means an enforced and recurring transgendered subjectivity, imposing on players a new and perhaps challenging relationship with their avatars. Queer performance becomes an imperative of the game.

CONCLUSION

World of Warcraft's player base has shifted over its history, and with this shift there has been a change in what is expected and accepted in the medievalist fantasy genre, driven by the popularity of other iterations of the genre (Lord of the Rings, Game of Thrones) as much as by the opening up of the video games market to women. The medieval figure of the armored woman is enjoyed readily within this genre but within a womanly body rather than disguised as a man. In World of Warcraft, breasts, waists, and hips are highly visible in the conventionally masculinized space of violent medieval battle, but they are not solely presented for the viewing pleasure of a presumed heterosexual male audience: the figure of the female body violently dominating the object world provides a different kind of pleasure to a different kind of player. The genred body of the armored woman is both an object and a subject, inhabiting this incongruous 'queer' space enabled by the premodern world being reimagined with modern technological tools. In the digital medieval environment of World of Warcraft, not only are limitations of time and history eased: bodily limitations are eased and possibilities for dynamic, contingent gender performance are opened up.

NOTES

1. World of Warcraft (Blizzard Entertainment, 2004); World of Warcraft: The Burning Crusade (Blizzard Entertainment, 2007); World of Warcraft: Wrath of the Lich King (Blizzard Entertainment, 2008); World of Warcraft: Cataclysm (Blizzard Entertainment, 2010).
2. John Funk, "Blizzard's Rob Pardo Talks Five Years of Warcraft," The Escapist, http://www.escapistmagazine.com/news/view/96113-Blizzards-Rob-Pardo-Talks-Five-Years-of-Warcraft (accessed July 19, 2012).

3. Lauryn S. Mayer, "Promises of Monsters: The Rethinking of Gender in MMORPGs," *Studies in Medievalism* 16 (2008): 191.
4. Judith Halberstam, *In a Queer Time and Place: Transgender Bodies, Subcultural Lives* (New York: New York University Press, 2005), 2.
5. Eddo Stern, "A Touch of Medieval: Narrative, Magic, and Computer Technology in Massively Multiplayer Computer Role-Playing Games," *Proceedings of Computer Games and Digital Cultures Conference* (Tampere, Finland: Tampere University Press, 2002), 258.
6. Guy Halsall, "An Introductory Survey," in *Violence and Society in the Early Medieval West*, ed. Guy Halsall (Woodbridge, Suffolk: Boydell and Brewer, 1998), 2; Mark D. Meyerson, Daniel Thiery, and Oren Falk, "Introduction," in *"A Great Effusion of Blood"? Interpreting Medieval Violence*, ed. Mark D. Meyerson, Daniel Thiery, and Oren Falk (Toronto: University of Toronto Press, 2004), 6.
7. Halsall, "Introductory," 3–4.
8. Meyerson, Thiery, and Falk, "Introduction," 5–6.
9. T. L. Taylor, "Multiple Pleasures: Women and Online Gaming," *Convergence*, 9, no. 1 (2003): 33.
10. R. Balzaretti, "'These Are Things that Men Do, Not Women': The Social Regulation of Female Violence in Lombard Italy," in *Violence and Society in the Early Medieval West*, ed. Guy Halsall (Woodbridge, Suffolk: Boydell and Brewer, 1998), 187.
11. Lena Norrman, "Woman or Warrior? The Construction of Gender in Old Norse Myth," in *Old Norse Myths, Literature and Society: Proceedings of the 11th International Saga Conference*, ed. Geraldine Barnes and Margaret Clunies Ross (Sydney: Centre for Medieval Studies, University of Sydney, 2000), 376.
12. William Layher, "Caught Between Worlds: Gendering the Maiden Warrior in Old Norse," in *Women in Medieval Epic*, ed. Sara S. Poor and Jana Schulman (New York: Palgrave, 2007), 184.
13. Layher, "Caught," 186.
14. Norrman, "Woman," 377.
15. Johnni Langer, "The Origins of the Imaginary Viking," *Viking Heritage Magazine* (December 2002): 2–4.
16. Mary Magoulick, "Frustrating Female Heroism: Mixed Messages in *Xena, Nikita,* and *Buffy,*" *Journal of Popular Culture* 39, no. 5 (2006): 743–44.
17. "Plate Bikinis?" *World of Warcraft Forums*, http://forums.worldofwarcraft. com/thread.html?topicId=18031368991&sid=1&pageNo=1 (accessed June 20, 2012).
18. "Comic Submission," *Blizzard Entertainment*, http://us.blizzard. com/en-us/ community/comics (accessed July 19, 2012).
19. Mia Consalvo, "Hot Dates and Fairytale Romances: Studying Sexuality in Video Games," in *The Video Game Theory Reader*, ed. Mark J. P. Wolf and Bernard Perron (New York: Routledge, 2003), 172.
20. Taylor, "Multiple Pleasures," 39.
21. Nick Yee, "Maps of Digital Desires: Exploring the Topography of Gender and Play in Online Games," in *Beyond Barbie and Mortal Combat: New Perspectives on Gender and Gaming*, ed. Yasmin B. Kafai, Carrie Heeter, Jill Denner, and Jennifer Y. Sun (Cambridge, MA: MIT Press, 2008), 93.
22. Hilde G. Corneliussen, "*World of Warcraft* as a Playground for Feminism," in *Digital Culture, Play, and Identity*, ed. Hilde G. Corneliussen and Jill Walker Rettberg, (Cambridge, MA: MIT Press, 2008), 76–78.
23. Corneliussen, "Playground," 65.
24. Corneliussen, "Playground," 70.

25. Derek A. Burrill, *Die Tryin': Videogames, Masculinity, and Culture* (New York: Peter Lang, 2008), 50.
26. Christian Schmieder, "World of Maskcraft vs. World of Queercraft? Communication, Sex, and Gender in the Online Role-playing Game *World of Warcraft*," *Journal of Gaming and Virtual Worlds* 1, no. 1 (2009): 18.
27. Halberstam, *Queer Time*, 21.
28. Stern, "A Touch," 262.
29. Iris Marion Young, *Throwing Like a Girl and Other Essays in Feminist Philosophy and Social Theory* (Ann Arbor, MI: UMI Books on Demand, 2002), 42–45.
30. Stern, "A Touch," 259.
31. Jeffrey J. Cohen, *Medieval Identity Machines* (Minneapolis: University of Minnesota Press, 2003), 8.
32. Carolyn Dinshaw, *Getting Medieval: Sexualities and Communities, Pre- and Postmodern* (Durham, NC: Duke University Press, 1999), 151.
33. Halberstam, *Queer Time*, 6.
34. See Stephen M. Whitehead, *Men and Masculinities: Key Themes and New Directions* (Cambridge, UK: Polity, 2002), 189.
35. Halberstam, *Queer Time*, 6.
36. Rudolf Simek, *Dictionary of Northern Mythology*, trans. Angela Hall (Woodbridge, Suffolk: D. S. Brewer, 1993), 283.
37. Although outside the scope of my example, it is worth noting that female players have a similar experience when on Netherwing quests in Shadowmoon Valley, where they are changed into a male orc.

Part IV

Case Study 2: *Dante's Inferno*

10 The Game's Two Bodies, or the Fate of *Figura* in *Dante's Inferno*

Bruno Lessard

haec omnia in figura

—St. Paul, 1 Corinthians 10:11

Often described by game critics as a mere clone of the *God of War* series (2005–12), *Dante's Inferno* (2010) has also been dismissed as an unsuccessful attempt at adapting Dante Alighieri's fourteenth-century canonical masterpiece, the *Inferno*, which opens the *Commedia* (1308–21). Reviewers having failed to put the video game in its proper cultural, literary, and philosophical context, assessing its merits or lack thereof is not so much a matter of addressing the issues of influence and faithfulness to the original poem as of understanding simulation in digital games, procedurality in game design, and the key role the neglected notion of *figura* has played throughout the centuries. Only then will it be possible to go beyond the misleading accounts that have characterized the critical reception of the video game.[1] *Dante's Inferno* departs from the scenarios of contemporary hack-and-slash video games such as *Bayonetta* (2010) or *Ninja Gaiden 3* (2012) in establishing a solid relationship with medieval poetics and art history via *figura*, and it allows us to consider video game adaptation in a way that eschews the pitfalls associated with the concept of influence so much discussed in game reviews.

As the latest installment in the afterlife of the *Inferno* in the visual arts and screen media, *Dante's Inferno* belongs to the long series of visual adaptations of Dante's *Commedia* taking us back to paintings, watercolors, and drawings by Botticelli, William Blake, and Gustave Doré; Dantesque visions of the modern world such as Goya's etchings *Los Caprichos* and *Los Desastres de la guerra* and Rodin's *La Porte de l'enfer;* early twentieth-century film adaptations of the *Inferno;* fin-de-millennium efforts such as Tom Phillips and Peter Greenaway's *A TV Dante* and William Barlowe's hellish drawings; James Nachtwey's *Inferno;* and Dariusz Nowak-Nova's website adaptation of the *Commedia.*[2]

What should deserve closer attention than the game's indebtedness to the aforementioned visual adaptations, or the *God of War* series for that matter, is that *Dante's Inferno* unwittingly embeds the medieval notion of *figura* and its actual *survival*[3] in the configuration and implementation of the virtual camera, the mobile perspective, the animated tapestry qua cutscene, and the quick-time event (QTE). Beyond its impressive frame rate (60 fps) and the undeniable capabilities of Visceral Games' proprietary engine, the path-breaking nature of *Dante's Inferno* would lie in allowing the notion of *figura* to survive in the world of digital gaming via its unvoiced demand to answer the Deleuzian question par excellence: What can a video game body do?

FIGURA AND THE SECULARIZATION OF REALISM

In his pioneering 1944 article published in *Neue Dantestudien* and in his invaluable chapter on Dante's poetics in his magnum opus, *Mimesis: The Representation of Reality in Western Literature*, German comparatist Erich Auerbach adroitly articulates what is at stake in the representation of reality in the *Commedia*. At the center of its poetics would lie the notion of '*figura*' and the type of interpretation a poem such as Dante's requires. Auerbach defines it as follows:

> Figural interpretation establishes a connection between two events or persons, the first of which signifies not only itself but also the second, while the second encompasses or fulfills the first. The two poles of the figure are separate in time, but both, being real events or figures, are within time, within the stream of historical life. Only the understanding of the two persons or events is a spiritual act, but this spiritual act deals with concrete events whether past, present, or future, and not with concepts or abstractions.[4]

Needless to say, such figural hermeneutics goes against the grain of causality and the way in which relations of space, time, and action are to be conceived of. Indeed, as Auerbach remarks, *figura* is predicated on divine providence and its eternal plan according to which "the temporal and causal, connection of occurrences is dissolved; the here and now is no longer a mere link in an earthly chain of events, it is simultaneously something which has always been, and which will be fulfilled in the future; and strictly, in the eyes of God, it is something eternal, something omni-temporal, something already consummated in the realm of fragmentary earthly event."[5]

Flying in the face of causality and rationality, figural interpretation raises many problems in light of *real* historical events involving *real* human beings. As early as Augustine, the figural interpretation of the Bible disclosed the tension between historical events that need to be explained in rational terms and the more elusive reading of the Bible that results from eternal fulfillment. Similarly, as a poem striving to imitate life realistically, Dante's *Commedia* presents an "astounding paradox"[6] and faces an almost unsolvable artistic problem: How does one reconcile an aesthetics and poetics predicated on an eternal scheme of things—which the figural reading is meant to reveal—and the poem's characters that derive from real historical events? Dante's quandary manifests itself in the problem of imitating reality and history, which, Auerbach reminds us, implies the "imitation of the sensory experience of life on earth—among the most essential characteristics of which would seem to be its possessing a history, its changing and developing."[7] A potential problem is that Dante's characters, eternally confined to hell, lead a "changeless existence."[8] How can the unfolding of secular history and eternal, changeless existence be reconciled?

In order to show how Dante solves this problem, Auerbach gives the example of two tomb dwellers, Farinata and Cavalcante, and points out that "This Hell has been visited by Aeneas and Paul and even by Christ; now Dante and Virgil are travelling through it; it has landscapes, and its landscapes are peopled by infernal spirits; occurrences, events, and even transformations go on before our very eyes."[9] The damned souls in the sixth circle (the heretics) are said to have "phenomenal appearance, freedom to speak and gesture and even to move about within limits, and thus, within their changelessness, a limited freedom of change."[10] Such concern about the issues of change and transformation in the poem would ultimately suggest the more understated problem of the "structure of events, in other words what conception of history, is the foundation for Dante's realism, this realism projected into changeless eternity."[11]

Auerbach's reflections on the problem of integrating eternity and change in one poetically unified whole cast new light on *figura*. In the case of characters such as Virgil and Beatrice, the figural interpretation maintains that their appearance in the eternal world is the fulfillment of their appearance on earth. The advantage of adopting such a figural perspective is that it helps to show how "both its poles—the figure and the fulfillment—[. . .] retain the characteristics of concrete historical reality."[12] The goal is to preserve the historical significance and imprint of the event beyond allegorical or symbolic interpretations, which is something the figural would allow, according to Auerbach. The eternal would thus tend to make of the phenomenal an unlikely ally; the changeless nature of eternity becomes inflected in Dante's all too historically charged events and characters.

Coming to the conclusion of his analysis, Auerbach briefly touches on another significant characteristic of *figura* in Dante's work, which can be described as its "becoming-secular." In a surprising turn of events, *figura* becomes something that had not been foreshadowed in the preceding pages. Indeed, it is as though the figural became so pregnant in its belated forcefulness that it breaks free from its eternal mooring to privilege its earthly aspect to the point that "The intensity of Dante's realism, its immensely powerful representation of human passions and irreducible individuality, broke the theological scheme from which it derived."[13] Dante's realism thus evolves into a powerful entity that cannot be contained by the promise of eternal fulfillment. Reveling in its realistic depiction of human suffering and emotions, *figura* undergoes an unlikely transformation in Dante's poetry whose consequences still remain to be assessed:

> And by virtue of this immediate and admiring sympathy with man, the principle, rooted in the divine order, of the indestructibility of the whole historical and individual man turns against that order, makes it subservient to its own purposes, and obscures it. The image of man eclipses the image of God. Dante's work made man's Christian-figural being a reality, and destroyed it in the very process of realizing it. The tremendous pattern was broken by the overwhelming power of the images it had to contain . . . In this fulfillment, the figure becomes independent: even in Hell there are great souls, and certain souls in Purgatory can for a moment forget the path of purification for the sweetness of a poem, the work of human frailty.[14]

As human reality and literary realism express themselves more and more concretely, leaving *figura* in the background and becoming more secular and "independent," the problem of realism turns into something that Auerbach hinted at but neglected to further develop in his final comments on "ontogenetic history" and the "history of man's inner life and unfolding."[15]

Auerbach's concluding reflections on Dante's poetry should give us pause, for they open the door to a radically different understanding of both the *Commedia* and, eventually, the video game adaptation of Dante's *Inferno*. *Figura*'s gradual independence calls for a different approach to its function in the legacy of Dante's poem, which would become more apparent in the visual arts, and the clash between *figura* and *historia* in perspectival painting. Going from Dante's poem into the visual realm, what exactly happened to the notion of *figura*? How does *figura* migrate from the page to the canvas, and what are the artistic and theoretical issues that this transition raises in terms of *figura*'s "becoming-secular"?

Expanding on Auerbach's analysis, it is essential to examine *figura*'s journey in quattrocento painting and the great shift to perspectivism that occurred in the age of Filippo Brunelleschi, Piero della Francesca, and Leone Battista Alberti. *Figura* becoming more "independent," as Auerbach put it, meant that its eternal component had to be discarded almost completely in the more realistic experience offered by perspectival painting. In the case of the painted image, art historical accounts tell us that *historia* would come to dethrone *figura* in the rise of perspective and would further concretize its "becoming-secular."

In his wide-ranging reflections on Fra Angelico's paintings, French art historian Georges Didi-Huberman offers nothing less than a radically innovative interpretation of the Italian painter's works based on the rehabilitation of *figura*.[16] Arguing that the very expression, *figurative painting*, has misguided art historians and art lovers alike for centuries, Didi-Huberman goes on to show that *figura*, derived from the Latin verbs *figurare* and *praefigurare*, does not refer to the readily identifiable object or person one can identify in a given painting but to the more complex process of hiding and displacing in an *Aufhebung* of the visible that was eclipsed after the rise of perspective. In short, common knowledge about figurative paintings, and the various figures they show, would express our collective forgetting insofar as *figura* is the opposite of figure. An art historical notion such as "figurative painting" would thus mistakenly privilege the *figurative aspect* instead of the *figural virtuality* in paintings such as Fra Angelico's.[17] Only in the age of perspective would the word *figure* acquire the entirely different meaning it has today.

To substantiate his provocative claim, Didi-Huberman uses the example of the Incarnation in Fra Angelico's works. Interestingly, the fifteenth-century painter's artistic problem recalls that of Dante, as discussed above. Indeed, Angelico faced a crucial problem: How was he to show the mystery of the Incarnation in the context of an art practice predicated on the medieval *figura*? How was he to distinguish between the vulgar bodies in his painting and the more noble, sacred body of the Virgin Mary? How was he to resolve the tension between the human body and the spiritual body? This has led Didi-Huberman to speak of the Incarnation as "the greatest *paradox of any figuration*,"[18] given that the painting must imitate reality. However, the problem is that *figura* cannot be a simple realistic representation; it must suggest more than it can show. This recalls Auerbach's reading of Dante's *Commedia* and the similar paradox the poet faced when trying to reconcile mimesis and *figura*, which is to say a realistic representation merging both history and eternal grand design. As far as Angelico's work is concerned, he solved this artistic conundrum by integrating various spots, stains, and blotches in his paintings, which denied the readily identifiable correspondence between the visual sign and its meaning, and they acted as mysterious entities in the painting and suggested a truly figural depiction of the Incarnation.

As in the case of Dante's poetic achievement, however, realism's unstoppable force in terms of generating what Auerbach described as the "ontogenetic history" and "man's inner life and unfolding" had the upper hand in the fate of *figura* and its becoming-secular by way of an excess of realism to the point of rendering *figura*'s metaphysical design irrelevant. This nascent interest in pictorial realism would culminate in the rise of perspective and the role *historia* would come to play in such a transition. As Alberti argues in his 1435 treatise *De Pictura*, *figura*, and its emphasis on invisibility, concealment, and eternity, was to be discarded in order for a more unambiguous representation of reality to emerge. Echoing this concern, Alberti gives his famous description of the true purpose of painting: "I call a sign anything which exists on a surface so that it is visible to the eye. No one will deny that things which are not visible do not concern the painter, for he strives to represent only the things that are seen."[19] Doing away with the figural understanding of the painter's task, and the underlying artistic and religious creed of a painter such as Angelico, Alberti goes on to privilege the "*historia*" in the painting—that is, the subject to be painted—over what the work would suggest figuratively.

Described as the "most important part of the painter's work,"[20] *historia* functions as the agent that counters any ambiguity resulting from *figura*. In fact, Alberti's *historia* mobilizes a new regime of visibility that does away with the suggestive power of *figura* and any ambiguity in the painting. The predominance of *historia* to the detriment of *figura* demonstrates that there is more at stake in the rise of perspective than a new worldview predicated on the unified vanishing point. When *historia* comes to displace *figura* in perspectival painting, the metaphysical world of Angelico's paintings faces a great challenge in the name of realism and what should and should not be shown in the picture plane. As a prescriptive text, Alberti's *On Painting* thus eliminates the elusive attributes of figural painting.

The displacement of *figura* in the name of *historia* and perspective had great impact. As Didi-Huberman argues on the subject of *figura*, it is said to be more than a mere artistic device; it is a way of making connections between things, worlds, and temporalities, further demonstrating *figura's* "*operational* and *differential* character."[21] As an interstitial device that is both relational and multidirectional, *figura* creates relations between two entities and demands a "*conversion of the gaze*"[22] that negates the common understanding of figurative painting in art history and the emphasis on *historia* in Renaissance painting. This is necessary because, as Didi-Huberman points out, *figura* is not in one single place; it is what engenders the very creation of somewhat incompatible spaces and the very possibility of confronting such spaces. *Figura's* relational abilities would be lost in perspectival painting and in what Erwin Panofsky has famously called the "translation of psychophysiological space into mathematical space; in other words, an objectification of the subjective."[23]

Privileging *historia* and objectifying the subjective thus have severe consequences for the spectator. While gaining a seemingly more realistic window onto the world, the spectator misses out on the more enigmatic and mysterious elements that are equally part of reality insofar as all of the real cannot be depicted in the picture plane, and this is what Fra Angelico was hinting at in his paintings' subtle interplay between concealment and revelation. The relations between incompatible worlds, spaces, events, and temporalities that *figura* favored would be lost in the reign of *historia* and the rise of perspective.

THE VIDEO GAME BODY: A FIGURAL CONSTRUCTION IN THREE PARTS

The tensions between *figura* and *historia*, between concealing the world and making it readily available for visual consumption, do not go away as easily as Alberti would have liked. What *Dante's Inferno* reminds us is that these tensions are far from being resolved in the world of digital gaming. Indeed, the design problems that exist in the implementation of the virtual camera and the mobile perspective, the type of cutscene to transition between game-play and plot development, and the imperative to perform in QTE scenarios all point to the impossibility of completely doing away with *figura* and dismissing its intriguing survival in Visceral Games' tripartite construction of the video game body.

The first manifestation of *figura*'s survival in its postmedieval secularized form is in the use of the virtual camera in *Dante's Inferno*. Combining the architectural and the cinematic, the virtual camera attempts to bridge the gap between these two types of spaces in order to provide the player with a challenging gaming experience that builds on both the affordances of architectural spaces to be explored and the great variety of cinematic camera shots that grace the big screen. Often used to give the player some perspective on the forthcoming tasks to be accomplished by showing where to look for clues, or simply to offer a scenic view in a 'fly-through' mode, this type of virtual camera is prerendered and does not allow the player to control it. This virtual camera-type is the one that most resembles the film camera insofar as it presents a single point of view that cannot be modified by player interaction. For instance, in *Dante's Inferno*, after reaching the City of Dis, the virtual camera gives a sweeping scenic view à la a film camera's establishing shot. On other occasions, the virtual camera will indicate where to look for a specific object such as a slider, thus facilitating the player's job in figuring out what to do next.

The other type of virtual camera offers something cinema cannot. The virtual camera's role in bridging the gap between camera types creates something new in the game body, given that the collision between architecture and cinema in this virtual space demands a camera type that will be responsive to the player's actions. Having to readjust itself all the time in the course of the game, responsive virtual cameras have thus become what Michael Nitsche calls "active performers."[24] Describing four virtual camera behaviors—the following camera, the overhead view, the first-person point of view, and predefined viewing frames—Nitsche goes on to show that, in a game such as *Dante's Inferno* that adopts the "following camera" behavior, "such a freely rotating camera opens up the visual exploration of the surrounding game space."[25] The use of such a camera type thus allows for the widening of the spatial representation and a more flexible gaming experience, thereby offering a mobile perspective.

As an active performer in the game that constantly changes perspective and redefines the viewing plane on the fly, the "following camera" in *Dante's Inferno* permits certain movements, but it would be inaccurate to claim that the virtual camera and the mobile perspective can be completely controlled by the player. For instance, one cannot perform 360-degree maneuvers in the game. One of the reasons preventing full control is the pervasive use of the 'invisible barrier' device that greatly impacts on the exploration of the game's virtual spaces and, therefore, what the virtual camera is capable of registering or not in real time. Able to see but unable to go beyond certain 'barriers' in the game in order to explore the hellish zones more freely, the player is confined to specific areas that open-ended games (aka 'sandbox games') such as *Just Cause 2* (2010) and *The Elder Scrolls V: Skyrim* (2011) have eliminated. This lack of control on the part of the player would make for a less immersive virtual body and, on the whole, a less enjoyable experience.

As is made evident to the player having to control the limited virtual camera and the mobile perspective in the presence of the invisible barrier, the tension between these three can be difficult to resolve. This tension in the game actually points to the survival of the tension between *figura* and *historia,* which is displaced onto the two virtual camera types and the invisible barrier. Indeed, as the invisible barrier device prevents the player from fully operating the virtual camera, it leaves interesting areas to explore in the dark. *Figura* leaving elements unrevealed and concealed, one sign of its survival in the world of *Dante's Inferno* is in such unexplorable areas. Going beyond the obvious secret passages or unseen areas in video games, *figura* functions in *Dante's Inferno* as a device connecting mobility, concealment, and a restrained third-person point of view and engendering these impossible spaces that the player sees but cannot access. As Didi-Huberman has argued, such tensions relate to *figura*'s creation of incompatible topoi, and this further manifests itself in the game in the impossibility of maneuvering the virtual camera to fully explore all spaces. This, in turn, causes the problematic relationship between camera types, the mobile perspective, and the invisible barrier to come to the fore in the player's exploration of the game space. As such game design problems make more concrete, *figura* does not disappear in the perspectival world of three-dimensional gaming. In the context of the virtual camera and the mobile perspective, which could be described as hallmarks of contemporary gaming, a device such as the invisible barrier unwittingly reinstates *figura*'s power to conceal despite advances in game design.

The perplexing work of *figura* in Visceral Games' construction of the video game body can be further analyzed by paying closer attention to the way in which traditional cutscenes are rethought. Indeed, moving from the virtual camera and the mobile perspective to the design of cutscenes, one is in better position to appreciate how *figura* reveals itself in the virtual camera's novel role in connecting dissimilar cutscene types. The purpose of cutscenes being to transition between the allegedly more interactive portion of the game and the more cinematic one that often serves as exposition and further plot development, such transitional scenes in *Dante's Inferno* provide a refreshing perspective given their hybrid nature and innovative implementation of an alternative to conventional cutscenes.

The player is treated to two types of cutscenes in *Dante's Inferno*. On the one hand, there is the noninteractive, three-dimensional animated cutscene with which we are familiar from other games. On the other, the game proposes an alternative to traditional cutscenes in mobilizing two-dimensional cel animation in the form of a moving tapestry that has been praised for its original design. Thus rethinking cutscenes, the game raises the issue of making not only transitions between gameplay and cutscenes, but also between the two types of cutscenes themselves that could be described as incompatible. This is a design problem that deserves further attention, especially in a game that allows *figura* to survive quite unexpectedly in the twenty-first century.

The game's introductory 'story movie' references the Third Crusade, the city of Acre, and the clash between Richard Lionheart and Saladin to reclaim the holy city in 1191. Dante is no poet in the opening sequence; he is cast as a veteran of the Crusade whose actions in battle have led him to question his destiny, and his *vita nova* is not to be found in either his love for Beatrice or the Christian faith at this early stage. Symbolizing the unforgettable memories of the Crusade that will accompany him forever, Dante, in Rambo-like fashion, is shown painfully sewing a cross made out of cloth onto his chest in the introductory sequence. Being present until the concluding sequence, in which Dante removes it from his chest and gives the impression of finally being free of his traumas and sins, the cross plays a special role in the game in giving the player access to Dante's memories. In fact, the cross functions as a portal into Dante's past that challenges the use and design of flashback in contemporary games. For example, in recent games such as *L.A. Noire* (2011) or *Dead Space 2* (2011), accessing a given character's memories is done in a fairly traditional manner, using a dissolve or a cut. In *Dante's Inferno*, flashbacks tap into the embodied impression of entering a character's body to access memories, thereby providing the player with a strikingly original use of cutscenes in game scenarios that merge the virtual feeling of embodied involvement with the loss of control that the cutscene implies.

The video game body uses a specific transition to trigger its fourteen animated tapestry sequences. This transition occurs when a traditional cutscene is playing, and Dante is seen in a low-angle camera shot or medium shot. Then, the virtual camera zooms in on Dante's chest and literally penetrates it in speedy forward motion, thereby triggering the animated tapestry sequence and offering an alternative to both traditional flashbacks and the three-dimensional cutscenes.[26] In these one-of-a-kind animated tapestries, the player gains access to Dante's memories of the Third Crusade, discussions with his beloved Beatrice, and past conversations with his antagonistic father, among others. These tapestries unfold in overlapping formations moving from left to right, right to left, and top to bottom, among other directions, as the multiplanar interplay between background and foreground generates further interest in this unexpected reconsideration of the traditional cutscene. These animated tapestries portray Dante as a traumatized fighter whose memories constantly return to haunt him whenever he is in the position of confronting someone from his past or sins he committed in the Crusade.

Surprisingly, few game critics have touched on the different cutscene scenarios in the game. One rare critic has noted a potential problem with cutscene design, pointing out that "These [cutscenes] are a mixture of Bayeux tapestry-style animated tableaux and simple 2D cartoons, which are excellent, and traditional CGI scenes, which often aren't."[27] Needless to say, the complementary use of traditional cutscenes and animated tapestries cannot but make us reflect on the notions of incompatibility and impossibility that *figura* itself calls to mind in the type of spaces it creates in its video game body.

Noteworthy is that what sutures the two types of cutscenes together is the noninteractive virtual camera that zooms in on Dante's chest, virtually entering his body and accessing his memories. Such emotionally charged moments in the game result from prerendered camera movements and the way in which they allow the player to go from one cutscene type to the other without much disruption. In such sequences, *figura* tries to make connections between worlds and temporalities to which the player could not have access were the game to include only one type of cutscene. It is in this sense that Didi-Huberman describes *figura*'s character as "operational" and "differential" given its unparalleled ability to relate various worlds and events in incompatible spaces.

In the case of the animated tapestries, the survival of *figura* is not so much a question of tension, as in the combined use of the virtual camera, the mobile perspective, and the invisible barrier, as of going from the two-dimensional animated tapestry to the three-dimensional animated cutscene in a way that will not look like too artificial. In other words, the goal is to make the transition between the two types of cutscenes in a way that will accentuate *figura*'s relational and multidirectional qualities. As such, using the noninteractive virtual camera to suture the gap between the two- and three-dimensional cutscenes resolves the tension between the two types in the construction of the video game body. As discussed above in the case of the virtual camera, the mobile perspective, and the invisible barrier, *figura* expresses the impossibility of joining together these three game design elements that are incompatible at heart. In the case of cutscenes, however, *figura* demonstrates its powers as an operational device that can be quite effective as a relational entity.

The analysis of the first video game body part, made up of the virtual camera, the mobile perspective, and the invisible barrier, and of the second part, featuring the two types of cutscenes and the noninteractive virtual camera, has shown how *figura* manages to counter *historia*'s perspectival imperative and realism. In the first instance, *figura* functions as the agent that highlights the incompatibility between the three game elements. In the second case, *figura* needs the help of prerendered virtual camera frames both to assemble two- and three-dimensional cutscenes and to simulate their quasi-operational function despite their incompatible nature. What these two video game body parts suggest is that the game events ensuing from their coming together in the gaming experience deserve closer attention in terms of simulation. In order to further explore this issue and the third part of the video game body, we need to return to the poem at the heart of *Dante's Inferno*.

In the *Commedia*, the narrator's journey is predicated on a series of events in the world of Dante's poetry. The salvation of Dante's soul being the most important event in the poem, it is imperative to examine how the game *simulates* this salvation process. The notion of simulation is key to understanding the artistic, ethical, and procedural configuration of the game itself, and the way in which it requires the player to act fast in QTEs, a predetermined sequence of button pushing, that decide on the fate of Dante and that of damned souls. Such QTEs equally define the player's moral compass in the end in the type of path (holy or unholy) he or she will privilege and its related upgrade system. *Dante's Inferno* thus offers a world in which events are simulated to generate a singular form of heroism in the player's mind in which good and evil constantly compete. This constant tension is presented through a simulated form of event that only digital games can offer, the QTE.

Dante's Inferno prompts the player to think and act quickly in the context of various QTE scenarios. The game has various types of QTEs: one involves hitting a series of buttons in random order to finish off a boss at the end of a circle; another requires that the player press one button furiously (usually the red [B] button) to regain control after a demon has got the upper hand, or to absolve it by blasting the holy cross in its face in a feat of strength; and another demands that the player push the left stick in the directions indicated on screen to dismember a demon. Depending on the type of entity the player faces—that is, a demon or a historically determined damned soul such as that of Pontius Pilate—punishing or absolving the entity will trigger different QTE scenarios. Noteworthy is that should the player choose to absolve the historical damned soul, the player then faces a peculiar game that, while not being a QTE per se, borders on the QTE's surprise effect due to its fast-paced final moments. Sarcastically described as a "sin-catching button-matching minigame frighteningly similar to Dance Dance Revolution,"[28] this game-within-a-game allows the player to earn as many souls as possible in less than thirty seconds by hitting the appropriate button when a coinlike soul reaches the corresponding button on the onscreen controller replica. This makes timing an important aspect of absolving, the coin-shaped souls increasing in speed as time winds down.

One of the potential dangers of the QTE is its predictability as the player explores the game world, faces eventful situations involving demons and bosses, and comes across similar scenarios repeatedly. A characteristic trait of a particular QTE scenario in *Dante's Inferno* is that the order in which the controller buttons must be hit does not change, making the button sequence fairly easy to memorize on a second or third attempt, and thus defeating the very purpose of QTEs and their challenge 'to think and act quickly.' Another repetitive and self-defeating QTE scenario is when the player approaches a door and plans to go through it; on this occasion, the player has to press the B button several times to stab the demon embedded in the door to go into the room. This type of QTE, which is most predictable and tiresome after several hours of gameplay, cannot but lead the player to reflect on the purpose of the QTE device in video games, especially in the context of the survival of *figura* in the game world.

The various types of QTEs in *Dante's Inferno* show how the survival of *figura* leads to the creation of a very idiosyncratic notion of simulated event in the game body. On the one hand, the events in the game stem from *figura*'s ability to create relations between hitherto incompatible temporalities and objects in requesting that the player act quickly and engage Dante's fate meaningfully. On the other hand, the repetitive and predictable nature of the QTEs, along with the two orientations (holy or unholy) to choose from, makes game design and player agency somewhat incompatible insofar as the latter is mostly effaced whenever a QTE is replayed. Such game design shies away from truly asking the player to confront the challenge the QTE scenario poses in order to maximize its user-friendliness to the detriment of the actual choices players have to make and actions they have to perform. The incompatible spaces *figura* creates send an ambiguous message in allowing the player to avoid facing the consequences of failure in QTEs, given the possibility of replaying the scene and memorizing the button sequence. Reaching the final battle against Lucifer, the game heroism the QTEs promote has a bittersweet taste to it in making the ultimate confrontation relatively too straightforward for the player.

CONCLUSION: *FIGURA* AND GAME ETHICS

The ethical implications of living the 'good life,' as is the case with Dante's persona in the *Inferno* and his salvation via the eternal truth of Beatrice's love and devotion, cannot but remind one of the question Alain Badiou raises in the conclusion to *Logics of Worlds*: "What is it to live?" What is it to live for Dante at the end of his journey? Badiou argues that to live is to incorporate oneself into a new body and follow the trace of an event: "It is necessary to enter into its [the new body's] composition, to become an active element of this body. The only real relation to the present is that of incorporation: the incorporation into this immanent cohesion of the world which springs from the becoming-existent of the eventual trace, as a new birth beyond all the facts and markers of time."[29] In the context of *figura*'s survival in *Dante's Inferno*, it is not so much issues of influence and originality that surface in the end, but the ethical ramifications underlying the new bodies involved and how different media conceive of the ideal life given their affordances.

Mark J. P. Wolf has made a very suggestive remark on video games' affordances and immensely crucial contribution to contemporary visual culture, noting that "video games are the cutting edge of interactive imagery, producing visually-convincing virtual worlds that can be entered vicariously, allowing them to occupy an ontological position somewhere between incarnation and imagination."[30] Bearing in mind the key role *figura* plays in *Dante's Inferno*, it goes without saying that Badiou's subjective "incorporation" and Wolf's performative "incarnation" come together to generate more questions than answers for both Dante, who is freed from his afterlife in hell at the end of the game, and for the player, who is told this story about the "becoming-subjective"[31] of Dante's postevental body in light of *figura's* own "becoming-secular" through the ages. As the salvation of Dante's soul is displaced onto the salvation of Beatrice's soul in *Dante's Inferno*, thereby turning one of the most memorable depictions of eternal love in Western poetry into a 'princess' to be saved à la *Super Mario Bros.* (1985) or *The Legend of Zelda* (1986), the ethical implications of heroism and salvation for Dante's new body and its incorporation of the amorous event are radically transformed in *figura's* journey from poetic device to video game mechanism.

Of course, such a reconsideration of the ethical stakes in *Dante's Inferno* in the context of the perennial conflict between *figura* and *historia* would deserve a longer treatment. Suffice it to note that the present study substantiates Auerbach's key insight into *figura* in showing how "a word [*figura*] may grow into a historical situation and give rise to structures that will be effective for many centuries."[32] Not so much a case of 'structures' as of *structural tensions*, the afterlife of *figura* first displayed its becoming-secular in Dante's poetry with an excess of realism, and the rise of perspective exacerbated the conflict between *figura* and *historia* to the point of crisis. Wanting to tame *figura* and doing away with the visual ambiguities in paintings such as Fra Angelico's, Alberti and Panofsky depicted the undeniable success of *historia* and perspective in a way that led us to believe that *figura* had completely disappeared by the time perspectival painting took the world by storm.

On the contrary, *Dante's Inferno* encloses *figura's* survival and radical transformation over several centuries and manifests itself in various game design elements more than seven hundred years after Dante first made sense of the tensions between earthly and divine bodies in his realistic representation of spiritual life. So when Jonathan Knight, the executive producer and creative director of the video game, retraces the artistic lineage between Botticelli and the game adaptation and downplays Visceral Games' achievement,[33] it is not so much a question of who deserves the greatest artistic merit, or whose adaptation will pass the test of time, as it is a case of how *figura* is made to survive in a visual work based on Dante's poem and how this survival is reflected in the video game body itself. In the end, reflecting on *Dante's Inferno* and going back to the question asked in the introduction, "What can a video game body do?," we can safely say a hell of a lot.[34]

146   *Bruno Lessard*

NOTES

1. Noteworthy is that Jonathan Knight, the game's executive producer, greatly
contributed to this type of discourse. Indeed, in countless interviews and in
the introduction to the new edition of the Longfellow translation of Dante's
Inferno that accompanied the publication of the video game featuring Dante
on its cover, massive scythe in hand, Knight singles out the notions of influence and fidelity to the detriment of other issues. See Jonathan Knight,
introduction to *Dante's Inferno*, by Dante Alighieri, trans. Henry Wadsworth
Longfellow (New York: Ballantine Books, 2010), ix–xxiv.
2. For an overview of Dante in the visual arts, see David Bindman, "Artists
Rediscover Dante," in *Dante Rediscovered: From Blake to Rodin*, ed. David
Bindman, Stephen Hebron, and Michael O'Neill (Grasmere, UK: The Wordsworth Trust, 2007), 23–43. For Dante and cinema, see Gianfranco Casadio,
ed., *Dante nel cinema* (Ravenna: Longo, 1996), and Antonella Braida and
Luisa Calè, eds., *Dante on View: The Reception of Dante in the Visual and
Performing Arts* (Burlington, VT: Ashgate, 2007). Nowak-Nova's website
adaptation, *Projekt Dante* (1998–2006), can be found at http://www.nova.
priv.pl/ (accessed August 14, 2012).
3. I derive the notion of 'survival' from Georges Didi-Huberman, *L'Image survivante. Histoire de l'art et temps des fantômes chez Aby Warburg* (Paris:
Editions de Minuit, 2002). In his monumental publication, Didi-Huberman
discusses Aby Warburg's montage techniques and the notions of 'survival'
and 'anachronism' as expressed in his 1929 *Bilderatlas*. See Aby Warburg,
Der Bilderatlas MNEMOSYNE, in *Gesammelte Schriften* II.1, ed. Martin
Warnke (Berlin: Akademie Verlag, 2012).
4. Erich Auerbach, "Figura," in *Scenes from the Drama of European Literature*, trans. Ralph Manheim (Minneapolis: University of Minnesota Press,
1984), 53.
5. Erich Auerbach, *Mimesis: The Representation of Reality in Western Literature*, trans. Willard R. Trask (Princeton: Princeton University Press, 1953), 74.
6. Auerbach, *Mimesis*, 191.
7. Auerbach, *Mimesis*, 191.
8. Auerbach, *Mimesis*, 191.
9. Auerbach, *Mimesis*, 191.
10. Auerbach, *Mimesis*, 191.
11. Auerbach, *Mimesis*, 194.
12. Auerbach, *Mimesis*, 195.
13. Catherine Gallagher and Stephen Greenblatt, *Practicing New Historicism*
(Chicago: University of Chicago Press, 2000), 35.
14. Auerbach, *Mimesis*, 202.
15. Auerbach, *Mimesis*, 202. For retrospective reflections on *figura*, see the contributions in Jayme Salomão, ed., *Erich Auerbach: 5° Colóquio UERJ* (Rio
de Janeiro: Imago Editora, 1994).
16. Georges Didi-Huberman, *Fra Angelico: Dissemblance and Figuration*, trans.
Jane Marie Todd (Chicago: University of Chicago Press, 1995).
17. Georges Didi-Huberman, "Puissances de la figure. Exégèse et visualité dans
l'art chrétien," in *L'Image ouverte. Motifs de l'incarnation dans les arts
visuels* (Paris: Gallimard, 2006), 211.
18. Didi-Huberman, *Fra Angelico*, 34, emphasis in original.
19. Leon Battista Alberti, *On Painting*, ed. Martin Kemp and trans. Cecil Grayson (New York: Penguin, 1991), 37.
20. Alberti, *On Painting*, 93.

21. Didi-Huberman, *Fra Angelico*, 59, emphases in original.
22. Didi-Huberman, *Fra Angelico*, 56, emphasis in original.
23. Erwin Panofsky, *Perspective as Symbolic Form*, trans. Christopher S. Wood (New York: Zone Books, 2005), 66.
24. Michael Nitsche, *Video Game Spaces: Image, Play, and Structure in 3D Worlds* (Cambridge, MA: MIT Press, 2008), 96.
25. Nitsche, *Video Game Spaces*, 97.
26. There is one noteworthy exception: when the camera penetrates Beatrice's eyes instead of Dante's chest in the second Circle of Hell, Lust.
27. Ellie Gibson, "Dante's Inferno Review," http://www.eurogamer.net/articles/dantes-inferno-review (accessed July 20, 2012).
28. Matthew Pellett, "Dante's Inferno. God of War Tumbles from Mount Olympus into the Depths of Hell," http://www.gamesradar.com/dantes-inferno-review/ (accessed July 29, 2012).
29. Alain Badiou, *Logics of Worlds: Being and Event, II,* trans. Alberto Toscano (New York: Continuum, 2009), 508.
30. Mark J. P. Wolf, "Z-Axis Development in the Video Game," in *The Video Game Theory Reader 2*, ed. Bernard Perron and Mark J. P. Wolf (New York: Routledge, 2009), 167.
31. On the subjectivation process in Badiou's *Logics of Worlds*, see Quentin Meillassoux, "Destinations des corps subjectivés," in *Autour de* Logiques des mondes *d'Alain Badiou*, ed. David Rabouin, Oliver Feltham, and Lissa Lincoln (Paris: Editions des archives contemporaines, 2011), 7–21.
32. Auerbach, "Figura," 76.
33. "I don't think it's Botticelli, to Gustav Dore [*sic*], to Rodin, to Visceral Games, I don't think we're playing as much of a lasting and sophisticated role in the history of Dante as those guys . . . our medium is sort of brief . . . Rodin's sculpture is what it is, and it endures; in video games, five years from now people don't even have the systems to run them. We have a less easily referenced record. I think in general you've got an issue where I don't know if video games will stand up in the way books and movies do where they're easy to go back and look at 20, 30, 50 years from now." Jonathan Knight in Ben Kuchera, "Dante's Inferno Interview: Of Marketing and Gods of War," http://arstechnica.com/gaming/2010/02/dantes-inferno-interview/ (accessed August 29, 2012).
34. The author wishes to acknowledge the research assistance of David Murphy and Scott Deeming.

11 Courtly Violence, Digital Play
Adapting Medieval Courtly Masculinities in *Dante's Inferno*

Oliver Chadwick

What kind of man are you?

—Cleopatra, *Dante's Inferno*

What kind of man is Dante in EA's and Visceral Games' *Dante's Inferno*? What medieval masculinities does he embody, enact, and mediate? Cleopatra's question is not only directed at Dante, but also at players who perform through him. What kinds of men are players (male or female) pretending to be through digital play? What kinds of subjective, embodied, and performative masculinities does *Inferno* insist players experience and enact through their extension into its digital space? *Inferno* is more than a medievalist adaptation of Dante's *Commedia*. By re-imagining Dante as a crusader-knight, and framing his digital performance within the courtly love paradigm, *Inferno* also becomes an adaptation of the courtly knight-lovers of Arthurian Romance.

Such creative infidelities to medieval sources continue to cause medievalists anxiety. Medievalist infidelity is a problematic intimately entwined with the entrenched alteritism that has sought, since the late medieval period itself, to define, know, and distill the culture of the European Middle Ages, thereby distancing the medieval past from contemporary presents. Medievalist texts such as *Inferno* place the problematics of alterity and adaptive infidelity squarely in the critical gaze. Drawing upon adaptation theory, I will reconceptualize medievalisms *as* adaptations; as *creative processes* that inherently re-imagine medieval culture, enabling coalescence and interaction between medieval past and contemporary present. Moreover, I will reconceptualize medievalisms as *receptive processes* of adaptation to interrogate the relationships between Dante's digital performance of courtly masculinities and the gender-constructive potentiality upon contemporary players (male or female) through digital play. Medieval culture demonstrates its contemporary functionality as a possible paradigm through which contemporary bodies may performatively construct and define masculinities through digital play. *Dante's Inferno*'s adaptive infidelities are the very mechanisms through which *en bloc* medieval alterity is problematized and the presentness and contemporary functionality of medieval culture demonstrated.

MEDIEVALISM AND ADAPTATION THEORY:
FIDELITY AND ALTERITY

Conceptions of the alterity of the medieval period arose from its construction as the flat, intermediary middle-space of cultural "barbarism, ignorance, and . . . persistent decline between the twin peaks of classical Rome and the Italian Renaissance at the end of the fifteenth century."[1] Moreover, the Western *grand récits* of intellectual and cultural progress by which "modernity identifies itself with the Renaissance and rejects the Middle Ages as . . . premodern" ascribes to the medieval period a specifically *premodern* alterity.[2] Medievalist alteritism, in all its guises, reinforces the temporal fixity and flatness of 'the medieval,' reproducing an "exclusionary model of temporalization" that enchains it within linear, progressivist narratives of teleological periodization as a distilled middle-space of premodernity.[3] Medievalist alteritism consequently defines the medieval period as the "dense, unvarying, and eminently obvious monolith against which modernity and postmodernity groovily emerge."[4]

Intimately bound to medievalist alteritism is the discourse of fidelity criticism, which ascribes critical significance to the ways in which medievalist texts are faithful or unfaithful to the medieval sources they adapt. Fidelity criticism reproduces the assumption that medieval culture is a distilled, knowable, and definable historical originary that can and should be faithfully reproduced. Such an approach fails to acknowledge the critical significance of how medieval culture, through *creative* adaptation, is unloosed from its temporal fixity and alterity and coalesces with multiple contemporary presents. My analysis of *Dante's Inferno* aims neither to vouch for, nor to dismiss medieval alterity, slipping as that would into the problematics of essentialism. Rather, I intend to examine how the medieval past converges and interacts with ideologies, discourses, and bodies in contemporary popular culture through the creative and receptive processes of adaptation. *Inferno* can be understood as a digital space in which linear, progressivist temporality is queered by the creative and receptive processes of adaptation, enabling medieval/modern coalescence, and demonstrating the ability of medievalism to "free up" and "undetermine" the historicity of the medieval period.[5] *Inferno* unlooses medieval culture from its *en bloc* alterity through the contemporary functionality of its subjective, embodied, and performative courtly masculinities, demonstrating how the *medieval* past is implicated in the construction and definition of *contemporary* masculinities.

Adaptation theory has yet to be brought into sustained dialogue with medievalism studies, despite its value as a methodology through which to reconceptualize medievalisms as creative and receptive *processes* and, in turn, move beyond questions of fidelity to a 'real' Middle Ages. Recent adaptation scholarship demonstrates a capacity to think beyond adaptive *products* (texts) to the creative *processes* through which sources are re-imagined. Linda Hutcheon, for example, argues that adaptations should be understood as processes of "(re-)interpretation and (re-)creation," "repetition without replication."[6] For Hutcheon, the creative agency of adapters is demonstrated through *appropriation,* or the "taking possession of another's story, and filtering it . . . through one's own sensibility, interests, and talents."[7] Acknowledgment of the reinterpretive processes of adaptation draws the critical gaze away from questions of fidelity and towards interrogation of the processes through which sources are re-imagined. The creative processes of medievalisms—those infidelities that, for example, re-imagine Dante as a scythe-sporting courtly knight (see Figure 11.1)—are the very mechanisms through which queer temporal spaces are opened for medieval/modern coalescences and interactions. These coalescences and interactions are where the greatest critical traction lies, and adaptation theory provides the methodology and vocabulary for their effective analysis.

Adaptation theory positions media as a primary mechanism shaping relationships between source and adaptation, past and present, re-creation and *reception.* The medium into which source materials are *transcoded* significantly affects how those source materials are reproduced and received in specific cultural contexts. For Hutcheon, remediation "always means change" because of the need to transcode source material "into a new set of conventions as well as signs."[8] Such intersemiotic transcoding inevitably affects how source materials are experienced by audiences. Players of video games, for example, performatively engage with digital heterocosms or virtual environments. For Espen Aarseth, *ergodicity*—that is, physicality and kinesthesia—characterizes players' interactions with virtual environments,[9] while Gordon Calleja argues that digital games enable a process of *transportation* into inhabitable virtual environments through players' kinesthetic, spatial, shared, narrative, affective, and ludic involvement.[10] Adaptation

Figure 11.1   EA's Re-imagined Figure of Dante as Crusading Knight

theory considers how such medium-specific receptive processes shape how source materials are re-imagined and received.

MASCULINITY AND MEDIEVALIST ADAPTATION

Medieval courtly masculinities in *Inferno* provide a. focal point for my analysis of the contemporary functionality of the re-imagined medieval, allowing me to move beyond analyses of adaptive processes to the gender-constructive potentiality enabled by those processes. If the digital *Inferno* enables medieval/modern coalescence, courtly masculinities are one primary site on which such coalescences are centered. Masculinities represent a multiplicity of socially, culturally, and historically produced ideas of maleness that are learned, assimilated, and performed by social bodies.[11] As such, masculinities are historically, culturally, and socially contingent codes or scripts of masculine subjectivity, embodiment, and performativity through which individuals construct and define their senses of masculine selfhood or otherness. Such constructive scripts may emerge in culture as discursive practices, images, or representations circulated by popular media,[12] or as "body-reflexive practices" (e.g., sport or violence) through which specific subjective, embodied, and performative masculinities and their contexts are enacted and maintained.[13] Analysis of *Inferno*'s adaptation of courtly masculinities is therefore a means of interrogating the contemporary *functionality* of the re-imagined medieval past. By adapting the medieval courtly masculinities of the knight-lover, *Dante's Inferno* provides a medieval performative paradigm within which contemporary players may construct and define their masculinities through digital play.

Jonathan Knight, the executive producer and creative director of *Inferno*, explains that the process of adapting the *Commedia* involved merging Dante's historical and textual identities.[14] Medieval manuscript illuminations visualized Dante-as-pilgrim as a nonidiosyncratic Christian Everyman, distancing the identity of the poet from that of his intradiegetic pilgrim.[15] However, drawing upon the Renaissance tradition of portraiture of Dante Alighieri, in particular Sandro Botticelli's "Portrait of Dante" (1495), *Dante's Inferno* merges historical poet and textual pilgrim to create an idiosyncratic corporeal and subjective construction of Dante-as-avatar. Consequently, Dante-as-pilgrim is not re-imagined as an Everyman, but rather as an idiosyncratic entity in the narrative with specific subjectivities, corporeality, and performativity through which players focalize and onto which players become sutured or fixed through digital play. Merging Dante's historical and textual identities also allowed the centralization of Dante's "unrealized relationship" with Beatrice Portarini as the "connective tissue between the literature and the game's narrative."[16] In the *Commedia*, Beatrice is an abstract, enlightening symbol of the "eternal life" and the "moral and intellectual" aspects of Christianity.[17] In *Dante's Inferno*, however, Beatrice shifts from marginal abstraction to a central position within the narrative as a wholly materialized romantic object-goal of the core gameplay. Dante's "driving purpose" in the game is to rescue and reclaim "the love of his life,"[18] thereby constructing the narrative as a primarily romantic rather than spiritual quest. Moreover, by re-imagining Dante as a crusader-knight and deploying courtly masculinities to frame his narrative performance, he is constructed as a courtly knight-lover, rather than as the "sleeping prophet" and "visionary dreamer" of the source text.[19]

Dante's Inferno re-imagines Dante as a warrior antihero who leaves the Crusades to return to his beloved Beatrice. However, an early narrative cutscene reveals to players that those hopes are dashed by Beatrice's death and subsequent capture by Lucifer:

> *Opening the front door of his father's villa in Florence, Dante surveys the scene: darkness, broken furniture, his father's corpse lying amidst the carnage, an ornate crucifix protruding from his eye-socket . . . "No, no!" . . . He crosses himself, then looks to the back door, as if suddenly aware of Beatrice's absence . . . Kicking down the door, Dante freezes, and his body goes limp as his gaze rests on the distant figure of Beatrice lying in the dirt, a sword plunged deep into her abdomen . . . his scythe slips from his hand, and he slumps down beside her, weeping . . . her shade rises from her lips, surrounded by brilliant white light . . . "I told him you would come for me" . . . dark shadows creep closer and take the form of Lucifer, who grasps her possessively . . ."I have to go with him, my love. I gave my word" . . . Beatrice is swept away, leaving Dante crying her name in anguish.[20]*

Aarseth argues that video games allow players the "pleasure of influence" through ergodicity, or through their ability "to explore, get lost, and discover secret paths" in the core gameplay.[21] While many video games grant players agency in the cocreation of narrative possibilities through gameplay, narrative cutscenes serve to "explain and motivate" that performative engagement.[22] Narrative cutscenes therefore function as part of the *scripted narrative* that delimits players' involvement by preconstructing the context of their digital play.[23] The aforementioned narrative cutscene of Dante's tragic homecoming therefore preconstructs the context within which Dante and player perform in the core gameplay, thereby delimiting players' collaboration in the creation of narrative by preconstructing the context of their digital play. The context within which players must perform is enforced in *Inferno*, because cutscenes are part of a scripted narrative that cannot be skipped and, therefore, players are denied the opportunity to ignore the script or to generate their own narratives through idiosyncratic or 'emergent' gameplay. Thus, *Inferno* insists Dante/player performs within the narrative context of a romantic quest to reclaim Beatrice from Lucifer.

COURTLY VIOLENCE IN THE DIGITAL INFERNO

Re-imagining Beatrice as the cause behind, and object-goal of, Dante/
player's romantic quest through the Inferno provides the foundation for
a range of courtly conventions to be played out within the narrative. Beatrice's death and capture position her, in Lacanian terms, as the "feminine
object" of Dante's desire who is introduced into the narrative through "the
door of privation or . . . inaccessibility."[24] Beatrice's eventual betrothal to
Lucifer—the "core plot of the game"[25]—reinforces Beatrice's inaccessibility and creates a love triangle that defines Dante's desire, in conventional
courtly terms, as adulterous or extramarital.[26] Beatrice is constructed as
Dante's unattainable *objet petit a,* and his quest becomes a cyclical performance of courtly proximity and distance, of *"amor interruptus."*[27] *Inferno*
allows only fleeting moments of proximity between Dante and Beatrice in
certain narrative cutscenes, before reintroducing distance upon resumption
of the core gameplay, thereby maintaining Beatrice's unattainability, sustaining Dante/player's desire for their object-goal, and, in turn, preventing
Beatrice's courtly desublimation.[28] Dante/player also remains subservient
and subordinate within a courtly "reversed gender hierarchy," in which he
plays vassal to Beatrice's "empowered feudal lord."[29] To explain Lancelot's condescension to Guinevere's desire to "restrain himself" during his
battle with Meleagant in *Lancelot, Le Chevalier de la Charrette,* Chrétien
de Troyes states that "[o]ne who loves totally is ever obedient and willingly
and completely does whatever might please his love."[30] In *Dante's Inferno,*
this gender hierarchy is established through Beatrice's authoritative commands during Dante/player's performances within the core gameplay. While
Dante/player negotiate obstacles and violently dispatch enemies, Beatrice's
voice often drifts into the gameplay, contextualizing those actions: "Dante,
I need you!," "You've got to save me!," "You must save me!," "If you love
me, you won't give up!"[31] The simultaneity of these commands with Dante/
player's performance establishes, in courtly fashion, female dialogic authority over male subservient action. As Calleja might say, Beatrice's dialogue
represents part of a *scripted narrative* that frames players' performative
generation of their own story, or "alterbiography," within the game.[32] Let
us examine more closely Dante/player's enactment of violence within this
preconstructed context of courtly servitude.

Violence is often conceptualized as a body-reflexive practice implicated in
the articulation, proving, and reinforcement of masculine identity.[33] Video
games, then, offer a "shadow sphere free of bodily pain" within which
players may prove their masculinity through digital violence.[34] *Inferno* was
marketed as a well-hard, violent warrior fantasy in the same vein as Sony
Entertainment's *God of War* series (2005–2012). Players may therefore
expect to experience and enact similar highly violent masculinities through
Dante as the scythe-sporting crusader-knight. Paradoxically, the courtly context within which Dante's violence is enacted insists players perform violence

as courtly knight-lovers rather than as archetypal warriors. Violence is not solely a performative through which players prove their masculine power to dominate and subjugate the object world, nor is it solely a means to assuage their anxieties over penetration and, by extension, effeminacy.[35] Rather, violence is specifically a performative means through which players prove their masculine identities and worth as Beatrice's *courtly lovers*.

In paradigmatic courtly texts, violence is a means through which knight-lovers prove their devotion to their ladies.[36] Similarly, courtly knight-lovers' physical wounding—a corporeal externalization of the "inborn suffering" associated with courtly love[37]—is integral to the affirmation of their masculine identities and worth.[38] Moreover, if the wounds of medieval knights are corporeal articulations of the significance of the causes for which they fight,[39] the wounds of *courtly* knights signify the strength of their love for their ladies and, by extension, bolster their masculine identities and worth as courtly knights. For example, in Chrétien's *Lancelot,* Bademagu says unto his son, Meleagant (who has captured Guinevere), that failing to "win the Queen from you in battle" would "cast shame" upon Lancelot, who would "rather regain her through battle than generosity, for it would enhance his fame."[40] The description of Tristram's confrontation with Palamides (who has captured La Beale Isoud) in Thomas Malory's *Le Morte D'Arthur* offers a similar conception of courtly violence: "[T]here began a strong battle on both parts, for both they fought for the love of one lady, and ever she lay on the walls and beheld them how they fought out of measure, and either were wounded passing sore, but Palamides was much sorer wounded."[41] Tristram and Palamides "fought *for* the love of one lady," which is an ambiguous phrase that defines the fight as a proving of Tristram's and Palamides' love for Isoud, and/or a proving of their worth as courtly lovers. Tristram's martial violence demonstrates both the love *he has* for Isoud and his worthiness to be loved *by her*. Similarly, Guinevere's presence at, and influence upon, Lancelot's battle with Meleagant in Chrétien's *Lancelot*—upon seeing Guinevere, Lancelot's "strength and courage grew because Love aided him"[42]—defines martial violence as both a performance and a proving of the strength of Lancelot's love for Guinevere and, by extension, his worthiness to be loved by her.

Success and failure in battle have specific consequences to the lady's attainability and to her lover's status as a courtly knight. For example, because Palamides is "much sorer wounded" than Tristram, the latter not only enables the repossession of Isoud—following the battle, Tristram "took the queen"—but is also declared by her as being comparable to Lancelot as a paragon of the courtly ideal. Palamides' failure in battle, however, results in his exile at Isoud's command: "thou shalt go out of this country while I am therein."[43] Similarly, in Chrétien's *Lancelot,* because of Meleagant's martial failure, Guinevere is passed into the possession of the victorious Lancelot.[44] However, Tristram and Lancelot are not inviolate masculine bodies: Tristram is "wounded passing sore" in his battle with Palamides, and Lancelot is "stunned and wounded . . . [by] powerful and treacherous blows" in his battle with Meleagant.[45] In both texts, then, wounding does not decrease the knight-lovers' courtly worth. After all, despite their wounding, both knight-lovers still attain their ladies. Wounding is a corporeal externalization of courtly "inborn suffering,"[46] an embodiment of the knight-lover's love for, and devotion to his Lady and, by extension, a corporeal affirmation of his masculine identity and worth as a courtly knight. *Inferno* also configures Dante's enactment and experience of martial violence as performative affirmations of his masculine identity and worth as Beatrice's lover. The configuration of Beatrice as the object-goal of Dante's quest defines the geography of the digital Inferno as a performative obstacle-space in which demonic foes—Lacan's "evil powers" that disrupt the proximity of courtly lovers[47]—are substitutive for conventional obstacles in courtly narratives (e.g., rival knights such as Palamides or Meleagant) seeking to maintain the Lady's inaccessibility and, consequently, maintain the knight-lover's desire for his sublimated *objet petit a*.[48]

Like Tristram and Lancelot, Dante in the game must repeatedly and successfully demonstrate his martial prowess from a position of courtly subservience to reclaim Beatrice. Beatrice's attainability, like Isoud's or Guinevere's, is contingent upon Dante's repeated violent domination of the corporeal obstacles within the courtly space of the Inferno. The transcoding of the *Commedia* into a digital, interactive medium insists players perform violence as courtly knight lovers. Such insistence occurs, first, through the preconstructed subjectivity and corporeality of the avatar through which players perform. Different types of avatars enable varying degrees of subjective immersion for players. Third-person avatars with preconstructed identities (like Dante), for example, are digital entities that are "distinct from the player's personality."[49] Because Dante-as-avatar has a preconstructed identity in *Dante's Inferno*, his subjectivity and narrative role are introduced and fixed *a priori* to players' involvement in the core gameplay, thereby corporeally, subjectively, and performatively framing their digital play. Put simply, *Dante's Inferno* insists players perform *as* Dante and, consequently, perform the preconstructed subjective, embodied, and performative courtly masculinities he represents.

MEDIEVAL VIOLENCE AND DIGITAL PLAY

Players' subjective and performative extensions onto Dante-as-avatar are most effectively understood as processes of *play*. George Herbert Mead suggests that players take on different "roles" through play, which involves the player "building a self" and temporarily creating and experiencing the subjective, corporeal, and performative aspects connected to that imagined self.[50] Similarly, Roger Caillois defines *mimetic* play as involving the player's temporary immersion in an "imaginary universe" in which she or he pretends to be someone other than him- or herself and, by doing so, "forgets, disguises, or temporarily sheds his [or her] personality in order to feign another."[51] Play can therefore involve not only a player's experience of a temporary self, but also his or her adoption of the subjective, corporeal, and performative aspects attached to that temporary self as substitutive for his or her own. Video game avatars can be understood as players' primary sites of digital agency, a digital "prosthesis" or "assumed alias" onto which the player is subjectively, corporeally, and performatively sutured through digital play.[52] In *Inferno*, Dante is the temporary self adopted by players through digital play, a digitally materialized medieval self through which players temporarily create and experience the preconstructed subjective, embodied, and performative masculinities of the courtly knight-lover. The digital environment of *Inferno* can therefore be understood as a violent masculine proving ground and courtly obstacle-space for players as much as it is for Dante. Violence becomes the sole means through which players may prove their masculine identities and worth as Beatrice's lovers within *Inferno*'s medievalized courtly paradigm.

Some video games, while giving the illusion of freedom, actually delimit digital play through spatial and performative limitations to players' actions within the core gameplay.[53] As a spatially labyrinthine video game, *Inferno* places environmental limitations upon navigable space, denying players the freedom to explore the visible space of the Inferno beyond those boundaries and, thereby, predefining a singular path by which players must traverse the geography of the Inferno. Unlike games such as *World of Warcraft*, players are forced along singular paths towards recurring battle-arenas, thereby denying their collaboration in the construction of narrative possibilities through spatial and ludic rules that enforce violent confrontation. For example, battle-arenas in *Dante's Inferno* are bounded by environmental limitations to movement such as walls, locked doors, flaming barriers, and sheer cliffs. Such limitations enforce violent confrontation by insisting that Dante/player dispatch all demonic foes within those closed battle-arenas to progress in the narrative. Once all demons within closed battle-arenas are vanquished, doors become operable, walls burst asunder (revealing exits), or flaming barriers are extinguished, allowing Dante/player to progress in the narrative. The parameters of players' digital play are therefore predefined by the structural constraints of the Inferno, preventing the exploration of alternative modes of play, and denying players the freedom to collaborate with game designers, developers, and writers in the creation of idiosyncratic or variable narrative possibilities within the core gameplay. Dante/player may only progress towards the ultimate goal of repossessing Beatrice through repeatedly and violently conquering every demonic obstacle to her attainability. Failure to conform to this preconstructed performativity results in death, repetition or, if the player exits the game in protest or frustration, cessation of *Inferno*'s narrative, thus condemning players, like Palamides, to be exiled from the digital world Beatrice inhabits. Interestingly, unlocked closed doors are also courtly obstacles to Beatrice's attainability that may only be overcome through violence. Upon such doors are living sculptures of demons, but rather than opening them conventionally, the player must thrust Dante's scythe into them and, with frantic button-mashing, through their bodies, splitting them from navel to neck. Thus, corporeal impediments (mobile *and* static) become courtly obstacles to Beatrice's attainability that players must violently overcome.

Insistence on Dante/player's enactment of violence upon others simultaneously insists, in courtly fashion, upon their repeated experience of wounding. It is the digital corporeality of Dante that wounds and is wounded during violent confrontations. Players, however, enact and witness that courtly wounding within the "shadow sphere" of digital play through the corporeality upon which she or he is sutured.[54] Moreover, players physically experience courtly violence through *Inferno*'s hard-coded haptics. *Haptics* refers to sensorial feedback experienced by players through the vibration of the controller[55] in response to certain actions and events occurring within the core gameplay.[56] In *Dante's Inferno*, players experience haptic feedback whenever dealing or receiving blows from enemies, increasing their physical and kinesthetic immersion in the performative courtly violence of the core gameplay. Violence enacted and experienced, courtly style, is the only performative means by which Dante *and* the player, medieval ghost/prosthesis *and* contemporary subject, may progress in their movement towards their *objet petit a* and, in turn, prove their masculine identities and worth as lovers within a medieval performative paradigm.

CONCLUSION

Through digital play, *Dante's Inferno* reveals "affective connections . . . across time" between medieval masculinities and contemporary bodies.[57] Medieval/modern coalescence occurs through players' subjective extension onto Dante-as-avatar, and through digital play, which insists upon their temporary adoption of the subjective, embodied, and performative masculinities of the medieval courtly knight-lover. The digital play enabled by *Inferno* not only results in players' temporary performance of medieval courtly masculinities, but also provides a contemporary space (a virtual sphere) within which players participate in medieval masculine body-reflexive practices through which their own masculinities may be "appropriated and defined."[58] Dante/player's violence reinforces traditionally hegemonic notions of embodied and performative masculinities that speak of the "force, hardness, toughness, [and] physical competence" of the male body and the ability of the male to "transcend space, or to place his body in aggressive motion within it, in so doing posturing to self and others the assuredness of his masculinity."[59] However, the courtly context within which such embodied and performative masculinities are played out establishes a specifically *medieval* paradigm of aggressive, violent masculine spatiality and motility within which *contemporary* subjects perform. As such, digital play in *Dante's Inferno* becomes a receptive process of medievalism through which contemporary bodies construct, define, and perform masculinities through medieval courtly paradigms. Medieval past and contemporary present interact and coalesce in these processes of digital play and through the resultant constructive potentiality between medieval courtly masculinities and contemporary bodies.

Thus, the *en bloc* alterity of European medieval culture dissolves. The medieval is shown to be implicated in the construction of contemporary masculinities through digital play, thereby freeing medieval culture from its *premodern* alterity. Medieval courtly masculinities in *Dante's Inferno* become present as functional palimpsests, digital ghosts of the medieval past that haunt, as Louise Fradenburg might say, "our attempts to design ourselves and our futures" at the corporeal level.[60] Medievalist queer coalescence is opened up in the digital Inferno, allowing players to engage in medievalist subject-building and performativity through digital play. Adaptation theory allows the reconceptualization of *Inferno*'s adaptive infidelities as the primary means through which medieval/modern coalescence is enabled. The infidelities that re-imagined Dante as a scythe-sporting crusader-knight, and re-imagine the Inferno as the violent courtly obstacle-space between knight-lover and beloved lady, are the very mechanisms through which medieval culture is made functional through digital play. To play *Inferno* is to play the re-imagined medieval knight-lover, to extend oneself into its masculine courtly subjectivities, bodies, and performativity in digital space, and to be contemporaneously receptive to its constructive potentiality upon our own bodies, identities, and ideas of masculinity. In *Inferno,* the medieval is not wholly self or other, it is self *and* other. In EA's and Visceral's digital Inferno, medieval subjectivities frame modern subjects, modern players control and animate medieval prosthetic flesh, medieval performativity shapes modern performer, and modern bodies coalesce with medieval masculinities.

NOTES

1. Norman F. Cantor, *Inventing the Middle Ages: The Lives, Works, and Ideas of the Great Medievalists of the Twentieth Century* (New York: William Morrow, 1991), 28–29.
2. Lee Patterson, "On the Margin: Postmodernism, Ironic History, and Medieval Studies," *Speculum* 65 (1990): 93.
3. Jeffrey Cohen, *Medieval Identity Machines* (Minneapolis: University of Minnesota Press, 2003), 2–3.
4. Carolyn Dinshaw, *Getting Medieval: Sexualities and Communities, Pre- and Postmodern* (Durham, NC: Duke University Press, 1999), 15–16.
5. Cohen, *Medieval Identity Machines,* 8.
6. Linda Hutcheon, *A Theory of Adaptation* (New York: Routledge, 2006), 7–8. See also Robert Stam, "Introduction: The Theory and Practice of Adaptation," *Literature and Film: A Guide to the Theory and Practice of Film Adaptation,* ed. Robert Stam and Alessandra Raengo (Malden: Blackwell,

2005), 3–17; Julie Sanders, *Adaptation and Appropriation: The New Critical Idiom*, ed. John Drakakis (New York: Routledge, 2006), 2–19; Rachel Carroll, "Introduction: Textual Infidelities," *Adaptation in Contemporary Culture: Textual Infidelities*, ed. Rachel Carroll (London: Continuum, 2009), 1–7.

7. Hutcheon, *Adaptation*, 18.
8. Hutcheon, *Adaptation*, 16. See also Hutcheon, *Adaptation*, 7–8, 14–18, 34; Stam, "Introduction," 11–13, 16–17.
9. Espen Aarseth, *Cybertext: Perspectives on Ergodic Literature* (Baltimore: Johns Hopkins University Press, 1997), 1–2.
10. Gordon Calleja, *In-Game: From Immersion to Incorporation* (Cambridge, MA: MIT Press, 2011), 35–165.
11. R. W. Connell, *Masculinities*, 2nd ed. (Berkeley: University of California Press, 2005), 35; John Beynon, *Masculinities and Culture* (Philadelphia: Open University Press, 2001), 1–2; David Buchbinder, *Masculinities and Identities* (Carlton: Melbourne University Press, 1994), 2–7; Tim Edwards, *Cultures of Masculinity* (New York: Routledge, 2006), 103; Michael S. Kimmel, *The Gendered Society*, 2nd ed. (Oxford: Oxford University Press, 2004), 93–94; Michael S Kimmel and Michael A. Messner, *Men's Lives*, 6th ed. (New York: Pearson, 2004), xii–xv; Stephen M. Whitehead, *Men and Masculinities: Key Themes and New Directions* (Cambridge, UK: Polity Press, 2002), 208.
12. Beynon, *Masculinities*, 64, 149; Susan Bordo, *The Male Body: A New Look at Men in Public and Private* (New York: Farrar, Straus, and Giroux, 1999); David Buchbinder, *Performance Anxieties* (St. Leonards, UK: Allen & Unwin, 1998), 2–26; Edwards, *Masculinity*, 15, 116, 160; Rebecca Feasey, *Masculinity and Popular Television* (Edinburgh: Edinburgh University Press, 2008); Kenneth MacKinnon, *Representing Men: Maleness and Masculinity in the Media* (London: Arnold, 2003); Whitehead, *Masculinities*, 182.
13. Connell, *Masculinities*, 52–65; R. W. Connell, *The Men and the Boys* (St. Leonards, UK: Allen & Unwin, 2000), 86.
14. Jonathan Knight, "Introduction," *Dante's Inferno*, trans. Henry Wadsworth Longfellow (New York: Del Rey, 2010), xviii–xix.
15. Rachel Owen, "The Image of Dante, Poet and Pilgrim," *Dante on View: The Reception of Dante in the Visual and Performing Arts*, ed. Antonella Braida and Luisa Calé (Aldershot, UK: Ashgate, 2007), 85. See also Peter H. Brieger, Millard Meiss, and Charles S. Singleton, *Illuminated Manuscripts of the Divine Comedy*, 2 vols. (Princeton: Princeton UP, 1969), 94.
16. Knight, "Introduction," xvi.
17. Kenelm Foster, *The Two Dantes and Other Studies* (London: Darton, Longman & Todd, 1977), 11–12.
18. Knight, "Introduction," xxi.
19. Owen, *Image of Dante*, 89.
20. *Dante's Inferno*, Visceral Games (Electronic Arts, 2010).
21. Aarseth, *Cybertext*, 1–4.
22. Espen Aarseth, "Quest Games as Post-narrative Discourse," *Narrative across Media: The Languages of Storytelling*, ed. Marie-Laure Ryan (Lincoln: University of Nebraska Press, 2004), 367.
23. See Calleja, *In-Game*, 121–22; Jesper Juul, *Half-Real: Video Games Between Real Rules and Fictional Worlds* (Cambridge, MA: MIT Press, 2005), 1, 133–35; Rune Klevjer, "In Defense of Cutscenes," *Computer Game and Digital Cultures Conference Proceedings*, ed. Frans Mäyrä (Tampere, Finland: Tampere University Press, 2002), 200; Simon Egenfeldt Nielsen, Jonas Heide Smith, and Susana Pajares Tosca, *Understanding Videogames: The Essential Introduction* (New York: Routledge, 2008), 176.

24. Jacques Lacan, "Courtly Love as Anamorphosis," *The Ethics of Psychoanalysis 1959–60, The Seminars of Jacques Lacan*, vol. 7, ed. Jacques Alain Miller, trans. Dennis Porter. (New York: Norton, 1988), 149.
25. Knight, "Introduction," xxi.
26. Andreas Capellanus, *The Art of Courtly Love*, trans. John J. Parry (New York: Ungar, 1959), 100.
27. Lacan, "Courtly Love," 152.
28. See Jacques Lacan, *Feminine Sexuality: Jacques Lacan and the École Freudienne*, ed. Juliet Mitchell and Jacqueline Rose, trans. Jacqueline Rose (London: Macmillan, 1982), 6; Slavoj Žižek, "Courtly Love, or, Woman as Thing," *The Metastases of Enjoyment: Six Essays on Woman and Causality* (London: Verso, 1994), 94; Lisa Coulthard, "Desublimating Desire: Courtly Love and Catherine Breillat," *Journal for Cultural Research* 14, no. 1 (2010): 60.
29. E. Jane Burns, "Courtly Love: Who Needs It? Recent Feminist Work in the Medieval French Tradition," *Signs* 27, no. 1 (2001): 32–33. See also Žižek, "Courtly Love," 90.
30. Chretien de Troyes, "*Lancelot, or the Knight of the Cart (Le Chevalier De La Charrete)*," *The Romance of Arthur: An Anthology of Medieval Texts in Translation*, ed. James J. Wilhelm, trans. William W. Kibler (New York: Garland, 1981), 163–64.
31. *Dante's Inferno*, 2010.
32. Calleja, *In-Game*, 115–22.
33. See Pierre Bourdieu, *Masculine Domination*, trans. Richard Nice (Cambridge, UK: Polity Press, 2001), 50–51; Derek Burrill, *Die Tryin': Videogames, Masculinity, Culture* (London: Peter Lang, 2008), 46, 75; Connell, *Masculinities*, 61–65; Connell, *Men and Boys*, 86; Hent DeVries and Samuel Weber, *Violence, Identity, Self-Determination* (Stanford: Stanford University Press, 1997), 1–2.
34. Burrill, *Die Tryin'*, 2–23.
35. Burrill, *Die Tryin'*, 14, 21–22.
36. Burns, *Courtly Love*, 32–33; Sarah Kay, "Courts, Clerks, and Courtly Love," *The Cambridge Companion to Medieval Romance*, ed. Roberta L. Krueger (Cambridge, UK: Cambridge University Press, 2000), 84; Gaston Paris, "Études Sur Les Romans De La Table Ronde: Lancelot Du Lac: *Le Conte De La Charrette*," *Romania* 12 (1883): 518.
37. Capellanus, *Courtly Love*, 28.
38. Kenneth Hodges, "Wounded Masculinity: Injury and Gender in Sir Thomas Malory's *Le Morte Darthur*," *Studies in Philology* 106, no. 1 (2009): 14.
39. Elaine Scarry, *The Body in Pain: The Making and Unmaking of the World* (New York: Oxford University Press, 1985), 16.
40. Chretien, *Lancelot*, 158.
41. Thomas Malory, *Le Morte D'Arthur: Sir Thomas Malory's Book of King Arthur and of His Noble Knights of the Round Table*, vol. 1 (London: MacMillan, 1908), 330–31.
42. Chretien, *Lancelot*, 163.
43. Malory, *Morte D'Arthur*, 331.
44. Chretien, *Lancelot*, 164–65.
45. Chretien, *Lancelot*, 162.
46. Capellanus, *Courtly Love*, 28.
47. Lacan, "Courtly Love," 149–51. See also Žižek, "Courtly Love," 94.
48. Žižek, "Courtly Love," 94. See also Lacan, *Feminine Sexuality*, 6; Coulthard, "Desublimating Desire," 60.

49. Toby Gard, "Building Character," *Gamasutra*, http://www/gamasutra.com/features/20000720/gard_pvf.htm (accessed May 26, 2010). See also Calleja, *In-Game*, 60.

50. George Herbert Mead, *Mind, Self, and Society: From the Standpoint of a Social Behaviorist*, ed. Charles W. Morris (Chicago: University of Chicago Press, 1967), 150–51.

51. Roger Caillois, *Man, Play, and Games*, trans. Meyer Barash (Chicago: University of Illinois Press, 2001), 19.

52. Burrill, *Die Tryin'*, 45–46, 75–79. See also Calleja, *In-Game*, 28, 60–62; Richard Rouse, *Game Design: Theory and Practice*, 2nd ed. (Plano, TX: Wordware, 2005), 7.

53. Juul, *Half-Real*, 163. See also Burrill, *Die Tryin'*, 39–40; Calleja, *In-Game*, 76–80; Nielsen, Smith, and Tosca, *Understanding Videogames*, 97, 175; Rouse, *Game Design*, xviii.

54. Burrill, *Die Tryin'*, 6.

55. *Dante's Inferno* was only released on Playstation 3 and Xbox platforms, both of which have haptic 'rumble packs' in their controllers.

56. Juul, *Half-Real*, 135–36, 207.

57. Dinshaw, *Getting Medieval*, 11–12.

58. Connell, *Masculinities*, 61.

59. Whitehead, *Masculinities*, 189; See also Beynon, *Masculinities*, 11; Bordo, *Male Body*, 36–58; Connell, *Masculinities*, 61–65; Connell, *Men and Boys*, 86, 137; Edwards, *Masculinities*, 153–60.

60. Louise Fradenburg, "'So That We May Speak of Them': Enjoying the Middle Ages," *New Literary History* 28, no. 2 (1997): 215.

12 Shades of Dante
Virtual Bodies in *Dante's Inferno*

Timothy J. Welsh and John T. Sebastian

Academic response to the 2010 release of Visceral Games' *Dante's Inferno*, an action-packed reboot of the Trecento poem, in which a hypermasculinized crusader with anger management issues and a really big scythe plumbs the depths of Hell in pursuit of his true love, was as chilly as the frozen banks of Lake Cocytus.[1] Several critics lamented that the narrative liberties taken by the design team would inevitably disappoint first-time readers of the *poema sacro* who came to Dante by way of the game. As it happens, Visceral anticipated accusations that its adaptation would "desecrate the original poem." In a developer's diary video entitled "Heresy," gameplay engineer Tom Wilson explains that they took their source material very seriously "without being literal and bound by the exact text because, come on, that would suck as a game."[2] Visceral consequently recast the poem's timid and philosophical pilgrim-protagonist as a warrior whose moral failings while in the Holy Land have devastating ramifications upon his return to Florence. Finding Dante's beloved Beatrice slain and her soul in the clutches of Lucifer, players guide the now brutish Dante through Hell where he must face his mortal imperfections in monstrous embodied forms.

Visceral's antifeminist revision of the Dante–Beatrice plotline prompted especially bilious reactions from commentators. In the words of eminent *dantista* Teodolinda Barolini:

> Of all the things that are troubling, the sexualization and infantilization of Beatrice are the worst. Beatrice is a human girl who is dead and is now an agent of the divine. She is not to be saved by him, she is *saving* him. That's the whole point! Here, she has become the prototypical damsel in distress. She's this kind of bizarrely corrupted Barbie doll.[3]

In defense of Beatrice's metamorphosis, EA Executive Producer Jonathan Knight explained that Visceral's designers decided to give Dante a motivation more easily recognizable to players. And so one of the most famously pious relationships in literary history is recast: the barrel-chested hero rushes to the aid of his somewhat sanctimonious girlfriend, who spends most of her time naked (or else dressed in a highly revealing outfit that resembles a vagina with teeth and probably wishing she were still *just* naked). Yet although Beatrice's depiction feels gratuitous, Visceral's recasting merely reinscribes her within the conventions of mainstream adventure games as the princess who is always in another castle, conventions that derive ultimately from medieval romances. Dante himself invokes these tropes—most memorably in his depiction of the lovers Paolo and Francesca—only to reject them in his pursuit of new poetic forms and subject matter.[4] Unquestionably, video game conventions regarding female bodies are grossly problematic.[5] Still, to stop at the troubling portrayal of Beatrice is to overlook the ways in which the game's focus on the body actually does engage its medieval source material.

Consciously or not, by turning Beatrice into a sex object and Dante into an action hero, Visceral redoubles a paradox inherited from Dante's image of an embodied afterlife. The tension that arises from Dante's allegorical use of physical punishments suffered by immaterial shades is echoed in Visceral's accentuating of the body as a way to make digital virtualities more, well, visceral. Expanding the focus on the body of Beatrice to consider the game's treatment of bodies in general, we argue that the paradox of virtual embodiment that underpins the game's mechanics resonates with Dante's own experiments with the bodies he encounters in Hell. Specifically, we examine how Visceral's efforts to give weightiness to on-screen virtualities might be understood within Dante's incorporation of the impossible weight of the shades into a metaphysics of sin. We suggest that Visceral's departures from the *Commedia*—though at times awkward and cynical—offer an unexpected entry point for considering the complex materiality of virtual bodies.

THE PARADOX OF VIRTUAL EMBODIMENT

About three-quarters through the Greed level, players of *Dante's Inferno* encounter a massive statue of Plutus, God of Wealth. Once the player has dispensed with a cadre of monsters, the statue directs a bright light onto a pile of sand, causing it immediately to take the form and physical properties of a four-pillared platform. The player rotates a plate on the floor that brings into the light's beam several more pillars of sand, each producing a larger platform than the last. Once the pillar moves out of the light, it begins to disintegrate. To reach the ledge that leads on to the next room, the player must climb the smallest pillar and quickly jump to the tallest before the materializing power of the light wears off. This platforming puzzle offers a simple metaphor for the 'magic' of video games. Game designers aspire to convince players that an arrangement of flickering lights on a two-dimensional surface manipulated by complex mathematical calculations has heft and depth. If successful, the virtual worlds they conjure support our material input just long enough for a meaningful experience.

Such was the task before the team at Visceral when they set out "to visualize what [Dante] wrote" in a video game.[6] In some respects, the medium of video games is ideally suited to generating the embodied experience of Hell Dante imagined. Knight observes that the poem is full of "adventure moments" in which Dante describes "how they descended this cliff, and they crossed this river, and they encountered this monster, and they talked to the judge of the dead."[7] The game's developers reported having "really latched onto" the Inferno as a setting.[8] Focusing on these elements, *Dante's Inferno* presents Hell as an epic, navigable environment that is, all in all, fairly true to the poem in terms of structure. The game's art design, L. B. Jefferies observes, draws inspiration from illustrations by Wayne Barlow and Gustave Doré to present Hell as not only filled with but built out of the suffering bodies of the damned, writhing in the walls for all eternity.[9] Charon, for example, ferries souls across Styx on his own bony back, his body the boat itself. The game's detailed, corporeal model offers players a chance to traverse the Nine Circles and interact with their woeful inhabitants. The player's scythe-based, violent exchanges take Dante's poem in quite a different direction; however, they certainly contribute to Visceral's efforts to "systematically bring [Dante's] vision to life in the game" as an extremely physical, interactive environment.[10]

Still, as impressive as *Dante's Inferno* appears on screen—and it certainly is stunning—any attempt to give (virtual?) body to Dante's original vision inherits a prominent paradox from the original poem: immaterial shades suffer bodily punishments for their sins. Dante addresses this paradox directly in *Purgatorio* 25 when the pilgrim-narrator, preparing to leave behind the Terrace of Gluttony in the company of his poet-guides Virgil and Statius, pauses to wonder about the physical appearance of the souls residing there:

> "How can thinness occur where there is
> no need for nourishment?"

> Come si può far magro
> là dove l'uopo di nodrir non tocca? (*Purg.* 25.20–21)[11]

The pilgrim's bafflement at the emaciated appearance of spirits whose lives were marked by unlicensed consumption but who nevertheless appear before him divorced from their physical bodies as they await the Final Judgment is met with a scholastic disquisition on human embryology.[12] Statius concludes his lengthy reply with a series of illustrative analogies that finally address the pilgrim's confusion:

> "And as the air, when it is full of rain,
> is adorned with rainbow hues not of its making
> but reflecting the brightness of another,
> so here the neighboring air is shaped
> into that form the soul, which stays with it,
> imprints upon it by its powers.

And, like the flame that imitates its fire,
wherever that may shift and flicker,
its new form imitates the spirit.
A shade we call it, since the insubstantial soul
is visible this way, which from the same air forms
organs for each sense, even that of sight.
Through this we speak and through this smile.
Thus we shed tears and make the sighs
you may have heard here on the mountain.
And, as we feel affections or desires,
the shade will change its form, and this
is the cause of that at which you marvel."

E come l'aere, quand' è ben pïorno,
per l'altrui raggio che 'n sé si reflette,
di diversi color diventa addorno;
così l'aere vicin quivi si mette
e in quella forma ch'è in lui suggella
virtüalmente l'alma che ristette;
e simigliante poi a la fiammella,
che segue il foco là 'vunque si muta,
segue lo spirto sua forma novella.
Però che quindi ha poscia sua paruta,
è chiamata ombra; e quindi organa poi
ciascun sentire infino a la veduta.
Qunidi parliamo e quindi ridiam noi;
quindi facciam le lagrime e ' sospiri
che per lo monte aver sentiti puoi.
Secondo che ci affliggono i disiri
e li altri affetti, l'ombra si figura;
e quest' è la cagion di che tu miri. (*Purg.* 25.91–108)

The appearance of leanness among the gluttons is, according to Statius, the result of the impression made by their misdirected desires on the surrounding air, an act that the soul performs *virtüalmente*. Deriving ultimately from Latin *virtu* meaning "power," *virtüalmente* is translated here by Jean and Robert Hollander and by others so as to suggest that the soul operates on the air through its, the soul's, own power. But as Charles Singleton following Bruno Nardi notes, Thomas Aquinas employs the phrase *in virtute* in a technical sense to describe the status of the vegetative and sensitive faculties of the soul—those responsible for growth and sensation but not rational thought, which is the preserve of the intellective faculty—once the body has been destroyed: they remain present in the soul only virtually, as potential formative powers but with no substance upon which to act.[13] This scholastic understanding of what it means to exist *in virtute* brings us much closer to contemporary notions of virtuality.[14]

Statius's explanation of the airy bodies of the shades undergoing purgation is almost immediately verified when, in the following canto, the denizens of the terrace of the lustful begin remarking to one another in astonished tones that the pilgrim's does not appear to be a "corpo fittizio," a fictitious body, like their own (*Purg.* 26.12). The virtual bodies of the departed in Dante's vision of the afterlife serve as screens on which the meanings of the desires buried deep in the shades' souls are projected for others, including Dante the pilgrim, to see and understand. Yet, the audience of those projections would also include Dante's readers, for whom all the characters of the *Commedia*, Dante included, inhabit fictitious bodies.

Statius's explanation of the gluttons' emaciated 'virtual bodies' in *Purgatorio* represents Dante's attempt to square retroactively the paradoxical embodiment of the souls in the *Inferno*. Even though it might seem contradictory for shades to suffer physical punishments, Dante's use of material metaphors depicts the abstract, 'virtual' phenomenon of sin as urgent and palpable. But, in his attempt to materialize sin through metaphors of physical suffering, Dante must contend with not only the abstractness of the subject matter but the representational shortcomings of language itself.[15] Dante is acutely aware of the limits of representation, and, to some extent, figuring Hell as a physical place where the dead suffer corporeal punishments can be taken as an attempt to mitigate the inevitable inadequacy of expression. But, poetic language can only go so far toward embodying abstract notions like sin and spiritual anguish. Hence, the irony of the lustful commenting on Dante's fictitious body. Despite the concreteness of Dante's imagery, the vision of the afterlife presented by the *Inferno* remains a virtual reality.

Adapting the *Inferno* into a playable environment is, therefore, more complicated than deploying some high-definition graphics and perspectival shading. Dante's project involves a twofold contradiction in that it represents the status of souls as physically suffering bodies in a virtual medium. As an attempt 'to visualize what he wrote' as a three-dimensional virtual environment, the game adds another layer of mediation to Dante's paradoxically embodied Hell. Dante's corporeal allegories must become interactive objects constructed of light and math that feel to the user like they have heft and volume. No doubt, the game's fascination with naked, mutilated bodies—going well beyond Doré and Barlow's visions—suggests a degree of overcompensation for the virtual aspects of the medium. Even so, as we will discuss in the next section, Visceral's attempt to give a sense of physicality to Dante the warrior in fact participates in Dante the poet's reflections on the weight of sin.

THE WEIGHT OF HELL

Dante's Inferno, the game, struggles with the limits of representation particular to that medium in its efforts to cultivate the overwhelming corporeality of its poetic predecessor. Take, for example, Visceral's decision to run *Dante's*

Inferno at sixty frames per second, double the rate of most contemporary games. Not only does a higher frame rate produce noticeably smoother animations, it also makes for more responsive controls. Because the computer redraws the display more times per second, it processes player input more frequently as well, resulting in a game world that feels more alive and interactive. By the same token, such fluidity of motion can also belie the feeling of weight and corporeality in gameplay. A higher frame rate helps in combat primarily; however, because the frames change more than four times as fast as we can recognize, the player will often not be able see the point of impact when Dante's scythe hits an opponent. Still, these indecipherable connecting blows need to feel like they have force and impact. Dante's massive strikes thus report with gore-splattered animations and a hearty vibration that shakes both the player's controller and the screen's viewport.[16] These vibrant clashings, however, are supposedly exchanges between spirits in the afterlife. Not only does Dante encounter shades in physical form, he hits them so violently that all of Hell quakes with each blow.

The game seems at times to overcompensate for the paradoxical embodiment of its digital shades with hulkingly physical gameplay. According to a frequent critique, Dante plays "heavy, inaccurate, and graceless," "a little too slow," and even "oafish."[17] It is certainly a fair criticism; even the giant monsters Dante rides drag their feet. Considered in relation to its source material, however, the extreme weightiness of the characters, gameplay, and environment seems wholly appropriate. The game, like the poem, attempts to overcome the immateriality of virtual representations by embodying sin through graphic metaphors of physical suffering. The (over)emphasis on the physicality of bodies in *Dante's Inferno* follows, even if a bit clumsily, the aesthetic conceit of the *Commedia*. In the first of many encounters with fellow Florentines in the *Inferno*, for instance, the pilgrim is informed by the shade of Ciacco that other former citizens of that city have sunk far deeper into Hell's bowels: "They are among the blacker souls. / Different vices weigh them toward the bottom, / as you shall see if you descend that far" (Ei son tra l'anime più nere; / diverse colpe giù li grava al fondo: / se tanto scendi, là i potrai vedere; *Inf.* 6.85–87). Sin's weight is physical as well as metaphorical here and in Purgatory, where the erasure of each P (for *peccatum*, sin) from the pilgrim's forehead lightens his progress up the mountain. The weightiness of the game's brutish Dante is thus entirely consistent with the poem's own literalization of the metaphor of sin's burden.

In fact, both poem and game compensate for their immateriality by deploying complex images intended to invoke a sense of sin's weightiness while nevertheless reminding us of the absent bodies that bear the load. In the bolgia of the hypocrites, Catalano, a Guelf from Bologna who betrayed Florence in 1266 when as *podestà* he supported Pope Clement IV's efforts to curtail the power of the city's Ghibellines, explains to the pilgrim the significance of the ponderous leaden cloaks worn by the shades slowly treading their eternal path there: "Our golden cloaks / are made of lead, and they're so dense, / like scales we creak beneath their weight" (Le cappe rance / son di piombo sì grosse che li pesi / fan così cigolar le lor bilance; *Inf.* 23.100–102).[18] Catalano's simile, comparing the tortured shades to creaky balances, offers parodic reinterpretations of both the scales of justice and the Crucifixion. But he also "compar[es] the structure of the human body, with the spine crossed by the shoulders and arms, to that of a traditional balance or scale," thereby closing the metaphorical circle: the body is a scale is the body.[19] We are again reminded that gravity is in full effect in Hell, exerting its force even on the noncorporeal shades who reside there.

Catalano's image of the body as a scale bearing the weight of past sins also looks forward to one of the most striking narrative devices employed in *Dante's Inferno*. In the game's atmospheric opening cutscene, the protagonist is depicted seated before a campfire as the first words of the poem waft through the dark night air over strains of faux-medieval chant. As we zoom in, we discover the hero sewing a cross-shaped embroidery directly onto his chest. The cross depicts scenes from Dante's time in the Holy Land, documenting his history of violence, lust, and treachery. Evocative of medieval narrative embroideries such as the Bayeux Tapestry, this unusual body art also draws on the conventions of the modern comic book in its representation of scenes from the life of Dante. These scenes are animated in subsequent cinematic interludes that recount Dante's past. Over the course of the game, the player learns that Dante made two promises to Beatrice before departing for the Holy Land: to remain celibate and to protect her brother Francecso, a fellow crusader. The individual panels of the embroidery gradually disclose Dante's failure to honor these vows. In one scene we return to Acre where one of the many thousands of Muslim captives taken by King Richard's army offers herself to Dante in exchange for her freedom and that of her brother. Dante accepts, only to discover later that the brother is in reality the husband. Worse still, the woman's aggrieved husband takes revenge by stabbing Dante in the back in Acre and murdering both Dante's father and Beatrice. In another scene from the embroidery, Francesco is depicted taking the blame for the slaughter of the remaining Muslim prisoners, a massacre that Dante ordered. Francesco is summarily executed, but not before instructing Dante to look after his sister. The panels on Dante's cross-shaped embroidery progressively reveal to the player as well as to Beatrice that the protagonist is by no means innocent of the evils he encounters in Hell.

A parody of the cross traditionally worn by crusaders as an emblem of their righteous cause, Dante's embroidery invokes Catalano's description of the golden cloaks of the hypocrites. Dante bears the weight of his sins physically, the shape of the embroidery recalling that of the body-as-balance. As the game's narrative progresses, it becomes evident that Dante's descent through Hell to rescue the distressed damsel is, in the tradition of medieval quest-romance, really a journey of self-discovery, in which the hero must confront the failures of his past in order to establish his own identity. Departing from the poem, Dante comes to recognize himself as sinner, deserving of punishment, and consequently the weight that had dragged him deep into Hell is lifted. In the game's final cutscene, the hero, having defeated Lucifer, emerges from a cave into the glaring brightness of a new world naked, except for his embroidery, which has now taken on an ashen hue. As he pauses on a shore to take in the sight of the tiered mountain of Purgatory looming before him, he rips the cross from his chest and tosses it aside. Freed from the weight of sin, he can now reverse trajectory, heading upward instead of down, the gravitational pull of Hell left behind.

EMBODIED PLAY AND INCORPOREAL MECHANICS

Gameplay in *Dante's Inferno* is not always a weighty affair, however. The most definitive aspect of that gameplay—the reliance of *Dante's Inferno* on quick-time events (QTEs)—exemplifies the paradox of the game's virtual bodies in a different way. The QTE, a prominent gameplay mechanic, requires players to relinquish control of the main action to an extended animation clip. As the scene plays out, icons appearing intermittently on screen prompt players to match a short sequence of scripted button presses, with failure to follow typically resulting in some penalty. Essentially a cutscene with limited interactivity, a QTE can offer much more elaborate, sensational action scenes because the player need not perform the sequence. *Dante's Inferno* takes advantage of these scripted animations to present some of the most graphic and grotesque violence in the game. Take, for example, the gut-turning way Dante finishes King Minos on a spring-loaded wheel of spikes. In order to achieve this cinematic gore, however, the game sacrifices the feeling of weight and atmosphere it cultivates elsewhere by letting players guide Dante through space. Dante's 'oafish' movement turns swift, precise, and even nimble, as decontextualized icons flash into the field of play and the rumble pack whirs disjointedly, decoupled from the player's input.

No matter how gratuitously violent, because it replaces player interaction with set-piece animation, the QTE is by nature a detached, incorporeal mechanic. By one interpretation, sprinkling in moments of interactivity throughout these cutscenes can maintain the player's physical engagement with the playable character. But, the player of a QTE enables rather than enacts on-screen events. It is Dante who deftly dispatches King Minos; the player merely permits a few sporadic actions to take place with some well-timed key sequences. For this reason, as Miguel Sicart notes, the QTE "seems like such an odd choice for controlling the action sequences of an adventure game, which has its origin in the intention of 'embodying' to a greater degree via the use of the console controller."[20] Indeed, the game's use of QTE reveals that the materiality of the *Inferno* has as much to do with the audience's embodiment as the visualization of physical suffering.

A few of the QTEs attempt to foster physical engagement by having the player mime the on-screen brutality with corresponding input gestures. Dante thwarts Cleopatra's advances in a sexually suggestive QTE that has players rock the left-analog stick back and forth as Dante penetrates her with his scythe. On another occasion, after the last head of Cerberus swallows Dante whole, the player invokes the power of Beatrice's crucifix, his secondary weapon, by making the sign of the cross with the analog stick. Even some more frequently occurring QTEs ask for player mimicry. Should the player decide to condemn a minotaur demon, one of the QTE animations has Dante rip the beast in two after the player quickly directs the analog sticks in opposite directions. In these instances, *Dante's Inferno* gives a sense of embodiment to the on-screen virtualities by drawing on the player's own embodied engagement with the game "by means of interface design."[21] Having to repeatedly press the circle button for Dante to force open a demon door is a form of physical resistance that players have to overcome to progress. These simple miming gestures, of course, bear little resemblance to the violent motions depicted in the QTE. Jesper Juul explains that in games like *Dante's Inferno* that "emphasize a fictional world, there has to be a metaphorical substitution between the player's real-world activity and the in-game activity performed."[22] Even so, these gamic metaphors externalize actions in the game world by translating them into corollary interactive experiences.

Some of the more interesting moments in *Dante's Inferno* occur when Dante's onscreen events resonate meaningfully with the player's offscreen actions. For example, in the wood of the suicides, Dante comes to a clearing where he must push a stone step to the edge of a slope, kick it up the hill with all his might, and then—before the step slides back down—jump onto the step and then on to the top of the hill. It is an infuriating passage that players likely will attempt more than once. Should the player fail a few times, the voice of Lucifer asks Dante if he's ever felt like he "just can't go on." In another example during the Greed level, a chest containing a collectible relic sits in clear view atop a central pillar in a circular room. To claim the relic, the player must make his or her way across a series of elevated platforms while avoiding three spiked spokes that rotate around the central column like an axis. Should the player fail a jump, Dante is knocked down to the bottom of the room, which features a full-wall mural of Sisyphus beginning his ascent. Dante must then battle a horde of challenging monsters before he can climb up and try again. Accessing the chest requires the player to get to the platform from which he or she can exit the room and then make a particularly difficult jump from the back wall toward the screen on to the axis, and then make the jump again to leave. The item in the chest, the Wasted Gold relic, gives Dante a small but ultimately unnecessary upgrade. Even so, its placement in this Sisyphean room will likely tempt the player's greedy impulses. Moments like these in *Dante's Inferno* invoke the player's investments as a gamer in their gamic metaphor. The embodied allegory for sin is thereby externalized, incorporated in the player's own material engagement with the media.

CONCLUSION

EA takes the logic of externalization to its furthest extreme through its inconsistent promotions for the game. Its onslaught of marketing stunts included clever press packets that posed a moral quandary to recipients in the form of a $200 check, a humorous trailer for a motion-controlled sacrament simulator, a mischievous Facebook application that let users place their friends in the Nine Circles, and a controversial staged religious protest conducted by paid actors. Perhaps the most prominent was the "Sin to Win" contest, which offered prizes to ComiCon conventioneers who "commit[ed] acts of lust" with models working at the exhibition booths and submitted photographic evidence.[23] Though intriguing for the ways they map virtual ethical acts onto actual physical bodies, thereby adding a final layer of material corporeality to the many virtual realities evoked by the game and through it the poem, the game's promotions emerge from the same deeply cynical impulses that lead to the tartification of Beatrice.

Ultimately, Visceral's appropriation of the *Inferno* is driven by the material realities of modern game publishing beyond any aspiration to truly adapt a classic work of literature, leaving *Dante's Inferno* in an awkward position relative to Dante's *Inferno*. From the beginning, the developers' interest in the poem was always as source material that they could mold into a defined, saleable formula. Even as EA and Visceral zeroed in on a demographic of gamers firmly established by the genre-defining *God of War* series—itself an adaptation of Greek mythology—they clearly labored under the cultural weight of Dante's literary masterpiece. Thus, Knight acknowledges that the game was "not meant to replace a reading of the poem" but then includes Longfellow's public-domain translation on the game disk, just in case hack-and-slash action inspires players to read the "much more sophisticated" version off their televisions.[24] The implication that the game might draw people to the poem, or that it has some kind of scholarly angle, seems disingenuous at best. More likely the elaborate website with historical information and brief literary analyses belongs to a misguided effort to borrow on the poem's cultural cachet to cross-promote it as educational. Random House in fact published a new edition of the Longfellow version of *Inferno* to coincide with the game's release; it features the same cover art as the game jacket and an introductory essay by Knight himself.

Yet to focus on the game's fidelity, or lack thereof, to the original poem is predicated on an undertheorized notion of authenticity as the sole—or at least the most significant—measure by which to judge the success of an adaptation like *Dante's Inferno*. Under greater scrutiny, such judgments reveal their indebtedness to medieval and especially Dantean understandings of *auctoritas*. Yet as Albert R. Ascoli has recently suggested in his masterful study of Dante's self-construction as an author/*auctor*, authority itself is not an ethically neutral category. In particular Ascoli wonders: "is the quest for authority, Dante's quest for authority, a righteous one? Does his achievement herald something new and valuable? Or the dawn of new regimes of social control? To begin an answer," he continues,

> one may consider precisely the extent to which the discourse of authority, in Dante and more generally, does depend upon positioning oneself in a relation of appropriation and/or domination with an *other*. In the first instance Dante, at some never entirely accessible discursive outset, posits the *auctor* as the absent and/or transcendent Other whose powers he both honors and seeks to expropriate.[25]

Having successfully achieved such authority for himself, Dante becomes the absent and transcendent Other for generations of future readers—and game designers. Of the many disembodied presences haunting *Dante's Inferno*, that of Dante himself presents the greatest obstacle to performing a sophisticated analysis of the relationship between game and poem. Visceral's imperative to make a game that does not 'suck' ultimately subverts any aspiration to the aesthetic innovation of the original. Still, in spite of itself, the game's distorted adaptation offers a new, digital entry point for reassessing traditional literary questions of textuality, virtuality, embodiment, and the claims of authority.

NOTES

1. *Dante's Inferno*, Visceral Games (Electronic Arts, 2010). See comments by academics reported in Dave Itzkoff, "Abandon All Poetry, but Enter Hell With an Attitude," *New York Times*, January 29, 2010, http://www.nytimes. com/2010/01/30/arts/television/30inferno.html (accessed June 18, 2012), and Benjamin Popper, "Dante Alighieri: Epic Poet, Ass Kicker," *The Atlantic* (February 2010), http://www.theatlantic.com/magazine/archive/2010/02/ dante-alighieri-epic-poet-ass-kicker/7936/ (accessed June 21, 2012).
2. Electronic Arts, "Developer Diary: Heresy," http://www.ea.com/dantes-inferno/ videos/63d8c7543c4e4210VgnVCM100000ab65140aRCRD (accessed July 26, 2012).
3. "An Ivy League Professor Weighs In," *Entertainment Weekly*, February 26, 2010, 79. By contrast, in an interview with *New York Times* culture reporter Dave Itzkoff in the weeks before the game's release, Barolini stated that she was "not in the least bit turned off" by alterations to the main storyline and looked forward to seeing the game. See Itzkoff, "Abandon All Poetry."

4. For a discussion of this trope as it applies to *Dante's Inferno*, see G. Christopher Williams, "Sorry Dante but Your Princess is in Another Castle," *PopMatters*, http://www.popmatters.com/pm/post/121718-sorry-dante-but-your-princess-is-in-another-castle (accessed May 26 2012).

5. For a recent example, see Erin Gloria Ryan, "The Rapey Lara Croft Reboot is a Fucked-Up Freudian Field Day," *Jezebel*, http://jezebel.com/5918222/the-rapey-lara-croft-reboot-is-a-fucked+up-freudian-field-day (accessed July 31, 2012).

6. Brian Crecente, "Should We Expect More from Electronic Art's Inferno," *Kotaku*, http://kotaku.com/5278242/should-we-expect-more-from-electronic-arts-inferno (accessed July 30, 2012).

7. Christian Nutt, "The Road To Hell: The Creative Direction of Dante's Inferno," *Gamasutra*, http://www.gamasutra.com/view/feature/4266/the_road_to_hell_the_creative_.php (accessed May 26, 2012).

8. Crecente, "Should We Expect More."

9. J. B. Jefferies, "The Literary Merits of Dante's Inferno," *PopMatters*, http://www.popmatters.com/pm/post/122719-the-literary-merits-of-dantes-inferno (accessed May 26, 2012).

10. Nutt, "The Road To Hell."

11. *The Divine Comedy of Dante Alighieri*, 3 vols., trans. Jean and Robert Hollander (New York: Anchor Books, 2002–2008). Subsequent references are to this edition and translation and appear parenthetically.

12. For Dante's embryology, see Bruno Nardi, "L'origine dell'anima umana secondo Dante," *Studi di filosofia medievale* (Rome: Edizione di storia e letteratura, 1960), 9–68, and Jennifer Fraser, "Dante/Fante: Embryology in Purgatory and Paradise," in *Dante and the Unorthodox: The Aesthetics of Transgression*, ed. James Miller (Waterloo, Ontario: Wilfrid Laurier University Press, 2005), 290–309.

13. Dante Alighieri, *The Divine Comedy: Purgatorio*, vol. 2: Commentary, ed. Charles Singleton (Princeton: Princeton University Press, 1973), 615–16.

14. Katherine Hayles, for instance, argues that the contemporary condition of virtuality, which presumes the primacy of information over materiality, "maps onto the older more traditional dichotomy of spirit/matter." See Hayles, "The Condition of Virtuality," *The Digital Dialectic: New Essays on New Media* (Cambridge, MA: MIT Press, 2000), 73.

15. For Dante's understanding of postlapsarian human speech as a debased and limited form language, see John M. Fyler, *Language and the Declining World in Chaucer, Dante, and Jean de Meun* (Cambridge, UK: Cambridge University Press, 2007), esp. chapter 1, "The Biblical History of Language."

16. Contemporary controllers have a 'rumble pack,' or small counterbalance weight, installed in the handle. When activated, the weight rotates on its axis causing the controller to 'rumble.' *Dante's Inferno* uses this haptic feedback incessantly, rattling the controller with each weapon swing, landed jump, and crumbling wall.

17. Daniel Bullard-Bates, "Dante's Inferno: A Failure on Two Fronts," *Press Pause to Reflect*, http://presspausetoreflect.blogspot.com/2010/01/dantes-inferno-failure-on-two-fronts.html (accessed May 26, 2012).

18. Michael Papio, "Catalano," in *The Dante Encyclopedia*, ed. Richard Lansing (New York: Routledge, 2010), 144.

19. *The Divine Comedy of Dante Alighieri*, vol. 1: *Inferno*, ed. and trans. Robert M. Durling (New York: Oxford University Press, 1996), 58.

20. Miguel Sicart, *The Ethics of Computer Games* (Cambridge, MA: MIT Press, 2009), 80.

21. Sicart, *The Ethics of Computer Games*, 80.
22. Jesper Juul, *Half-Real: Video Games between Real Rules and Fictional Worlds* (Cambridge, MA: MIT Press, 2005), 173.
23. See Brian Crecente, "EA Provides the Girls, Asks Gamers to Sin to Win," http://kotaku.com/5322216/ea-provides-girls-asks-gamers-to-sin-to-win (accessed July 31, 2012).
24. Nutt, "The Road to Hell."
25. Albert Russell Ascoli, *Dante and the Making of a Modern Author* (Cambridge, UK: Cambridge University Press, 2008), 61.

13 The Middle Ages in the Depths of Hell

Pedagogical Possibility and the Past in *Dante's Inferno*

Angela Jane Weisl and Kevin J. Stevens

> *You are Dante, in Cocytus, encountering Lucifer . . . and saving Beatrice from him. You are also a crusader and have carved a crusader cross into your exposed chest. . . .*

Even this brief reference to Visceral Games' *Dante's Inferno* video game places the player in a state of anachronism, engaging simultaneously with the game's literary inspiration and own fiction.[1] In a recent lecture at Seton Hall University, Marcello Simonetta, author of *The Montefeltro Conspiracy* and historical consultant to the video game *Assassin's Creed: Brotherhood* (2010), discussed how historically-based video games can educate gamers about a particular period. His example, *Assassin's Creed: Brotherhood*, accurately depicts the architecture in Italy circa 1500 and includes Pope Alexander VI, Niccolò Machiavelli, and Leonardo da Vinci in its integral characters. Games like *Dante's Inferno* and *Assassin's Creed* prove that history makes for compelling game plots, and Simonetta anticipates that drawing from reality may move a gamer to explore a historical subject further (and thus galvanize the educational process).[2]

One might question this impulse to educate when looking at the video game rendition of Dante's *Inferno*. Video games are not textbooks, so one might ask why interrogating their pedagogical potential is necessary. However, by claiming a connection to a famous historical work, this game (and others like it, which announce their ties to the past thus overtly) set up certain expectations of authenticity and responsibility to the past moments they claim as their origin. Dante's poem is not Italy in the 1500s, but it is tied to a particular time, history, and set of attitudes that locate it in the medieval past. *Dante's Inferno* is a game with a huge story that has nearly nothing in common with the plot of the original. So why bother? Are the creators simply trading on a famous name? After all, people have heard of Dante's *Inferno*. Before the game's release, its website offered an extended look at "The Poem," providing an overview of Dante's life and works; however, the current site has dropped these attempts to connect the video game with the *Divine Comedy* from which it ostensibly comes. As an introduction to one's Dante studies, the game leads the player down a path to perdition, rather than to the "l'amor che move il sole e l'altre stelle" ("the love that moves the sun and other stars" (*Paradiso* 33.145),[3] and in place of Dante the Poet and Dante the Pilgrim, we are offered Dante the Action Hero, a crusader condemned to Hell for his own sins and the sins of his family, such as his father's avarice and merciless theft. Those sins separate him from Beatrice, whom he must rescue to win the game. Hell may look familiar, but what happens in it is not.

As an alternative to the 'real' *Divine Comedy,* the game essentially produces what might best be called 'counterfactual thinking,' providing a simulated past, a past perhaps more exciting for a gamer than Dante's thirteenth-century Florence, but one whose intentions and meanings deviate sharply from the *Divine Comedy*'s. The consequences of this approach to Dante may be beneficial in sustaining an interest in the poem and its history, but they are also dangerous. In a sense the creators at Visceral have taken an essential medieval figure (Dante) and the essential medieval narrative of the love quest, and a little bit of the Orpheus legend, and put them together with some science-fiction trappings, collapsing the Middle Ages into a unitary project in which any one element can be imposed on any other element.[4] Under these circumstances, then, is Simonetta's suggestion about historical/literary games' educational purposes possible, or is the most we can find in these games a modern Middle Ages, a bricolage of fact and fiction that may resemble medieval fictions in its nexus of archaic locations and contemporary fascinations, but which finally offers the past only as a mirror of the present?

VIDEO GAMES AND EDUCATION

Many scholars insist that video games can be used as valuable pedagogical tools; James Paul Gee, for instance, suggests that "a new research field is emerging around the hypothesis that video games are good for learning."[5] However, it becomes fairly clear from an investigation of this field that the educative possibilities for video games do not lie in teaching history or engaging players/students with the past in any particular way. Although few games descend gamers into Hell to battle Lucifer, the setting of *Dante's Inferno* in medieval times is not a novel concept; popular games such as *The Sims Medieval* and the *Assassin's Creed, Stronghold,* and *Age of Empires* series have all, among many others, broached the Middle Ages on personal computers and gaming systems. But while video games persistently return to the Middle Ages as the locus for epic battles and tests of chivalry and honor, scholars repeatedly ignore the pedagogical possibilities (and pitfalls) of historical representation in these games. In discussing the educational benefits of games, Gee offers a list of potential loci for education in video games; "video game technologies hold out great promise, beyond entertainment, for building new learning systems for serious purposes in and out of school,"[6] and he lists these principles as "empathy for a complex system, simulation of experience and preparations for action, distributed intelligence via the creation of smart tools, cross-functional teams, situational meaning, and open-endedness," which he defines as "melding the personal and the social."[7] None of these suggest that games can provide knowledge about or insight into the pasts they claim to represent. Although he does see "situational meaning" as specifically focusing on language use in context and the situational meanings of words,[8] historical video games cannot even participate in this process, because they are removed linguistically from their sources. *Dante's Inferno* may quote translations of the original, as is demonstrated below, but it is not played in medieval Italian, nor are other medieval examples—*Assassin's Creed, Sims Medieval*—engaging in any use of original languages either. Although certain kinds of authentic language may permeate these games, that "situational meaning" seems unlikely to develop the significant appreciation for the historical past that Simonetta suggests. Additionally, in *Teaching Videogames,* James Newman and Barney Oram never consider history or historical material at all in their detailed analysis of video games and their pedagogical potential. Although they offer materials, guidelines, and rubrics for an entire course on video games, engaging ideas such as gender, violence, interactivity, design, and the representation of conflict, none of this occupies a historical mode, even those areas that are specifically played out in historical games, such as conflict, gender, and violence.[9]

Attempting to define what games are, Katie Salen and Eric Zimmerman suggest that "a game is a system in which players engage in an artificial conflict, defined by rules, that results in a quantifiable outcome."[10] This definition would certainly suggest a connection to historical understanding, because any study of past conflicts inevitably treats them as rule defined and quantified, making them somewhat artificial, or perhaps attaching to them arbitrary beginnings and endings, much as games do. Yet Gordon Calleja and Ivan Collins quantify this by adding that "the artificial aspect of games envisages a mode of experience different from everyday life."[11] However, in relating that difference to Johan Huizinga's "Magic Circle,"[12] which both sets of authors do, they connect it to a historical mode of play, tied, as Huizinga notes, to both transmission and tradition, elements certainly present in the historical antecedents from which these games are drawn. Indeed, Dante's poetry is built almost entirely on these same principles of transmission and tradition; when Huizinga calls a game "a new-found creation of the mind, a treasure to be retained by the memory," he might be comfortably speaking of the *Divine Comedy* itself.[13]

In additionally noting that "all games embody a contest of powers,"[14] observing that by their nature they "create the possibility of a *verifiable and quantifiable* outcome—a state of affairs that is objectively final at the end of the game and *valorized* by the players involved," and adding that "some of the possible outcomes are objectively better than others and harder to obtain, and are valued for their emergence from *player effort*,"[15] Calleja and Collins also suggest historical potential. These notions of conflict and contest, after all, apply very well to history, particularly the historical representations found in video games, which tend to focus on conflicts, wars, and battles, and operate by various kinds of contests that are won by the efforts of the players themselves. To look specifically at Dante for a moment, the *Comedy* itself can be said to create the possibility of a "verifiable and quantifiable" outcome (the location of the various souls in the afterlife and the reader's consciousness of this process and how it affects him or her), and certainly some of the possible outcomes are better than others (Purgatory is better than Hell; Paradise better than Purgatory), and achieving these can certainly be seen as emerging from someone's effort on earth to achieve a more transcendent future. Yet this observation is essentially an exercise in pointlessness, because although these definitions of 'game' can be allied with the historical material the game purports to present, the game itself does not take advantage of allowing these definitions to align with each other; the game may observe the 'rules of play,' but it does not observe the rules or goals of the material from which it claims its inspiration. That is not to say that one cannot learn anything from the *Dante's Inferno* video game, or from any other medieval or historical games, but what one is likely to learn is not precisely about Dante, history, or the Middle Ages as a specific period of the past. Rather, the game exhibits the modern idealization of the Middle Ages (a counterfactual fantasy), revealing more about the present perception of the Middle Ages than the period itself.

DANTE'S INFERNO

The game's deviation from the 'real' text becomes apparent in its opening scene. Taking place in 1191, following the Third Crusade when European knights capture Acre, the game begins with a loose translation of the opening lines of *Inferno*—"At the midpoint on the journey of life I found myself in a dark forest with a clear path that was lost"—as Dante, a crusader garbed in knightly armor, stitches a cross-shaped tapestry onto his torso in the dimly lit forest. Unlike Dante the Pilgrim, who must enter Hell after three beasts infamously block his path uphill, Dante the Crusader finds his way out of the forest to fight heretics in the Citadel of Acre, where he is killed in battle by a prisoner. To return to the point Salen and Zimmerman make about conflicts, we see a real conflict being exchanged for an artificial one; there was certainly a battle in Acre in 1191, but Dante didn't fight in it; the Crusades are exchanged for the Guelph/Ghibelline conflict which so engages Dante the author in the *Divine Comedy*. Rather than taking advantage of a real past, the game's creators chose a symbolic one; the Crusades do multiple duties as representative of the Middle Ages as the 'Age of Faith,' setting up a context for Dante the game character's semireligious engagement with Hell and sin, although those ideas are also detached from any medieval theological understanding of those terms and their meaning. The game, for instance, does not employ the perfect nature of Hell's punishments as a part of the larger divine plan, a lesson that Dante learns as he increasingly gives up feeling pity for the shades, nor does it understand the dichotomy of reason and grace which Dante grows to comprehend by his progress through the three realms of the afterlife.

In the video game, much to our action hero's dismay, the dark apparition of death appears and grants Dante "everlasting damnation for [his] sins," despite promises of absolution from Christian priests, but this Dante refuses to die; instead of transcending death through knowledge of the penitential process, Dante must 'beat death' by killing him. Once successful, Dante returns to Italy where he denounces the Crusades—"The bishop said our cause was holy. Holy had nothing to do with it"—and pines for "the warmth of my devoted Beatrice and for the chance to redeem the past—to start again." However, when he returns home, he finds the deceased bodies of his father and Beatrice. Beatrice's soul appears, but the shadowy spirit of Lucifer pulls her away, and Dante follows her to the gates of Hell, where he willingly, rather than apprehensively, descends to save his beloved, propelling the gamer into the depths of the Inferno.

After the game's reinvented plot propels Dante into Hell, the gaming experience begins to resemble Dante's text experientially. Once gamers enter and progress through the Inferno, they experience the levels of Hell both with and as Dante; controlling Dante's every action through a third-person vantage, the gamers views themselves as Dante, paralleling the readers-as-Dante identification in the *Inferno*: the readers are "nel mezzo del cammin di nostra vita" ("In the middle of the road of our life") (*Inferno* 1.1). In his distinguishing of first-person shooters from roleplaying games, David Golumbia notes that "in FPS [first-person shooter] games, even more than RPGs [role-playing games], a great deal of emphasis is placed on the suturing of the player's identity and activity with the apparent 'main character' in the game."[16] Although the camera angle differs between first- and third-person shooters, *Dante's Inferno* stresses a similar connection between gamers and Dante; Dante's moral and theological experience is as much the reader's/gamer's as it is his own. As the game's original website explained, "In the upcoming EA third person adventure, *Dante's Inferno, you are Dante*. Death has come to steal *your* love Beatrice's soul and take her to Hell—but on his way out, *you* grab his scythe and follow behind."[17] Such identification enables the game to reenact the experience of reading Dante's *Inferno* during the Middle Ages (and, indeed, now); gamers descend with/as Dante through Hell one level at a time, only here they visually, rather than imaginatively, experience the author's harrowing vision of the underworld.

Jeff Howard asserts that Dante's quest exemplifies the pedagogically useful elements of video games, demonstrating the components of quest narratives that can be traced from the *Odyssey* through postmodernism: "Stronger connections between the literary history of quest narratives and quest games can also offer strategies for how to teach a rich tradition of literature through technologies associated with a more recent but equally valuable selection of games, from early adventure games of the 1980's to next-generation RPG's."[18] Although Howard writes before the release of *Dante's Inferno,* his definition of the quest and its hero, influenced by Northrop Frye and Joseph Campbell, accurately describes both the game and its originary text: "Quests in games and literature often take place in mazes, which proliferate in the 'descents into the underworld' of myth and the 'dungeon crawls' of role-playing games."[19] However, although fruitful in new media approaches to canonical literature, Howard's structuralist approach to the study of quests in video games equates Greek, medieval, Victorian, and postmodern quests, compressing all pasts under one umbrella and, again, overlooking historical potential. Golumbia also argues that the quest, and the experience one's avatar or character gains during it, is particularly what makes video games fun, as he details gamers' satisfaction after enhancing their avatars or characters in role-playing games: "Even advocates for social transformation and 'games as teaching tools' would acknowledge that leveling up is one of the main pleasurable parts of gameplay and that the pursuit of higher levels is a main 'addictive' quality of all RPGs."[20] The same concept applies in *Dante's Inferno,* only in an ironic twist the gamer receives satisfaction from leveling *down* further into Hell. Thus, although the 'addictive' elements of video games are intrinsically built into the *Inferno* text, the game nevertheless trades the 'authentic' past for a counterfactual fantasy, suggesting that the shift from Dante's public to private journey represents more than a necessary alteration to create the most exciting (and most lucrative) action game possible.

In addition to the experientially similar qualities the video game shares with Dante's text, the Hell in *Dante's Inferno*—although primarily a reproduction of upper Hell, the circles of the seven deadly sins, and Cocytus—clearly draws its matter from the poem itself. From the precise framework of Hell to the deformed souls and frightening monsters that inhabit it, the game visualizes the Inferno with commendable accuracy and in stunning detail; for instance, after Dante fights the three-headed beast, Cerberus, "grandine grossa, acqua tinta e nove" ("enormous hailstones, water colored by filth") (6.10) pour on him as he runs through Gluttony, or as Dante reaches the seventh circle (Violence), he views the Phlegethon River: a river of boiling blood that scorches the tormented souls floating in it: "La riviera del sangre in la qual bolle / qual che per violenza in altrui noccia" ("the river of blood in which boil / those who by violence injured others") (12.47–48). In this light, the video game has comparable benefits to an exceptionally designed movie: it brings a text to life, although often at the expense of readers' imaginations, and, as Simonetta suggests, can arouse and help to sustain newfound interest in Dante's text from players who may have otherwise never considered reading the *Inferno*.

Nevertheless, stimulating educational interest cannot be conflated with the actual educational process: although the game simulates the Dantean gamer-as-pilgrim identification, captures a vision of the Inferno adherent to the text, and will perhaps assist undergraduates in memorizing the circles of Hell before their Western literature finals, the fabricated plot of *Dante's Inferno* remains the centerpiece of the game. Not unlike *Assassin's Creed: Brotherhood,* which balances highly accurate detail and flights of narrative fancy in its depiction of its 'historical' characters, *Dante's Inferno* is selectively meticulous in its accurate portrayal of Dante's *Inferno;* both games emphasize the importance of their architecture—that is, the circles, ditches, flames, ice, rivers, immobile characters, etc. in the *Inferno*—yet reinvent the circumstances that lead the games' figures to these settings. *Dante's Inferno,* in particular, takes great liberties in constructing Dante the Crusader/Action Hero's alternative existence once the gamer enters Dante's Hell. As Dante navigates through the circles of Hell, flashbacks of his fictionalized past intermittently appear, gradually informing the player of the events that have led to the game's beginning: the gamer learns that Dante is asked to 'babysit' 3,000 prisoners while Richard negotiates an exchange with Saladin for the 'true cross'; that Dante and Beatrice are lovers, and that Beatrice implores Dante to protect her crusading brother, Francesco; that bishops, subhumanly depicted with beaming white eyes and black mouths, promise to absolve all the crusaders' sins; and that an imprisoned woman offers to 'comfort' Dante in exchange for the protection of her brother, which Dante ultimately accepts. The game distinguishes the past from the present moments in the game by depicting the flashbacks in animated cartoons, creating a break from the gameplay as well as a distinct departure from Dante's text. As Dante progresses further into Hell, his sins and their ramifications are further exposed through these flashbacks: the brother that the imprisoned woman had protected kills Dante's father and Beatrice and reveals himself as the woman's husband; Dante mercilessly has the prisoners of the Crusades killed, shouting "spill the blood of heathens!" (a line that seems to come from the *Song of Roland* rather than from Dante's original text); and, when in danger of being punished for the bloodshed he had caused, Dante blames his actions on Beatrice's brother, consequently condemning the innocent man to death.

Dante's Inferno reinvents (and, to a gamer unfamiliar with Dante, potentially tarnishes) not only the reputation of Dante, but also that of his parents, who appear in the game in similarly peculiar roles, considering their complete absence from Dante's *Inferno*. Indeed, little is known about Dante's family, other than that they were noble, but likely quite poor, yet the game presents Dante's father as a wealthy, hedonistic, gluttonous tyrant, whom Dante must fight to prove to himself that, as he says, "I will not be damned like you." After defeating his father, Dante descends to The Wood of the Suicides where he finds his mother hanging from a tree. As Virgil explains, "When a soul quits a body from which it has uprooted itself, Minos judges it to the seventh circle. There it sprouts, shoots up like a sapling, no body, only the pain," which echoes the speech to Dante from the anonymous man who committed suicide in the *Inferno*: "Quando si parte l'anima feroce / dal corpo ond'ella stessa s'è disvelta, /Minòs la manda a la settima foce / Cade in la selva, e non l'è parte scelta; / ma là dove fortuna la balestra, /quivi germoglia come gran di spelta" ("When the savage spirit / leaves the body from which it has torn itself / Minos then sends it to the seventh mouth / It falls into the wood, and there's no place / but wherever fortune has placed it / there it germinates like a grain of spelt") (13.94–99). Here the game reveals surprising conformity to a text that it so glaringly ignores in its essential plot; in fact, directly preceding Virgil's speech, the game most patently demonstrates its juggling of accuracy and anachronism, as Dante's mother confesses, "I despised your father's cruelty, but I was too weak to defy him. And so I took my own life . . . And you—you've learned his ways. . . . Some men change, son."

To redeem himself and his family's legacy, Dante must fight through the various stages of Hell, where he encounters villains of the game's fictional and the author's actual past (his parents, Francesco, his political enemy Filippo Argenti, etc.) and also of history and fiction (Marc Antony, Semiramis, Cerberus, etc.). On his path to redemption, Dante redeems the souls of Francesco and his mother with his illuminative cross and has the opportunity to punish (by impaling) or to absolve various historical figures in Hell. That the gamer is granted the autonomy to make these decisions signifies a notable departure from Dante's *Inferno,* in which Virgil informs Dante of the Harrowing of Hell, the one instance in which the "Great Lord" redeems the souls of Adam, Abel, Noah, and others (4.53), transporting them from Limbo into Paradise. Thus, in *Dante's Inferno,* Dante and, by extension, the gamer, is given divine power to save and condemn; Dante not only is transformed into a fallen, medieval crusader on a quest to save his beloved, but he is also imbued with omnipotence, a significant alteration from the text that proves essential to the outcome of the game: when Dante approaches the final layer of Hell, he finally reaches Beatrice and gives her his cross, allowing her to ascend into Heaven. This overtly reverses their roles from the *Divine Comedy,* in which Beatrice descends from Heaven to save Dante from his despair, first charging Virgil to lead him through Inferno and Purgatory and then taking over the task herself in the Earthly Paradise, leading Dante most of the rest of the way to the Empyrion. Subsequently, in Lake Cocytus, Dante encounters and defeats Lucifer, at which point, the souls he has absolved during his journey save him from the Inferno and force Lucifer back into the ice. As the game concludes, a naked Dante reaches an angelic Beatrice, they touch in a gesture resembling Adam and Eve, Beatrice disappears, and Dante emerges from the Inferno staring at the spiraling, volcanic mountain of Purgatory, perhaps suggesting that he has emerged "a riveder le stelle" ("once more to see the stars") (*Inferno* 34.139), or possibly suggesting a video game sequel to come.

CONCLUSIONS

As the above examination of the game has shown, this Dante has little in common with earlier visions; the medieval philosophical background of the poem has been removed, and a new identity is written on the empty space. Dante becomes a representation of a generic (albeit fictionally generic) 'Middle Ages,' divorced from any specificity, where time, geography, history, and literature are collapsed into an all-encompassing definition of 'the past.' This relationship to the past may be a function of the medium itself; Zach Whelan and Laurie N. Taylor, in *Playing the Past,* suggest that "video games are playing an increasing role in communicating complex ideas—real world history, media ecologies, and gaming histories."[21] Yet their section that deals with historical games is enticingly called "Playing with the Past: Real and Revisionist History in Video Games," implying that any lucid engagement with the past is essentially a recreation: any attempt to make historical material adequate to gaming is to revise it. This offers an intriguing sense that "video games frequently operate . . . in imagined worlds and eras with their own histories and timelines."[22] Games may provide the opportunity to grapple with the past, but they are essentially conveying "narratives about the past, . . . offering nostalgists an opportunity to 'relive' the past" while playing "with the narrative and the setting."[23] Ideologies, ideas, relationships, and constructions of the past are built into the game as a part of the history it conveys. "The effects of these changes on historical representation," they suggest, "operate similarly to nostalgia's desired return to a particular moment or to a mythical state of innocence. In this context, play becomes a way of relating to the past and a means of addressing our loss of innocence by temporarily allowing us access to that innocent condition."[24] Susan Stewart, in her discussion of longing, explains, "the direction of force in the desiring narrative is always a future-past, a deferment of experience in the direction of origin and thus eschaton, the point where narrative begins/ ends, both engendering and transcending the relation between materiality and meaning. Yet the particular content of this desire is subject to historical formation."[25] Historical video games, then, engage this longing through their formulations of the past and their relationships to present and future.

What we may learn from the *Dante's Inferno* video game, then, is not about either Dante or the Middle Ages, besides the aesthetic and experiential qualities of descending through Dante's vision of the Inferno as (a heavily fabricated) Dante, but instead about contemporary audiences' longing for a return to a particular state of innocence, where the fiction of the video game exemplifies the modern age's reimagining of a highly fictional Middle

Ages. Here the Middle Ages represent an idealized vision of a simplistic time of structure and clarity, where good and evil lack ambiguities and when evil could be conquered with a sword (or scythe); as explained earlier, the physiognomy of the game's antagonists, such as the amoral priests, Dante's gluttonous father, and even Dante himself at times, distinguishes them from the innocent, and when Dante encounters evil, he triumphs so long as the gamer can master several battle techniques. Moreover, in this gaming universe, morality and actions are specifically linked to progress towards transcendence. These deceptively simple interconnections get called 'medieval' and linked to Dante because of the Middle Age's multiple identification as an age of faith, an age of magic, an age of primitivism, and an age of violence—all qualities that the game's version of Dante embodies. Although any real understanding of Dante shows a highly complex relationship between human action, sin, and transcendence, the *Divine Comedy* has come to be identified, at least, with this redemptive process. Dante emerges at the end of *Paradiso* transformed by "l'amor che move il sole e l'altre stelle" ("the love that moves the sun and other stars") (*Paradiso* 33.146), having learned the relationship of human action on earth to one's transcendent afterlife, as well as coming to understand the role and limits of human reason and the function of divine grace. As such, a video game may prove a particularly appropriate way to represent certain basic premises of this transformative experience, if not its specific medieval and theological details. Thomas Malaby sees games as "*processual*. Each game is an ongoing process. As it is played it always contains the potential for generating new practices and new meanings."[26] Although it seems unlikely that players of *Dante's Inferno* will see their success in the game as a theological commitment to avoiding an afterlife in Hell, it is at least possible to suggest that the game engages a desire for that kind of transformation—a kind of moral 'leveling up' with Dante. At the end of Sandow Birk and Sean Meredith's animated film of *Dante's Inferno*, a hoodie and jeans wearing Dante escapes from the Inferno and declares, "I'd better watch what I do."[27] This film, like the video game, collapses the past's complexity into a simple message, working out contemporary anxiety and longing by locating it in an ostensibly simplified history.

It is this engagement that the *Dante's Inferno* video game can instruct, and, ironically, this anachronistic use of the past is, in itself, inherently medieval. This 'past' is not so different in spirit from the 'past' constructed in medieval narrative, such as the collapsing of time we see in Arthurian romances which hearken back to a Golden Age that looks almost exactly like the poem's historical present, and this is what makes the game most interesting. As with the anachronistic presentation of the past in medieval literature, including Dante's *Comedy*, where classical, biblical, and historical figures all inhabit the same time frame, speak the same language, and all look remarkably medieval, *Dante's Inferno* coalesces elements of the poem, classical mythology, fantasy and gaming tropes, and special effects into a whole that stands for the Middle

Ages themselves. If Dante himself can use the past in the *Divine Comedy* to work out the theological and political problems of his own present, the video game treats Dante's work with the same anachronistic sensibility that Dante treats his own sources. By using a collage of various pasts to stand for 'the past,' and by then having the reader/player interact with those in the present, both works engage a similar kind of nostalgia and a similar method of analysis.

NOTES

1. *Dante's Inferno*, Visceral Games (Electronic Arts, 2010).
2. Marcello Simonetta, "Assassin's Creed" (lecture, Seton Hall University, South Orange, NJ, April 18, 2011).
3. Translations from the *Divine Comedy* are by Angela Jane Weisl. The Italian text is taken from the online Digital Dante Project, http://dante.ilt.columbia.edu/comedy/index.html (accessed October 2, 2012).
4. In doing this, the game's creators have something in common with medievalizers like Stephen Weeks, whose two films of *Sir Gawain and the Green Knight*, 1984's *The Sword of the Valiant*, starring Sean Connery as the Green Knight, and 1973's *Sir Gawain and the Green Knight*, starring Murray Head as Sir Gawain, seem to lose sight of their medieval antecedent, bringing in elements of Chrétien's *Yvain*, other medieval stories, and some odd new-age spirituality, as if 'paganism' and 'medievalism' were equivalents, despite the strongly Christian message of the poem itself.
5. James Paul Gee, "Are Video Games Good for Learning?" in *Worlds in Play: International Perspectives on Digital Games Research*, ed. Suzanne de Castell and Jennifer Jenson (New York: Peter Lang, 2007), 323.
6. Gee, "Are Video Games Good for Learning?" 323.
7. These terms are Gee's, and each begins a section heading in his article.
8. Gee, "Are Video Games Good for Learning?" 328–29.
9. James Newman and Barney Oram, *Teaching Videogames* (London: British Film Institute, 2006).
10. Katie Salen and Eric Zimmerman, *Rules of Play: Game Design Fundamentals* (Cambridge, MA: MIT Press, 2003), 80.
11. Gordon Calleja and Ival Collins, "Game Studies," in *The Routledge Companion to Literature and Science*, ed. Bruce Clarke and Manuela Rossini (London: Routledge, 2011), 324.
12. Johan Huizinga, *Homo Ludens: A Study of the Play Element in Culture* (Boston: Beacon Press, 1950), 10. Huizinga sees this "magic circle" as a space "marked off beforehand either materially or ideally" and subject to "an absolute and peculiar order" (10).
13. Huizinga, *Homo Ludens*, 9–10.
14. Calleja and Collins, "Game Studies," 324.
15. Calleja and Collins, "Game Studies," 325.
16. David Golumbia, "Games Without Play," *New Literary History* 40 (2009): 179–204.
17. "NECA Takes You to Hell and Back with New Dante's Inferno Collectible Figure," http://youbentmywookie.com/news/neca-takes-you-to-hell-and-back-with-new-dantes-inferno-collectible-figures-7611 (accessed October 2, 2012).
18. Jeff Howard, "Interpretative Quests in Theory and Pedagogy," *Digital Humanities Quarterly* 1, no. 1 (2007), http://digitalhumanities.org/dhq/vol/1/1/000002/000002.html (accessed July 6, 2012).

19. Jeff Howard, "Interpretative Quests."
20. Golumbia, "Games Without Play," 188.
21. Zach Taylor and Laurie N. Whelan, "Playing the Past: An Introduction," in *Playing the Past: History and Nostalgia in Video Games*, ed. Zach Taylor and Laurie N. Whelan (Nashville: Vanderbilt University Press, 2008), 2.
22. Taylor and Whelan, "Playing the Past," 11.
23. Taylor and Whelan, "Playing the Past," 11.
24. Taylor and Whelan, "Playing the Past," 12.
25. Susan Stewart, *On Longing: Narratives of the Miniature, the Gigantic, the Souvenir, the Collection* (Durham, NC: Duke University Press, 1993), x.
26. Thomas N. Malaby, "Beyond Play: A New Approach to Culture," *Games and Culture* 2, no. 2 (2007): 98.
27. *Dante's Inferno*, directed by Sean Meredith (Santa Monica, CA: Dante Film, 2008), DVD.

Part V

Theoretical and Representational Issues in Medieval Gaming

14 We Will Travel by Map
Maps as Narrative Spaces in Video Games and Medieval Texts

Thomas Rowland

Maps are one of those texts that we have become so used to that their function seems evident, obvious, and commonsense: with the advent of online street and satellite maps, such as those Google provides, they are more accessible, easier to use, and cover very nearly not only every surface of the earth, but also some deep places, too. Since the Enlightenment and global maritime navigation, maps have always been expected to represent for us a true and accurate image of the land, sea, and space, for the purposes of helping us to navigate that space. It is hard for us to conceptualize how a map may function in any other way.

This is why medieval maps have been so puzzling—for the most part, they refuse to operate within accurate scales of proportion and representation. Continents lack their familiar outlines, while seas are sometimes bigger than their adjoining landmass. Orientation is rarely set to the north. An early map dating from Anglo-Saxon England (Cotton Tiberius B.V. 56) renders Western Europe nearly unrecognizable. These *mappaemundi* (maps of the world) have traditionally been explained as primitive, premodern, or unsophisticated attempts to represent the world as an untraveled monk with limited technology might have perceived it.[1]

This explanation, however, is itself mostly obsolete: much worthy research on medieval maps recently has revised and eliminated most of the scorn once placed on medieval cartography. Any casual examination of these *mappaemundi* reveals the careful detail and effort put in these deliberately constructed elaborate cosmologies. The key to understanding medieval maps is to start by denying the assumption that maps must be defined as scaled, proportional representations of geography and instead to consider that they work as discursive texts, creating a space wherein narration occurs: one should read them in a manner that "involved a slow, meditative ingestion and rumination in order to draw out various levels of meaning."[2] Medieval maps are a place for telling stories and making virtual journeys, and these functions make them unfamiliar to us.

Not so unlike the medieval maps, we have in video games a reconceptualization of maps: video game maps have been a constant companion to games, and in this close proximity they have slowly but undeniably changed the way we read them. From the earliest video games, maps were quickly integrated to the game experience: games like *Pac-Man* (1980) and the original *Legend of Zelda* (1986) render the substrate of the game as a sort of map on which the action of the game occurs. Maps in a way we would recognize were soon added to accentuate the historical aesthetic of the game. Games such as *Secret of Monkey Island* (1990) and *Myst* (1993) made maps integral to gameplay, because in these games players used maps to move through various segments of the narrative, and in the case of *Myst* sometimes these maps appeared within the virtual game space as highly rendered three-dimensional models. But of all the game designers utilizing maps as part of the game design, Nintendo led the way. Its highly successful *Super Mario Bros.* series and *The Legend of Zelda* games both integrated maps as integral elements of the gameplay. The function of maps revolutionized gameplay, and it so happens in so doing they reintroduced a very medieval understanding of maps.

MAPS: MEDIEVAL AND MODERN

Most of us today expect maps to reproduce or represent real geographies in proportional and scaled manner that can be used both for scientific measurement (how far is it?) and navigation (how do we get there?). Normally, they are tied to geography, wherein "each point in the representation correspond[s] to an actual geographic position according to a fixed scale or projection."[3] Key to reading maps is differentiating *place* and *space,* that *places* occupy *space* in a scaled and predictable way. Yi-Fu Tuan is noted for reconceptualizing both *space* and *place* as social encounters, wherein *space* occupies the area between *places*—stable places for visiting or pausing. *Space* allows movement, *place* gives direction.[4] The distinction has been useful for video game studies, as Eric Hayot and Edward Wesp show in their anthropological discussion of space in games such as *Everquest* (1999).[5]

A better conceptualization, however, identifies *place* as a spatial marker (I'm ten miles away) and *space* as a chronological marker (I'm ten minutes away). In massively multiplayer online role-playing game (MMORPG) geographies, maps provide organization of the gameplay by giving *places* where players meet and set off to explore spatially, while the area between these discrete *places* is set off by *space* that, unlike *places,* has no virtual experience associated with it. For instance, in *Guild Wars* (2005), the characters move from place to place on the map, but the act of moving has no representation on the map—it happens in a virtual landscape, and accessing this *space* could only occur by moving into a *place.* Once explored, the map became a surface with which the player can access any *place* from any other. *World of Warcraft* (2004) works similarly: moving between *places* by griffin or ship or some other means only required an elapse of *time,* less of *space.*

Ultimately, the maps in MMORPGs function according to a familiar principle of cartography, namely that the representation of the place should be proportional and scaled, that we may use it to better understand our position within that world. But what about maps that are wildly disproportionate, such as those found in games like the *Super Mario Bros.* series? These games feature linear, disproportionate maps that chronicle the player's progress in the game, but look little like the elaborate world maps of *World of Warcraft*. The answer I propose lies in a medieval understanding of maps.

When we start looking at how medieval maps function, we can begin to see parallels with video game maps. By the fourteenth century, there were (as with so many other elements of medieval society) two courses of cartography: the newer trend, developing in Italy, required a scaled representation of the waterways of the Mediterranean for use by the traders crisscrossing it—these 'portolan maps' will begin the modern tradition of cartography that relies on proportionally accurate representation of land and water. The older tradition, however, one emerging from the privilege of the word over image,[6] is associated closely with the discussion of the spiritual nature of man and his environment (both spatially and chronologically). Of the few maps remaining to us today, some formed part of larger chronicles, such as Matthew Paris's *Chronica Majora*, and some of devotional texts, as in the beautiful Psalter World Map (in the British Library, MS Additional 28681). Rarely but notably, some maps appeared within architectural contexts—the most famous being the elaborate and intricate thirteenth-century Hereford Cathedral *mappamundi,* with over 1,000 illustrations and clusters of text covering a vellum surface over five feet high.[7] The Psalter World Map, too, gives evidence of maps as decoration: it was likely a copy of a much larger version adorning the bedchamber wall of King Henry III. The Hereford *mappamundi*[8] contains numerous written entries showing historical incidents, theological concepts, and even the shape of the world and the inclusion or exclusion of certain elements, and which in its setting creates a semiotic emphasis on man's understanding of himself in space and time against the events dictated by God. In all of these cases, however, the setting (whether a manuscript or a cathedral) of maps emphasizes the function of the map *within* the context of a larger text—hence, the map both provides contextualization but also requires it, and like the video game map, it is hard to appreciate the map outside the text it accompanies.

Nearly all of the maps we still have—most notably the Hereford *mappamundi*, the Psalter World Map, and the Ebstorf wall map[9]—are intricate and cluttered with writing and information to the point that they are difficult to read. They are impossible to read quickly, and that is the point: the medieval map is a complicated and sophisticated text, one intended to slow down the reader and make him meditate upon the complexities of the world and his own worldview. It is a deliberative space, a meditative space, and, in many instances, a virtual space allowing for spiritual travel. In other words, medieval maps, like video game maps, evoke and chronicle a certain sort of narrative experience as one reads them that seeks to present an understanding of the world as Creation, as a tool by which one can virtually travel this world, and finally as a piece of art: these three functions, I maintain, link maps from our two very different historical periods together.

MAPS AS ONTOLOGICAL CONTEXT

The first of three functions of the medieval map is to present the world as a creation of God's design—not unlike the essential intentional quality of video game maps, and in this way they provide substantial context for understanding and traveling within this virtual geography. These maps do so by organizing essential information into one space, collapsing both chronological and geographical distance into the simultaneous and continuous *tabulae* of the map (both events and places exist side-by-side). The map serves as an anchor for reading whatever text it accompanies (usually a chronicle). The twelfth-century theologian Hugh of St. Victor advocated using maps to help the memory retain details necessary for a sound education, because the map as an image could serve as a

> kind of brief summary . . . which the soul can most easily comprehend and the memory retain. There are three matters on which the knowledge of past actions especially depends, that is, the *persons* who performed the deeds, the *places* in which they were performed, and the *time* at which they occurred. Whoever holds these three by memory in his soul will find that he has built a good foundation for himself, onto which he can assemble afterward anything by reading and lecture . . . and retain it for a long time.[10]

This use of maps is not altogether unfamiliar to the modern reader: when encountering fantasy maps in books often readers will keep a finger on the page to reference events in the story, but we have become accustomed to the bad habit of reading books by focusing our attention on the writing itself. But medieval manuscripts—and by implication, maps, too—present information in complex patterns involving not only the prose text, but also the interlayering of illuminations both within and outside the text, as well as the organization of the texts within a manuscript. Hence, to understand the message of a text, one must 'read' the entire page as something intentional: the illuminations in the margin, the oversized initial, the boxes interspersed in the text, and finally the text itself.

Maps function as part of the overall text, but they also organize a considerable amount of interpretation just in the layout of the map itself as well, a design that is both deliberative and evocative. In most of these maps, the circle containing the world is superimposed on a figure of Christ, such that his hands and feet and head are evident at certain points around the circle: the implication is obvious—that Christ exists in all parts of the world and oversees the progress of history. Within the circle of the world, the most common pattern is what is known as a T-O map, referring to its shape as a circle but divided into thirds, usually by a combination of the Mediterranean Sea and various rivers making the shape of a T. In most cases the purpose of this is to draw the reader's eye to the center, nearly always occupied by Jerusalem, because its prominence in Christian theology made it the metaphorical center of the world.

All significance of other parts of the world then drew on their proximity to Jerusalem; hence, Constantinople, Rome, and Egypt appear distorted and indecipherable but linked closely to the Holy Land. France, Spain, England, and far parts of the East are sometimes omitted or at least distorted beyond recognition to reflect their position as boundaries or liminal edges. The overall focus of these maps is on the Holy Land for its connection to Christ and that all efforts to understand one's place in the world must account for the marginal relevance of oneself to Jerusalem: this organization promoted the spiritual exercise of pilgrimages and crusading. The design encouraged movement towards the center in a way that the reader should feel compelled to visit Jerusalem, if not physically, then spiritually.

Sometimes this ontological awareness moved to extremes as, for example, the strange maps of Opicinus who drew the Mediterranean world to resemble a man and lover embracing. Like Bede, who described the shape and condition of the island of Britain to mirror the spirituality of the Anglo-Saxons, the connection of land (real) and the divine are analogically linked, such that the land reflects the spiritual condition of its people. In video games, the map can reflect the spiritual corruption of the action: consider how the final world of *Super Mario Bros. 3* (1988) is presented on the map consumed in flames, with a preponderance of blacks, browns, grays, and off-whites. So, too, does the Isle of Delfino in *Super Mario Sunshine* (2002) reflect the culture of the people, shaped as it like a dolphin. In the independent game *Braid* (2009), the map takes the form of a house, providing both context and commentary on the character. The maps in these games attempt to layer meaning onto the narration by organizing the narrative sequence with recognizable symbols (i.e., flames, houses, dolphins, trees, clouds, colors, swords, deserts) reflective of their virtual cultures.

The video game map, therefore, is intended to provide context to the narration but in a way that adds ontological awareness: we know Bowser in *Super Mario* is bad because he is surrounded, on the map, by flames. We know that Hyrule in *Zelda* is supreme because it occupies a central position. The presence of the fixed map, framed and bounded, with a center and edges, encourages movement towards the center, like a spiritual pilgrimage, because we understand intuitively (and by experience) that that is where we must complete the quest to find a narrative and spiritual fulfillment.

Like the T-O maps, most video game maps are organized to promote movement towards the center. In some cases, like the early *Super Mario Bros.* maps, the movement tends to happen left to right, but by the release of *Super Mario World* (1990) and in other games, such as the popular *The*

Legend of Zelda: The Ocarina of Time (1998), in which the town, market, and castle are positioned prominent in the top center (in almost the same place as Jerusalem in a medieval T-O map), the map has moved into a circular design with the center as a position of prominence. The map for the game *Robin Hood: Legend of Sherwood* (2002) centers Sherwood Forest in the middle. This organization becomes increasingly important when we consider the margins in video game maps, like medieval maps, are intended to cut off, alienate, and disenfranchise.

The implication of movement in maps further establishes the necessity of limits. Because in video games infinite movement in any direction is still not yet possible (nor is it desirable), video games must establish boundaries to movement, and hence maps must work within frames to establish boundaries and to create frontiers, edges, and wilderness. In Google Maps and global positioning systems (GPS), which are capable of moving along with the user, the edge or boundary recedes constantly as the traveler approaches it, making it impossible to reach. This eliminates the boundary and the margin of the map and removes any 'no man's land,' frontier, or netherland.

In postmedieval maps, the edge was replaced by absence, or by blank space, perhaps identified as *terra incognita,* but in the Middle Ages, the possibility of additional space beyond what was known was unacknowledged, and the known world was compactly presented within strict frames.[11] Hence, the medieval map presented Creation where certain areas were marginal and hence spiritually handicapped—the corollary to the rule of relation to Jerusalem. If the center represents spiritual purity, the edges represent barbarism and monstrosity—thus, the Psalter World Map ornaments the African edge with images of monsters and distorted men, and likewise the Ebstorf World Map labels and illustrates such men next to Christ's left hand, which casts the wicked into Hell. Gerald of Wales describes the Irish as a "wild and inhospitable people . . . so removed in these distant parts from the ordinary world of men, as if they were in another world altogether and consequently cut off from well-behaved and law-abiding people, they know only of the barbarous habits in which they were born and brought up."[12] He accompanies this description with a map of waterway accesses to England and Ireland in which Ireland is framed by France and Spain, two areas where King Henry II had already established control: the lower center (Ireland) extends beyond the colonized areas and lies well outside the spiritual city of Rome. Thus, Gerald justifies Henry's desire to conquer Ireland.[13]

The space between the spiritual center (Jerusalem) and the barbaric edges gives room for the people of Europe to dwell, and the circular geometry means the edge and the center create a dialectic of center and margin[14] on which to find the normal or mundane: Michael Camille insightfully suggested the one depends on the other, the edge and the center, for its continued existence.[15] When movement is circular, therefore, we can read the video game map in terms of narrative and diegetic organization: the crisis occurs in the center and consequently the catharsis as well. The center is plagued by elements from the fringe: in *The Legend of Zelda*, Hyrule castle's central position means it is surrounded by the monstrous, exotic, or oriental—the rocklike Gorons, the fishlike Zora, the gnomelike Kokiri, and the Arab-based Shiekah tribe. In *Dragon Age: Origins* (2009), corruption comes to the center from the margin, and it is this area that must be redeemed.[16]

In many MMORPGs, when players approach the edge they remove themselves from other players, useful quests, or narrative elements and are instead surrounded by random (read: meaningless) mobs or spawned creatures, useful only for gathering loot (called 'farming'). In addition, approaching the edge in a game means isolating the character amongst tall mountains, long deserts, oceans, cliffs, or other equally inhospitable terrain and geography intended to limit the player's movement. These unscalable edges resemble the boundaries of the manuscript or the medieval map: here there be monsters, savage men, and cruel beasts. But in games and medieval maps, the edge is also useful for hiding secrets: in *Super Mario Bros. 3*, secret 'bonus' sections of the game are hidden by mountains or clouds or other impassable boundaries; likewise, Matthew Paris transgresses the normal edge of the manuscript space by sewing flaps that fold back onto the page. Hence, the edge also becomes associated with secrets, mystery, and the arcane.

Thus the map in the video game and the medieval manuscript helps us to understand how the world is organized and what places are spiritually purer and what places are savage and monstrous: the map is like an arcane text, containing both knowledge and secrets to be sought, revealing its knowledge through position and proximity, center and margin, space and place, to show spiritual fulfillment and descent into barbarism.

MAPS AS AESTHETIC ENDEAVOR

Since the Enlightenment, map-makers have increasingly deemphasized the elements of maps that have no or little relevance to the information to be conveyed. From the highly ornate and elaborate navigational maps of the eighteenth century to the moderns maps of government and scientific institutions (such as the U.S. Army Corp of Engineers or NASA), maps have steadily relied less on decorative elements. And although Google Maps has a sort of pleasing simplicity in its design, there are nevertheless no elements not associated with transportational or topographical features. This is simply because the maps are tools, not art. This, of course, is in direct contrast to medieval and video game maps. Medieval maps were designed artifacts, meaning they were conceived not only to provide information, but also to impress onto the reader the beauty associated with God's Creation and thus to serve as a spiritual exercise in worship. Medieval maps, like the manuscripts and cathedrals in which they appeared, served a spiritual purpose in their beauty and design.

The thirteenth-century Psalter World Map, for instance, occurs at the beginning of the manuscript (originally as the first page of the Psalter, or collection of Psalms for worship), and upon thumbing through the added pages of heavily gold-leafed illuminations now proceeding it, the reader is impressed by the map's finely wrought detail and bold colors. As with the Hereford *mappamundi,* the elements of the map are intended to slow down the reader, to make the reader pause to deliberate on the map, and to consider the connection between Christ (holding the world in his hands) and Creation (ornamented with several rings of details, contrasting colors, and amusing images). The wall-map from which it was copied was as much decoration as edification.

Although modern cartography has moved so firmly towards a simplification of the map, however, video games quickly realized that with fictional geographies, detail and clarity were not as critical as aesthetic quality. The map is so integral to the experience of the game that a considerable effort goes into making the map as pleasing as possible. Hence, we have games today with elaborate pen-and-ink designs that are intended to resemble 'primitive' hand-drawn maps of an earlier age, such as 'pirate maps' in *Sid Meier's Pirates!* (2007), reflecting a preference for hand-drawn maps.[17] Newer games such as *Dragon Age: Origins* (2009) and *Elder Scrolls: Skyrim* (2011) have elaborately hand-drawn maps discolored to suggest historical authenticity.

But even early video games put much attention on creating attractive maps. The simplicity of the old 8-bit maps had a certain appeal that has continued today.[18] Some games were notable for early game-map innovation, such as *The Legend of Zelda* (where the map was the playing surface), *Super Mario Bros. 3,* and particularly the early neomedievalist games such as Sierra On-line's *King's Quest* series[19] and New World Computing's *Might and Magic* series, which included in the early games a printed map poster.[20] These games set the precedent that maps in games should be artistically produced and visually appealing, even when they must be programmed for the screen (or else, as in *Might and Magic* above, a printed map would accompany the game as an extradiegetic object). As computers have become increasingly more powerful and capable of handling more demanding graphics, these carefully executed maps have simply gone from paper to screen. *New Super Mario Bros.: Wii* (2009) has re-created the early game maps, albeit with considerably smoother and more nuanced color and design. These maps are intentional works of art in their own right, and the effect these have, like the medieval maps of manuscripts, cannot be separated from the overall work of narrative or literary art they accompany.

MAPS AS NARRATIVE SPACE

The most important function of medieval and video game maps, however, is in containing the narrative events of the text. The map exists physically as a text but provides virtual space in which we can view the sequence (both chronologically and geographically) of events via markers (sometimes as dots, icons, or written text), a space which is to be read not left to right, but holistically, circularly, and diegetically. This is why *mappaemundi* are so difficult to decipher—the markers exist in deliberate relation to each other, but not in the way we expect them to be. So, too, with video game maps. We read the relationship of one place to another in terms of *winning* access to it, and so distance and proportion are both important and irrelevant—moving from one dot in the *Super Mario Bros.* games is not difficult based on the span to the next dot (most locations are equidistant from the next or last), but in the narrative event *within* the dot to progress forward.[21] Hence video game maps and *mappaemundi* contain space and places in which moving through each *place* requires a considerable effort, but which space does not suggest difficulty, but is instead there to require pause and deliberation.

The most illustrative example from medieval maps comes from an elaborate strip-map accompanying Matthew Paris's *Chronica Majora*. The map he presents (see Figure 14.1) lays out a sequence of cities one passes through from London en route to Jerusalem, the Holy Land. In terms of scale and navigation, the route itself is not very useful and contains errors.[22] But assuming it is intended as a sort of road atlas in the way we use Google Maps today, or the way the extensive Gough medieval road map might be useful, is to fall into our old habits of expecting modern functions of medieval texts. Daniel Connolly points out we should be concerned with how "medieval intellectual culture understood ideas of space and time, ideas of place and the memories, institutional and personal, that could shape space into something palpably meaningful, and perhaps most importantly, desirable."[23] Reading a map as this, particularly as it is bound in a volume much too large for easy transport (especially for a pilgrim) and thus stationary, it becomes evident that the journey to Jerusalem is intended to be entirely virtual, an experience of meditation and rumination, of spiritual imagination as an act of devotion. The map leads the reader through each step along the road to Jerusalem so that he may visualize the encounter without ever actually taking it. Matthew's maps too were not unique in this: other *mappaemundi* such as the Hereford World Map hint at pilgrim itineraries.[24]

The strip-map works by using symbolic icons and scale to invite individuals to partake in an "imagined journey"[25] by visualizing themselves progressing through the various points on the map: it provided a useful substitute for the actual pilgrimage, particularly for those who were too poor, disabled, or otherwise oath bound to remain at one place (such as a monastery). The symbolic scale worked as an allegory, the map inducing a virtual, corporal pilgrimage towards the center, towards Jerusalem, and hence the map presented a narrative experience of moving through space towards a place of spiritual significance.

These itineraries work by symbols to direct the reader to imagine a familiar narrative and to engage in an imagined pilgrimage as a practice of devotion, a substitute for the worshipful act of visiting the Holy Land. This is

Figure 14.1   Map of *Super Mario Bros. 3*, World III. Strip-map for traveling to Jerusalem, Matthew Paris's *Chronica Majora* (CCC MS 26). Image reproduced by kind permission of the Master and Fellows of Corpus Christi College, Cambridge.

accomplished by what Connolly calls "translocative thinking,"[26] of moving into the text in a bodily fashion by engaging the senses of sight, hearing, and touch. For a manuscript, this means holding the text in the lap, handling the pages, reading, and perhaps listening. In the case of the Hereford *mappamundi*, Kline points out that given the likelihood of a viewer being literate, the map was likely read aloud, engaging the sense of hearing, sight upon viewing the text, and touch insofar as it exists as an object of many media, including vellum (calfskin) and wood.[27] The nature of the *mappaemundi*, like the itineraries, forces the reader to "provide narrative structure in order to link diverse pictures, to make connections where no connections are apparent, to create dramatic incident where few emotive clues are provided: in short, to use the map as a vehicle for imaginative comprehension."[28] She continues, "the maps obviously elicited visions of distant travel, but they also provided a field for imaginative rumination about creation and history whose narrative depended upon the viewer's personal invention that occurs between the boundaries of images and words."[29] In other words, then, the map provided medieval readers a substrate, a sort of *tabula rasa* onto which they could project their own vision of traveling through the lands described in the map.

If Matthew Paris's maps worked by creating a *tabula rasa* onto which one could project an encounter with a virtual destination, it makes sense that the *mappaemundi* in general could also work this way: the connection of place and event, simultaneous and synchronous, over all of Europe leads the viewer to experience each place, each event, in a virtual, imagined way. The touch and feel of the map, the sensory elements of color and texture, of the dyes and gold leaf, of the orientation through Christ, made the maps a corporal, pseudo-physical experience of journey and storytelling to a spiritual encounter with the Creator.

This description of a virtual journey should be familiar to most video game players: in games we find maps that work analogously. The map in the video game, ultimately, is there to establish the journey of the game—one not taken in reality, but virtually, through the mediation of the video game system or computer. Scale and proportion are no longer relevant except to differentiate locations, and the purpose is to draw movement from the reader directed towards a specific destination (though not perhaps spiritually significant, as a culmination of the *muthos* or plot of the game, the destination is imminently important).

In *Super Mario Bros. 3*, the maps resemble closely the strip map of Matthew Paris (see Figure 14.1 for a visual comparison), with locations (symbolized by dots, castles, huts, pyramids, pipes, etc.) connected through a single strip (visually very similar to the *signum* of the strip-maps[30]) along which Mario travels. Mario as an avatar is only a stand-in for the player, who travels *through* each place and must struggle to win access to the next place—the distance between giving the player time to rest and to deliberate: the time and space between each dot is irrelevant, and though we see the avatar move through this space, it is automatic and brief.

Traveling through the map then tracks our progress through the narrative. Hence, the map is carefully tied in to storytelling and narration, and the map as indicator of progress means that it exists as a *tabula rasa* for the experience we have in the story. The map, then, serves as a space in which narrative experience is organized and undertaken, the space and the action inseparably and intrinsically tied (the map *is* the substrate where we play the game), and the corporal nature of the text (the feel of the controllers, the colors and textures of the graphics, the sounds of the game) invite the reader to project himself bodily through the avatar as a substitute for the reader, for the self, into the journey, into the narrative. Consider how in the *Super*

Mario Bros. games the map features a circular fade into the world upon selecting a level, as though we are falling into a hole, into the narrative. The maps act as one part of the video game in which the reader is invited to experience the text, to move into the text, and to begin the process of negotiating self-identity, much the same way that these itineraries and *mappaemundi* invite the faithful reader to enter into the imagined spaces of the pilgrimage and renegotiate his or her own identity as a devoted Christian.

The maps of medieval texts, whether on walls or in books, were intended to reveal the world as a created object, to show themselves as objects of beauty for gazing and deliberation, and to contain narrative as an enticing, spiritual pilgrimage. None of these three primary functions survive into the twentieth-century maps as they are most commonly used, except that in video games we see again a resurgence, a renaissance, of maps in this style. The digital maps of games, whether explicitly 'neomedieval' or not, have returned to seeing maps not as scaled and proportional representations of real geography to aid and facilitate travel but as narrative spaces, intended to provide context and make sense of the narrative structure of the game as a story, as a place in which the reader is invited to encounter the narrative in a very corporal fashion. And finally it is there as an object of art, of design, if for no other reason, to impress upon the reader its existence as a beautiful artifact.

NOTES

1. See David Woodward, "Medieval *Mappaemundi*," in *History of Cartography: Prehistoric, Ancient, and Medieval Europe and the Mediterranean*, vol. 1, ed. J. B. Harley (Chicago: University of Chicago Press, 1987), 288. See especially his note on Beazley in the early twentieth century, note 17.
2. Asa Simon Mittman, *Maps and Monsters in Medieval England* (New York: Routledge, 2006), 2.
3. Oxford English Dictionary, "Map," http://www.oed.com (accessed August 1, 2012).
4. Yi-Fu Tuan, *Space and Place: The Perspective of Experience* (Minneapolis: University of Minneapolis Press, 2001).
5. Eric Hayot and Edward Wesp, "Towards a Critical Perspective of Virtual-World Geographies" *Game Studies* 9, no. 1 (2009), http://gamestudies.org/0901/articles/hayot_wesp_space (accessed April 2010).
6. Woodward, "Medieval *Mappaemundi*," 286.
7. See Naomi Reed Kline, *Maps of Medieval Thought: The Hereford Paradigm* (Woodbridge, UK: Boydell, 2001), for more information on this beautiful wall map.
8. The signature of the author at the base labels the map as *c'est estoire* ("this history"), giving us another way to think of the map. See P. D. A. Harvey, *Mappa Mundi: The Hereford World Map,* (Toronto: University of Toronto Press, 1996), 7; and Michael Gaudio, "Matthew Paris and the Cartography of the Margins," *Gesta* 39, no. 1 (2000): 52.
9. Now destroyed, but we have record of it by an early photograph and several reconstructions made in the last century.
10. Hugh of St. Victor, *De Tribus Maximiis Circumstantiis Gestorum,* translated by Mary Carruthers, *The Medieval Craft of Memory: An Anthology of Texts*

and Pictures (Philadelphia: University of Pennsylvania Press, 2004), 39. Also see William H. Green, "Hugo of St. Victor: *De Tribus Maximis Circumstantiis Gestorum*," *Speculum* 18, no. 4 (1943), 484–93. Emphasis is mine.

11. Consider Matthew Paris's comment ("If the page allowed it, this island should be longer") on his map of England, where he laments not being able to represent England better because of space constraints: as Michael Gaudio phrases it, "his geography finds its limits at the borders of the page." Michael Gaudio, "Matthew Paris and the Cartography of the Margins," *Gesta* 39, no. 1 (2000): 50.

12. Gerald of Wales, *Topographia Hibernica*, translated by J. J. O'Meara, *Gerald of Wales: The History and Topography of Ireland* (Harmondsworth: Penguin, 1982).

13. Diarmuid Scully, "Gerald of Wales and the English Conquest of Ireland: Map, Text, and Marginal Illustration in MS 700, National Museum of Ireland" (conference presentation, International Medieval Congress, Leeds, 2012).

14. Gaudio, "Matthew Paris," 52.

15. Michael Camille, *Image on the Edge: The Margins of Medieval Art* (Cambridge, MA: Harvard University Press, 1992), 10.

16. Although we may note, *Dragon Age: Origins* (2009) and the MMORPG *World of Warcraft* emphasize the collapse into chaos of a decentralizing world by moving the action into the margins: *Dragon Age* makes the center the point of collapse (invasion) and the edge the place of fighting, and *World of Warcraft* places in the center a maelstrom, a vestige of cataclysmic events from previous game narratives.

17. One can see how hand-drawn maps do in fact maintain a sort of simple beauty and how these are being preserved through websites such as http:// www.handmaps.org, which solicits viewers to upload images of maps they have drawn or received.

18. In April 2012, Google Maps revealed a special 8-bit presentation of the online maps and images of Streetview.

19. According to the review in *Compute!* magazine issue 130 (1991), Sierra On-line scanned artist-produced images for the game *King's Quest V* and rendered them in 256-color mode, giving the game its colorful and pleasing artistic feel.

20. The limitations of computing at the time of release of *Might and Magic* made it difficult to integrate map graphics into gameplay; hence, the solution was to release the game with a printed map.

21. In other words, it is much harder to navigate the map near the end, where the levels are harder, than at the beginning, even though the distance of any two sequential levels is the same.

22. These itineraries are not noted for their accuracy; in fact, as several scholars note, these maps have been disregarded by academic cartographical studies until recently, dismissed as grossly inaccurate approximations demonstrating the medieval inability to measure or represent accurately.

23. Daniel Connolly, *The Maps of Matthew Paris: Medieval Journeys through Space, Time, and Liturgy* (Woodbridge, Suffolk: Boydell, 2009), 5.

24. See Gaudio's note on this topic, "Matthew Paris," 53.

25. Connolly, *The Maps of Matthew Paris*, 28.

26. Connolly, *The Maps of Matthew Paris*, 30.

27. Kline, *Maps of Medieval Thought*, 56.

28. Kline, *Maps of Medieval Thought*, 89.

29. Kline, *Maps of Medieval Thought*, 89.

30. See Michael Gaudio's discussion of the *signum* in Matthew Paris's strip-maps in "Matthew Paris," 54–55.

15 Author, Text, and Medievalism in *The Elder Scrolls*

Michelle DiPietro

The land of Tamriel has been home to the critically acclaimed *The Elder Scrolls* (*TES*) series of computer games since the 1990s. Like the settings of many fantasy role-playing computer and video games (RPGs), Tamriel is an original setting independent from any single cultural influence, engaging players with unique places, characters, and stories vaguely reminiscent of our own past. Throughout its career, fantasy has carried a tinge of the medieval, less the recasting of the Middle Ages than the application of medieval culture, technology, and aesthetic qualities to fictional worlds, from stylized weapons and armor to walled castles. Yet the bona fide seal of 'medievalism' in *TES* is not its heroes or its strongholds, but its books.[1]

Narratology of the past two decades has lent legitimacy to the analysis of games as texts,[2] but the study of texts within games remains a new frontier. Perhaps this is because although modern games use the written word to convey lore—fabricated backstory corresponding to the game's world—it is often a footnote of gameplay. In BioWare's *Dragon Age: Origins* (2009), players encounter bits of parchment relating a rich history and mythos, only to find said information quickly relegated to the ether of the user interface. *World of Warcraft* (2004) contains many stationery books that impart lore, but all its collectible books, however amusing or interesting, prove little more than "vendor trash."[3]

The developers of *TES*, conversely, built a veritable book culture into their games. Across three games—*III: Morrowind* (2002), *IV: Oblivion* (2006), and *V: Skyrim* (2011) (henceforth *Morrowind*, *Oblivion*, and *Skyrim*)—the series includes hundreds of in-game books as digitally tactile as its weapons and armor.[4] Authored by denizens of Tamriel, books enlighten players figuratively and literally. Some relate lore, whereas others, often cleverly titled, award skill points that advance the player's character when opened: *Mace Etiquette* (*Oblivion*, *Skyrim*) boosts the blunt-weapons skill, whereas *Liminal Bridges* (*Oblivion*, *Skyrim*) improves the ability to conjure magical items and allies. Herein lies the immediate value of the books for players less amused by setting development than by the raw hack-and-slash typical of fantasy RPGs.

For those who take a bit more interest, though, the texts themselves, toted around in realistic-looking leather covers with interactive capabilities, visibility on bookshelves, and accruing weight in one's 'inventory,' witness the vibrant intellectual culture and rich history crafted for Tamriel.

In keeping in step with the fantasy genre, *TES* lore bears a distinctly medieval flavor. In literature and gaming, high fantasy deviates in setting from what C. W. Sullivan III calls "contemporary consensus reality by creating a separate world," while maintaining enough familiar features to be accessible.[5] Elements of medieval technology and material culture are often employed to maintain this foothold, at once a "distillation of [tropes] which have come down to the twentieth century as the Arthurian tradition" and a departure from the contemporary.[6] This tendency of fantasy in popular culture has been dubbed a kind of 'medievalism,' "a nostalgic impulse to rework or recreate or gesture towards the Middle Ages" involving "consideration of the Middle Ages as an aesthetic object."[7] High-fantasy video games establish the pseudohistorical via an arsenal of tropes from "castles and forests and mountains" to "heroes," "quests," and magical elements.[8] *TES* adds the codex to what M. J. Toswell deems this "useful shorthand" of medievalism.[9]

Just as the medieval grounds the *TES* games in recognizable fantasy, books and the texts within the games form elegant signifiers of the game's world. User interaction with game spaces and the objects within those spaces is key to any game's immersive quality, making players feel present within the game.[10] As Michael Nitsche has said of player relation to game spaces, "Players can only interact with the game elements as they are presented to them via the narrating entities (like the virtual camera)."[11] The physicality of *TES*'s books is thus an important world-building tool: players may engage with a book (by pressing a key or controller button), open it, scroll through its pages, and even cart it away (thievery being a series hallmark). Through their own agency, players determine how much of a text they want to read before moving on. The books' physical features steer the player's imagination toward a pseudohistorical milieu. Title pages reference books' fictional publishers, while copious quills and inkwells atop desks throughout the game, attest to the prevalence of writing. These mixed messages on book production evoke a sense of transitional technology akin to that of late fifteenth-century Europe and contribute to a premodern aesthetic.[12]

Like Nitsche's "virtual camera" analog, books in *TES* are, fittingly, "narrating entities," building the world in dribs and drabs via their contents. Through reading, players can learn about inaccessible geographical regions and glimpse a history spanning millennia, facets of the setting that simply cannot fit in the games themselves. Of most interest to this study are the authors who present unabashedly biased views on Tamriel's history and culture. Historians in *TES* employ the medieval chronicle style. The topoi of Tamrielic royal biography parallel medieval ideas of rulership. Men of letters dabble in cartography to functional and revealing ends. Scholars of magic and lore elucidate Tamriel's arcane aspects with a kind of honesty and vigor that renders the truth far from static. Such narrative vehicles transform the often tedious trudge through fantasy lore into an intellectual expedition.

This study cannot attempt to be exhaustive of the over 500 titles found throughout the series, ranging in length from one paragraph to several thousand words.[13] The texts in question witness Tamriel's historical, cultural, and academic discourses and conjure parallels to iconic medieval texts. This historically inspired content adds depth to the game world, influencing in-game choices and transforming Tamriel into a living world richer than the digitally rendered space in which it exists.

HISTORY AND BIOGRAPHY

In *Skyrim*, players face a world beset by vengeful dragons who stir from their ancient graves, bewildering and terrorizing the masses. At one stage, players must seek advice from a lore keeper who, amidst doling out much-needed perspective on the crisis, places a book upon a table: the rare and valuable *Annals of the Dragonguard (Skyrim).*[14]

Immediately the historically minded player may recall a pervasive medieval mode of historical record-keeping. While Egyptian and Babylonian rulers had long kept annual records and Roman consular lists adopted a similar format,[15] the Easter tables of the fifth and sixth centuries CE, "slowly and busily filled in with local interests by monks and scribes," made the resultant annalistic genre a medieval tradition unto itself.[16]

The *Annals of the Dragonguard* illuminate Tamriel's historical traditions in several ways. They only appear once and in reproduction at that. The scribe, Brother Annulus, who has clearly come from beyond the fourth wall, prefaces, "I have faithfully copied the following from the *Annals of the Dragonguard of Sky Haven Temple* for the years 2800–2819" (*Annals of the Dragonguard*). In essence, he has streamlined history for us. Annulus's version is also hundreds of years old in the game's present day, distancing the player from the original text's provenance. In our own Middle Ages, annalistic records traveled from abbey to abbey where monks would extract and add entries as years passed.[17] For modern historians, Beryl Smalley has likened the art of gleaning a set of annals' origination point and subsequent spread to peeling an onion: more layers continually reveal themselves.[18] For example, the Irish were prolific annalists in the Middle Ages. A set of Irish records known as the *Chronicle of Ireland,* believed extant in the early tenth century, were dispersed, interpolated, and "savagely abbreviated" over time so as to become four ostensibly different texts, one of which, the *Chronicon Scottorum*, survives only in a seventeenth-century copy.[19] By mimicking this medieval written tradition, the *Annals of the Dragonguard* lends historical weight to Skyrim's central conflict. Simultaneously, it whets players' curiosity about the similar dragon-induced catastrophes in Skyrim's past, propelling them forward in the quest for answers. Inasmuch as we have inherited variations on medieval annals, the Tamrielic reader is separated from the *Annals of the Dragonguard* in their original and entirety, left to wonder what befell those first scrawled records.

In the political landscape contemporary with gameplay, Tamriel consists of nine provinces—with each game thus far set in a different one—and ten 'races,' from the lizard-like Argonians and feline Kahjiit to Tolkienesque orcs and sundry flavors of elves and humans. Many histories center on the deeds of the Empire (whose native humans are the 'Imperials'), the ruling body with its nexus in Imperial City, Cyrodiil, and its reach extending into every province.

Third Era: A Short Timeline (Skyrim) records major events in Tamriel's past five centuries in an abbreviated chronicle style. Having debuted in *Skyrim*, the most recent installment of *TES* to date, it acquaints new players with events like the 'Oblivion Crisis' that ravaged Cyrodiil in the previous game *Oblivion* and the related assassination of Emperor Uriel Septim VII. It is otherwise a terse summary of the coronations and deaths of the Septim Imperial line. Even disputes in outlying Vvardenfell—cheekily deemed "opened for settlement" in year Third Era (3E) 414—and the founding of the province Orsinium are cast as Imperial achievements in an array of successions (*Third Era: A Short Timeline*). The Imperial author's inclination to focus history through the lens of the Empire resembles the tendency of medieval annals to favor political powers, such as the ninth-century *Royal Frankish Annals*, records of the Carolingian court from 741 to 829.[20] These medieval annals take almost exclusive interest in military achievements, foreign relations, and conquest, with Charlemagne (r. 768–814) at their epicenter as monarch, legislator, and Christian leader.[21] In an iconic entry for 772, Charlemagne's forces march deep into the heart of Saxony and destroy a religious tree called the Irminsul.[22] This combined assault on an enemy power and a final frontier of paganism in the medieval West portrays Charlemagne as a righteous expansionist in a historical source that is wholly a "powerful triumphalist narrative."[23] Though more willing to admit blemishes in the Imperial reputation, the *Third Era: A Short Timeline* remains a similarly propagandistic assertion of Imperial power over the historical record and therefore history itself.

Unlike chronicle records, medieval biographies were rhetorical and often dramatic, although allegedly nonpartisan.[24] In *TES*, *A Short Life of Uriel Septim VII (Oblivion, Skyrim)* immortalizes a ruler in such a way. The biography begins with Emperor Uriel's ascent into power and progresses to his role in leading the Empire to peace. Each chapter endows Uriel with a persona—woefully betrayed, restorer of peace, bringer of the true faith to outlying lands—consistent with the theme that he produced efficacious policies and transformed the political face of Tamriel. In all matters, Uriel ultimately proves triumphant. Though miniature by comparison, Uriel's biography bears resemblance to the medieval *Life of Charlemagne*.[25]

Charlemagne, Rosamond McKitterick writes, "is one of the few major rulers in European history for whom there is an agreed stereotype"; history has fashioned him as equal parts warrior, conqueror, and champion of faith and learning.[26] This persona applies almost verbatim to Uriel, including in his regime's promotion of learning and worldliness; the court under Uriel touted its role in publishing, to be examined below, and Charlemagne was a great lover of Latin, Greek, and the liberal arts.[27]

Even their cults are similar. Uriel's biography appears in *Oblivion*, in which Uriel himself exists briefly, much as the cult of Charlemagne resonated in literature and history not long after his death.[28] In *Skyrim*, a game set 200 years later and in a different province, Uriel's biography appears in practically every third household. From this the player can interpret Uriel as a posthumous hero, a sort of Tamrielic Charlemagne whose deeds have made him a legend in his own right. Tamriel's history feels mutable and alive, and the events of *Oblivion*, in which players may have taken part, have become inextricably enmeshed in that history. By the same token, the prevalence of Imperial texts attests to the extensive spread of Imperial power, even when that power does not view all its constituents favorably.

OUTSIDERS AND EMPIRE

When the Collector's Edition of *Oblivion* shipped in 2006, it contained a booklet called *A Pocket Guide to the Empire* by the Imperial Geographical Society.[29] This world handbook never actually appears in-game, yet *Third Era: A Short Timeline* records its third-edition printing as though it were an in-game text. This unique entry in Tamriel's historical record offers two important revelations: the Empire envisions its territory as encompassing all of Tamriel and monopolizes the very process of charting that territory. Within *Third Era: A Short Timeline*, *A Pocket Guide to the Empire* is one facet of an Imperial panegyric, a cartographic and cultural achievement wedged between the military feats of a political monolith. In-game texts on geography and travel reveal that this sense of dominance over distant lands extends to the populations therein, with less-than-diplomatic effects. Despite their roles as geographers and observers, the authors of these texts interweave fact and bias into a body of world views more scintillating than any map or atlas.

An Explorer's Guide to Skyrim (*Skyrim*) by Imperial Viscount Marcius Carvain is a guide to more adventurous feats in the Norse-inspired province, Skyrim. Carvain writes for an audience of noble Imperials who seldom visit Skyrim's countryside as it is "far from hospitable, a place of fierce, wild beauty" that one must possess "refinement to truly appreciate" (*An Explorer's Guide to Skyrim*). Although Skyrim has been assimilated into the Empire, a diminutive view of the population prevails: its local rulers appear worldly, while the "provincials and village folk" harbor old superstitions

(*An Explorer's Guide to Skyrim*). To Carvain, Skyrim is a playground for the wealthy elite with an exploratory impulse, and the Nords who populate it are simpletons ruled by gracious 'jarls' eager to host and indulge an Imperial.

Having witnessed and read about the Empire's expansionism, it is difficult for any player not to develop opinions about Tamriel's political landscape. In every *TES* game so far, players have been presented with the chance to join any number of factions, sometimes including the Imperial Legion. In *Skyrim*, the eponymous province has grown restless under Imperial domination, which has led to civil war. The rebel Stormcloaks, also a joinable faction, abound in Skyrim. Historical context can inform whether players feel drawn to join the sprawling superpower that is the Imperial armed forces, or to outright rebel against it to defend Skyrim's independence.

Provinces of Tamriel (Morrowind, Oblivion) is a cursory introduction to the geography and culture of each Imperial province. For the unnamed author, Skyrim's people are bold and warlike, while only their ancestors were unrestrained. Other nations merit less gentle opinions. Valenwood has few Imperial roads and mainly "undeveloped footpaths," fashioning it wild and rustic (*Provinces of Tamriel*). Of the Khajiit territory, Elsweyr the author contrasts the northern Khajiit, "aggressive and territorial tribal raiders periodically united under tribal warlords" with the "settled south," which "has been quick to adopt Imperial ways" (*Provinces of Tamriel*). Summing up, the Imperial city's home province of Cyrodiil is dubbed "the cradle of Human Imperial high culture," making the author's heritage less than dubious (*Provinces of Tamriel*).

To the Empire, these populations that "[dare] to stand invitingly at their borders"[30] share two common qualities: they are Imperial acquisitions and they are geographically distant or distinct from the heart of the empire. Cartographers of Tamriel see outlying provinces as wild and alien, views which extend to the populations therein. Margins and political frontiers similarly influenced how medieval populations saw the world. As Robert Bartlett explains, "When the Anglo-Normans looked west to Wales and Ireland they saw what were ostensibly barbarians."[31] John Gillingham has pointed out that such attitudes became prominent in the Anglo-Norman world of the twelfth century, deeper than the nationalistic 'us' and 'them' distinction, a "view that certain people are so inferior as to belong to a distinctly lower order of society."[32]

William of Malmesbury (1080–1143) and Gerald of Wales (1146–1223) promulgated such attitudes. William envisioned a world in which Anglo-Norman England was the height of civilization and culture.[33] His contemporary barbarians were the poverty-stricken and provincial Irish. William asserts that Irish soil "lacks all advantages, and so poor ... are its cultivators that it can produce only a ragged mob of Irishmen outside the towns," whereas the English and French, being civilized town-dwellers, "carry on trade and commerce."[34] Decades later, Gerald of Wales made similar observations of Ireland and Wales. The Welsh lack sophisticated agriculture and "pay no attention to commerce, shipping, or industry."[35] The Irish, too, lack mechanical arts and live in primitive settlements, with "little use for the money-making of towns."[36] Absence of manufacturing, in the case of the northern Khajiit of Tamriel and of discernible towns for the inhabitants of Valenwood, brings Tamrielic outsiders as much disdain as the medieval Irish and Welsh faced from the Anglo-Normans.

Societies peripheral to an empire, whether the Anglo-Norman world or Tamriel's Empire, suffer judgment of their worth based on agrarian development and settlement, a judgment that extends to their people and is rooted in the fundamental desire of the observers to compare outsiders to themselves. *Provinces of Tamriel* cares not for traditions or broader culture; a hostile, undeveloped landscape solidifies a population's barbarism, be that Valenwood's scattered settlements and disused roads or Elsweyr's dry northern grasslands, resistant to the plantations that drive commerce in the aristocratic south. Northern Elsweyr may border the Imperial nation, but its geography removes it from the same model of civilization. As Jeffrey Jerome Cohen has noted, in perpetuating the idea that fringe populations were beastly or barbaric, Anglo-Norman writers made their subjects "primitive, subhuman, incomprehensible in order to render the taking of their lands unproblematic."[37] In *Morrowind*, *Oblivion*, and *Skyrim*, conquest is not especially recent and the political face of Tamriel is no stranger to change, but the attitudes of the conquerors pervade.

At the same time, *Provinces of Tamriel* takes care to separate the Empire from acts of outright subjugation. When playing *Morrowind*, players encounter Argonians in shackles, the result of regular raids by the citizens of Morrowind to seize Argonians from their home province of Black Marsh and bring them back as slaves. *Provinces of Tamriel* informs us that slavery is banned under Imperial law, yet some unruly areas of Morrowind persist in it. Similarly, when William of Malmesbury briefly mentions slavery in England, he portrays it as owing to the Danes' corruptive influence.[38] In *TES*, freeing slaves is an optional course of action, though it often leads to players being branded as criminals and pursued by local authorities. Apart from empathy, the context offered by *Provinces of Tamriel* can inform players' decisions to either stand up to slavery or abide by Morrowind's Imperially disavowed laws. In Tamriel and historical reality, authors may convey negative attitudes towards outsiders but still distance their favored political powers from any truly atrocious acts.

Despite their pejorative appearances, Anglo-Norman observations proved formative to medieval ethnography. Their methods, developed independently of classical exemplars, emphasized "detail, a sense of society as an organic whole, and a skilful use of comparative method."[39] Such inclinations also work in the favor of Tamriel's geographical texts. Without access to such regions as Valenwood, Elsweyr, and Black Marsh in-game, these descriptive texts engage players in a kind of armchair tourism, learning as much from the biases of their tour guides as from the facts they convey.

SCHOLARS

Some nods to medieval textual traditions are unapologetically bold. The *TES* book *De Rerum Dirennis* (*Oblivion, Skyrim*), apart from being a pleasure to say out loud, is an obvious play on the topical titles of medieval and classical treatises. Isidore of Seville in the seventh century and the Venerable Bede (c. 672–735) in the eighth produced works known as *De natura rerum*, "On the nature of things," inspired by Lucretius' first-century poem *De rerum natura*.[40] Both medieval works aimed to "[demystify] natural phenomena through reason," especially meteorology and cosmology.[41] *De Rerum Dirennis*, roughly "On the deeds of the Direnni," finds itself an odd fit in this company, being a biography of Tamrielic alchemist Vorian Direnni's clan. Amidst his ancestors' ins and outs with the Mage's guild and brushes with historical rulers over his 600 years of life, Vorian Direnni expertly weaves his knowledge on the origin of the dangerous alchemical solvent 'Glow Dust.' The book's effect on the player is twofold. On the one hand, its grasp at Latin evokes the medieval. The Latin legacy as inherited from the Roman Empire was established in the medieval West through the writings of the Latin fathers and came to dominate the learned writing of the early medieval west.[42] By emulating a well-known Latin title, the designers of *TES* simultaneously grant Vorian Direnni's work authority in the field of alchemy and allow his name to be mentioned in the same breath as influential thinkers such as Isidore and Bede. At the same time, the obviously authoritative Vorian Direnni also informs the player's perspective on alchemy, an optional part of gameplay that allows players to concoct potions and poisons from ingredients found throughout the game world. *De Rerum Dirennis* allows players to see alchemy as more than a fun game mechanic. It is an ancient practice with a storied history, put through generations of painstaking tests (and that remains unperfected as fledgling alchemists will notice). Alchemy's boons, from restoring health to poisoning foes, are only available thanks to the efforts of dedicated scholars such as Vorian Direnni.

Another text further shows that authority is paramount among Tamriel's learned elite. In *The Varieties of Faith in the Empire* (*Morrowind*), author Brother Mikhael Karkuxor adopts the persona of 'scholar as compiler of knowledge,' astutely cataloging the deities native to Tamriel. Brother Karkuxor describes eight pantheons and sixty-one deities past, present, and foreign, only a fraction of whom appear in-game. Yet his knowledge of the gods of the subjugated Argonian race is incomplete. "The omission of any reference to the worships of the Argonians of Black Marsh," he explains, "is a result of my complete inadequacy in reconciling the obscure and contradictory accounts available to me on that subject" (*Varieties of Faith in the Empire*). This corroborates the Argonians' marginalized status as seen in-game. Yet Karkuxor's statement is also an appeal to authority. It reveals that his book is a compilation of sources, sometimes too many to reconcile, and he will only dignify it with authoritative sources. In his seventh-century *Etymologies*, Isidore of Seville describes the pagan gods in a similarly detailed fashion.[43] In doing so, he repeatedly defers to authority, culling information from at least eleven authors, from Tertullian to Augustine.[44] Like Isidore, Brother Karkuxor wants to be thorough for his readers' benefit. If anything, Karkuxor's disclaimer simply shows a restraint absent from Isidore, who was wont to include every opinion available, dissonance be damned.[45] *Varieties of Faith* exposes players to an intellectual landscape so dynamic that conflicting opinions sometimes obscure the truth.

Nowhere is this climate of diverging minds more evident than in *Response to Bero's Speech* (*Morrowind, Oblivion, Skyrim*). Here Malviser, a Battlemage—a hired combatant skilled in 'Destruction' magic—deals in a brand of skepticism that fans the flames of scholarly debate within *TES*. Malviser reacts to the speech given by Berevar Bero, a practitioner of 'Illusion' magic, over the purity of Destruction magic in a Battlemage's arsenal. Says Malviser of his opponent, "His intent was to show that where it matters, the Battlemage relies on other Schools of Magicka, not the School of Destruction which is supposedly a Battlemage's particular forte" (*Response to Bero's Speech*). Destruction magic is more complex than his opponent, an outsider, can understand, a remark that leaves Malviser so flabbergasted that he implores, "How can one respond to this?" The answer: with acerbity and tried rhetorical techniques.

In *Morrowind* and *Oblivion*, mages such as Malviser belong to a guild and in *Skyrim* occupy a remote college. Their status as an intellectual elite beyond monastic confines resembles the scholastics of the twelfth century, especially the fiery Peter Abelard (1079–1142), whose theological works provoked controversy and accusations of heresy, and Bernard of Clairvaux (1090–1153), a powerful ecclesiast and intellectual adversary of Abelard's.[46] Letters exchanged between these two men reveal elements of their discourse that Malviser also employs. In Peter Abelard's letter, relating a collision of minds over his controversial *Theologia*, he admonishes Bernard, "a secret enemy, who has . . . now blazed out into such great envy that he could not bear the fame of my writings."[47] This accusation undermines the legitimacy of Bernard's claims while not cutting so deep as to devalue him as a rival. Malviser also dignifies Bero's misguided points by deigning to respond, but he has a less gentle opinion of the man; it must be Bero's deceptive character as an Illusion mage that drove him to mislead the public with his false ideas. "Illusion is, after all, all about masking the truth," he writes (*Response to Bero's Speech*). Through his well-informed text, Malviser educates the player on the history and theory of magic while demonstrating that Tamriel's intellectual culture is mixed and contentious.

Magic is very real in Tamriel, and players may customize their magical proficiencies to fit their preferred play style. One can seamlessly blend Illusion and Destruction magic, turning frenzied enemies against each other before unleashing a firestorm upon them, thus getting the best of Malviser's and Bero's worlds. Essentially, players take away from *Response to Bero's Speech* a sense that their choices have meaning and that magic carries complex connotations. They may strive for consistency with this context or eschew it completely.

Tamriel's academic texts, infused with the imagined and the medieval, make great strides towards building a believable world that will immerse players. More visibly, they denote a climate of energetic debate, populating Tamriel with a host of minds, both modest and ruthless. Some use knowledge to educate, in the manner of Vorian Direnni, while those like Brother Karkuxor can find the wealth of it overwhelming. Simultaneously, they convey rigorous discourse without always proving who is right. Players presented with divergent opinions and unresolved questions become enmeshed in debates that define game-world culture simply by reading about them. Much the way medieval thinkers are forever separate from us in time, *TES* players must decide by written evidence alone whose version of the truth is more worthy.

CONCLUSION

This modest selection of texts demonstrates the power of the written word to enrich a fantasy setting, but we have barely scratched the surface of Tamriel's book culture. Much more could be said about the physicality of these books and trends in their ownership. No single library or shop in any *TES* game contains all of Tamriel's texts. Perhaps trends in ownership parallel relationships between status, literacy, and possession of books in the Middle Ages.[48] To further address content, a Scandinavian specialist may reveal parallels nestled amidst *Skyrim*'s Norse-influenced tales, derivative runic alphabet, and heroic themes. Religious texts are also well represented in the *TES* corpus, but Tamriel's pantheons so diverge from medieval Europe's predominant monotheisms—not to mention that several Tamrielic gods actually appear in-game—that a comparison would prove a colossal undertaking. From hagiographies like *Trials of St. Alessia* (*Oblivion*, *Skyrim*), to the nebulous boundary between miracles and player-accessible magic, theology is a creature worthy of its own study. As more games join the series in future years, medievalists and bibliophiles face endless possibilities.

On the relationship between medieval authorship and time, M. T. Clanchy has noted that medieval monastic writers most often dedicated their works to God or posterity, not their contemporaries: "Monasticism gave writers the humility or the arrogance, depending on one's point of view, to care about posterity."[49] In all their appreciation for future readers, medieval authors, monastic or otherwise, could never have envisioned that their works would influence the intellectual landscapes of imagined worlds. The books of *TES* make Tamriel familiar to the collective medieval fantasy imagination without the baggage of historical accuracy. Inasmuch as any RPG lends escapism, the books of *TES* encourage players to take pause between slaughtering supernatural foes and experience immersion through textual discovery.

NOTES

1. I owe thanks to Timothy Anstedt for suggestions at the start of this project and to Karl Kinsella of the University of Oxford for his invaluable feedback throughout.
2. Jan Simons, "Narratives, Games, and Theory," *Gaming Studies* 7, no. 1 (2007): http://gamestudies.org/0701/articles/simons (accessed July 28, 2012).
3. *WoWWiki*, "Vendor Trash," http://www.wowwiki.com/Vendor_trash (accessed July 28, 2012). The term describes items that "have little or no function in the game except to be sold to [a non-playable character] vendor for money."
4. Other *TES* games contain considerably fewer texts and have been excluded for brevity.
5. C. W. Sullivan, "High Fantasy," in *The International Companion Encyclopedia of Children's Literature*, 2nd ed., ed. Peter Hunt (London: Routledge, 2004), 436, 437.
6. Sullivan, "High Fantasy," 438.
7. M. J. Toswell, "The Tropes of Medievalism," *Studies in Medievalism* 17 (2009): 69.
8. Toswell, "Tropes," 69–71.
9. Toswell, "Tropes," 70.
10. Werner Wirth et al., "A Process Model of the Formation of Spatial Presence Experiences," *Media Psychology* 9 (2007): 496.
11. Michael Nitsche, *Video Game Spaces* (Cambridge, MA: MIT Press, 2008), 56.
12. Christopher de Hamel, *A History of Illuminated Manuscripts*, 2nd ed. (London: Phaidon Press, 1994), 13
13. *The Unofficial Elder Scrolls Pages*, "Lore: Books," http://www.uesp.net/wiki/Lore:Books (accessed June 8, 2013). The total represents individual titles and does not account for the multiple discrete volumes of some texts, which would bring the total to 700.
14. All texts are quoted as they appear in the listed game(s).
15. Bernhard Walter Scholz with Barbara Rogers, introduction to *Carolingian Chronicles: The Royal Frankish Annals and Nithard's Histories* (Ann Arbor: University of Michigan Press, 1972), 3.
16. Beryl Smalley, *Historians in the Middle Ages* (London: Thames and Hudson, 1974), 56–58.
17. Smalley, *Historians*, 58.
18. Smalley, *Historians*, 58.
19. Kathleen Hughes, *Early Christian Ireland: Introduction to the Sources* (London: Camelot Press, 1972), 114.
20. *Royal Frankish Annals* in *Carolingian Chronicles: The Royal Frankish Annals and Nithard's Histories*, ed. and trans. Bernhard Walter Scholz with Barbara Rogers (Ann Arbor: University of Michigan Press, 1972).
21. Scholz, introduction to *Carolingian Chronicles*, 3.
22. *Royal Frankish Annals*, 48–49.
23. Rosamond McKitterick, *Charlemagne: The Formation of a European Identity* (Cambridge, UK: Cambridge University Press, 2008), 31.
24. Alan Thacker, "Bede and History," in *The Cambridge Companion to Bede*, ed. Scott DeGregorio (Cambridge, UK: Cambridge University Press, 2010), 170.
25. Einhard, *Life of Charlemagne*, trans. Samuel Epes Turner (New York: Harper and Brothers, 1880), on *Fordham Medieval Sourcebook*, http://www.fordham.edu/Halsall/basis/einhard.asp (accessed July 30, 2012).
26. McKitterick, *Charlemagne*, 1.
27. Einhard, *Life of Charlemagne*, ch. 7.

28. McKitterick, *Charlemagne*, 22–27: McKitterick points to the ninth-century works of the Poeta Saxo.
29. *The Unofficial Elder Scrolls Pages*, "Pocket Guide to the Empire 3rd Edition," http://www.uesp.net/wiki/Lore:Pocket_Guide_to_the_Empire,_3rd_Edition (accessed July 29, 2012).
30. Jeffrey Jerome Cohen, "Hybrids, Monsters, and Borderlands," in *The Postcolonial Middle Ages*, ed. Jeffrey Jerome Cohen (Bakingstoke, UK: MacMillan, 2000), 86.
31. Robert Bartlett, *Gerald of Wales: 1146–1223* (Oxford: Clarendon Press, 1982), 158.
32. John Gillingham, "The Beginnings of English Imperialism," *Journal of Historical Sociology* 5, no. 4 (1992): 397.
33. William of Malmesbury, *Gesta Regum Anglorum: The History of the English Kings*, ed. and trans. R. A. B. Mynors, Rodney M. Thompson, and Michael Winterbottom, 2 vols. (Oxford: Clarendon Press, 1998–99), 1:134–35; cf. Bartlett, *Gerald of Wales*, 158.
34. William of Malmesbury, *History*, 1:738–41; cf. Bartlett, *Gerald of Wales*, 159.
35. Gerald of Wales, *The Description of Wales*, in *The Journey through Wales and the Description of Wales*, ed. and trans. Lewis Thorpe (Harmondsworth, UK: Penguin, 1978), 233.
36. Gerald of Wales, *History and Topography of Ireland*, ed. and trans. John J. O'Meara, (Atlantic Highlands, NJ: Humanities Press, 1982), 102; cf. Bartlett, *Gerald of Wales*, 159.
37. Cohen, "Hybrids," 87.
38. William of Malmesbury, *History*, 1:362–63.
39. Bartlett, *Gerald of Wales*, 175.
40. Calvin B. Kendall and Faith Wallis, introduction to *Bede: On the Nature of Things and On Times* (Liverpool: Liverpool University Press, 2011), 7–9, 1; cf. Kendall and Wallis, 191. Lucretius was known to Isidore, but not to Bede.
41. Kendall and Wallis, *Bede*, 2.
42. Rosalind Love, "The World of Latin Learning," in *The Cambridge Companion to Bede*, ed. Scott DeGregorio (Cambridge, UK: Cambridge University Press, 2010), 43.
43. Isidore of Seville, *Etymologies*, 183–190.
44. Katherine Nell Macfarlane, "Isidore of Seville on the Pagan Gods (Origines VIII.11)," *Transactions of the American Philosophical Society* 70, no. 3 (1980): 7.
45. Macfarlane, "Isidore of Seville," 4.
46. Jan M. Ziolkwoski, introduction to *Letters of Peter Abelard: Beyond the Personal*, trans. Jan M. Ziolkowski (Washington, DC: Catholic University of America Press, 2008), xiv, xxxiii.
47. Peter Abelard, "Letter 15" in *Letters of Peter Abelard: Beyond the Personal*, trans. Jan M. Ziolkowski (Washington DC: Catholic University of America Press, 2008), 108–109.
48. Rosamond McKitterick, *The Carolingians and the Written Word* (Cambridge, UK: Cambridge University Press, 1989), 157–58. McKitterick describes these trends in an early medieval context.
49. M. T. Clanchy, *From Memory to Written Record: England 1066–1307*, 2nd ed. (Oxford: Blackwell, 1993), 146.

16 Technophilia and Technophobia in Online Medieval Fantasy Games

Nick Webber

The settings of massively multiplayer online role-playing games (MMORPGs) are, in many cases, worlds that draw heavily on a mixture of historical medieval societies (usually European or Japanese) and the traditions of other computer games, fantasy literature, and offline games (e.g., *Dungeons & Dragons* and similar 'sword and sorcery' games). According to one survey site, more than 85 percent of MMORPGs can be classified as part of the fantasy genre (as opposed to science fiction, for example).[1] Among this group are the most populous games of this kind, including *World of Warcraft* (2004–10) and *Aion* (2008), as well as notable others, such as *Everquest* (1999) and *Rift* (2011).[2] All of these could reasonably be characterized as 'medieval fantasy.' Of particular significance in the construction of these 'medieval' settings is the treatment of science and technology, especially contemporary (modern) science and industrial technology. As one might expect of a pseudomedieval environment, computers and cell phones are not in ready supply, but fantasy MMORPGs do accommodate and adapt to ideas of science and technology in various ways that can feel uncomfortable against the medievalized background otherwise portrayed.

In what follows I will engage with treatments of science and technology in two MMORPGs, Blizzard Entertainment's hugely successful *World of Warcraft* (2004)[3] and Trion Worlds' smaller, but arguably more complex, *Rift* (2011).[4] I will explore three main areas: the representation of science and technology, the relationship between science/technology and religion, and the relationship between science/technology and magic. In the course of this engagement I will also bring out three themes: the notion of technophobia and the opposition between contemporary and medieval constructions of technology; the use of medieval games not as ways to represent the past, but rather as ways of saying something about ourselves; and the way in which MMORPGs interpret and respond to contemporary attitudes to technology, in particular the technophilia of the societies that produce and play them. Although this analysis can by no means be exhaustive, I aim to present some ideas that can help us to understand these two games more fully as cultural objects that have some more general application to our understanding of medieval fantasy games and that offer a perspective on our relationship with science and technology.

MEDIEVALISM, TECHNOLOGY, AND GAMES

A relatively small amount of existing literature considers video games as a locus of medievalism. Video games have come to the medievalism debate rather late, a combination no doubt of their relatively recent nascence and scholarly struggles to establish whether or not they were an appropriately 'serious' object of study.[5] And although scholars have given quite extensive consideration to the relationship of technology and games, the vast majority of this has concerned technology external to the game, focusing on the use of technology as a mechanism to access, facilitate, and experience games. In short, most previous work has discussed games in the context of science and technology, as opposed to science and technology in the context of games.

Understandably, more attention has been paid to the presentation of science and technology in science-fiction literature and games than in medieval fantasy literature and games. Yet in inflecting the contemporary through analysis of the imagined future, some approaches to science fiction have a useful bearing on my attempt here to inflect the contemporary through an analysis of a fantasy past. The divide between science fiction and fantasy is anyway indistinct, and Brent Moberly and Kevin Moberly note that the two blur together in the popular imagination.[6] In this regard, we might beneficially draw upon Daniel Dinello's work, which attempts to understand the relationship between the utopian technological visions of contemporary scientists and the technological pessimism of science fiction.[7]

In terms of the context of science and technology, David Noble has explored the close historical link between technology and religion, arguing that the modern assumption that science and religion are opposites or in some way functionally at odds with one another ignores centuries of interleaved development.[8] Eddo Stern offers an interesting reflection on the relationship between technology and magic, considering them as narrative elements that, through their affordances and limitations, structure the play experience of MMORPGs.[9] The role of magic as a narrative device has also been considered by Amy Kaufman[10] in terms of its relationship to gender, and Celia Pearce has referred to fantasy MMORPGs as "an environment where nature and magic are integrally intertwined."[11] .

We must also be aware of the perceived connection between industrial technology and capitalist economic approaches on which some analyses of video games have drawn. Moberly and Moberly suggest that medievalism in science-fiction games offers "a compelling antidote to the worst excesses of technological, third-stage capitalism," even though the creation of such games depends on these conditions.[12] Oliver Traxel observes that the 'pseudomedieval' elements of many game titles are driven by market forces, set against aspects that are either authentic or slight elaborations on a true medieval past (although technology is one element that is treated authentically in Traxel's experience).[13] Elsewhere, Scott Rettberg considers *World of Warcraft* as a locus of corporate ideology, and Andrew Baerg explores the idea that the rationality and risk management elements of computer role-playing games (RPGs) respond to a modern, neoliberal context.[14]

At first glance, this all seems very much about technology and very little about science. However, it is important to note that technology, as it appears here, is, in many ways, science articulated in physical or tangible form; thus, it becomes difficult to disentangle the two on close examination. Furthermore, science is a mechanism through which the world can be understood and explained, and in what follows it will play a significant role. For much as these games manifest messages and ideologies through technology, they also do so in a more subtle manner through the way in which they treat knowledge of the functioning of the world.

SCIENCE AND TECHNOLOGY

The rejection of science and (industrial) technology is a commonplace central principle of medievalizing ideas, both historically and in more modern contexts. The notionally anti-industrial Arts and Crafts movement of the nineteenth century conceived of a simpler world devoid of the oppressive technology of the Industrial Revolution; one prominent member, William Morris, wrote of what Dinello has called a "pastoral earthly paradise of the future that recreated the pre-industrial past."[15] In the twentieth century, J.R.R. Tolkien's imagined Middle Earth set the gentle rural Englishness of the Shire, home of his famous *Hobbit*, against the dark protoindustrial gloom of Mordor.[16] More recently, we might see ideas of organic farming and concerns about the health effects of cell phone masts as indicative of a cultural tendency to reject technological intervention, especially when it is seen as intruding upon or disrupting a loosely conceived 'nature.'

To generalize from Moberly and Moberly's point above, video games seem a strange place to look for discourses of this kind, as to reject science and technology would be to reject the medium through which such games are accessed and experienced. Even where elements of computer culture seek an alternative to the most widely applied model of computer consumption, by expressing a countercultural ideology or Do It Yourself (DIY) ethic in contrast to a perceived industrial capitalist appropriation of a technological 'commons,' the facts of the technology and the underpinning science remain constant. It is not, then, usual for computer culture to practice rejection of itself. For MMORPGs, this technological association is even more pronounced, and the requirement to remain online in order to play, and the sense of compulsion to play as much as you can (and thus be online as much as you can), may evoke, for some, echoes of the technological dystopias of cyberpunk fiction.[17]

But fantasy video games do, of course, draw upon a rich legacy of pre-industrial settings depicted in literature, in the creative arts, and in games. Fantasy literature, popularized by writers such as Tolkien, has grown into a huge market: many writers are now household names (J. K. Rowling, for example), and nonliterary forms abound across a multitude of media. In game terms, *Dungeons & Dragons*, published originally in 1974,[18] was one of the first prominent RPGs, offering in essence an interpretation of a literary fantasy setting that balanced game mechanics with rich, character-focused narratives. The corresponding flood of tabletop RPGs may represent only a small economic presence in the contemporary entertainment market, but their systematization of the fantasy experience provides the inspiration for many highly successful video games, *World of Warcraft* and *Rift* included. This, then, is a pedigree couched firmly in constructions of medieval worlds. Following Traxel, we might conceive of these worlds therefore as balancing three aspects, those of authenticity, elaboration, and pseudomedievalism, and thus the extent to which they focus on authenticity in many ways conditions their capacity to reflect attitudes to (industrial) technology and, to a lesser extent, science.

The world of Azeroth, the setting for *World of Warcraft*, is extensively pseudomedieval in nature. With its variety of nonhuman (albeit humanoid) races, pervasive magic, and islands that float in midair, it is clearly not in pursuit of any essential authenticity as a medieval world. It does, however, draw upon many of the standard tropes of medieval *fantasy* worlds: characters' weapons include swords and bows, player organizations are called guilds, and dragons and undead abound, for example. In this respect, *World of Warcraft* evidences a conservatism in its approach to the notion of a fantasy world but adds to this numerous popular culture references to things outside the game. As such, Azeroth as a world is easy for players to understand: it draws upon well-known conceptions of medieval fantasy and marries them to the players' real-world (entertainment) context.

How then might science and technology in such a world be imagined? In *World of Warcraft*, the portrayal of postmedieval technology in particular is intriguing; not only does *World of Warcraft* include gunpowder weapons, but also a broad spectrum of more modern technology: motorbikes, zeppelins, and biplanes. Furthermore, technology is written into the landscape of *World of Warcraft*: where there are forests, there are logging machines; where there is oil, there are refineries. Modern technology is thus omnipresent and yet not key to the gameplay experience, providing narrative and aesthetic elements but in most cases sitting quietly alongside less-technological innovations and offering equivalent (or sometimes inferior) performance, such that guns are only as powerful as longbows and motorbikes travel only as fast as horses run.

Within this modern technological aesthetic, however, can be seen much of the pessimism Dinello identifies in science fiction. Examining the presentation of war and history in *World of Warcraft*, Esther MacCullum-Stewart highlights the associations the player is invited to make when confronted with a vision of zeppelins and smoking oil refineries. She reminds us of the link between zeppelins and dystopic progress, noting that, even though these are tubby, comedic zeppelins as opposed to sleek ships that conjure fascist associations, in-game dialogue still references the Hindenburg disaster of 1937. Elsewhere, she records, biplanes sit unused in abandoned airfields or crashed on mountainsides, while the Alliance that owns them instead employs griffons and other 'low-tech' flying beasts.[19] Significant, also, are the oil refineries and other activities of resource exploitation. In *World of Warcraft*, these are generally the activities of the Venture Trading Company, which can be found in various game locations "deforesting and plundering the world" as one game-related site suggests.[20] Venture Co. refineries belch fumes, their logging machines deforest whole zones, and they leave pools of pollution behind them.

For technology at its most dystopic, though, we must look to the underground city of Gnomeregan, once the home of the gnomish race. According to game lore, a race of troggs, reminiscent of Wellsian brutes, invaded the city, prompting its defenders to flood the halls with radioactive gas, unwittingly turning the city into an uninhabitable wasteland.[21] Now only troggs, twisted leper gnomes, and robots inhabit the halls, along with a few 'boss' monsters, including the evil overlord, Mekgineer Thermaplugg. Thermaplugg sits inside a great mechanical battle suit and is portrayed as the engineering equivalent of a mad scientist; it was his idea, so the story runs, to deploy the radioactive gas in the first place. And, indeed, Thermaplugg is not the only mad scientist character we can locate among the villains of *World of Warcraft*: elsewhere we find a selection of mad scientists responsible for a variety of typically science-fiction sins, creating stitched together flesh giants or refining deadly plague viruses. Indeed, this theme is used widely enough that there is a specific mad scientist model to convey the principle: typically undead, sporting mismatched glasses and a chemical tank backpack, and on occasion a bloodied meat cleaver.[22]

Clearly the discourse of technology in *World of Warcraft* is not a positive one. MacCullum-Stewart's analysis, in connecting many of these things to ideas of twentieth-century war, reminds us of the attitudes to technology that came out of the mechanical age. As Dinello observes, the use of machines in war hastened the demise of the sense of techno-utopianism that had flourished in many corners of society during the nineteenth century (the Arts and Crafts movement, of course, excepted).[23] But the breadth of the pessimism in *World of Warcraft*, and the number of science-fiction tropes on which it draws, suggest a more substantial rejection of technology than just that for military purposes. We might see in the Venture Co. a cynicism about capitalism and industrial production more generally and a comment on the exploitative and destructive tendencies identified by Moberly and Moberly in the Star Wars universe, where they perceive a "vast technological and commercial conspiracy."[24]

However, *World of Warcraft* makes comment not only upon industrial technology but also upon science, too, and indeed upon nonindustrial technology. For in *World of Warcraft*, players can produce their own technology via the Engineering trade skill. Through this, players can produce a wide-spread collection of eclectic and occasionally useful equipment, including explosives, the aforementioned motorbikes, mechanical chickens, and teleportation devices. And yet while the devices created may offer gameplay-affecting powers and are limited in many cases exclusively to engineers, there is here, again, a tacit rejection of technology. Attractive but tremendously expensive, engineered devices are also inherently flawed: there is a continual risk of malfunction. Goblin Rocket Boots may speed your character forward along his or her way or, if you are unlucky, they may explode. The Ultrasafe Transporter is anything but: the unfortunate may be temporarily transformed along the way to a different race, gender, size, or, in extreme cases, into a chicken.[25]

So *World of Warcraft* takes a critical stance not only on industrial technology, but also on technologies that we might consider akin to the products of an eccentric inventor. The greater the technological scale, the greater the negative outcome, but it is a scale that effectively starts with exploding footwear and works up. *World of Warcraft* does not reject technology in pursuit of authenticity, as is evident from its heavily pseudomedieval aesthetic. Nor, too, would the critique it offers make sense in a medieval context: in rejecting both technology and science, *World of Warcraft* rejects not only Enlightenment constructions of progress but also medieval conceptions of perfection and the strong association between salvation and the useful arts.[26] Indeed, we can only conclude that *World of Warcraft* offers no true commentary on the medieval past and makes no pretense to offer a commentary on the future. The presentation of technology—of a radiation-blighted city, rapacious exploitation of the land, and dangerously unreliable flying machines—offers comment only on our contemporary situation. MacCullum-Stewart observes that, "In putting forward a vision of a world in which war was a fundamental part of the economy, history and landscape, Blizzard is also sending out less overt messages about the rightness of warfare as an everyday activity."[27] In its portrayal of science and technology, Blizzard conveys similar, albeit more explicit, messages about the nature of human progress and our relationship to the planet on which we live.

SCIENCE, TECHNOLOGY, AND RELIGION

Andrew Higson has observed that a medieval setting offers us a space to explore taboo subjects or socially uncomfortable behaviors;[28] in *World of Warcraft*, we can see a medieval game used not to represent the past but as a way of saying something about ourselves. But perhaps because *World of Warcraft* was designed with mass appeal in mind and has a large user base, it makes quite simple and unsophisticated statements about what are actually subtle and nuanced debates. These are, certainly, comfortable mainstream positions, and although they are not indisputable, they are not particularly alienating. In *Rift*, conversely, the smaller audience perhaps allows a more complicated engagement with a more complicated debate, and rather than inviting us to share a position, *Rift* positions us to ask some questions about a relationship. In this instance, the relationship in question is that between technology and religion. Once again wearing the trappings of pseudomedieval fantasy, *Rift* reflects a division between extreme positions of both a scientific and religious nature and the concept that the two are in direct opposition. Thus, *Rift* presents not only a pseudomedieval aesthetic but also evokes a popular conception of medieval Western Europe, of a Church beleaguered by heretics, and of the persecution of Galileo.

Within the world of *Rift*, players can opt to join one of two sides, Guardian or Defiant, functionally identical (in terms of game mechanics) yet divided on matters of principle and ideology, sharing a common (notionally evil) enemy. *Rift*'s world, Telara, is being invaded from other planes by six dragons, led by Regulos, the dragon of death. The game introduces players into the world through a short prelude before bringing them into the persistent realm in which the majority of gameplay takes place and in which Guardians and Defiant fight one another and (occasionally together) the planar invaders. All player-characters are of a type known as Ascended— superhuman(oid)s in an epic-heroic mold.

It is in the difference in principles and ideologies, however, that *Rift* poses its questions, through a basic division. The Guardians worship the five gods of the Vigil, whom they see as the key to defeating Regulos; but at the time the main game takes place, the gods are silent. The Defiant, conversely, seek success through technological innovation combined with powerful magic. To the Guardians, the Defiant are blasphemers and heretics; to the Defiant, the Guardians are foolish and deluded, denying their own agency in shaping their future. The exploration of these ideas begins even as the player, through a newly created character, experiences the prelude. For a Guardian character, the 'moment' of *Rift* lies in the future; the prelude occurs twenty years previously, when Regulos emerges from a death rift onto Telara. Slain during the ensuing battle, the character is chosen by the Vigil to return to fight Regulos once again when the prelude ends, and the new incarnation occurs at the point the full game begins. For a Defiant, the prelude takes place in the past; Defiant characters watch the triumph of Regulos play out in a future where the Ascended are defeated and are sent back in time to try to change that future.

Key to the understanding of *Rift* is the concept of the Ascended. Guardian Ascended are chosen by the Vigil at the point of death and brought back to life to defend Telara. Although the Defiant eschew the Vigil's aid, they see the worth of Ascension, and the purpose of the prelude is to articulate the Defiant's achievement as much as their downfall. Through the power of technology—the ancient technology of a fallen empire—and their magic, the Defiant succeed in re-creating the process of Ascension and creating their own superheroes from their dead. And thus, at the moment of their defeat, the Defiant use this knowledge to send heroes back into the past to prevent defeat in the future. As the Guardians in the game can be heard to remark, the Defiant Ascended are "machineborn."

There is much here to consider in terms of the relationship of science, technology, and religion, and in terms of the human relationship to all three. Immediately, the technological breakthrough of the Defiant situates them in the role of Shelley's Dr. Frankenstein or Wells's Dr. Moreau: through their scientific knowledge and their technological skill, they intervene in the natural order of things, returning the dead to life and sending them back in time, and all without the aid of the gods. Not only do the Defiant usurp the power of the gods, but they also raise their own to a kind of demi-godhood; we are reminded of numerous pessimistic presentations of similar scenarios.[29] Yet if the Defiant may damn themselves through their own action, the Guardians may do so through inaction. Their faith drives them to wait for the Vigil to save them, an almost millenarian expectation that the gods will return to sort everything out. And although each side is dismissive and condemnatory of the other's approach, it is notable that both groups fare equally well and equally poorly by turns and that, in the moments of greatest challenge, it is only by working together that they succeed in defeating their greater enemy.

As with *World of Warcraft*, then, *Rift* offers us a fantasy world that displays, in some regard, the problems of our own. We are pushed to consider the relationship of religion and science/technology and are reminded of the apparent divide between them that is rehearsed in the real world, especially in the West. In some ways, we might see Guardian and Defiant positions as representing pre- and post-Enlightenment attitudes towards religion, but the approach to science and technology confounds this picture. For Noble, such a division has no historical basis; it is something new, a post-Enlightenment phenomenon that sets secularist polemic and ideology against religious accusations of the "spiritually sterility" of technological rationality, forgetting that "religion and technology have evolved together and that, as a result, the technological enterprise has been and remains suffused with religious belief." In Noble's interpretation, they are neither complements nor opposites, nor are they successive markers of progress; rather, they are merged.[30] This connection is further complicated in *Rift* by the pervasiveness of magic, a power available to both sides and operating not only in connection with their religion or technology but also separate from it. In this, *Rift* perhaps reflects the complexity of medieval understandings of magic, accepting the historic notion of magic as something that occupies an intersection between science and religion while extending both, but rejecting early Christian conceptions of magic as a demon-driven force incompatible with religion.[31]

Importantly, the Defiant are not unreligious. They accept the existence of the Vigil—indeed, game lore implies that they blame the Vigil for the situation in which they find themselves[32]—but they believe that they must save themselves and that the Vigil will not do this for them. In this, they represent strongly the ideas that drove the Enlightenment—a sense that humans were agents in the world and should not assume that God will act for them. And much as with many great Enlightenment scientists—Newton, for example, or Leibniz—religion can be accommodated within this world-view. Conversely, however, we can also see in the Defiant a more genuinely medieval perspective, in their fulfillment of the promise of technology and of the "useful arts," the promise of transcendence.[33] For as the Defiant succeed in creating their own Ascended, they achieve this promise; but in doing so, they appear to displace the gods.

Yet remarkably, for all their technological skill, the Defiant are defeated in the prelude. Achieving transcendence alone is, it would appear, not suffi-cient. The Guardians, conspicuous in their absence from the Defiant prelude, clearly also cannot stand alone. The underlying message of *Rift* would thus appear to be one of cooperation, of stepping past divisions of ideology to resolve problems which affect us all. Traditionalism and progressivism must stand together.

SCIENCE, TECHNOLOGY, AND MAGIC

In both *Rift* and *World of Warcraft*, then, science and technology play a role predominantly as narrative devices. They have relatively little effect on gameplay, and those who have access to science, and the products of science, have no significant advantage over those who do not. Notably, how-ever, many activities are possible within both Azeroth and Telara that would be unachievable in our modern world without access to technology. In MMORPGs, these feats are accomplished through the application of magic.

Here, then, we come to the curious contradiction that lies at the heart of games of this kind. We have seen how both *Rift* and *World of Warcraft* employ science and technology to explore contemporary concerns about industrialization and technological progress, the idea of man as god, and debates about religion. Yet to set these technologies up as issues of debate, they are required to be absent from some segments of the game world—one cannot create opposition in a world where everything is uniform. In an authentic medieval construction, the removal of industrial technology at least would be unproblematic, and this approach to technology is com-monly practiced.[34] Returning, however, to Stern's point, that game narrative is structured at least in part by some combination of magic and real-world technology, we can see that technology continues to have a direct effect upon the game: logging out and saving, for example, are "metaphorically patched" through the idea of setting up camp for the night.[35] So, we have worlds without technology affected by technology, and those technologies are hidden behind a metaphor of magic.

However, it is possible to take Stern's analysis a stage further and to suggest that magic is not simply a metaphor for the external technological conditions of these games but that it is, in fact, a metaphor for technology in society more generally. In medieval fantasy MMORPGs, magic constitutes part of the full presentation of technology. In *World of Warcraft*, for example, technology accepts and reflects the dystopian perspectives that have been so prevalent and so prominent in science fiction's attempts to imagine "the problematic consequences brought about by these new technologies and the ethical, political, and existential questions they raise."[36] Technology is thus inherently flawed. Magic, conversely, is not: although it can be misused, it is broadly neutral in aspect; it always works; and, perhaps fundamentally, it was not created by humans. In some sense, it is also a commons, beyond ownership, in rejection of the commercial imperatives discussed previously. In the less technophobic *Rift*, technology depends on magic, and the Defiant innovations are referred to as 'technomagic.'

In a more explicit sense, magic responds to player expectations, not of magic but of experience. As Stern observes, players will not willingly spend three hours of play time traveling from one city to another on horseback, so magic portals and speed-increasing spells are introduced to remove this inconvenience.[37] This and other constraints of the medievalized world are eroded and removed through the action of magic, in part because unsanitized medieval realism would not be greatly entertaining and in part because an authentic medieval world would offer so few of the affordances of our modern experience that it would be almost incomprehensible. Noble refers to our "widespread infatuation with technological advance"[38]— we are technophilic and, moreover, we are technologically *dependent.*

Here, then, lies the key to understanding the role of magic, in *World of Warcraft* and *Rift* at least, and, in so doing, more clearly understanding the role and representation of science and technology in these games. Magic provides both explanations of the world and solutions for its problems. The massively destructive diseases of the medieval world can be cured through the direct application of magic power or via medicines prepared by alchemists (semiscience that evokes magic). Through magic, transport is sped, food and drink created, and darkness dismissed. Pearce has observed that the interplay of magic and nature can be seen as a metaphor for the computer itself, as "a mysterious realm of darkness which seldom behaves as anticipated, even while we try to harness and control it."[39] But a computer *can* be understood, though not by everyone, and is the product of science as a system of knowledge that explains the world. Thus, not only does magic replace and yet replicate the affordances of modern technology, magic also replaces and replicates the systematic understanding of modern science. Magic in these games is inherently systematic—it obeys rules; there are powerful and knowledgeable experts in magic; and, through the interaction of these things, magic offers explanations. So magic helps us to understand the medievalized world or, in places where understanding eludes us, know that the world *can* be understood. And such an understanding is more fulfilling for the contemporary gamer than an approach which seeks to directly replicate the (mis)understandings of authentic medieval knowledge.

CONCLUSION

In MMORPGs, the medieval setting draws on common tropes of medieval fantasy with a lengthy literary pedigree and a more recent but still rich history in gaming. By adopting pseudomedieval approaches to the presentation of the world, these games reflect this broad selection of influences and also their fundamental connection to technology and, through technology, modern science. Yet although the external technology used to deliver the game experience has a direct effect on the mechanics of the game, science and technology also appear within the games themselves. Although science and technology form part of the narrative structures of both *Rift* and *World of Warcraft*, neither game portrays them with the same utopian ideals that appear in some real-world presentations about our scientific future. Science and technology in *World of Warcraft* are actively dystopian, in *Rift* more complex and yet still imperfect.

In both cases, however, the fantasy medieval context allows them to present constructions of the world that are allegorical with our own and to offer opinions or provoke debates about contemporary and potentially contentious issues. In so doing, however, they remove technology from a universally legitimate role within the game world and render the world more medieval and correspondingly less comprehensible to the modern player. Perhaps as a result, magic is invoked as a way to 'shore up' the medievalizing fantasy and to deliver the fulfillment of our technologically informed expectations of fast transport and medical health. In addition, magic provides an alternate to science as a means of making sense of the world, allowing this space to be coherent and comfortable and yet to seem medieval and utopic. Thus, online medieval fantasy games allows us to explore technophobia even as they use magic to feed our technophilia.

NOTES

1. Ibe Van Geel, "MMOData.net," http://mmodata.net (accessed October 10, 2012).
2. *World of Warcraft*, Blizzard Entertainment (Blizzard Entertainment, 2004); *Aion: The Tower of Eternity*, Aion Team Development Department (NCsoft, 2008); *Everquest*, Sony Online Entertainment (Sony Online Entertainment, 1999); *Rift*, Trion Worlds (Trion Worlds, 2011).
3. *World of Warcraft* has the largest active subscription base of any MMORPG, at 10 million active accounts (Van Geel, "MMOData.net").
4. *Rift* has around 250,000 active accounts at the time of writing (Van Geel, "MMOData.net").
5. Game studies is often considered to have been constituted in 2001, with the launch of the journal of that name. See Espen Aarseth, "Computer Game Studies, Year One," *Game Studies* 1, no. 1 (2001): http://www.gamestudies.org/0101/editorial.html (accessed October 28, 2012.)

6. Brent Moberly and Kevin Moberly, "Revising the Future: The Medieval Self and the Sovereign Ethics of Empire in *Star Wars: Knights of the Old Republic*," *Studies in Medievalism* 16 (2008): 159.

7. Daniel Dinello, *Technophobia! Science Fiction Visions of Posthuman Technology* (Austin: University of Texas Press, 2005).

8. David F. Noble, *The Religion of Technology* (New York: Penguin, 1999).

9. Eddo Stern, "A Touch of Medieval: Narrative, Magic and Computer Technology in Massively Multiplayer Computer Role-Playing Games," in *Proceedings of Computer Games and Digital Cultures Conference*, ed. Frans Mäyrä (Tampere, Finland: Tampere University Press, 2002), 268.

10. Amy S. Kaufman, "Romancing the Game: Magic, Writing, and the Feminine in *Neverwinter Nights*," *Studies in Medievalism* 16 (2008): 143–58.

11. Celia Pearce, "Emergent Authorship: The Next Interactive Revolution," *Computers & Graphics* 26, no. 1 (2002): 24.

12. Moberly and Moberly, "Revising the Future," 161–62.

13. Oliver M. Traxel, "Medieval and Pseudo-Medieval Elements in Computer Role-Playing Games: Use and Interactivity," *Studies in Medievalism* 16 (2008): 131, 133–34.

14. Scott Rettberg, "Corporate Ideology in *World of Warcraft*," in *Digital Culture, Play, and Identity: A World of Warcraft Reader*, ed. Hilde Corneliussen and Jill Walker Rettberg (Cambridge, MA: MIT Press, 2008), 19–38; Andrew Baerg, "Risky Business: Neo-liberal Rationality and the Computer RPG," in *Dungeons, Dragons and Digital Denizens: The Digital Role-Playing Game*, ed. Gerald A. Vorhees, Joshua Call, and Katie Whitlock (New York: Continuum, 2012): 153–73.

15. Dinello, *Technophobia!*, 33.

16. J. R. R. Tolkien, *The Hobbit* (London: Grafton, 1991); J. R. R. Tolkien, *The Lord of the Rings* (London: HarperCollins, 1993).

17. See Dinello, *Technophobia!*, 13 for a brief resumé.

18. Baerg, "Risky Business," 155.

19. Esther MacCullum-Stewart, "'Never Such Innocence Again': War and Histories in *World of Warcraft*," in *Digital Culture, Play, and Identity: A World of Warcraft Reader*, ed. Hilde Corneliussen and Jill Walker Rettberg (Cambridge, MA: MIT Press, 2008), 49–53. The Alliance are one of two player factions in *World of Warcraft*, the Horde being the other.

20. *Wowwiki*, "Venture Trading Company," http://www.wowwiki.com/Venture_Trading_Company (accessed October 10, 2012).

21. *World of Warcraft*, "Gnomeregan," http://us.battle.net/wow/en/zone/gnomeregan/ (accessed October 10, 2012).

22. *Wowwiki*, "Undead Mad Scientists," http://www.wowwiki.com/Mad_scientist (accessed October 10, 2012).

23. Dinello, *Technophobia!*, 49.

24. Moberly and Moberly, "Revising the Future," 177.

25. *Wowwiki*, "Goblin Rocket Boots," http://www.wowwiki.com/Goblin_Rocket_Boots; Wowwiki (accessed October 10, 2012), "Ultrasafe Transporter: Toshley's Station," http://www.wowwiki.com/Ultrasafe_Transporter:_Toshley's_Station (accessed October 10, 2012).

26. See Noble, *Religion*, 12–15 for the relationship between technology and transcendence in the Middle Ages.

27. MacCullum-Stewart, "Never Such Innocence," 59–60.

28. Andrew Higson, "'Medievalism,' the Period Film and the British Past in Contemporary Cinema," in *Medieval Film*, ed. Anke Bernau and Bettina Bildhauer (Manchester, UK: Manchester University Press, 2009), 203–24.

29. On this, see Dinello, *Technophobia!*, 41–44.
30. Noble, *Religion*, 4–5.
31. Richard Kieckhefer, *Magic in the Middle Ages* (Cambridge, UK: Cambridge University Press, 1989), 1, 9, 14, 37, 200.
32. *Telarapedia*, "The Defiant," http://telarapedia.com/wiki/ The_Defiant (accessed October 10, 2012).
33. Noble, *Religion*, 9.
34. Traxel, "Medieval and Pseudo-Medieval," 131.
35. Stern, "Touch of Medieval," 267.
36. Dinello, *Technophobia!*, 5–6, 17.
37. Stern, "Touch of Medieval," 268.
38. Noble, *Religion*, 3.
39. Pearce, "Emergent Authorship," 24.

17 The Consolation of Paranoia

Conspiracy, Epistemology, and the Templars in *Assassin's Creed*, *Deus Ex*, and *Dragon Age*

Harry J. Brown

The lunatic is all idée fixe, and whatever he comes across confirms his lunacy. You can tell him by the liberties he takes with common sense, by his flashes of inspiration, and by the fact that sooner or later he brings up the Templars.

—Umberto Eco, *Foucault's Pendulum* (1988)

1 + 1 = 11

In the spring 2002 issue of *Paranoia* magazine, Richard Hoagland, widely known to listeners of *Coast to Coast AM* for postulating the existence of alien ruins on the Moon and Mars, published the shocking truth about the September 11 attacks. He begins by noting some suspicious numerical coincidences. The attacks took place on 9/11 . . . 9 + 1 + 1 = 11. Each tower of the World Trade Center had 110 floors . . . a multiple of 11. American Airlines Flight 11, which struck the North Tower, carried 11 crew members and 65 people in total . . . 6 + 5 = 11. American Airlines Flight 77, another multiple of 11, struck the Pentagon. September 11 is the 254th day of the year . . . 2 + 5 + 4 = 11. After September 11, 111 days remain in the year. 'New York City' consists of 11 letters, and New York was the 11th state admitted to the union. Clearly, Hoagland says, someone meant to send a message.

Then he brings up the Templars. The order of crusader knights, he explains, formed in Jerusalem in 1118 . . . 1 + 1 + 1 + 8 = 11. Between that year and 2001, 883 years had passed . . . 8 + 8 + 3 = 19, the same as the number of hijackers. By no coincidence, Hoagland explains, the number 19 is sacred in Koranic numerology. The Templars' arch enemies, the Islamic Order of Assassins, or *hashshashin,* formed in 1090 . . . 2001 − 1090 = 911. Hoagland sees only one logical conclusion: 9/11 represented an attack by modern Assassins against the United States, a nation founded by the Masonic heirs of the Templars, in order to instigate an apocalyptic war between Christianity and Islam.[1] *Q.E.D.*

In his novel *Foucault's Pendulum,* Eco sports with such theories, portraying three editors, Belbo, Casaubon, and Diotallevi, wearied by manuscripts like Hoagland's, who propose to dupe their publisher by concocting an elaborate Templar hoax of their own. Imagination turns to conviction, however, as they come to believe in their own imaginary history. Historians as well as paranoiacs, Eco suggests, harbor an "idée fixe" in their shared passion for meaning. Both weave elegant skeins of narrative, rendering coherent patterns from incoherent phenomena. Knowledge and lunacy differ only in degree. In *A Culture of Conspiracy,* Michael Barkun offers the same diagnosis of the whole of American culture, which he sees as increasingly susceptible to millennialist beliefs like Hoagland's. Like the careful novelist, Barkun suggests, "the conspiracy theorist must engage in a constant process of linkage and correlation in order to map the hidden connections."[2] For both Barkun and Eco, the Templars are not shadowy forms looming behind the curtain of history, but rather projections of the desire for knowledge that any student of the past inevitably shares with Eco's three warped editors. They are a versatile cognitive tool, serving to repair broken connections or to supply an explanation where one is lacking. When in doubt, Casaubon applies the fundamental axiom: "The Templars have something to do with everything."[3]

Collaborative in authorship, interactive in use, and intertextual in content, digital games provide a fertile medium for Templar conspiracism. Like Hoagland, the *Assassin's Creed* series[4] (2007–12) envisions the medieval conflict between the Templars and Assassins merely as the beginning of an endless crusade continuing through the Italian Renaissance and the American Revolution to the present day, when we can anticipate its apocalyptic consummation. In the *Deus Ex* series[5] (2000–11), the Templars play an integral role in an imagined future history, when they emerge as a fanatical branch of the Illuminati, dedicated to purifying humanity of the evil of nanotechnology. The *Dragon Age* series[6] (2009–11) removes the Templars from any recognizable historical context to the 'Forgotten Realms' of *Dungeons & Dragons,* where they retain their role as holy warriors and appoint themselves to subject dangerous magicians to their righteous authority.

As we will see, the peculiar appropriation of Templar conspiracism in these games demonstrates an ambivalent approach to history, symptomatic of a moment, as Barkun suggests, when traditional political and moral certainties have been subverted by the ascendance of formerly marginalized forms of knowledge. We find in them the manias about secret societies, mind control, and the end of days, familiar from conspiracy theories. At the same time, we also find a silhouette of the medieval knights who roused in their contemporaries resentment of their vast wealth and fear of their unaccountable power. What medieval chroniclers feared about the Templars in the twelfth and thirteenth centuries continues to resonate in our own time, as the games recast the Templars as avatars of modern corporatism or dictatorship, regimes that wield absolute power through the possession and regulation of forbidden wisdom or technology. As dramas that invite the player's participation in this epistemological struggle, the *Assassin's Creed*, *Deus Ex*, and *Dragon Age* series afford the same consolations that conspiracy theorists find in their own arabesque delusions: subjective intervention in the historical narrative and empowerment through the imagined control of knowledge.

TEMPLAR CONSPIRACISM

The twelfth-century historian William of Tyre records that, following the capture of Jerusalem by the First Crusade, nine French knights formed an order of warrior-monks to protect pilgrimage routes and to defend newly formed Christian kingdoms. They established their headquarters in the al-Aqsa mosque on the Temple Mount and called themselves the Order of the Poor Knights of Christ and the Temple of Solomon.[7] Their reputation for military and spiritual discipline won the order numerous initiates and patrons. Even as the Muslims regained control of the Holy Land, the Templars consolidated their wealth and power in Europe, inviting the resentment of rivals, particularly those indebted to the order. In the early fourteenth century, Philip IV of France and Pope Clement V conspired to seize Templar possessions, accusing the knights of homosexuality, defiling the cross, and paying homage to the pagan idol Baphomet. Many Templars fled France to join other orders, while others were imprisoned, tortured, and burned. In 1312, Clement formally dissolved the order.

In the middle eighteenth century, Scottish Freemasons revived the dormant Templar myth and adopted the order as their forebears. In 1737 Andrew Michael Ramsay identified the crusader knights as bearers of "ancient signs and symbolic words" and guardians of "the most sublime truths."[8] Ramsay's successors drew a more direct connection between the Templars' occupation of the Temple of Solomon and the secret wisdom inherited by the Freemasons.[9] The Masonic appropriation of the Templars prompted Friedrich Schlegel and other scholars to search medieval romances for connections between the Templars and the Holy Grail, originating the tradition linking the Templars to occult knowledge and buried treasure.[10]

In the revolutionary climate of the early nineteenth century, these speculations assumed political significance, as conservative writers revived the charges of heresy against the Templars in order to implicate the Freemasons in imagined revenge plots against the French monarchy and other Roman Catholic governments. In 1797, the French exile and former Jesuit Augustin Barruel published an elaborate indictment of Freemasonry, which interprets the Reign of Terror as the bloody consummation of a conspiracy against the monarchy and papacy, hatched by the last Templars and nurtured in subsequent centuries by the Illuminati and Freemasons. In 1818, the Austrian scholar Joseph von Hammer-Purgstall likewise blamed the Templars and Freemasons for contemporary social upheavals, attributing the wave of revolution in Europe to the clandestine sway of their Gnostic dogma and idol worship.[11] Like Hoagland, both Barruel and Hammer-Purgstall find Templars lurking behind the traumas of their era.

In our own time, the Templars' most compelling role in the popular imagination remains as guardians of "the most sublime truths." Bolstered by speculative and often specious scholarship, this erstwhile Masonic claim has gone viral. In *Holy Blood, Holy Grail* (1982), Michael Baigent, Richard Leigh, and Henry Lincoln identify the Templars as key players in an epochal conspiracy to obscure the true origin of Christianity, encoded in the medieval grail romances.[12] In *The Sign and the Seal* (1992), Graham Hancock proposes that the Templars discovered the secret location of the Ark of the Covenant, in fact a radioactive alien weapon, during their occupation of the Temple Mount, likewise encoding their discovery in grail romances.[13] In bestselling novels such as Dan Brown's *The Da Vinci Code* (2003) and Raymond Khoury's *The Last Templar* (2005) and in popular films such as Steven Spielberg's *Indiana Jones and the Last Crusade* (1989) and Jon Turteltaub's *National Treasure* (2004), the Templar conspiracy originating with Ramsay, Barruel, and Hammer-Purgstall has become one of the most commercially successful conceits of our generation.

TEMPLARS IN *ASSASSIN'S CREED, DEUS EX,* AND *DRAGON AGE*

Digital games have seized this cultural moment, when Templar conspiracy theories, long seeded at the fringes of culture, have blossomed into a collective medievalist fantasy. *Assassin's Creed* literally represents the medieval knights as dreams, or 'genetic memories,' buried in the unconscious mind of the game's protagonist, the young slacker Desmond Miles. In the frame narrative set in the present, the unsuspecting Desmond is abducted by operatives of mysterious Abstergo Industries and wired to Animus, a prototype machine designed to unlock deeply embedded memories, including genetic memories encoded in DNA. In the embedded narrative, set within Desmond's mind in the year 1191, the player enacts these memories as Desmond's distant ancestor Altaïr ibn-La'Ahad, a Saracen Assassin who battled the Templars to possess the Piece of Eden, a mystical, perhaps alien, artifact that the Templars unearthed beneath the Temple Mount. By accessing Desmond's genetic unconscious, Abstergo seeks to discover the hiding place of the artifact, now lost to the ages.

Throughout the game, the Templars act as foils to the Assassins, bullying and deceiving both Muslims and fellow Christians as part of their secret plan to dominate the Holy Land through the mind-control power contained in the artifact. Altaïr inevitably foils the conspiracy, killing Templar Grand Master Robert de Sablé in single combat. Upon emerging from the Animus, however, Desmond learns that Abstergo is a front for the Templars, who have survived as a powerful covert organization and are now using him as a pawn in their continuing plans for world domination. In *Assassin's Creed II*, *Assassin's Creed: Brotherhood*, and *Assassin's Creed: Revelations*, Desmond uses the latent powers of his Assassin forebears to continue the millennial struggle against the Templars in Renaissance Italy, adopting the persona of the Florentine nobleman Ezio Auditore da Firenze. *Assassin's Creed III* introduces a new historical setting and a new embodiment of Desmond's genetic memory, as the half-Mohawk scout, Connor Kenway, searches for the Piece of Eden behind the grand scenes of the American Revolution.

As an order of medieval knights now incarnate as a diabolical transnational corporation, the Templars of the *Assassin's Creed* series represent a composite of previous Templar conspiracy theories. Like Ramsay's and Schlegel's adepts, they guard secret knowledge. Like Hancock's treasure hunters, they unearth an alien artifact beneath the Temple. Like Baigent, Leigh, and Lincoln's supreme conspirators, they operate covertly throughout the centuries, growing more powerful as they adapt their schemes to each new age. The *Assassin's Creed* games not only look for secret motives behind historical events but undertake a complete revision of human history, imagining ancient texts and artifacts as encoded evidence of an epochal secret. Glyphs locked within the Animus reveal humanity's origin as a slave race created by godlike aliens known as the 'First Civilization,' which became extinct when a solar flare struck the Earth sometime in prehistory. As Ezio, Desmond discovers that the ancient war between the Templars and Assassins is a struggle to reclaim the lost knowledge of the First Civilization, so that humanity can avoid the same fate in 2012, the year prophesied to witness the same cosmic catastrophe. The Templars see the prospect of planetary destruction as an opportunity to remake a better world, using the Piece of Eden and other artifacts of the First Civilization to control the minds of the survivors and elevate themselves as enlightened despots.

Like the *Assassin's Creed* series, the *Deus Ex* series adapts elements of Templar conspiracy theories familiar since the nineteenth century, framing them not as an alternative narrative of the past but rather as a future history. In *Deus Ex*, the player enters the dystopian twenty-first century as J. C. Denton, an antiterrorism agent who, like Desmond, gradually awakens to knowledge of the shadowy powers at work in his world. Like *Assassin's Creed*, *Deus Ex* foregrounds technocratic conspiracies, envisioning a world where transnational corporations and ruthless secret societies have eclipsed the influence of national governments. At the same time, new and dangerous technologies, such as sentient artificial intelligence systems, genetically engineered plague viruses, and nanotechnology, threaten to upset the balance of power. The United Nations uses the threat of terrorism to expand its powers, while the Federal Emergency Management Agency (FEMA) quietly dismantles American civil liberties. On a more covert supranational plane, the elegant tyrants of the Illuminati vie for supremacy against the amoral militarists of Majestic-12, competing for a device to disperse the

Gray Death, a virus they plan to use a means of social control through the selective distribution of a cure.

The Templars appear most prominently in *Deus Ex: Invisible War,* where they seek to purge the world of the evil influence of nanotechnology. Their crusade for biological purity inevitably erases the boundary between holy warrior and mass murderer with the jarring scene of a Templar agent destroying the city of Chicago, an uncomfortable reverberation of September 11. While the Templars in the *Deus Ex* series reprise their role as violent fanatics, the moral system evoked by the games remains ambiguous. At the conclusions of both *Deus Ex* and *Deus Ex: Human Revolutions*, the player may form an alliance with a variety of factions, including the Illuminati and Majestic-12, all of whom desire to destroy the world in order to re-create and improve it. In this apocalyptic scenario, common in conspiracy theories, the ideals of liberal democracy and human rights seem quaint. The contending forces in the *Deus Ex* dystopia equally manifest tyrannical amorality, differing only in their means of achieving supremacy, with the reactionary dogma of the Templars on one end of the spectrum and the cybernetic hive mind of runaway artificial intelligence on the other.

Dragon Age: Origins and *Dragon Age II* represent the Templars as an order of holy knights pledged to protect the world against the excesses of 'blood mages,' who too often become possessed by demons and make trouble for innocent folk. They feature most prominently in the climactic chapter of *Dragon Age II*, where a recent battle with the Quanari, a barbaric warrior race, has left the city of Kirkwall without a ruler. Meredith, the Templar commander, quickly seizes power and begins a systematic persecution of mages, whom she intends to subject to 'Tranquility,' a magical rite that removes the ability to perform magic but also obliterates free will and personality, leaving the mage in the same content but mindless state that the Templars in *Assassin's Creed* mean to impose on the world. As Hawke, the player may support either the oppressive Templars or the destructive mages, who resort to the killing of innocent clergy as a means of retaliating against the Templars. Whichever alliance the player makes, the final confrontation reveals the source of Meredith's power as an idol composed of the magical substance lyrium, a kind of Baphomet, that compels obedience in her followers, twists her intentions to evil, and gives her the godlike ability to enervate inanimate objects with supernatural life. Like the Templars in the *Assassin's Creed* and *Deus Ex* series, the Templars in the *Dragon Age* games are warmongers fashioning themselves as peacekeepers, becoming corrupted by the arcane knowledge they pledge to control.

THE TEMPLAR SILHOUETTE

While the *Assassin's Creed*, *Deus Ex*, and *Dragon Age* series freely appropriate and recombine Templar conspiracy theories, a silhouette of the historical Templars remains, signaling a relevance in these games beyond that of a pluralistic pastiche. According to William of Tyre's chronicle, what made the Templars "exceedingly troublesome" to their contemporaries was a "neglect of humility" that caused them to "deny obedience" to the Patriarch of Jerusalem and other rightful superiors.[14] Their rule stated that the Templars answered to no one but the Pope. When Christian knights donned the white cowl, they absolved themselves of all temporal debts and obligations. The Templars existed independently of the hierarchy of vassalage, free to pursue an independent agenda with secrecy and impunity.

The source of William's apprehension, widely shared by medieval chroniclers, originates in the papal bull *Omne datum optimum*, "All the Best Gifts," issued by Innocent II in 1139, which granted the order unprecedented privilege and autonomy in exchange for its allegiance to the papacy. As the bull mandates, the order owed obedience only to the Pope. No lord could command homage from the order, nor could any bishop exact tithes. The order could dispose of spoils taken in battle with the Muslims as it wished, without dividing them with Christian allies. The order could build its own chapels, appoint its own chaplains, and attend to its own burials. None could compel the order to admit or expel a member or to change its rule. Supporting the defenders of the faith, Innocent claimed, necessitated such preference.[15]

At the same time, the privileges granted to the Templars often seemed to undermine the larger goals of the Crusade. In his account of the capture of Ascalon by the Second Crusade in 1153, for example, William alleges that the Templars rushed into a breech in the city wall in order to seize any potential spoils for themselves. When reinforcements did not follow, they were quickly surrounded and killed by the Muslim defenders, their headless corpses displayed on the city walls the next day. William regards the incident as one of many illustrations of Templar greed subverting the military and diplomatic efforts of other Christian rulers. "Everyone could have entered without distinction and taken the city," he writes, "and there would have been sufficient loot for the victors, but when an evil stems from an evil root and wicked intentions it rarely produces a good result."[16]

William's account of the siege represents a particularly vivid illustration of a widespread perception of Templars during the twelfth and thirteenth centuries. They hoarded their spoils, some witnesses alleged, refusing to finance Christian expeditions or ransom Christian rulers. In spite of their reputation for valor, they only joined battle on their own terms and would not submit to the command of any Christian leaders. They brokered separate treaties with Muslim factions in order to sustain their own trade networks, or, when war better served, broke treaties made by other Christian leaders, perpetuating the Crusade as a kind of private business venture.[17]

The Templars' belief that the privileges granted by *Omne datum optimatum* superseded older and more entrenched fealties, their tendency to operate outside the rules, and their creation of a continental system of trade and finance that outstripped its original purpose of supporting Crusade, have led historians to compare them to modern transnational corporations or banking syndicates, a characterization that bridges traditional historiography and Templar conspiracism.[18] The refiguring of the Templars as an ultramodern, ultrapowerful corporation in the *Assassin's Creed* series, as agents of the Illuminati in the *Deus Ex* series, and as an oppressive police force in the *Dragon Age* series, suggests that they continue to embody the popular suspicion of covert and unaccountable power, just as they had for William. Although far removed in time, the Jerusalem that William describes in the twelfth century bears clear resemblance to the Jerusalem in *Assassin's Creed* or Kirkwall in *Dragon Age II*, where Templars roam the streets as arrogant thugs, using their divine mandate to justify the brutal enforcement of their dogma over an innocent and defenseless populace. The connection between William of Tyre and the *Assassin's Creed*, *Deus Ex*, and *Dragon Age* games is the populist desire to expose power, to reveal and foil its conspiracies, whatever they are.

EPISTEMOLOGICAL DRAMAS

In their indiscriminate deployment of both conspiracy and history, their equitable embrace of Graham Hancock and William of Tyre, the games illustrate what Michael Barkun describes as a form of ideological bricolage that draws simultaneously from "Eastern and Western religion, New Age ideas and esotericism, and radical politics, without any sense that the resulting mélange contains incompatible elements." This leveling of "incompatible elements" into an improvisational "mélange," Barkun explains, flourishes in the current climate of "epistemological pluralism," a condition resulting from the erosion of belief in traditionally authoritative sources of meaning.[19] As historical and political discourse drifts from a consensus reality in which contested questions of fact may be reasonably resolved, conspiracy theory fills the void of meaning with an alternative historical narrative of a world governed by hidden design and sharply divided between the forces of good and evil. As Barkun suggests, there no longer seems to be "a consensus reality about the causes of events and the reliability of evidence."[20] Conspiracism is the art of a relativistic age, when a growing number of people, nurtured by the Internet and entertainment media, "seem to inhabit a different epistemic universe, where the usual rules of for determining truth and falsity do not apply."[21]

We find evidence for these claims in the Vatican's reaction to *The Da Vinci Code,* a romantic fictionalization of the theory proposed by Baigent, Leigh, and Lincoln. Alarmed that Vatican tourists were using the novel as guide to religious history, the Church had to remind the world's Catholics that *The Da Vinci Code* is indeed a work of fiction. They appointed as publicist and debunker Cardinal Tarcisio Bertone, who told an Italian newspaper in 2005, "[t]here is a very real risk that many people who read [*The Da Vinci Code*] will believe that the fables it contains are true. [Dan Brown] even perverts the story of the holy grail, which most certainly does not refer to the descendants of Mary Magdalene. It astonishes and worries me that so many people believe these lies."[22] The following year, the Vatican called for Catholics to boycott Ron Howard's film adaption of the novel.

Like Bertone, academic debunkers diligently attempt to quash Templar conspiracy theories, warning against the same narrative seductions that consume the editors in *Foucault's Pendulum*. In *The New Knighthood*, Malcolm Barber writes: "So great is the appeal of a comprehensive explanation of history that writers have been attracted to it ever since, undeterred by lack of evidence. . . . Such links are inherently satisfying to proponents of conspiracy theories of history, for they abhor loose ends, often seeing history as one vast jigsaw puzzle in which the participants leave 'clues' for latter-day Hercule Poirots to investigate."[23] In spite of such appeals to 'evidence,' however, the Templars of romance, suspense fiction, and digital games have somehow supplanted the Templars of the historical record, at least in the popular mind. According to the backwards logic of the people who propagate and subscribe to these theories, Bertone's denial of the story only confirms its truth. That scolding churchmen and stuffy academics rise in defense of orthodoxy merely bolsters the indictment of orthodoxy While Baigent, Leigh, and Lincoln, for example, dismiss many of the esoteric claims about the Templars as "ridiculous" and "extravagant," they tempt the reader with suggestive rhetoric and the promise of their own true revelation:

> [W]as there some genuine mystery connected with [the Templars]? Could there have been some foundation for the later embellishments of myth? We first considered the accepted accounts of the Templars—the accounts offered by respected and responsible historians. On virtually every point these accounts raised more questions than they answered. They not only collapsed under scrutiny, but suggested some sort of "cover-up." We could not escape the suspicion that something had been deliberately concealed and a "cover story" manufactured, which later historians had merely accepted.[24]

Baigent, Leigh, and Lincoln momentarily nod to "respected and responsible" accounts like Barber's only to undermine them as incomplete, flimsy, or even indirectly complicit in their gullible acceptance of the "cover story," making them, in fact, seem untrustworthy and irresponsible. For both Bertone and Barber, the Templar conspiracy theory, though ridiculous, creates an epistemological crisis, where the normally steady anchors of historical knowledge have slipped loose and left us spinning in an eddy where revelations materialize from the unknown only to dissolve into deeper questions, and those who unravel the conspiracy become indistinguishable from those who spin it.

The epistemological pluralism that has transformed *The Da Vinci Code*, a seemingly innocuous work of suspense fiction, into a potentially subversive account of alternative history likewise provides fertile ground for digital games featuring Templar conspiracies. In the *Assassin's Creed*, *Deus Ex*, and *Dragon Age* series, the Templars are uprooted from "respected and responsible" history and transplanted in the radioactive soil of imaginary history, where they are free to mutate into fantastic new forms. This notion of the conscious detachment from history and the consequent distortion of medieval material into something we no longer recognize as historical preoccupy recent attempts to define "neomedievalism" as a peculiarly postmodern phenomenon, a more acute symptom of the chronic dislocation of meaning described by Barkun. Carol L. Robinson and Pamela Clements, for example, call neomedievalism an "alternate universe of medievalisms, a fantasy of medievalisms," created by manipulating the "illusion" rather than the reality of the Middle Ages.[25] Neomedievalism, they continue, demonstrates that "all medievalisms are constructs, made from prefabricated materials."[26] Amy S. Kaufman likewise suggests that "[n]eomedievalism is thus not a dream of the Middle Ages, but a dream of someone else's medievalism. It is medievalism doubled upon itself."[27] In *The Da Vinci Code*, *Assassin's Creed*, *Deus Ex*, and *Dragon Age*, medievalism "doubles upon itself" to construct an illusion of the Middle Ages from the residue of previous illusions. Here Ramsay, Schlegel, and Hammer-Purgstall return like vaguely remembered dreams, becoming the "prefabricated materials" of our more familiar Templar myths, copies of copies.

In a 1977 interview, "Truth and Power," Michel Foucault anticipates the epistemological crisis that finds expression in these neomedievalist fantasies. Addressing the fundamental processes through which truth is produced, distributed, regulated, and dismissed, Foucault claims that truth is "linked in a circular relation with systems of power which produce and sustain it, and to effects of power which it induces and which extends it. A 'regime' of truth."[28] He continues: "Each society has its regime of truth . . . that is, the types of discourse which it accepts and makes function as true; the mechanisms and instances which enable one to distinguish true and false statements, the means by which each is sanctioned; the techniques and procedures accorded value in the acquisition of truth; the status of those who are charged with saying what counts as true."[29] For Foucault, truth is contingent with ideology, and therefore constantly challenged by competing ideologies. "There is a battle 'for truth,'" he concludes.[30] Historical knowledge becomes plastic, and each event, no matter how familiar, becomes available for constant reinterpretation.

In these terms, Baigent, Leigh, and Lincoln's rejection of "respected and responsible historians" represents a sidelong challenge to the dominant idea of what counts for historical truth and who may distinguish between truth and falsehood. In their prominent role in conspiracy theories like *Holy Blood, Holy Grail* and the games informed by these theories, the Templars represent the fulcrum between two opposing regimes of truth, with one side occupied by Barber and his kind, who see an order of warrior-monks defunct since the fourteenth century, and the other by Baigent and his kind, who see an immortal secret society manipulating the fate of the world.

Although the *Assassin's Creed, Deus Ex*, and *Dragon Age* series obviously differ in narrative content, the games share some essential formal elements. Each one features a narrative contesting accepted truths, a reconstruction of events and causal connections that compels us to question familiar sources of truth and power. Each narrative positions itself at a nexus between competing regimes of truth. Who will control the dangerous forms of knowledge figured respectively as the secrets of the First Civilization, nanotechnology, and blood magic? Synonymous with occultism and secret knowledge since the nineteenth century, the Templars play a crucial role in these epistemological dramas, in each case constituting a regime of truth standing in opposition to the player's own attempt to control this knowledge.

THE CONSOLATION OF PARANOIA

In the *Assassin's Creed, Deus Ex*, and *Dragon Age* series, the recurrence of secret societies, mind control, and apocalyptic visions that lure us with the promise of ultimate knowledge, reflect Barkun's sense that contemporary culture has lost its mooring from traditional sources of meaning. As a consequence, we witness the proliferation of chameleon narratives that change hue, but not form, as they flit from history to conspiracism to digital entertainment. Of course, playing games that feature Templar conspiracy theories does not constitute a belief in such theories. For most of us, imagination does not give way to conviction, as it does for Belbo, Casaubon, and Diotallevi. Digital games package conspiracy for consumption, but they do not argue its truth in the same way that Hoagland, Baigent, and Hancock do. In this sense, these games represent little more than slick but nonetheless predictable iterations of the conspiracist tradition, beginning with Ramsay, Barruel, and Hammer-Purgstall. As interactive media, however, they also represent something entirely new with respect to this tradition. More so than *Holy Blood, Holy Grail* or *The Sign and the Seal*, the *Assassin's Creed, Deus Ex*, and *Dragon Age* games afford players the unique cognitive appeal that Eco's editors find in their own project: the sense of taking control of knowledge and making an active intervention in the formerly baffling flux of history.

In his influential 1964 essay, "The Paranoia Style in American Politics," Richard Hofstader explains the cyclical resurgence of conspiracism and paranoia in American political discourse as a reaction to crisis or social change by reactionary minds who feel dispossessed under the new conditions. He writes:

> America has been largely taken away from them and their kind, though they are determined to try to repossess it and to prevent the final destructive act of subversion. The old American virtues have already been eaten away by cosmopolitans and intellectuals; the old competitive capitalism has been gradually undermined by socialistic and communistic schemers; the old national security and independence have been destroyed by treasonous plots, having as their most powerful agents not merely outsiders and foreigners as of old but major statesmen who are at the very centers of American power.[31]

Barkun likewise connects the ascendancy of conspiracism in the second half of the twentieth century to the slackening influence of religious and political traditions. In their ambivalent approach to history and myth, the games seem to indicate a desire for knowledge when true knowledge seems elusive or relative. They are expressions of a pluralistic historical moment, manifesting an antiauthoritarian attitude to power and an antifoundational approach to history, knowingly appropriating these millennial sentiments for commercial purpose but nonetheless reviving medieval fears of unaccountable power, unwonted wealth, and unnatural privilege.

At the same time, the games, as interactive narratives, offer a particularly effective means for quelling the sense of anxious dispossession that fuels conspiracism and constantly threatens to escalate into real violence, according to Hofstatder and Barkun. Digital games exploit the contingent nature of historical truth by giving the player an active role in the construction of an alternative historical narrative that stands in opposition to the accepted understanding of history. Players may indulge in a temporary state of lunacy, adopting the paranoid frame of mind of a conspiracy theorist who enters into a subjective and playful relation to history. These games, though dressed in the motley trappings of recycled fantasies, promise a momentary 'repossession' of history. For Hofstader, this is the consolation of paranoia, and for us, this is the consolation of gaming.

NOTES

Parts of this chapter have been adapted from my previous study, "Baphomet Incorporated: A Case Study in Neomedievalism," *Studies in Medievalism* 20 (2011): 1–10, and have been reprinted with the permission of Boydell & Brewer.

1. Richard Hoagland, "The Twin Towers and the Great Masonic Experiment: Has the 'End of Days' Begun?" *Paranoia* 20 (Spring 2002): 52–58.
2. Michael Barkun, *A Culture of Conspiracy: Apocalyptic Visions in Contemporary America* (Berkeley: University of California Press, 2003), 4.
3. Umberto Eco, *Foucault's Pendulum*, trans. William Weaver (New York: Harcourt, 1989), 364.

4. *Assassin's Creed*, Ubisoft Montreal (Ubisoft, 2007); *Assassin's Creed II*, Ubisoft Montreal (Ubisoft, 2009); *Assassin's Creed: Brotherhood*, Ubisoft Montreal (Ubisoft, 2010); *Assassin's Creed: Revelations*, Ubisoft Montreal (Ubisoft, 2011); *Assassin's Creed III*, Ubisoft Montreal (Ubisoft, 2012).

5. *Deus Ex*, Ion Storm (Eidos Interactive, 2000); *Deus Ex: Invisible War*, Ion Storm (Eidos Interactive, 2004); *Deus Ex: Human Revolution*, Eidos Montreal (Square Enix, 2011).

6. *Dragon Age: Origins*, Bio Ware Edmonton (Electronic Arts, 2009); *Dragon Age II*, Bio Ware (Electronic Arts, 2011).

7. William of Tyre, *Historia rerum in partibus transmarinis gestarum*, XII, 7, ed. and trans. James Brundage, in *The Crusades: A Documentary Survey* (Milwaukee, WI: Marquette University Press, 1962), 70–73.

8. Richard Barber, *The Holy Grail: Imagination and Belief* (Cambridge, MA: Harvard University Press, 2004), 307.

9. Malcolm Barber, *The New Knighthood: A History of the Order of the Temple* (New York: Cambridge University Press, 1994), 317–18.

10. Richard Barber, *The Holy Grail*, 306–07.

11. Malcolm Barber, *The New Knighthood*, 318–21.

12. Michael Baigent, Richard Leigh, and Henry Lincoln, *Holy Blood, Holy Grail* (New York: Bantam Dell, 2004), 64–95.

13. Graham Hancock, *The Sign and the Seal* (New York: Touchstone, 1992), 89–120.

14. William of Tyre, *Historia*, 70–73.

15. Malcolm Barber, *The Trials of the Templars* (Cambridge, UK: Cambridge University Press, 1978), 8; Stephen Howarth, *The Knights Templar* (New York: Dorset Press, 1991), 80.

16. William of Tyre, *Historia*, 126–36.

17. Peter Partner, *The Templars and Their Myth* (New York: Oxford University Press, 1982), 24–26; Malcolm Barber, *The New Knighthood*, 103, 110, 271–72; Malcolm Barber, *The Trials of Templars*, 12; Howarth, *The Knights Templar*, 220.

18. Malcolm Barber, *The New Knighthood*, 2, 103, 153, 282.

19. Barkun, *Culture of Conspiracy*, 11.

20. Barkun, *Culture of Conspiracy*, 36.

21. Barkun, *Culture of Conspiracy*, 186–87.

22. Michelle Pauli, "Vatican Appoints Official Da Vinci Code Debunker," *The Guardian*, March 15, 2005, http://www.guardian.co.uk/books/2005/mar/15/catholicism.religion (accessed July 30, 2012).

23. Barber, *The New Knighthood*, 319–20.

24. Baigent, Leigh, and Lincoln, *Holy Blood, Holy Grail*, 65, 81.

25. Carol L. Robinson and Pamela Clements, "Living with Neomedievalism," *Studies in Medievalism* 18 (2009): 81, 90.

26. Robinson and Clements, "Living with Neomedievalism," 99, 105.

27. Amy S. Kaufman, "Medieval Unmoored," *Studies in Medievalism* 19 (2010): 5.

28. Michel Foucault, "Truth and Power," in *Power/Knowledge: Selected Interviews and Other Writings, 1972–1977*, ed. Colin Gordon, trans. Colin Gordon, Leo Marshall, John Mephan, Kate Soper (New York: Pantheon, 1980), 133.

29. Foucault, "Truth and Power," 131.

30. Foucault, "Truth and Power," 132.

31. Richard Hofstader, "The Paranoid Style in American Politics," *Harper's*, November 1964, 77–86, http://karws.gso.uri.edu/jfk/conspiracy_theory/the_paranoid_mentality/the_paranoid_style.html (accessed July 30, 2012).

Part VI

Sociality and Social Media in Medieval Gaming

18 Casual Medieval Games, Interactivity, and Social Play in Social Network and Mobile Applications

Serina Patterson

Facebook's release of its development platform in January 2007 resulted in an explosion of games, amusements, and general entertainment applications, soon followed by the proliferation of application platforms on other social networks. For the first time, social networks provided ubiquitous gameplay via computers and handheld electronics and uniquely integrated a player's own interpersonal relationships into a game's core design. When I began research for this paper in 2009, social game applications for the mobile market had not yet reached a critical mass. With the advent of new forms of social gaming, including genres such as location-based gaming, alternative-reality gaming, and massively multiplayer games on mobile devices, web browsers, and social networks, we have witnessed considerable growth in the number of casual games within the game industry.[1]

Social gaming is not an entirely new phenomenon: MUDs (multi-user dungeons), virtual fantasy worlds that garnered wide popularity in the late 1970s, also incorporated social features such as online chatting and competitive play between players.[2] Yet these immersive text-based worlds often required extensive time commitments and were not attached to an individual's digital life beyond the game itself. Gaining popularity around the year 2000, casual social games—defined as games that contain social aspects, fit into a player's lifestyle, support asynchronous play across multiple platforms, and are easy to engage without a large time commitment or deep-seated knowledge of game history—have enjoyed somewhat of a rediscovery in the game industry. Game theorist Jesper Juul remarks, "not everyone feels the pull [of a hardcore game]: not everybody knows what to do";[3] casual games fill this niche. Social casual games also extend the potential of games to appeal to 'nontraditional gamers,' encouraging participation among friends through sharing, wide competition, joint gameplay, and other social activities. The game industry has responded to this broader demographic of people who do not consider themselves game experts; casual gamers currently comprise over 200 million players worldwide, and over 400 commercial titles are released annually within this genre, making casual gaming one of the fastest growing sectors in the entertainment industry.[4]

This chapter explores the relationship between pseudomedieval elements and social play in these popular social casual games, focusing on applications developed for Facebook, Twitter, and mobile devices. Although medieval social games have also appeared on other social networks (such as MySpace and Bebo), Facebook has enjoyed the greatest success to date as a gaming platform and, as a result, many of the games featured on Facebook are simply mirrored on other social networks.[5] The last section of this paper discusses two particular social games, *Elven Blood* (2008) and *Tweetlord* (2009), which have been adapted for the microblogging platform Twitter and thus provide alternate examples of the ways in which games are developed to suit their platforms. Additionally, the scope for this chapter focuses on *social* casual games. Although single-player casual medieval games also exist for Facebook and mobile devices, such as simple renditions of archery games under the guise of 'Robin Hood' and the like,[6] the innovation of these two platforms as socially integrative devices drives the creation of social games that challenge these traditional game models. By virtue of their construction, social networking sites are used primarily for maintaining personal social connections. Social networks are not only a method of communication, but also function as a modern electronic 'agora'—or, a virtual third place, which comprises a place to socialize with others online.[7] Building on a design platform that focuses on user relationships and interactivity, games must therefore work to meet these needs.[8] Although games such as the widely popular massively multiplayer online game (MMO) *World of Warcraft* enable complex social organizations using proprietary tools to organize 'guilds' and groups of friends,[9] games on social networks and mobile devices are able to utilize the user's preexisting social relationships and the network's inherent user interface in order to provide a simple, playful user experience. If game design for social networks and mobile devices differs considerably from that of MMOs and strategy games, as posited by Aki Järvinen,[10] then how does this design influence the inclusion of medieval elements and the player's interaction with them? Do these medievalisms still reflect a fantasy-like escapism, as Umberto Eco suggests of traditional print and film,[11] or do their narratives provide a different form of individual fulfillment?

To date, medievalists studying the characteristics of medievalism in digital gaming have for the most part focused on 'hardcore' role-playing and strategy games such as *Neverwinter Nights* (2002), *Medieval: Total War* (2002), and *Lord of the Rings Online* (2007), paying little attention to the relationship between interactivity, game design, and medievalism in *casual* games despite their overwhelmingly greater popularity.[12] What is more, medieval games display this sustained popularity across platforms; in November 2011 Zynga's *Castleville* (2011), for instance, boasted over 5 million active users *per day*.[13] On Apple's iPad tablet device, *Kingdoms of Camelot* (2009)—one of the longest running social-strategy games available on multiple platforms—is currently the second top-grossing application.[14]

I argue that medieval social casual games on social networks and mobile devices form pseudomedieval fictional worlds constructed in part by online user relationships, which, in turn, project a digital fictionalization of the self through inclusion on user profiles, news feeds, and achievement boards; specifically, their visual user interfaces and group dynamics compose part of an individual's desired identity and status. Within the digital community of large preexisting social networks, the medieval realm sheds many of its historical roots in favor of an imaginary "possibility space"[15] ripe with opportunities to build individualized medieval worlds and economies. 'Medieval' elements have thus become a part of an individual's playful identity both inside and outside of the game world.

CASUAL MEDIEVAL GAMES

Unlike those elements in 'hardcore' medieval games such as *Great Battles: Medieval* (2011) and *War of the Roses* (2012), which attempt to re-create the War of the Roses between France and England in the fifteenth century,[16] references to historical moments and periods in social casual games become mere markers of aesthetics, genres, and mechanics. The browser-based game *1100AD* (2009–11), which players can access through Facebook, encompasses a simplified strategy game. Apart from the title, the game has little to do with twelfth-century European economics, architecture, or culture. Although the game states that it provides an "online browser game based in a parallel version of the Middle Ages,"[17] the term 'Middle Ages' becomes a catch-word for the type of experience players receive. Players can effectively conquer territories, ally with other players, and exchange resources; in *1100AD*, the idea of the 'medieval' becomes synonymous with war. Not surprisingly, the motives behind the design of the majority of medieval games, as Oliver Traxel notes, stems from popular imagination: designers appeal to "what [they] believe their audiences kno[w] about the Middle Ages";[18] thus, war, knights, and castles act as a pretext for a game wherein game designers can take great liberties with medieval content, mingling historical facts with fantastical fiction.

Even within games that promise a historical experience, such as the social strategy game *Medieval Times* (2009), the premise is still fundamentally bound to the user's ability to play with his or her friends; the game description for *Medieval Times* reads:

> Take a journey through Medieval Europe's dark ages with your friends by your side, and go from serf to king by joining Medieval Times! In this epic journey through time, you start your lowly existence as a serf in medieval Europe. As you travel through this wretched period in Europe's history you gain power by acquiring wealth through: weapons, land, and of course money. Eventually, if it be so deemed, you will rise

to the top of the food chain and become a king. It is your destiny. Take hold. Join the journey today. Your future awaits you.[19]

The rags-to-riches narrative that drives this game, and other social-strategy games such as *Knights of Honor* (2005) and *Medieval Clash* (2009), display a Western ideal of the effect of capitalism, which, in turn, projects personal wish fulfillment, a path of upwards power and success based on personal achievement. The iPhone and iPad strategy MMO *Lords* (2011) also modernizes medieval manorialism by integrating social aspects: players can play as a duke, baron, knight, marquis, or other medievalized figure and build a fortress by hiring other players as vassals, buying and selling within a thriving market economy, and creating alliances with friends.[20] Similar to *Medieval Times*, players in *Lords* begin as a commoner who was born to a noble family but orphaned by war and subsequently raised by peasants, a plot sometimes found in medieval romance. The goal of the game is to gain back possessions that were supposedly lost. All relationships and ties to other players, whether they are vassals, allies, or enemies, reinforce the competitive, strategic nature of the game—that is, to increase rankings on the game's leaderboard by amassing large sums of money and building a strong kingdom.

MEDIEVAL GAMES ON SOCIAL NETWORKS AND MOBILE APPLICATIONS

Medieval elements—such as quests, weaponry, and knighthood—are thus portrayed in their most rudimentary form, downplayed in order to create an asynchronous 'medieval' experience with one's friends. Although they often retain elements from their parent genres—that is, strategy, role-playing, and massively multiplayer games—the emphasis on social aspects that are integrated interpersonally across several platforms fundamentally alters the ways in which players engage with medieval elements. In 2010, I classified medieval elements in Facebook applications and concluded that they were primarily deployed through six different application models:[21]

1. Social-Strategy: Graphical
   - Real-time strategy
   - Isometric graphical-based interface, often built on Adobe Flash
   - Prompts friends to join an ad-hoc network as an ally in order to build a strong force against opposing players
2. Social-Strategy: Limited Graphics
   - Uses text-based lists rather than a graphical interface
   - Employs simple mechanics (e.g., point-and-click quest progression)
   - Prompts friends to join an ad-hoc network as an ally in order to build a strong force against opposing players

3. MMO-style
   - Three-dimensional graphics
   - Prompts friends to join an ad-hoc network as an ally in order to build a strong force against opposing players
4. Quizzes
   - Personality quizzes
   - Tests knowledge of subjects such as literature and history
   - Showcases results on published status updates
5. Gift-Giving
   - Enables sending 'medieval' items to friends (e.g., a longsword)
   - Each gift sent grants the player points that can be collected in exchange for items
6. Miscellaneous
   - Displays objects such as flags, family escutcheons, and other items on a user's page

Applications ranged from strategy games in which players could rise to become the leader of a kingdom to gift-giving applications that allow players to send medieval weaponry to someone within their network. More recently, these models can also be applied to pseudomedieval applications on mobile devices. Players can purchase medieval castles as a wallpaper for their phone, for instance, or enact stylized swordplay using the device's gyroscope and accelerometer.[22] This wide range of application models indicates that medieval elements, like those of other genres, are not limited to games alone and that these games can often straddle the line between casual game and free play. Sending a fleet of minions to a friend in need in the game *Warbook* (2007), for instance, does not seem to encompass many of the desired features of a modern electronic game—including an immersive world or an engaging narrative.[23] Yet those same minions could nonetheless help stave off an attack from another player, indicating an emphasis on competition and strategy in order to create a social experience.[24] As Järvinen argues in his work on game design for social networks, gameplay on sites like Facebook and MySpace are "filtere[ed] through the emotional disposition of playfulness," so it "may become more casual (random, fleeting, effort-aversive)" than players engaged with MMOs, role-playing, and strategy games.[25] What we see from this list is not an eradication of traditional medieval game genres such as real-time or turn-based strategy, but a transformation—a repackaging of these genres for an audience that wants to reinforce external social connections in a casual environment. The inclusion of medieval and pseudomedieval elements in these games, as Carol Robinson observes, usually "ha[ve] little to do with the Middle Ages."[26]

Due to the ease of development with Facebook's Application Programming Interface (API), the majority of strategy games are modeled on a simplistic version of their parent genre: in general, users must build up their rank or kingdom by completing goals (quests), exploring the land, fighting other players, and creating buildings. Unlike hardcore strategy games, any action can usually be completed using a single user interaction (e.g., a click of a mouse). In the multiplatform strategy game *Castle Age* (2011), for example, players can complete goals by repeatedly acting (e.g., clicking) on a button that reads 'quest,' which rewards them with experience and money to buy new items (e.g., armor). The ever-present battle mechanics also operate asynchronously: players can recruit fellow allies to help defeat a monster by prompting their friends via their news feed and in-game messages.[27] In *Robin Hood* (2009), a game built on similar mechanics to *Castle Age*, players are encouraged to invite friends by sending them free virtual gifts, such as a sparkling ring or a pear. The more friends a player invites, the stronger that player (and subsequently his or her friends) become as a team. Although a player does not have to invite friends to a game, constant reminders on a friend's activity stream and the emotional value placed on virtual items reinforces the concept that sociality is a key gameplay element.[28]

The appeal of the 'medieval,' then, does not solely stem from the act of playing the games themselves—indeed, mechanisms such as restrictive timers and finite resources which deplete with every action performed serve as an intrinsic limiting factor; rather, motivations to play a medieval social-strategy game often lie in the player's visible association with the associated gaming culture. A player's Facebook profile and personal feed act as a public play space that shapes the construction of a player's desired online persona and enables him or her to socialize with others. As with many games on Facebook, most medieval social games not only showcase a players' in-game actions to their friends but also publish actions those friends perform for them as well. One news item for *Castle Age* may announce that the individual has killed a monster and include the number of friends who helped defeat the foe. And in *Armies of Magic* (2012) the news item entices fellow friends to collect a 'bonus item' if they click on the player's newly discovered troop unit or research.[29] In one newsfeed post, *Kingdoms of Camelot* (2009) not only rewards the player for gaining a level, but also similarly promises a bonus reward for five friends (Figure 18.1).

Notably, sharing in-game items and news on the player's personal profile page (and friends' newsfeeds) is completely optional: in most games, the interface prompts the player with a 'share' button, but sharing is not required to advance in the game. As a result, many games include bonus rewards or extra quests if players decide to broadcast their status and thus extend the boundaries of the game's influence. This mechanic not only provides free advertising for the game, but also helps create a larger virtual community within the game. Using this strategy to attract new players, *Kingdoms of Camelot* currently boasts over 300,000 monthly active users on Facebook alone. Playing *Castle Age, Robin Hood, Armies of Magic*, and other social-strategy games on Facebook showcases a player's interest in strategy games and provides a 'third space' oriented toward communities across platforms.

Figure 18.1   Kingdoms of Camelot, post on a personal Facebook profile

Because many elements that exist in medieval social games are also found in other nonmedieval games, playing in a medieval world can be ostensibly a conscious choice for the player. Medieval elements, then, become iconic in nature—swords, kings, castles, and quests stand in as personal status symbols, completely divorced from their historical origins. What is more, the numerous personality and knowledge quizzes, including "What medieval torture device are you?" "Would you survive a medieval battle?" and "What profession would you be in the medieval times?" all attest to the use of medieval iconography and ideas as individualizing agents and sources of personal distraction. Medieval social-strategy games, gift-giving, and quizzes certainly cleave to this purpose, promoting a persona that a player builds within a social network through engaging in activities defined by the game. For many medieval games on mobile devices, a display of achievement is further centralized: *Lords & Knights* (2011), a massive multiplayer strategy found on iPhone, iPad, Android, and Facebook, connects to Apple's Game Center, which enables players to join friends' games, chat, and showcase unlocked game achievements (e.g., owning five castles or stationing 3,000 troops in an owned castle) to fellow players.[30] For social casual games, then, the 'medieval' not only defines a place one goes, but also something one *does*. As Ines Di Loreto and Abdelkader Gouaïch observe in their psychological study of Facebook users, "the motivation that pushes the users to show their achievements—e.g., publishing on the Facebook wall—[is] linked to the social acknowledgement and approval of their achievement."[31] Intermixed with other aspects of an individual's digital persona—such as messages, status updates, and other interests—medieval social casual game progression makes up part of a person's public identity. Thus, these games extend beyond the virtual: they construct, and help fictionalize, an individual's identity.

But the emphasis on a game's social and public aspects does not rest only on these iconographic status-symbols appearing in newsfeeds, achievement boards, and profile pages. In some cases, developers adapt the medieval aspects of a game for a specific audience, fully integrating socializing mechanics into the game's core design. When the developer team for 6Wave's Facebook game *Ravenshire Castle* (2012) began conceptualizing the game's core mechanics, they asked their player-base, consisting largely of middle-aged women, how they wanted to conduct player-versus-player conflicts.[32] While the majority of medieval social-strategy games emphasize the need to conquer enemy kingdoms through force and siege, *Ravenshire Castle*'s players took a different approach: female players would rather sneak into a friend's castle to seduce characters and steal possessions (Figure 18.2).[33]

A study of casual game demographics on Facebook reveals that content and aesthetics are not the only criteria people use to choose which game to play: middle-aged female players typically formed 66 to 78 percent of the player-base for *Farmville*, *Yoville*, and *Treasure Isle*.[34] All of these games emphasize collaboration and joint gameplay through achieving goals (quests), resource collection, and item acquisition. In *Ravenshire Castle* players can lay traps for guards and gain progression in the game by successfully stealing items from friends and other players. In these simulated medieval worlds, then, friends become an integral part of this playful gameplay. Indeed, friend slots, which show portraits of a player's friends, constitute a major portion of the user interface, often located in a row beside the main menu. After constructing a 'Maiden's Tower' for the castle in *CastleVille*, the game prompts the player to add crew by recruiting friends.[35] *CastleVille* and *Ravenshire Castle* also

Figure 18.2   Sneaking into a castle in *Ravenshire Castle*

integrate social relationships into quests: in one *CastleVille* quest, the player must defeat a monster in a friend's kingdom. Castles, which can be built, customized, and decorated, act as not only spaces for individual expression but also sites for socialization. Although players can play the game alone, the game rewards social actions such as sharing and gifting and, in some cases, the only way players can advance in the game is to play with friends.

Ravenshire Castle's and *CastleVille*'s successful integration of social features into their pseudomedieval game worlds illustrates a new development in the design of social games: social city-building. In recent years, social medieval simulation games have increased on Facebook and other platforms, adding to the previous six application models. Although games such as *Castle Age* invite allies to help fight monsters, text-based messages provide the only mechanism with which to create a communal space to socialize with other players. For social simulation games, each player maintains an individual visual space: in practice, a plot of land that can be expanded as a player progresses through the game. Notably, players can not only visit their friends' kingdoms, but also interact with their friends' space by tending gardens, defeating enemies, and placing special items. Influenced in part by Zynga's widely successful game *FarmVille*, social simulation games create possibility landscapes wherein players can effectively create their own versions of a world. For medieval games such as *Ravenshire Castle*, players are tasked to restore a kingdom to greatness—again adopting the rags-to-riches concept—by constructing new rooms and guarding against sneaky intruders. *CastleVille* similarly shares in an idyllic, idealized medieval world: their slogan reads, for instance, "Build a Happy Kingdom with Your Fiery Friends."[36] And in Ubisoft's *Castle & Co* (2010), players must also manage their citizens' happiness meter: clicking 'cheer' on non-player characters (NPCs) increases their overall productivity.[37] Medieval objects and landscapes shift, in other words, from a historical sociotemporal space to an imaginary one. The 'medieval' is an Othering space, but no longer represents remnants of a past age.

Why do simulation games turn to fantastical medieval worlds again and again? Due to the long history of fantasy and role-playing games, largely attributed to Tolkien's *Lord of the Rings*, *Dungeons & Dragons*, and early adventure games, one could argue that medieval modalities easily correspond to genre mechanics (or, conversely, mechanics such as tower defense are inspired by medieval modalities). As we have already witnessed, medieval iconography often determines a specific form of gameplay. For casual games, which have lower situational and immersive context, these medieval elements provide visual literacy for expected gameplay and a realm that they alone control. But the persistence and appeal of the Middle Ages goes beyond mere convenience; the imaginary spaces it builds fulfill fundamental emotional needs. Social simulation games targeted toward a female player-base, for instance, emphasize collaboration rather than conflict, so imaginary medieval worlds can effectively reflect this unique relationship.

Players of the pet-breeding simulation game *Dragon City* (2012) can help care for their friends' baby dragons, for instance.[38] In *CastleVille,* players can purchase a 'Unicorn Cottage' for a friend. As Valentina Rao notes, "Facebook Applications seem to appeal to the sphere of emotions (fun and playful mood) rather than actions (gameplay)."[39] By infantilizing pseudomedieval landscapes, the Middle Ages is no longer associated with historical realities such as war, plague, or manorialism. Rather, for medieval worlds in many social simulation games, castles, dragons, crowns, and similar trappings evoke a playful mood in a childlike atmosphere. The infantilism illustrated by the cartoonized aesthetics and anthropomorphized characters—figures with big eyes, large heads, small bodies, delicate facial features, and customizable wardrobes—speaks to a manifestation of pedomorphosis: medieval elements are rendered infantile because players respond positively, increasing their retention, playfulness, curiosity, and nurturing behavior. Therefore, game designers turn to medieval worlds to promote alternate imaginary and fun playspaces, and aesthetically pleasing medieval elements are, in turn, ushered to stimulate these desired moods.

MEDIEVAL GAMES ON TWITTER

Games on Twitter are a relatively new phenomenon. Although sites such as Twitter are also social platforms, their differing user demographics, lack of a graphical interface, and focus on microblogging provide a unique platform for designing games. In a nutshell, Twitter is a free social networking service that allows users to post and read short 140-character messages (tweets). The emphasis is on public information dissemination and aggregation. Developers can tap into a huge player-base, with over 140 million active users,[40] but there is no closed environment for games or visual interfaces.

Due to Twitter's restricted user-input model, medieval casual games have branched into two different designs: cross-platform games and text-based games. *Elven Blood*, a medievalized fantasy game, follows the same social-strategy game model we see on Facebook with one-click quest completion, energy depletion, and the ability to equip and trade digital items with friends.[41] Similar to other social-strategy games, *Elven Blood* is focused on gaming through relationships. On Twitter, the game invites players to build their 'party' by sending requests to friends (called 'followers') on their Twitter contact list to join the game. Actions players perform in the game show up in their Twitter feed, where a follower can see the player's progress. Although *Elven Blood* does build in the need for social interaction by requiring extra party members in order to complete certain quests or explore the game world, medieval elements are not intrinsic to the platform structure or user experience. For *Elven Blood,* players can quickly switch to their other games, including a vampire or apocalyptic theme, while maintaining the same interface and core mechanics. In essence, 'the medieval' experience simply becomes a thematic aesthetic layering over the core mechanics. Due to this freedom of choice, the popularity of *Elven Blood* reveals that the public has a conscious desire to play with medieval, as opposed to, for example, vampiric content.

Where *Elven Blood* works around Twitter's limitations, the role-playing Twitter game *Tweetlord* works directly through Twitter's core functionality. In *Tweetlord,* users can perform any action in the game world by simply creating a hashtag of that action, such as #grapple or #pickpocket, and directing the tweet to the game world, '@TLgame.'[42] Actions are tied to a moral system, called 'karma,' where players can 'kill' other players or, alternatively, 'help' them. In keeping with other social games, each action spends finite resources and players can improve their characters by performing a certain quantity of actions. *Tweetlord* is completely text-based, so it is able to seamlessly integrate with everyday life more readily than other social medieval games due to Twitter's ubiquity across several devices. For players, individual fulfillment for this game is achieved through their creative use of their tweets and the game's ubiquity. For instance, a player can amalgamate game actions into their everyday tweets such as "I #swam in the ocean @TLgame" in order to earn points. The space between the modern and the pseudomedieval is virtually indistinguishable because the game can be played anywhere through a Twitter application, whether on a mobile phone or a computer. Player avatars may include images of swords, bows, feathered caps, and breeches on various cartoon birds, but they are used as a level indicator rather than as a main identifier for a given player. In *Tweetlord,* the imaginary Middle Ages is thus not a nostalgic environment, but rather actions reflected on a public persona, mingled with the player's other relationships.

CONCLUSION

Social gaming is a relatively immature market in the game industry. As new technologies become increasingly cross-platform and available to more consumers—spurred by the growth of social games across consoles, computers, mobile phones, tablets, and other devices—medieval and pseudomedieval elements will no longer be restricted to immersive, graphical game worlds, but rather work to help form the public personas of individuals and communities. Location-based games, in particular, are beginning to emerge across various social platforms and mobile devices. In *Parallel Kingdoms* (2009), for instance, the player begins the game with a tutorial set in New York. The game designers have overlaid a map of the city with monsters, caverns, treasure troves, and other items to explore.[43] In *GeoEmpires* (2012), available on Android, iPhone, and iPad devices, players can not only conquer real neighboring territories, but also access local leaderboards. More than other social casual games, these games create a feeling of a regional community because players can declare their local streets as territories and their local neighbors as allies or enemies.[44] That medieval landscapes are one of the most popular forms of location-based gaming testifies to the appeal of blurring our world with alternate, fantastical realms. Overlaying castles on maps and forcing a neighbor to pay feudal taxes keeps a sense of presence, an awareness of our location in time.

Medieval applications are far from the majority on these networks, but their persistent presence does give us a context for examining the use of medieval elements within a unique social environment, especially when they are compared to hardcore single-player or massively multiplayer games. Although these social games borrow elements from their parent genre and other social games, medieval applications create imaginary worlds that serve a variety of social and emotional needs. For social casual medieval games, the 'medieval' is a way to not only escape the real world, but also further define oneself within it.

NOTES

1. As of July 2012, mobile devices have become the most-valued gaming platform, overtaking both browser-based and social networking games in customer time and spending. See Michael Barnett, "Mobile Plays Lead Role in Growth of Gaming," *Marketing Week*, http://www.marketingweek. co.uk/trends/mobile-plays-lead-role-in-growth-of-gaming/4002633.article (accessed July 19, 2012).
2. Matt Barton, *Dungeons & Desktops: The History of Computer Role Playing Games* (London: AK Peters, 2008), 37–43.
3. Jesper Juul, *A Casual Revolution: Reinventing Video Games and Their Players* (Cambridge, MA: MIT Press, 2010), 4. Juul also discusses casual gaming as a revolutionary moment in this history of games: casual games, he notes, are "a cultural reinvention of what a video game can be, a reimagining of *who* can be a video game player" (4).
4. See "Casual Games Association: FAQ," http://www.casualgamesassociation. org/news.php#casualgames (accessed July 19, 2012).
5. As of September 2011, Facebook has reached over 750 million users around the world. Popular games on Facebook can attract millions of players. Zynga's *CityVille*, for instance, boasted 31 million active users on June 20, 2012. For data and statistics on various applications, see http://www. appdata.com/.
6. See, for instance, *Longbow: Archery 3D*, Jason Allen (Android, 2012); *Bowmaster*, Chromegekko (iOS, 2012); and *Sherwood Forest Archery*, Revolution Games (iOS, 2010).
7. Oldenburg argues that with the rise of virtual and digital communities, we are losing physical, neutral 'third places' between work and home life, which serve to define and strengthen communities (e.g., a coffee shop). See Ray Oldenburg, *The Great Good Place: Cafes, Coffee Shops, Community Centers, Beauty Parlors, General Stores, Bars, Hangouts, and How They Get You Through the Day* (New York: Marlowe, 1991). Howard Rheingold also argues that the development of virtual communities is "in part a response to the hunger for community that has followed the disintegration of traditional

communities around the world." See his *The Virtual Community: Home-steading on the Electronic Frontier* (Cambridge, MA: MIT Press, 2000), 418.

8. In their psychological study of Facebook games, Ines Di Loreto and Abdelkader Gouaïch remark that social casual games not only aim to create a sense of community, but also fulfill Harold Murray's criteria for appealing to fundamental psychological needs—that is, materialism, power, affection, ambition, and information. See "Social Casual Games Success is Not So Casual," Research Report #RR-10017 LIRMM, University of Montpellier CNRS, http://hal.archives-ouvertes.fr/docs/00/48/69/34/PDF/FunAndGames2010–03–22.pdf (accessed June 17, 2012).
9. *World of Warcraft*, Blizzard Entertainment (Blizzard Entertainment, 2004–2012).
10. Aki Järvinen, "Game Design for Social Networks: Interaction Design for Playful Dispositions," in *Proceedings of the 2009 ACM SIGGRAPH Symposium on Video Games* (New York: Association for Computing Machinery, 2009), 97.
11. Umberto Eco, "Dreaming the Middle Ages," in *Travels in Hyperreality*, trans. W. Weaver (New York: Harcourt Brace, 1986), 65.
12. Casual games generate revenues of approximately $6 to $8 billion dollars per year. See Emily Parkhurst, "Casual-gaming Industry: $8 Billion and Counting," *Puget Sound Business Journal*, http://www.bizjournals.com/seattle/blog/techflash/2012/07/casual-gaming-8-billion-and-counting.html?page = all (accessed July 19, 2012).
13. Leena Rao, "Zynga's CastleVille Crosses 5M Daily Active Users, Now Growing Faster Than CityVille," *Tech Crunch*, http://techcrunch.com/2011/11/21/zyngas-castleville-crosses-5m-daily-active-users-now-growing-faster-that-cityville/ (accessed July 21, 2012).
14. As of July 21, 2012.
15. Will Wright, "Sculpting Possibility Space" (keynote address, Accelerating Change, Stanford University, Palo Alto, CA, November 6, 2004), http://itc.conversationsnetwork.org/shows/detail376.html# (accessed May 4, 2012).
16. *Great Battles: Medieval*, War Drum Studios (Slitherine Software, 2009); *War of the Roses*, Fatshark (Paradox Interactive, 2012).
17. *1100AD*, Amber Games (Web, 2009–2012).
18. Oliver Traxel, "Medieval and Pseudo-Medieval Elements in Computer Role-Playing Games: Use and Interactivity," *Studies in Medievalism* 16 (2008): 132.
19. *Medieval Times*, Generation Me (Facebook, 2009).
20. *Lords*, Trinix3, LLC (iOS, 2011).
21. Serina Patterson, "'My Friends and Allies:'" Medieval Games, Interactivity, and Social Play in Social Network Applications" (paper presented at the 45th International Congress on Medieval Studies, Kalamazoo, MI, 2010).
22. See, for instance, *Sword!*, Mass Orbit Software (Android, 2009).
23. Jesper Juul, *Half-Real: Video Games between Real Rules and Fictional Worlds* (Cambridge, MA: MIT Press, 2005), 190.
24. *Warbook*, SGN (Facebook, 2007).
25. Järvinen, "Game Design for Social Networks," 97.
26. Carol Robinson, "An Introduction to Medievalist Video Games," *Studies in Medievalism* 16 (2008): 124.
27. *Castle Age*, Phoenix Age (Android, Facebook, and iOS, 2011).
28. *Robin Hood*, Zynga (Facebook, 2009).
29. *Armies of Magic*, Playdom (Facebook, 2012).
30. *Lords & Knights*, XYRALITY GmbH (Android, Facebook, and iOS, 2011).
31. Di Loreto, "Social Casual Games Success is Not So Casual," 5.

32. *Ravenshire Castle*, Silverlake, 6Waves (Facebook, 2012).
33. John Osborne, "On Ravenshire Castle, Curing Fatigue and Pushing Envelopes," *Games.com*, http://blog.games.com/2012/05/07/ravenshire-castle-interview/ (accessed July 15, 2012).
34. "Facebook Casual Game Demographics," *DataGenetics,* http://www.data genetics.com/blog/december12010/index.html (accessed July 19, 2012).
35. *CastleVille*, Zynga (Facebook, 2011).
36. *CastleVille*, Zynga (Facebook, 2011).
37. *Castle & Co*, Ubisoft (Facebook, 2010).
38. *Dragon City*, SocialPoint (Facebook, 2012). As of July 31, 2012, *Dragon City* has just under 8 million monthly active users.
39. Valentina Rao, "Playful Mood: The Construction of Facebook as a Third Place," MindTrek Conference 2008, Tampere, Finland, http://prtal.acm.org/ citation. cfm?id = 1457199.1457202&coll = Portal&dl = GUIDE&CFID = 24746181&CFTOKEN = 85617762 (accessed April 10, 2010).
40. Angela Moscaritolo, "Twitter Turns Six with 140 Million Active Users," *PC Mag.com*, http://www.pcmag.com/article2/0,2817,2401955,00.asp (accessed July 19, 2012).
41. *Elven Blood*, 140blood (Twitter, 2008).
42. *Tweetlord*, Multi Axis Games (Twitter, 2009).
43. *Parallel Kingdoms*, PerBlue (Facebook and iOS, 2009).
44. *GeoEmpires*, Archae s.r.o (Android and iOS, 2012).

Appendix A
List of PC and Console Games

The titles here conform to *Game Title*. Developer. Publisher, date.

Age of Empires II: The Age of Kings. Microsoft Game Studios. Ensemble Studios, 1999.

Aion: The Tower of Eternity. Aion Team Development Department. NCsoft, 2008.

Anarchy Online. Funcom. Funcom, 2001.

Assassin's Creed. Ubisoft Montreal. Ubisoft, 2007.

Assassin's Creed II. Ubisoft Montreal. Ubisoft, 2009.

Assassin's Creed III. Ubisoft Montreal. Ubisoft, 2012.

Assassin's Creed: Brotherhood. Ubisoft Montreal. Ubisoft, 2010.

Assassin's Creed: Revelations. Ubisoft Montreal. Ubisoft, 2011.

Bayonetta. Platinum Games. Sega, 2010.

The Beast Within: A Gabriel Knight Mystery. Sierra On-Line. Sierra On-Line, 1995.

Beowulf: The Game. Ubisoft. Ubisoft, 2007.

Braid. Number None. Independent release, 2008.

Conan. Nihilistic Software. THQ, 2007.

Crusader Kings. Paradox Development Studio. Paradox Interactive, 2004.

Crusader Kings: Deus Vult. Paradox Development Studio. Paradox Interactive, 2007.

Dante's Inferno. Visceral Games. Electronic Arts, 2010.

DC Universe Online. WBIE. Sony Online Entertainment, 2011.

Dead Space 2. Visceral Games. Electronic Arts, 2011.

Deus Ex. Ion Storm. Eidos Interactive, 2000.

Deus Ex: Human Revolution. Eidos Montreal. Square Enix, 2011.

Deus Ex: Invisible War. Ion Storm. Eidos Interactive, 2003.

Dragon Age: Origins. BioWare Edmonton. Electronic Arts, 2009.

The Elder Scrolls III: Morrowind. Bethesda Game Studios. Bethesda Softworks, 2002.

The Elder Scrolls IV: Oblivion. Bethesda Softworks. 2K Games, 2006.

The Elder Scrolls V: Skyrim. Bethesda Game Studios. Bethesda Softworks, 2011.

Eve Online. CCP. Simon and Schuster, 2003.

Everquest. Sony Online Entertainment. Sony Online Entertainment, 1999.

Everquest II. Sony Online Entertainment. Sony Online Entertainment, 2004.

Fallout 3. Bethesda Game Studies. Bethesda Softworks, 2008.

Fallout: New Vegas. Obsidian Entertainment. Bethesda Softworks, 2010.

Gabriel Knight: Sins of the Fathers. Sierra On-Line. Sierra On-Line, 1993.

Gabriel Knight 3: Blood of the Sacred, Blood of the Damned. Sierra On-Line. Sierra On-Line, 1999.

God of War. SCE Santa Monica. Sony, 2005.

God of War II. SCE Santa Monica. Sony, 2007.

God of War III. SCE Santa Monica. Sony, 2010.

God of War Saga. SCE Santa Monica. Sony, 2012.

Great Battles: Medieval. The History Channel. Slitherine Software, 2011.

Guild Wars. ArenaNet. NCsoft North America, 2005.

Just Cause 2. Avalanche Studios. Eidos Interactive, 2010.

King's Quest V: Absences Makes the Heart Go Yonder. Sierra On-line. Sierra On-line, 1990.

Knights of Honor. Black Sea Studios. Paradox Interactive, 2005.

L.A. Noire. Team Bondi. Rockstar Games, 2011.

The Legend of Zelda. Nintendo. Nintendo, 1986.

The Legend of Zelda: Ocarina of Time. Nintendo. Nintendo, 1998.

The Legend of Zelda: Windwaker. Nintendo. Nintendo, 2003.

Lord of the Rings Online. Turbine. Midway, 2007.

Mass Effect. Bioware. Demiurge Studies, 2007.

Medieval: Total War. The Creative Assembly. Activision, 2002.

Medieval 2: Total War. The Creative Assembly. Sega, 2006.

Might and Magic. NEC Avenue. NEC Avenue, 1992.

Myst. Cyan. Broderbund Software, 1993.

Neverwinter Nights. Bioware. Atari, 2002.

New Super Mario Brothers: Wii. Nintendo. Nintendo, 2009.

Ninja Gaiden 3. Team Ninja. Tecmo Koei, 2012.

Pac-Man. Namco. Namco Midway, 1980.

Pong. Atari. Atari, 1972.

Resident Evil. Capcom. Virgin Interactive, 1997.

Rift. Trion Worlds. Trion Worlds, 2011.

Robin Hood: Legend of Sherwood. Spellbound. Strategy First, 2002.

Secret of Monkey Island. Lucasfilm Games. Softgold, 1990.

Sid Meier's Pirates! Firaxis Games. 2K Games, 2007.

The Sims Medieval. The Sims Studio. Electronic Arts, 2011.

Stronghold. Firefly Studios. Gathering, 2001.

Super Mario Bros. Nintendo. Nintendo, 1985.

Super Mario Bros. 3. Nintendo. Nintendo, 1988.

Super Mario Sunshine. Nintendo. Nintendo, 2002.

Super Mario World. Nintendo. Nintendo, 1990.

Vanguard: Saga of Heroes. Sony Online Entertainment. Sony Online Entertainment, 2007.

War of the Roses. Fatshark AB, Paradox Interactive, 2012.

Warcraft: Orcs & Humans. Blizzard Entertainment. Blizzard Entertainment, 1994.

Warcraft II: Tides of Darkness. Blizzard Entertainment. Blizzard Entertainment, 1995.

Warcraft III: Reign of Chaos. Blizzard Entertainment. Blizzard Entertainment, 2002

Warhammer Online: Age of Reckoning. Mythic Entertainment. Electronic Arts, 2008.

Warlock: Master of the Arcane. Paradox Interactive. Ino-co Plus, 2012.

World of Warcraft. Blizzard Entertainment. Blizzard Entertainment, 2004.

World of Warcraft: Cataclysm. Blizzard Entertainment. Blizzard Entertainment, 2010.

World of Warcraft: Mists of Pandaria. Blizzard Entertainment. Blizzard Entertainment, 2012.

World of Warcraft: The Burning Crusade. Blizzard Entertainment. Blizzard Entertainment, 2007.

World of Warcraft: Wrath of the Lich King. Blizzard Entertainment. Blizzard Entertainment, 2008.

Appendix B
List of Social Media/Mobile Games

The titles here conform to *Game Title*. Developer. Platform, date.

1100AD. Amber Games. Web, 2009–2012.

Armies of Magic. Playdom. Facebook, 2012.

Bowmaster. Chromegekko. iOS, 2012.

Castle Age. Phoenix Age. Android, Facebook, and iOS, 2011.

Castle & Co. Ubisoft. Facebook, 2010.

CastleVille. Zynga. Facebook, 2011.

Dragon City. SocialPoint. Facebook, 2012.

Elven Blood. 140blood. Twitter, 2008.

GeoEmpires. Archae s.r.o. Android and iOS, 2012.

Kingdoms of Camelot. Water Cooler. Facebook, 2009.

Longbow: Archery 3D. Jason Allen. Android, 2012.

Lords. Trinix3. LLC, iOS, 2011.

Lords & Knights. XYRALITY. GmbH, Android, Facebook, and iOS, 2011.

Medieval Clash. Vincler Conceptions. Flash, 2009.

Medieval Times. Generation Me. Facebook, 2009.

Parallel Kingdoms. PerBlue. Facebook and iOS, 2009.

Ravenshire Castle. Silverlake. 6Waves, Facebook, 2012.

Robin Hood. Zynga. Facebook, 2009.

Sherwood Forest Archery. Revolution Games. iOS, 2010.

Sword! Mass Orbit Software. Android, 2009.

Tweetlord. Multi Axis Games. Twitter, 2009.

Warbook. SGN. Facebook, 2007.

Bibliography

Aarseth, Espen. "Computer Game Studies, Year One." *Game Studies* 1, no. 1 (2001). Accessed October 28, 2012. http://www.gamestudies.org/0101/editorial.html.
———. *Cybertext: Perspectives on Ergodic Literature.* Baltimore: Johns Hopkins University Press,1997.
———. "How We Became Postdigital: From Cyberstudies to Game Studies." In *Critical Cyberculture Studies,* edited by David Silver and Adrienne Massanari, 37–46. New York: New York University Press, 2006.
———. "Quest Games as Post-Narrative Discourse." In *Narrative across Media: The Languages of Storytelling,* edited by Marie-Laure Ryan, 361–76. Lincoln: University of Nebraska Press, 2004.
Abdalla, Laila. "Theology and Culture: Masculinizing the Woman." In *Varieties of Devotion in the Middle Ages and Renaissance,* edited by Susan C Karant-Nunn, 17–37. Turnhout, Belgium: Brepols, 2003.
Abelard, Peter. Letters. In *The Letters of Peter Abelard: Beyond the Personal.* Edited and translated by Jan M. Ziolkowski. Washington, DC: The Catholic University of America Press, 2008.
Abrams, Sandra S. "A Gaming Frame of Mind: Digital Contexts and Academic Implications." *Educational Media International* 46 (2009): 335–47.
Abulafia, David, and Nora Berend, eds. *Medieval Frontiers: Concepts and Practices.* Aldershot: Ashgate, 2002.
Alberti, Leon Battista. *On Painting.* Edited by Martin Kemp and translated by Cecil Grayson. New York: Penguin, 1991.
Alighieri, Dante. *The Divine Comedy.* Translated by Henry Wadsworth Longfellow. London: George Routledge and Sons, 1867.
———. *Divine Comedy.* Digital Dante. http://dante.ilt.columbia.edu/comedy/index.html.
———. *The Divine Comedy of Dante Alighieri.* 3 vols. Translated by Jean and Robert Hollander. New York: Anchor Books, 2002–2008.
———. *The Divine Comedy of Dante Alighieri,* Vol. 1: *Inferno.* Edited and translated by Robert M. Durling. New York: Oxford University Press, 1996.
———. *The Divine Comedy: Purgatorio.* Edited by Charles Singleton. Princeton: Princeton University Press, 1973.
"All Your Base Are Belong To Us." *Wikipedia.* Accessed August 18, 2011. http://en.wikipedia.org/wiki/All_your_base_are_belong_to_us.
Allmand, Christopher. *The De Re Militari of Vegetius: The Reception, Transmission and Legacy of a Roman Text in the Middle Ages.* Cambridge, UK: Cambridge University Press, 2011.
Allston, Aaron. *Strike Force.* Charlottesville, VA: Iron Crown Enterprises, 1988.

Appadurai, Arjun. *The Social Life of Things: Commodities in Cultural Perspective.* Cambridge, UK: Cambridge University Press, 1980.

Arneson, Dave. *The First Fantasy Campaign.* Decatur, IL: Judges Guild, 1977.

Ascoli, Albert Russell. *Dante and the Making of a Modern Author.* Cambridge, UK: Cambridge University Press, 2008.

Ashe, Laura. "*Sir Gawain and the Green Knight* and the Limits of Chivalry." In *The Exploitations of Medieval Romance,* edited by Laura Ashe, Ivana Djordjeviá, and Judith Weiss, 159–72. Cambridge, UK: D. S. Brewer, 2010.

Ashley, Kathleen. "Material and Symbolic Gift-Giving: Clothes in English and French Wills." In *Medieval Fabrications: Dress, Textiles, Clothwork, and Other Cultural Imaginings,* edited by E. Jane Burns, 137–46. New York: Palgrave Macmillan, 2004.

Auerbach, Erich. *Mimesis: The Representation of Reality in Western Literature.* Translated by Willard R. Trask. Princeton: Princeton University Press, 1953.

———. "Figura." In *Scenes from the Drama of European Literature.* Translated by Ralph Manheim, 11–76. Minneapolis: University of Minnesota Press, 1984.

Bachrach, Bernard S. "L'Art de la guerre angevin." In *Plantagenêts et Capétiens: confrontations et héritages,* edited by Martin Aurell and Noël-Yves Tonnerre, 267–84. Turnhout, Belgium: Brepols, 2006.

———. "Medieval Military Historiography." In *Companion to Historiography,* edited by Michael Bentley, 203–20. New York: Routledge, 1997.

———. "The Practical Use of Vegetius' *De Re Militari* During the Early Middle Ages." *The Historian* 47 (1985): 239–55.

Backhaus, Wilf K. "Once Upon a Time." *Places to Go, People to Be.* Accessed July 23, 2012. http://ptgptb.org/0015/retro.html.

———. "Readers' Forum." *Places to Go, People to Be.* Accessed July 26, 2012. http://ptgptb.org/0015/forum.html.

Badiou, Alain. *Logics of Worlds: Being and Event, II.* Translated by Alberto Toscano. New York: Continuum, 2009.

Baerg, Andrew. "Risky Business: Neo-Liberal Rationality and the Computer RPG." In *Dungeons, Dragons and Digital Denizens: The Digital Role-Playing Game,* edited by Gerald A. Vorhees, Joshua Call, and Katie Whitlock. 153–73. New York: Continuum, 2012.

Baigent, Michael, Richard Leigh, and Henry Lincoln. *Holy Blood, Holy Grail.* New York: Bantam Dell, 2004.

Bainbridge, William Sims, and Wilma Alice Bainbridge. "Electronic Game Research Methodologies: Studying Religious Implications." *Review of Religious Research* 49 (2007): 35–53.

Bakhtin, M. M. "Author and Hero in Aesthetic Activity." Translated by Vadim Liapunov. In *Art and Answerability: Early Philosophical Essays,* edited by Michael Holquist and Vadim Liapunov, 4–256. Austin: University of Texas Press, 1990.

Baldwin, John W. *The Government of Philip Augustus: Foundations of French Royal Power in the Middle Ages.* Berkeley: University of California Press, 1986.

Balzaretti, R. "'These Are Things that Men Do, Not Women': The Social Regulation of Female Violence in Lombard Italy." In *Violence and Society in the Early Medieval West,* edited by Guy Halsall, 175–92. Woodbridge, Suffolk: Boydell and Brewer, 1998.

Barber, Malcolm. *The New Knighthood: A History of the Order of the Temple.* New York: Cambridge University Press, 1994.

———. *The Trials of the Templars.* Cambridge, UK: Cambridge University Press, 1978.

Barber, Richard. *The Holy Grail: Imagination and Belief.* Cambridge, MA: Harvard University Press, 2004.

Barclay, David E. "Medievalism and Nationalism in Nineteenth-Century Germany." *Studies in Medievalism* 5 (1993): 5–22.

Barker, M. A. R. *Empire of the Petal Throne*. Lake Geneva, WI: TSR, 1975.

Barkun, Michael. *A Culture of Conspiracy: Apocalyptic Visions in Contemporary America*. Berkeley: University of California Press, 2001.

Barnett, Michael. "Mobile Plays Lead Role in Growth of Gaming." *Marketing Week*. Accessed July 19, 2012. http://www.marketingweek.co.uk/trends/mobile-plays-lead-role-i growth-of-gaming/4002633.article.

Barthes, Roland. "The Imagination of Signs." In *Critical Essays*, by Roland Barthes, translated by Richard Howard, 205–11. Evanston, IL: Northwestern University Press, 1972.

Barthes, Roland. *The Fashion System*. Translated by M. Word and D. Howard. New York: Hill and Wang, 1983.

———. "The Imagination of Signs." In *Critical Essays*, by Roland Barthes, translated by Richard Howard, 205–11. Evanston, IL: Northwestern University Press, 1972.

Bartlett, Robert. *Gerald of Wales, 1146–1223*. Oxford: Clarendon Press, 1982.

Bartlett, Robert, and Angus MacKay, eds. *Medieval Frontier Societies*. Oxford: Oxford University Press, 1989.

Barton, Matt. *Dungeons & Desktops: The History of Computer Role Playing Games*. London: AK Peters, 2008.

Baudrillard, Jean. *The System of Objects in Jean Baudrillard: Selected Writings*. Translated by James Benedict. London: Verso, 1996.

Bell, D. A. *The First Total War: Napoleon's Europe and the Birth of Modern Warfare*. London: Bloomsbury, 2007.

Benton, John F. "'Nostre franceis n'unt talent de fuïr,' the *Song of Roland* and the Enculturation of a Warrior Class." In *Culture, Power and Personality in Medieval France*, edited by Thomas N. Bisson, 147–78. London: Hambledon, 1991.

"*Beowulf* Review—Xbox 360 Review at IGN." *IGN*. Accessed June 28, 2012. http://xbox360.ign.com/articles/835/835410p1.html.

"*Beowulf: The Game* for Xbox 360 Reviews, Ratings, Credits, and More—Metacritic." *Metacritic*. Accessed June 28, 2012. http://www.metacritic.com/game/xbox-360/beowulf-the-game.

Beowulf: The Movie. Directed by Robert Zemeckis. Hollywood, CA: Paramount Pictures, 2007. DVD.

Berend, Nora. "Medievalists and the Notion of the Frontier." *The Medieval History Journal* 2 (1999): 55–72.

Beynon, John. *Masculinities and Culture*. Philadelphia: Open University Press, 2001.

Biggam, C. P. "Aspects of Chaucer's Adjectives of Hue." *Chaucer Review* 28 (1993): 41–53.

Bindman, David. "Artists Rediscover Dante." In *Dante Rediscovered: From Blake to Rodin*, edited by David Bindman, Stephen Hebron, and Michael O'Neill, 23–43. Grasmere: The Wordsworth Trust, 2007.

Bisson, Thomas N. *The Crisis of the Twelfth Century: Power, Lordship and the Origins of European Government*. Princeton: Princeton University Press, 2009.

Blackburn, Francis Adelbert. "The Christian Coloring in the *Beowulf*." *PMLA* 12 (1897): 205–25.

Blanning, Tim. *The French Revolutionary Wars, 1787–1802*. London: Arnold, 1996.

———. *The Pursuit of Glory: Europe, 1648–1815*. London: Allen Lane, 2007.

Bliese, John R. E. "Rhetoric and Morale: A Study of Battle Orations from the Central Middle Ages." *Journal of Medieval History* 15 (1989): 201–26.

Bolter, David J. "Digital Essentialism and the Mediation of the Real." In *Moving Media Studies: Remediation Revisited*, edited by Heidi Philipsen and Lars Qvortrup, 195–210. Frederiksberg: Samfundslitteratur Press, 2007.

———, and Richard A. Grusin. *Remediation: Understanding New Media.* Cambridge, MA: MIT Press, 1999.

Bonjour, Adrien. "Grendel's Dam and the Composition of *Beowulf*." *English Studies* 30 (1949): 290–99.

Boss, Emily Care. "Key Concepts in Forge Theory." In *Playground Worlds: Creating and Evaluating Experiences of Role-Playing Games,* edited by Markus Montola and Jaakko Stenros, 232–47. Jyvaskyla, Finland: Ropecon ry, 2008.

Bordo, Susan. *The Male Body: A New Look at Men in Public and Private.* New York: Farrar, Straus, and Giroux, 1999.

Bouchard, Constance. *Strong of Body, Brave and Noble: Chivalry and Society in Medieval France.* Ithaca, NY: Cornell University Press, 1998.

Bourdieu, Pierre. *Masculine Domination.* Translated by Richard Nice. Cambridge, UK: Polity, 2001.

Bradbury, Jim. *The Medieval Siege.* Woodbridge, Suffolk: Boydell, 1992.

Braida, Antonella, and Luisa Calè, eds. *Dante on View: The Reception of Dante in the Visual and Performing Arts.* Burlington, VT: Ashgate, 2007.

Brehe, S. K. "Reassembling the *First Worcester Fragment*." *Speculum,* 65, no. 3 (1990): 521–36.

Breizmann, Natalia. "*Beowulf* as Romance: Literary Interpretation as Quest." *Modern Language Notes* 113, no. 5 (1998): 1022–35.

Brieger, Peter H., Millard Meiss, and Charles S. Singleton. *Illuminated Manuscripts of the Divine Comedy.* Princeton: Princeton University Press, 1969.

Brown, Governor of California, et al. v. Entertainment Merchants Association, et al., No. 08-1448, 1–92. Accessed August 15, 2011. http://www.supremecourt.gov/opinions/10pdf/08-1448.pdf.

Brown, Harry J. "Baphomet Incorporated: A Case Study in Neomedievalism." *Studies in Medievalism* 20 (2011): 1–10.

"Brown v. Entertainment Merchants Association." *Wikipedia.* Accessed January 15, 2013. http://en.wikipedia.org/wiki/Brown_v._Entertainment_ Merchants_ Association.

Browne, Ray B. "Hero with 2000 Faces." In *Profiles of Popular Culture: A Reader,* edited by Ray B. Browne, 16–23. Madison: University of Wisconsin Press, 2005.

Buchbinder, David. *Masculinities and Identities.* Carlton: Melbourne University Press, 1994.

———. *Performance Anxieties.* St. Leonards, NSW: Allen & Unwin, 1998.

Buettner, Brigitte. "Past Presents: New Year's Gifts at the Valois Courts, ca. 1400." *The Art Bulletin* 83 (2001): 598–625.

Bullard-Bates, Daniel. "Dante's Inferno: A Failure on Two Fronts." *Pause to Reflect.* Accessed May 26, 2012. http://presspausetoreflect.blogspot.com/2010/01/dantes-inferno-failure-on-two-fronts.html.

Burns, E. Jane. "Courtly Love: Who Needs It? Recent Feminist Work in the Medieval French Tradition." *Signs* 27, no. 1 (2001): 23–57.

Burrill, Derek A. *Die Tryin': Videogames, Masculinity, Culture.* London: Peter Lang, 2008.

Caie, Graham D. "The Manuscript Experience: What Medieval Vernacular Manuscripts Tell Us About Authors and Texts." In *Medieval Texts in Context,* edited by Denis Renevey and Graham D. Caie, 10–27. London: Routledge, 2008.

Caillois, Roger. *Man, Play, and Games.* Translated by Meyer Barash. Champaign: University of Illinois Press, 2001.

Calleja, Gordon. *In-Game: From Immersion to Incorporation.* Cambridge, MA: MIT Press, 2011.

———, and Ival Collins. "Game Studies." In *The Routledge Companion to Literature and Science,* edited by Bruce Clarke and Manuela Rossini, 323–34. London: Routledge, 2011.

Camille, Michael. *Image on the Edge: The Margins of Medieval Art.* Cambridge, MA: Harvard University Press, 1992.

———. *The Medieval Art of Love.* London: Harry N. Abrams, 1998.

Campbell, J. "Stubbs, William (1825–1901)." In *Oxford Dictionary of National Biography,* edited by H. C. G. Matthew and Brian Harrison. Oxford: Oxford University Press, 2004. Accessed August 27, 2012. http://www.oxforddnb.com/view/article/36362.

Cantor, Norman F. *Inventing the Middle Ages: The Lives, Works, and Ideas of the Great Medievalists of the Twentieth Century.* New York: William Morrow, 1991.

Capellanus, Andreas. *The Art of Courtly Love.* Translated by John Jay Parry. New York: Ungar, 1959.

Carlson, Signe. "The Monsters of *Beowulf*: Creations of Literary Scholars." *The Journal of American Folklore* 80, no. 318 (1967): 357–64.

Carpenter, David. *The Struggle for Mastery: Britain, 1066–1284.* London: Penguin, 2004.

Carroll, Rachel. "Introduction: Textual Infidelities." *Adaptation in Contemporary Culture: Textual Infidelities,* edited by Rachel Carroll, 1–7. London: Continuum, 2009.

Carruthers, Mary, and Jan M. Ziolkowski. *The Medieval Craft of Memory: An Anthology of Texts and Pictures.* Philadelphia: University of Pennsylvania Press, 2004.

Cartlidge, Neil. Introduction to *Heroes and Anti-Heroes in Medieval Romance,* edited by Neil Cartlidge, 1–5. Cambridge, UK: D. S. Brewer, 2012.

"Casual Games Association: FAQ." *Casual Games Association.* Accessed July 19, 2012. http://www.casualgamesassociation.org/news.php#casualgames.

Ceccola, Russ. "King's Quest V." *Compute! Magazine,* June 1990, 116. Accessed July 1, 2012. www.atarimagazines.com.

Chadwick, Nora. "The Monsters and Beowulf." In *The Anglo-Saxons: Studies in Some Aspects of the History and Culture Presented to Bruce Dickins,* edited by Peter Clemoes, 171–203. London: Bowes, 1959.

Chambers, R. W. "*Beowulf* and the Heroic Age." In *Beowulf: Translated into Modern English Rhyming Verse,* translated by Archibald Strong. London: Constable, 1925.

Chance, Jane. "The Structural Unity of *Beowulf*: The Problem of Grendel's Mother." In *New Readings on Women in Old English Literature,* edited by Helen Damico and Alexandra Hennessey, 248–67. Bloomington: Indiana University Press, 1990.

Chapman, Robert L. "Alas, Poor Grendel." *College English* 17, no. 6 (1956): 334–37.

Childs, John. *Armies and Warfare in Europe, 1648–1789.* New York: Holmes and Meier, 1982.

Chin, Elliott. "Medieval: Total War Review." *Gamespot UK.* Accessed July 23, 2012. http://uk.gamespot.com/medieval-total-war/reviews/medieval-total-war-review-2878535/.

Chrétien de Troyes. "*Lancelot, or the Knight of the Cart (Le Chevalier De La Charrete).*" In *The Romance of Arthur: An Anthology of Medieval Texts in Translation,* edited by James J. Wilhelm. Translated by William W. Kibler, 121–99. New York: Garland, 1994.

Clanchy, M. T. *From Memory to Written Record: England 1066–1307.* 2nd ed. Oxford: Blackwell, 1993.

Cohen, Jeffrey Jerome. "Hybrids, Monsters, and Borderlands: The Bodies of Gerald of Wales." In *The Postcolonial Middle Ages,* edited by Jeffrey Jerome Cohen, 85–104. Basingstoke, UK: Macmillan, 2000.

———. *Medieval Identity Machines.* Minneapolis: University of Minnesota Press, 2003.

———. *Medieval Identity Machines.* Kindle Edition.

Combs, James. "Celebrations: Rituals of Popular Veneration." In *Profiles of Popular Culture: A Reader,* edited by Ray B. Browne, 277–84. Madison: University of Wisconsin Press, 2005.

"Comic Submission." *Blizzard Entertainment.* Accessed July, 19, 2012. http://us.blizzard.com/en-us/community/comics.

Connell, R.W. *Masculinities.* 2nd ed. Crows Nest, NSW: Allen & Unwin, 2005.

———. *The Men and the Boys.* St. Leonards, NSW: Allen & Unwin, 2000.

Connolly, Daniel. "Imagined Pilgrimage in the Itinerary Maps of Matthew Paris." *The Art Magazine* 91, no. 4 (1999): 598–622.

———. *The Maps of Matthew Paris: Journeys in Space, Time, and Liturgy.* Berkeley: University of California Press, 1987.

Consalvo, Mia. "Hot Dates and Fairytale Romances: Studying Sexuality in Video Games." In *The Video Game Theory Reader,* edited by Mark J. P. Wolf and Bernard Perron, 171–94. New York: Routledge, 2003.

Contamine, Philippe. *War in the Middle Ages.* Translated by Michael Jones. Oxford: Blackwell, 1984.

Corneliussen, Hilde G. "*World of Warcraft* as a Playground for Feminism." In *Digital Culture, Play, and Identity,* edited by Hilde G. Corneliussen and Jill Walker Rettberg, 63–87. Cambridge, MA: MIT Press, 2008.

———, and Jill Walker Rettberg, eds. *Digital Culture, Play, and Identity: A World of Warcraft Reader.* Cambridge, MA: MIT Press, 2008.

Coulthard, Lisa. "Desublimating Desire: Courtly Love and Catherine Breillat." *Journal for Cultural Research* 14, no. 1 (2010): 57–69.

Crane, Susan. "Anglo-Norman Cultures in England 1066–1460." In *The Cambridge History of Medieval English Literature,* edited by David Wallace, 35–60. Cambridge, UK: Cambridge University Press, 1999.

Crecente, Brian. "EA Provides the Girls, Asks Gamers to Sin to Win." *Kotaku.* Accessed July 31, 2012. http://kotaku.com/5322216/ea-provides-girls-asks-gamers-to-sin-to-win.

———. "Should We Expect More from Electronic Art's Inferno." *Kotaku.* Accessed July 30, 2012. http://kotaku.com/5278242/should-we-expect-more-from-electronic-arts-inferno.

Crichton, Michael. *Eaters of the Dead.* New York: Bantam, 1976.

Crusader Kings Wiki. Accessed August 1, 2012. http://crusaderkings.wikia.com/wiki/Crusader_Kings_Wiki.

Curry, Anne. *Agincourt: A New History.* Stroud: Tempus, 2005.

The Dante Encyclopedia. Edited by Richard Lansing. New York: Routledge, 2010.

Dante's Inferno. Directed by Sean Meredith. 2007. Santa Monica, CA: Dante Film, 2008.

Dargis, Manohla. "Confronting the Fabled Monster, Not to Mention His Naked Mom." *New York Times,* November 16, 2007. Accessed July 4, 2012. http://movies.nytimes.com/2007/11/16/movies/16beow.html.

Dawkins, Richard. *The Selfish Gene.* 2nd ed. Oxford: Oxford University Press, 1989.

De Charny, Geoffroi. *A Knight's Own Book of Chivalry.* Translated by Elspeth Kennedy. Philadelphia: University of Pennsylvania Press, 2005.

de Hamel, Christopher. *A History of Illuminated Manuscripts.* 2nd ed. London: Phaidon Press, 1994.

de Mas-Latrie, Louis, ed. *Chronique d'Ernoul et de Bernard le Trésorier.* Paris: Société de l'histoire de France, 1871.

De Vries, Hent, and Samuel Weber, ed. *Violence, Identity, Self-Determination.* Stanford: Stanford University Press, 1997.

"The Defiant." *Telarapedia.* Accessed October 10, 2012. http://telarapedia.com/wiki/ The_Defiant.

Delaborde, Henri-François, ed. *Œuvres de Rigord et de Guillaume le Breton*. Paris: Société de l'histoire de France, 1882–85.

Dell, Helen. "Past, Present, Future Perfect: Paradigms of History in Medievalism." *Parergon* 25 (2008): 58–79.

Dettwyler, Zac. "[Chronica Feudalis] Not What I Expected." *Abby's Place*. Accessed July 31, 2012. http://abbysgamerbasement.blogspot.com/2010/11/chronica-feudalis-not-what-i-expected.html.

Devries, Shane. "History of C&S as I Know It." *Chivalry & Sorcery RPG Fan Site*. Accessed July 23, 2012. http://chivalrysorcery.myfastforum.org/History_of_C_amp_S_as_I_know_it__about14.html.

Didi-Huberman, Georges. *Fra Angelico: Dissemblance and Figuration*. Translated by Jane Marie Todd. Chicago: University of Chicago Press, 1995.

———. *L'Image survivante. Histoire de l'art et temps des fantômes chez Aby Warburg*. Paris: Editions de Minuit, 2002.

———. "Puissances de la figure. Exégèse et visualité dans l'art chrétien." In *L'Image ouverte. Motifs de l'incarnation dans les arts visuels*, 195–231. Paris: Gallimard, 2006.

Di Loreto, Ines, and Abdelkader Gouaïch. "Social Casual Games Success is Not So Casual," Research Report #RR-10017 LIRMM, University of Montpellier CNRS. Accessed June 17, 2012. http://hal.archives-ouvertes.fr/docs/00/48/69/34/PDF/FunAndGames2010–03-22.pdf.

Dinello, Daniel. *Technophobia! Science Fiction Visions of Posthuman Technology*. Austin: University of Texas Press, 2005.

Dinshaw, Carolyn. *Getting Medieval: Sexualities and Communities, Pre- and Postmodern*. London: Duke University Press, 1999.

Duby, Georges. *The Legend of Bouvines: War, Religion and Culture in the Middle Ages*. Translated by Catherine Tihanyi. Berkeley: University of California Press, 1990.

Durkheim, Emile. *The Division of Labor in Society*. Translated by W. D. Halls. New York: Free Press, 1984.

Ebert, Roger. "Video Games Can Never Be Art." *Roger Ebert's Journal*. Accessed January 15, 2013. http://blogs.suntimes.com/ebert/ 2010/04/video_games_can_never_be_art.html.

Eco, Umberto. "Dreaming of the Middle Ages." In *Travels in Hyperreality: Essays*. Translated by William Weaver, 61–72. New York: Harcourt, Brace, Jovanovich, 1986.

———. *Foucault's Pendulum*. Translated by William Weaver. New York: Harcourt, 1989.

———. "Living in the New Middle Ages." In *Travels in Hyperreality: Essays*. Translated by William Weaver, 73–85. New York: Harcourt, Brace, Jovanovich, 1986.

Edwards, Tim. *Cultures of Masculinity*. New York: Routledge, 2006.

Edwards, Ron. "All-out Dissection (Long and Brutal)." *The Forge Forums Read-Only Archives*. Accessed August 1, 2011. http://indie-rpgs.com/archive/index.php?topic = 24.0.

———. "A Hard Look at Dungeons & Dragons." *The Forge Forums Read-Only Archives*. Accessed July 17, 2012. www.indie-rpgs.com/ articles/20.

———. "Understanding the Pool." Accessed August 1, 2011. http://adept-press.com/wordpress/wp-content/media/Understanding_The_Pool.pdf.

———, and Vincent Baker. "The Forge." *The Forge Forums Read-Only Archives*. Accessed September 29, 2008. http://www.indie-rpgs.com/forums.

Einhard. *Life of Charlemagne*. Edited and translated by Samuel Epes Turner. New York: Harper and Brothers, 1880. Accessed July 25, 2012. http://www.fordham.edu/Halsall/basis/einhard.asp.

Eisenmann. "Chronica Feudalis: Witness." *RPG.net Forums*. Accessed July 31, 2012. http://forum.rpg.net/showthread.php? 452092-Chronica-Feudalis-Witness.

Electronic Arts. "Developer Diary: Heresy." Accessed July 26, 2012. http://www.ea.com/dantes-inferno/videos/63d8c7543c4e4210VgnVCM100000ab65140aRCRD.

Emerson, Oliver. "Legends of Cain, Especially in Old and Middle English." *PMLA* 21 (1906): 831–929.

Emery, Elizabeth. "The 'Truth' About the Middle Ages: *La Revue des Deux Mondes* and Late Nineteenth-Century French Medievalism." *Prose Studies* 23 (2000): 99–114.

Everett, Daniel L. "Cultural Constrains on Grammar and Cognition in Pirahã: Another Look at the Design Features of Human Language." *Current Anthropology* 46 (2005): 621–46.

"Facebook Casual Game Demographics." *DataGenetics*. Accessed July 19, 2012. http://www.datagenetics.com/blog/december12010/index.html.

Fantosme, Jordan. *Chronique*. In *Chronicles of the Reigns of Stephen, Henry II and Richard I,* edited by Richard Howlett, Rolls Series 82, 3: 202–377. London: Longman, 1884–89.

Feasey, Rebecca. *Masculinity and Popular Television*. Edinburgh: Edinburgh University Press, 2008.

Fedorenko, Gregory. "The Crusading Career of John of Brienne, c. 1210–1237." *Nottingham Medieval Studies* 52 (2008): 43–79.

Felix. "[Let's Read] Fantasy Wargaming (Seriously)." *RPG.net Forums*. Accessed July 27, 2012. http://forum.rpg.net/showthread.php?422199-Let-s-Read-Fantasy-Wargaming-(seriously).

Fine, Gary Alan. *Shared Fantasy: Role-Playing Games as Social Worlds*. Chicago: University of Chicago Press, 1983.

Finke, Laurie, and Martin B. Shictman. *Cinematic Illuminations: The Middle Ages on Film*. Baltimore: Johns Hopkins University Press, 2009.

Foster, Kenelm. *The Two Dantes and Other Studies*. London: Darton, Longman and Todd, 1977.

Foucault, Michel. "Truth and Power." In *Power/Knowledge: Selected Interviews and Other Writings, 1972–1977*. Edited by Colin Gordon. Translated by Colin Gordon, Leo Marshall, John Mephan, and Kate Soper, 109–33. New York: Pantheon, 1980.

Fox, Michael, and Stephen R. Reimer. *Mappae Mundi: Representing the World and its Inhabitants in Texts, Maps, and Images in Medieval and Early Modern Europe*. Exhibition and Catalogue, Bruce Peel Special Collections Library, February–April 2008. Edmonton, Alberta: University of Alberta, 2008.

Fradenburg, Louise. "'So That We May Speak of Them': Enjoying the Middle Ages." *New Literary History* 28, no. 2 (1997): 205–30.

France, John. *Western Warfare in the Age of the Crusades*. London: University College of London Press, 1999.

Frasca, Gonzalo. "Simulation versus Narrative: Introduction to Ludology." *The Video Game Theory Reader,* edited Mark J. P. Wolf and Bernard Perron, 221–36. New York: Routledge, 2003.

Fraser, Jennifer. "Dante/Fante: Embryology in Purgatory and Paradise." In *Dante and the Unorthodox: The Aesthetics of Transgression,* edited by James Miller, 290–309. Waterloo: Wilfrid Laurier University Press, 2005.

Funk, John. "Blizzard's Rob Pardo Talks Five Years of *Warcraft,*" *The Escapist,* November 14, 2009. Accessed July 19, 2012. http://www.escapistmagazine.com/news/view/96113-Blizzards-Rob-Pardo-Talks-Five-Years-of-Warcraft.

Fyler, John M. *Language and the Declining World in Chaucer, Dante, and Jean de Meun*. Cambridge, UK: Cambridge University Press, 2007.

Gage, John. *Colour and Culture: Practice and Meaning from Antiquity to Abstraction.* London: Thames and Hudson, 1993.

———. *Colour and Meaning: Art, Science and Symbolism.* London: Thames and Hudson, 1999.

Gaiman, Neil, and Roger Avary. *Beowulf: The Script Book.* London: Harper, 2007.

Gallagher, Catherine, and Stephen Greenblatt. *Practicing New Historicism.* Chicago: University of Chicago Press, 2000.

Galloway, Bruce. *Fantasy Wargaming.* New York: Stein and Day, 1981.

Gard, Toby. "Building Character." *Gamasutra.* Accessed May 26, 2010. http://www.gamasutra.com/features/20000720/gard_pvf.htm.

Gaudio, Michael. "Matthew Paris and the Cartography of the Margins." *Gesta* 39, no. 1 (2000): 50–57.

Geary, Patrick J. *The Myth of Nations: The Medieval Origins of Europe.* Princeton: Princeton University Press, 2002.

Gee, James Paul. "Are Video Games Good for Learning?" In *Worlds in Play: International Perspectives on Digital Games Research,* edited by Suzanne de Castell and Jennifer Jenson, 323–35. New York: Peter Lang, 2007.

———. *What Video Games Have to Teach Us About Learning and Literacy.* New York: Palgrave Macmillan, 2004.

George, Jodi-Ann. Beowulf: *A Reader's Guide to Essential Criticism.* Houndsmill, UK: Palgrave Macmillan, 2010.

Georgianna, Linda. "King Hrethel's Sorrow and the Limits of Heroic Action in *Beowulf.*" *Speculum* 62 (1987): 829–50.

Gerald of Wales. *The Description of Wales.* In *The Journey through Wales and The Description of Wales.* Edited and translated by Lewis Thorpe, 211–88. Harmondsworth: Penguin, 1978.

———. *Giraldi Cambrensis opera.* Edited by J. S. Brewer, J. F. Dimock and G. F. Warner. Rolls Series 21. London: Longman, 1861–91.

———. *History and Topography of Ireland.* Edited and translated by John J. O'Meara. Harmondsworth: Penguin, 1982.

Gibson, Ellie. "Dante's Inferno Review." *Eurogamer.net.* Accessed July 20, 2012. http://www.eurogamer.net/articles/dantes-inferno-review.

Gillingham, John. "The Beginnings of English Imperialism." *Journal of Historical Sociology* 5, no. 4 (1992): 392–409.

———. *Richard I.* New Haven: Yale University Press, 1999.

———. "Up with Orthodoxy! In Defense of Vegetian Warfare." *Journal of Medieval Military History* 2 (2003): 149–64.

———. "William the Bastard at War." In *Anglo-Norman Warfare: Studies in Late Anglo-Saxon and Anglo-Norman Military Organisation and Warfare,* edited by Matthew Strickland, 143–60. Woodbridge, Suffolk: Boydell, 1992.

Golumbia, David. "Games Without Play." *New Literary History* 40 (2009): 179–204.

Green, William H. "Hugo of St. Victor: *De Tribus Maximis Circumstantiis Gestorum.*" *Speculum* 18, no. 4 (1943): 484–93.

Gregory, Clairellyn Rose. "Who Gender-Bends and Why? A Qualitative Study of *World of Warcraft.*" PhD diss., Portland State University, 2011.

Grindley, Carl James. "The Hagiography of Steel: The Hero's Weapon and Its Place in Pop Culture." In *The Medieval Hero on Screen: Representations from Beowulf to Buffy,* edited by Martha W. Driver and Sid Ray, 151–66. Jefferson, NC: McFarland, 2004.

Gygax, E. Gary, and Dave Arneson. *Dungeons & Dragons.* Lake Geneva, WI: Tactical Studies Rules, 1974.

Haber, Tom Burns. *A Comparative Study of the* Beowulf *and the* Aeneid. Princeton: Princeton University Press, 1931.

Halberstam, Judith. *In a Queer Time and Place: Transgender Bodies, Subcultural Lives.* New York: New York University Press, 2005.

Halsall, Guy. "An Introductory Survey." In *Violence and Society in the Early Medieval West,* edited by Guy Halsall, 1–45. Woodbridge, Suffolk: Boydell and Brewer, 1998.

Hammond, Wally. "Beowulf." *Time Out.* Accessed July 4, 2012. http://www.time-out.com/film/reviews/84501/beowulf.html.

Hancock, Graham. *The Sign and the Seal.* New York: Touchstone, 1992.

Harley, J. B. *A History of Cartography, Vol. I: Prehistoric, Ancient, and Medieval Europe and the Mediterranean.* Chicago: University of Chicago Press, 1987.

Harty, Kevin J. *The Reel Middle Ages.* Jefferson, NC: McFarland, 2006.

Harvey, P. D. A. Mappa Mundi: *The Hereford World Map.* Toronto: University of Toronto Press, 1996.

Harwood, Britton J. "Gawain and the Gift." *PMLA* 106 (1991): 483–99.

Hastings, Adrian. *The Construction of Nationhood: Ethnicity, Religion and Nationalism.* Cambridge, UK: Cambridge University Press, 2007.

Hayles, Katherine. "The Condition of Virtuality." In *The Digital Dialectic: New Essays on New Media,* edited by Peter Lunenfeld, 69–94. Cambridge, MA: MIT Press, 2000.

Hayot, Eric, and Edward Wesp. "Towards a Critical Aesthetic of Virtual-World Geographies." *Game Studies* 9, no.1 (2009). Accessed April 15, 2010. http://gamestudies.org/0901/articles/hayot_wesp_space.

Heaney, Seamus, trans. *Beowulf.* Bilingual ed. New York: W. W. Norton, 2001.

Heller, Sarah-Grace. *Fashion in Medieval France.* Cambridge, UK: D. S. Brewer, 2007.

Hennequin, Wendy. "We've Created a Monster: The Strange Case of Grendel's Mother." *English Studies* 89, no. 5 (2008): 502–23.

Henry of Huntingdon. *Historia Anglorum: The History of the English People.* Edited by Diana Greenway. Oxford: Clarendon Press, 1996.

Henthorne, Tom. "Boys to Men: Medievalism and Masculinity in *Star Wars* and *E.T.: The Extra-Terrestrial.*" In *The Medieval Hero on Screen: Representations from Beowulf to Buffy,* edited by Martha W. Driver and Sid Ray, 73–89. Jefferson, NC: McFarland, 2004.

Higson, Andrew. "'Medievalism,' the Period Film and the British Past in Contemporary Cinema." In *Medieval Film,* edited by Anke Bernau and Bettina Bildhauer, 203–24. Manchester: Manchester University Press, 2009.

Hill, John M. *The Narrative Impulse of* Beowulf: *Arrivals and Departures.* Toronto: University of Toronto Press, 2009.

Hoagland, Richard. "The Twin Towers and the Great Masonic Experiment: Has the 'End of Days' Begun?" *Paranoia* 20 (2002): 52–58.

Hodges, Kenneth. "Wounded Masculinity: Injury and Gender in Sir Thomas Malory's *Le Morte Darthur.*" *Studies in Philology* 106, no. 1 (2009): 14–31.

Hodges, Laura F. "Sartorial Signs in *Troilus and Criseyde.*" *Chaucer Review* 35 (2001): 223–59.

Hofstader, Richard. "The Paranoid Style in American Politics." *Harper's,* November 1964. Accessed July 30, 2012. http://karws.gso.uri.edu/jfk/conspiracy_theory/the_paranoid_mentality/the_paranoid style.html.

Holland, Dorothy, and Jean Lave. "History in Person: An Introduction." In *History in Person: Enduring Struggles, Contentious Practice, Intimate Identities,* edited by Dorothy Holland and Jean Lave, 3–33. Santa Fe, NM: School of American Research, 2001.

Holsinger, Bruce. *Neomedievalism, Neoconservatism, and the War on Terror.* Chicago: Prickly Paradigm Press, 2007.

Hopkins, Amanda. "Female Vulnerability as Catalyst in the Middle English Breton Lays." In *The Matter of Identity in Medieval Romance*, edited by Philippa Hardman, 43–58. Cambridge, UK: D. S. Brewer, 2002.

Hosler, John D. *Henry II: A Medieval Soldier at War.* Leiden: Brill, 2007.

Housley, Norman. "European Warfare: c. 1200–1320." In *Medieval Warfare: A History*, edited by Maurice Keen, 113–35. Oxford: Oxford University Press, 1999.

Howard, Jeff. "Interpretative Quests in Theory and Pedagogy." *Digital Humanities Quarterly* 1, no. 1 (2007). Accessed July 6, 2012. http://digitalhumanities.org/dhq/vol/1/1/000002/000002.html.

Howarth, Stephen. *The Knights Templar.* New York: Dorset Press, 1991.

Hughes, Kathleen. *Early Christian Ireland: Introduction to the Sources.* London: Camelot Press, 1972.

Huizinga, Johan. *Homo Ludens: A Study of the Play Element in Culture.* Boston: Beacon Press, 1950.

Hutcheon, Linda. *A Theory of Adaptation.* New York: Routledge, 2006.

Ingham, Patricia Clare. *Sovereign Fantasies: Arthurian Romance and the Making of Britain.* Philadelphia: University of Pennsylvania Press, 2001.

Isidore of Seville. *Etymologies.* Edited and translated by Stephen A. Barney, W. J. Lewis, J. A. Beach, and Oliver Berghof. Cambridge, UK: Cambridge University Press, 2006.

Itzkoff, Dave. "Abandon All Poetry, but Enter Hell With an Attitude." *New York Times,* January 30, 2010. Accessed June 18, 2012. http://www.nytimes.com/2010/01/30/arts/television/30inferno.html.

"An Ivy League Professor Weighs In." *Entertainment Weekly,* February 26, 2010, 79.

Jackson, K. H., ed. *A Celtic Miscellany.* Harmondsworth: Penguin, 1971.

Järvinen, Aki. "Game Design for Social Networks: Interaction Design for Playful Dispositions." In *Proceedings of the 2009 ACM SIGGRAPH Symposium on Video Games,* 95–102. New York: Association for Computing Machinery, 2009.

Jefferies, J. B. "The Literary Merits of Dante's Inferno." *PopMatters.* Accessed May 26, 2012. http://www.popmatters.com/pm/post/122719-the-literary-merits-of-dantes-inferno.

Jenkins, Henry. *Fans, Bloggers, and Gamers: Exploring Participatory Culture.* New York: New York University Press, 2006.

Jewitt, Carey, and Gunther Kress. "Introduction." In *New Literacies and Digital Epistemologies: Vol. 4. Multimodal Literacy,* edited by Carey Jewitt and Gunther Kress, 1–18. New York: Peter Lang, 2008.

Johansen, David. "Bwahahaahahahah!!! I Have It and I Just Might Run It." *RPG. net Forums.* Accessed July 27, 2012. http://forum.rpg.net/archive/index.php/t-219474.html.

Johnson, Haynes. *The Best of Times: The Boom and Bust Years of America Before and After Everything Changed.* New York: Harcourt, 2001.

Johnson, Margaret. "The Developing World: Comparing Medieval Maps from Around the Globe." Website accompanying Hereford Cathedral Exhibition of *Mappae Mundi,* 1999. Accessed July 1, 2012. http://www.britannia.com/history/herefords/mapmundi.html.

Joy, Eileen A., and Craig Dionne. "Before the Trains of Thought Have Been Laid Down So Firmly: The Premodern Post/Human." *Postmedieval* 1 (2010): 1–9.

Juul, Jesper. *A Casual Revolution: Reinventing Video Games and Their Players.* Cambridge, MA: MIT Press, 2010.

———. "Games Telling Stories." *Game Studies* 1, no. 1 (2001). Accessed August 18, 2011. http://www.gamestudies.org/0101/juul-gts/.

————. *Half-Real: Video Games between Real Rules and Fictional Worlds.* Cambridge, MA: MIT Press, 2005.

Kaske, Robert E. "Sapientia Et Fortitudo as the Controlling Theme of *Beowulf.*" *Studies in Philology* 55 (1958): 423–57.

Kaufman, Amy S. "Medieval Unmoored." *Studies in Medievalism* 19 (2010): 1–11.

————. "Romancing the Game: Magic, Writing, and the Feminine in *Neverwinter Nights.*" *Studies in Medievalism* 16 (2008): 143–58.

Kay, Sarah. *The* Chansons de Geste *in the Age of Romance: Political Fictions.* Oxford: Clarendon, 1995.

————. "Courts, Clerks, and Courtly Love." In *The Cambridge Companion to Medieval Romance,* edited by Roberta L. Krueger, 81–96. Cambridge, UK: Cambridge University Press, 2000.

————, ed. and trans. *Raoul de Cambrai.* Oxford: Clarendon Press, 1991.

Keen, Maurice. *Chivalry.* New Haven: Yale University Press, 1984.

Keller, Jeremy. *Chronica Feudalis: A Game of Imagined Adventure in Medieval Europe.* Minneapolis: Cellar Games, 2009.

————. "[Chronica Feudalis] Pinging Your Radar, Medievally." *Story Games.* Accessed July 31, 2012. http://www.story-games.com/forums/discussion/comment/234941.

Kendall, Calvin B., and Faith Wallis. *Bede: On the Nature of Things and On Times.* Liverpool: Liverpool University Press, 2011.

Kieckhefer, Richard. *Magic in the Middle Ages.* Cambridge, UK: Cambridge University Press, 1989.

Kim, John H. "The Threefold Model Faq." Accessed July 19, 2012. http://www.darkshire.net/jhkim/rpg/theory/threefold/faq_v1.html.

Kimmel, Michael S. *The Gendered Society.* 2nd ed. Oxford: Oxford University Press, 2004.

————, and Michael A. Messner. *Men's Lives.* 6th ed. New York: Pearson, 2004.

Klevjer, Rune. "In Defense of Cutscenes." In *Computer Game and Digital Cultures Conference Proceedings,* edited by Frans Mäyrä, 191–202. Tampere, Finland: Tampere University Press, 2002.

Kline, Naomi Reed. *Maps of Medieval Thought: The Hereford Paradigm.* Woodbridge, Suffolk: Boydell, 2001.

Kline, Stephen, Nick Dyer-Witheford, and Greig De Peuter. *Digital Play: The Interaction of Technology, Culture, and Marketing.* Montreal: McGill-Queen's University Press, 2003.

Knight, Jonathan. Introduction to *Dante's Inferno.* Translated by Henry Wadsworth Longfellow, ix–xxiv. New York: Ballantine Books, 2010.

Knowles, David. *Great Historical Enterprises: Problems in Monastic History.* London: Nelson, 1963.

Koslin, Désirée G. "Value-Added Stuffs and Shifts in Meaning: An Overview and Case Study of Medieval Textile Paradigms." In *Encountering Medieval Textiles and Dress: Objects, Texts, Images,* edited by Désirée G. Koslin and Janet E. Snyder, 233–49. New York: Palgrave MacMillan, 2002.

Kuchera, Ben. "Dante's Inferno Interview: Of Marketing and Gods of War." *Arstechnica.* Accessed July 29, 2012. http://arstechnica.com/gaming/2010/02/dantes-inferno-interview/.

Lacan, Jacques. "Courtly Love as Anamorphosis." In *The Ethics of Psychoanalysis 1959–60,* volume 7, *The Seminars of Jacques Lacan.* Edited by Jacques Alain Miller. Translated by Dennis Porter, 139–54. New York: Norton, 1988.

————. *Feminine Sexuality: Jacques Lacan and the École Freudienne.* Edited by Juliet Mitchell and Jacqueline Rose. Translated by Jacqueline Rose. London: Macmillan, 1982.

Lair, Jules. "Mémoire sur deux chroniques latines composées au XIIe siècle à l'abbaye de Saint-Denis." *Bibliothèque de l'école des chartes* 35 (1874): 543–80.

Langer, Johnni. "The Origins of the Imaginary Viking." *Viking Heritage Magazine,* December 2002, 1–7.

Langland, William. *Piers Plowman.* Edited by Elizabeth Robertson and Stephen H. A. Shepherd. New York: W. W. Norton, 2006.

Layher, William. "Caught Between Worlds: Gendering the Maiden Warrior in Old Norse." In *Women in Medieval Epic,* edited by Sara S. Poor and Jana Schulman, 183–208. New York: Palgrave, 2007.

Leerssen, Joep. *National Thought in Europe: A Cultural History.* Amsterdam: Amsterdam University Press, 2006.

Lewis, Suzanne. *The Art of Matthew Paris in the "Chronica Majora."* Berkeley: University of California Press, 1987.

"Looking Back: Medieval II: Total War." *Computer and Video Games.* Accessed July 23, 2012. http://www.computerandvideogames.com/166477/interviews/looking-back-medieval-ii-total-war/.

Lord Gorath. "Fantasy Wargaming, by Bruce Galloway." *Dragonsfoot Forums.* Accessed July 26, 2012. http://s123723500.websitehome.co.uk/forums/viewtopic.php?f=20&t=12045&sid=8e8145fafa73290de20b455f2a4db1b7.

Love, Rosalind. "The World of Latin Learning." In *The Cambridge Companion to Bede,* edited by Scott DeGregorio, 40–53. Cambridge, UK: Cambridge University Press, 2010.

Lull, Ramon. *The Book of Knighthood and Chivalry.* Translated by William Caxton. Union City, CA: Chivalry Bookshelf, 2001.

Lynn, John A. "Towards an Army of Honour: The Moral Evolution of the French Army, 1789–1815." *French Historical Studies* 16 (1989): 152–82.

MacCullum-Stewart, Esther. ""Never Such Innocence Again": War and Histories in *World of Warcraft.*" In *Digital Culture, Play, and Identity: A World of Warcraft Reader,* edited by Hilde Corneliussen and Jill Walker Rettberg. 39–62. Cambridge, MA: MIT Press, 2008.

Macfarlane, Katherine Nell. "Isidore of Seville on the Pagan Gods (*Origines* VIII.11)." *Transactions of the American Philosophical Society* 70, no. 3 (1980): 1–40.

MacKinnon, Kenneth. *Representing Men: Maleness and Masculinity in the Media.* London: Arnold, 2003.

Magoulick, Mary. "Frustrating Female Heroism: Mixed Messages in *Xena, Nikita,* and *Buffy.*" *Journal of Popular Culture* 39, no. 5 (2006): 729–55.

Malaby, Thomas N. "Beyond Play: A New Approach to Culture." *Games and Culture* 2, no. 2 (2007): 95–113.

Malone, Kempe. "Hildeburg and Hengest." *Journal of English Literary History* 10, no. 4 (1943): 257–84.

Malory, Thomas. *Le Morte Darthur.* 2 vols. New York: Penguin, 2004.

———. *Le Morte D'arthur: Sir Thomas Malory's Book of King Arthur and of His Noble Knights of the Round Table.* Volume 1. London: MacMillan, 1908.

Marshall, David W., ed. *Mass Market Medieval: Essays on the Middle Ages in Popular Culture.* Jefferson, NC: McFarland, 2007.

———. "Introduction: The Medievalism of Popular Culture." In *Mass Market Medieval,* ed. David W. Marshall, 1–12. Jefferson, NC: McFarland, 2007.

Mauss, Marcel. *The Gift: Forms and Functions of Exchange in Archaic Societies.* Translated by Ian Cunnison. London: Cohen and West, 1954.

Mayer, Lauryn. "Promises of Monsters: The Rethinking of Gender in MMORPGs." *Studies in Medievalism* 16 (2008): 184–203.

McArthur, J. A. "Digital Subculture: A Geek Meaning of Style." *Journal of Communication Inquiry* 33, no. 1 (2009): 58–70.

McCracken, Peggy. "The Poetics of Sacrifice: Allegory and Myth in the Grail Quest." *Yale French Studies* 95 (1999): 152–68.

McGlyn, Sean. *By Sword and Fire: Cruelty and Atrocity in Medieval Warfare.* London: Weidenfeld & Nicolson, 2009.

———. "The Myths of Medieval Warfare," *History Today* 44, no. 1 (1994): 28–34.

McKitterick, Rosamond. *The Carolingians and the Written Word.* Cambridge, UK: Cambridge University Press, 1989.

———. *Charlemagne: The Formation of a European Identity.* Cambridge, UK: Cambridge University Press, 2008.

Mead, George Herbert. *Mind, Self, and Society: From the Standpoint of a Social Behaviorist.* Edited by Charles W. Morris. Chicago: University of Chicago Press, 1967.

"Medieval 2: Total War Interview." *IGN PC.* Accessed July 23, 2012. http://uk.pc.ign.com/articles/699/699515p2.html.

Meillassoux, Quentin. "Destinations des corps subjectivés." In *Autour de Logiques des mondes d'Alain Badiou,* edited by David Rabouin, Oliver Feltham, and Lissa Lincoln, 7–21. Paris: Editions des archives contemporaines, 2011.

Mellinkoff, Ruth. *Outcasts: Signs of Otherness in Northern European Art of the Late Middle Ages.* 2 vols. Berkeley: University of California Press, 1994.

Mendlesohn, Farah, and Edward James. *A Short History of Fantasy.* London: Middlesex University Press, 2009.

Merleau-Ponty, Maurice. *The Phenomenology of Perception.* Translated by Colin Smith. London: Routledge, 1962.

———. *The Visible and the Invisible.* Translated by A. Lingis. Evanston, IL: Northwestern University Press, 1968.

Meyerson, Mark D., Daniel Thiery, and Oren Falk. "Introduction." In *"A Great Effusion of Blood?" Interpreting Medieval Violence,* edited by Mark D. Meyerson, Daniel Thiery, and Oren Falk, 3–16. Toronto: University of Toronto Press, 2004.

"Midgets, Trolls, and 2 Headed Dragons Oh My." Accessed 18 February 2007. http://www.youtube.com/watch?v=Hrb4n-x7CJ4&feature= youtube_gdata_player.

Millar-Heggie, Bonnie. "The Performance of Masculinity and Femininity: Gender Transgression in *The Sowdone of Babylone.*" *Mirator* (2004): 1–11.

Mitchell, Bruce, and Fred Robinson, eds. *Beowulf: An Edition.* Rev. ed. Malden, MA: Blackwell, 2006.

Mittman, Asa Simon. *Maps and Monsters in Medieval England.* London: Routledge, 2006.

Moberly, Brent, and Kevin Moberly. "Revising the Future: The Medieval Self and the Sovereign Ethics of Empire in *Star Wars: Knights of the Old Republic.*" *Studies in Medievalism* 16 (2008): 159–83.

Mona, Erik. "From the Basement to the Basic Set: The Early Years of Dungeons & Dragons." In *Second Person: Role-Playing and Story in Games and Playable Media,* edited by Pat Harrigan and Noah Wardrip-Fruin, 25–30. Cambridge, MA: MIT Press, 2007.

Monaco, Mike. "Bruce Galloway's Fantasy Wargaming." *Swords & Dorkery.* Accessed July 26, 2012. http://mikemonaco.wordpress.com/bruce-galloways-fantasy-wargaming/.

Montola, Markus. "The Invisible Rules of Role-Playing: The Social Framework of Role-Playing Process." *International Journal of Role-Playing* 1, no. 1 (2008): 22–36.

Morgan, Gwendolyn A. "Medievalism, Authority, and the Academy." *Studies in Medievalism* 17 (2009): 55–67.

Morillo, Stephen. *Warfare under the Anglo-Norman Kings, 1066–1135.* Woodbridge, Suffolk: Boydell, 1994.

Morpurgo, Michael. "Children's Author Michael Morpurgo on *Beowulf.*" *Guardian,* November 20, 2007. Accessed July 9, 2012. http://www.guardian.co.uk/film/2007/nov/20/booksforchildrenandteenagers.poetry.

Morris, William, and A. J. Wyatt. *The Tale of Beowulf.* London: Kelmscott Press, 1895.

Moscaritolo, Angela. "Twitter Turns Six with 140 Million Active Users." *PC Mag.com.* Accessed July 19, 2012. http://www.pcmag.com/article2/0,2817,2401955,00.asp.

Munro, John H. "The Medieval Scarlet and the Economics of Sartorial Splendour." In *Cloth and Clothing in Medieval Europe: Essays in Memory of Professor E. M. Carus-Wilson,* edited by N. B. Harte and K. G. Ponting, 13–70. London: Heinemann, 1983.

Nachtwey, James. *Inferno.* London: Phaidon, 1999.

Nardi, Bruno. "L'origine dell'anima umana secondo Dante." In Bruno Nardi, *Studi di filosofia medievale,* 9–68. Rome: Edizione di storia e letteratura, 1960.

Ncube, Brad. "Chivalry and Sorcery Playtest (Retroactive Analysis)." *Skull Crushing for Great Justice.* Accessed July 26, 2012. http://crushingskulls.blogspot.com/2011/07/chivalry-sorcery-playtest-retroactive.html.

"NECA Takes You To Hell And Back With New Dante's Inferno Collectible Figure." *Youbentmywookie.* Accessed October 2, 2012. http://youbentmywookie.com/news/neca-takes-you-to-hell-and-back-with-new-dantes-inferno-collectible-figures-7611.

Newman, James, and Barney Oram. *Teaching Videogames.* London: British Film Institute, 2006.

Nichols, Kathleen. "Many Monsters to Destroy." *Arthurian Legend.* Accessed June 25, 2011. http://www.uiweb.uidaho.edu/student_orgs/arthurian_legend/quests/monsters/agiants.html.

Nielsen, Simon Egenfeldt, Jonas Heide Smith, and Susana Pajares Tosca. *Understanding Videogames: The Essential Introduction.* New York: Routledge, 2008.

Nissen, Christopher. "The Motif of the Woman in Male Disguise from Boccacio to Bigolina." In *The Italian Novella: A Book of Essays,* edited by Gloria Allaire, 201–17. New York: Routledge, 2003.

Nitsche, Michael. *Video Game Spaces.* Cambridge, MA: MIT Press, 2008.

Noble, David F. *The Religion of Technology.* New York: Penguin, 1999.

Norrman, Lena. "Woman or Warrior? The Construction of Gender in Old Norse Myth." In *Old Norse Myths, Literature and Society: Proceedings of the 11th International Saga Conference,* edited by Geraldine Barnes and Margaret Clunies Ross, 375–85. Sydney: Centre for Medieval Studies, University of Sydney, 2000.

North, Richard. "Poetry in Motion." *Time Out.* Accessed July 9, 2012. http://www.time-out.com/film/features/show-feature/3815/Dr_Richard_North_on-Beowulf-.html.

Nutt, Christian. "The Road To Hell: The Creative Direction of Dante's Inferno." *Gamasutra.* Accessed May 26, 2012. http://www.gamasutra.com/view/feature/4266/the_road_to_hell_the_creative_.php.

Oldenburg, Ray. *The Great Good Place: Cafes, Coffee Shops, Community Centers, Beauty Parlors, General Stores, Bars, Hangouts, and How They Get You Through the Day.* New York: Marlowe, 1991.

Oman, Charles. *A History of the Art of War in the Middle Ages.* 2nd ed. London: Methuen, 1924.

Osborne, John. "On Ravenshire Castle, Curing Fatigue and Pushing Envelopes." *Games.com.* Accessed July 15, 2012. http://blog.games.com/2012/05/07/ravenshire-castle-interview.

Osmond, Andrew. "*Beowulf.*" *Sight and Sound* 18, no. 1 (2008): 61–62.

Owen, Rachel. "The Image of Dante, Poet and Pilgrim." In *Dante on View: The Reception of Dante in the Visual and Performing Arts,* edited by Antonella Braida and Luisa Calé, 83–94. Aldershot, UK: Ashgate, 2007.

Oxford English Dictionary. "Map." Accessed August 1, 2012. http://www.oed.com.

Palmer, R. R. "Frederick the Great, Guibert, Bülow: From Dynastic to National War." In *Makers of Modern Strategy from Machiavelli to the Nuclear Age,* edited by Peter Paret, 91–119. Oxford: Clarendon Press, 1986.

Panofsky, Erwin. *Perspective as Symbolic Form.* Translated by Christopher S. Wood. New York: Zone Books, 2005.

Paradox Interactive. "Forum: Crusader Kings." *Paradox Interactive.* Last accessed August 1, 2012. http://forum.paradoxplaza.com/forum/forumdisplay. php?81-Crusader-Kings.

Paris, Gaston. "Études Sur Les Romans De La Table Ronde: Lancelot Du Lac, Ii: Le Conte De La Charrette." *Romania* 12 (1883): 459–534.

Parkhurst, Emily. "Casual-gaming Industry: $8 billion and Counting." *Puget Sound Business Journal.* Accessed July 19, 2012. http://www.bizjournals.com/seattle/ blog/techflash/2012/07/casual-gaming-8-billion-and-counting.html?page=all.

Partner, Peter. *The Templars and Their Myth.* New York: Oxford University Press, 1982.

Pastoureau, Michel. *Blue: The History of a Color.* Translated by Markus I. Cruse. Princeton: Princeton University Press, 2001.

———. *The Devil's Cloth: A History of Stripes and Striped Fabric.* Translated by Jody Gladding. New York: Columbia University Press, 2001.

———. *Heraldry: An Introduction to a Noble Tradition.* New York: Harry N. Abrams, 1997.

———. *L'Hermine et le sinople: Études d'héraldique médiévale.* Paris: Le Léopard d'or, 1982.

———. *Noir: Histoire d'une couleur.* Paris: Seuil, 2008.

Patterson, Lee. "On the Margin: Postmodernism, Ironic History, and Medieval Studies." *Speculum* 65, no. 1 (1990): 87–108.

Patterson, Serina. "'My Friends and Allies': Medieval Games, Interactivity, and Social Play in Social Network Applications." Paper presented at the 45th International Congress on Medieval Studies, Kalamazoo, MI. May 13, 2010.

Pauli, Michelle. "Vatican Appoints Official Da Vinci Code Debunker." *The Guardian,* March 15, 2005. Accessed July 30, 2012. http://www.guardian. co.uk/books/2005/mar/15/catholicism.religion.

Pearce, Celia. "Emergent Authorship: The Next Interactive Revolution." *Computers & Graphics* 26, no. 1 (2002): 21–29.

Pellett, Matthew. "Dante's Inferno: God of War Tumbles from Mount Olympus into the Depths of Hell." *Gamesradar.* Accessed August 20, 2012. http://www.games-radar.com/dantes-inferno-review/.

Pleij, Herman. *Colors Demonic and Divine: Shades of Meaning in the Middle Ages and After.* Translated by Diane Webb. New York: Columbia University Press, 2004.

Popper, Benjamin. "Dante Alighieri: Epic Poet, Ass Kicker." *The Atlantic,* February, 2010. Accessed June 21, 2012. http://www.theatlantic.com/magazine/ archive/2010/02/dante-alighieri-epic-poet-ass-kicker/7936/.

Powell, James M. *Anatomy of a Crusade, 1213–1221.* Philadelphia: University of Pennsylvania Press, 1986.

Power, Daniel, and Naomi Standen, eds. *Frontiers in Question: Eurasian Borderlands, 700–1700.* Basingstoke: Macmillan, 1999.

Putter, Ad. "Gifts and Commodities in *Sir Amadace.*" *Review of English Studies* 51 (2000): 371–94.

Ralph of Coggeshall. *Chronicon anglicanum.* Edited by Joseph Stevenson. Rolls Series 66. London: Longman, 1875.

Rao, Leena. "Zynga's CastleVille Crosses 5M Daily Active Users, Now Growing Faster Than CityVille." *Tech Crunch.* Accessed July 21, 2012. http://techcrunch.com/2011/11/21/zyngas-castleville-crosses-5m-daily-active-users-now-growing-faster-that-cityville.

Rao, Valentina. "Playful Mood: The Construction of Facebook as a Third Place." MindTrek Conference 2008, Tampere, Finland. Accessed April 10, 2010. http://prtal.acm.org/citation.cfm?id=1457199.1457202&coll=Portal&dl=GUIDE&CFID = 24746181&CFTOK EN = 85617762.

Rettberg, Scott. "Corporate Ideology in *World of Warcraft.*" In *Digital Culture, Play, and Identity: A World of Warcraft Reader,* edited by Hilde Corneliussen and Jill Walker Rettberg, 19–38. Cambridge, MA: MIT Press, 2008.

Rheingold, Howard. *The Virtual Community: Homesteading on the Electronic Frontier.* Cambridge, MA: MIT Press, 2000.

Ridoux, Charles. *Évolution des études médiévales en France de 1860 à 1914.* Paris: Champion, 2001.

Robinson, Carol. "An Introduction to Medievalist Video Games." *Studies in Medievalism* 16 (2008): 123–24.

———. "Some Basic Definitions." *MEMO: Medieval Electronic Multimedia Organization.* Accessed August 24, 2011. http://medievalelectronic multimedia.org/definitions.html.

———, and Pamela Clements. "Living with Neomedievalism." *Studies in Medievalism* 18 (2009): 78–106.

———, eds. *Neomedievalism in the Media: Essays on Film, Television, and Electronic Games.* Lewiston, ME: Edwin Mellen, 2011.

Rosen, Judith. "Distribution in a Digital Age." *Publishers Weekly,* April 16, 2012, 18–23.

Rothenberg, Gunter. "The Age of Napoleon." In *The Laws of War: Constraints on Warfare in the Western World,* edited by Michael Howard, George J. Andreopoulos and Mark R. Shulman, 86–97. New Haven: Yale University Press, 1994.

Rouse, Richard. *Game Design: Theory and Practice.* 2nd ed. Plano, TX: Wordware, 2005.

Rowland, Thomas, and Amanda Barton. "Outside Oneself in *World of Warcraft:* Gamers' Perception of the Racial Self-Other." *Transformative Works and Culture* 8 (2011). Accessed November 15, 2011. http://journal.transformativeworks.org/index.php/twc/article/view/258/242.

Ryan, Erin Gloria. "The Rapey Lara Croft Reboot is a Fucked-Up Freudian Field Day." *Jezebel.* Accessed July 31, 2012. http://jezebel.com/5918222/the-rapey-lara-croft-reboot-is-a-fucked+up-freudian-field-day.

Sabbath, Roberta. "Jane Jensen's *Gabriel Knight: Sins of the Fathers/*The Numinous Woman and the Millennium Woman." *Journal of Popular Culture* 31, no. 1 (1997): 131–47.

Sainato, Susan Butvin. "Not Your Typical Knight: The Emerging On-Screen Defender." In *The Medieval Hero on Screen: Representations from Beowulf to Buffy,* edited by Martha W. Driver and Sid Ray, 133–46. Jefferson, NC: McFarland, 2004.

Salen, Katie, and Eric Zimmerman. *Rules of Play: Game Design Fundamentals.* Cambridge, MA: MIT Press, 2003.

Salomão, Jayme, ed. *Erich Auerbach – 5° Colóquio UERJ.* Rio de Janeiro: Imago Editora, 1994.

Sanders, Julie. *Adaptation and Appropriation: The New Critical Idiom.* Edited by John Drakakis. New York: Routledge, 2006.

Scarry, Elaine. *The Body in Pain: The Making and Unmaking of the World.* New York: Oxford University Press, 1985.

Schmeider, Christian. "World of Maskcraft vs. World of Queercraft? Communication, Sex, and Gender in the Online Role-playing Game *World of Warcraft.*" *Journal of Gaming and Virtual Worlds* 1, no. 1 (2009): 5–21.

Scholz, Bernard Walter, with Barbara Rogers, ed. and trans. *Royal Frankish Annals.* In *Carolingian Chronicles: The Royal Frankish Annals and Nithard's Histories.* 35–126. Ann Arbor: University of Michigan Press, 1972.

Schut, Kevin. "Desktop Conquistadors: Negotiating American Manhood in the Digital Fantasy Role-Playing Game." In *Gaming as Culture: Essays on Reality, Identity, and Experience in Fantasy Games,* edited by J. Patrick Williams, Sean Q. Hendricks, and W. Keith Winkler, 100–19. Jefferson, NC: McFarland, 2006.

Scott, Margaret. *Medieval Dress and Fashion.* London: British Library, 2007.

Scully, Diarmuid. "Gerald of Wales and the English Conquest of Ireland: Map, Text, and Marginal Illustration in MS 700, National Museum of Ireland." Conference presentation, International Medieval Congress, Leeds, 2012.

Sheehan, James J. *German History, 1770–1866.* Oxford: Clarendon Press, 1989.

Shippey, Tom. "Medievalisms and Why They Matter." *Studies in Medievalism* 17 (2009): 45–54.

Sicart, Miguel. *The Ethics of Computer Games.* Cambridge, MA: MIT Press, 2009.

Simbalist, Edward E., and Wilf K. Backhaus. *The C&S Red Book.* Camrose, Alberta: Gamestuff, 2000.

Simek, Rudolf. *Dictionary of Northern Mythology.* Translated by Angela Hall. Woodbridge, Suffolk: D. S. Brewer, 1993.

Simonetta, Marcello. "Assassin's Creed." Lecture at Seton Hall University, South Orange, NJ, April 18, 2011.

Siskoid. "Rpgs That Time Forgot . . . Fantasy Wargaming." *Siskoid's Blog of Geekery.* Accessed July 27, 2012. http://siskoid.blogspot.com/2007/07/rpgs-that-time-forgot-fantasy-wargaming.html.

Sklar, Elizabeth S. "Marketing Arthur: The Commodification of Arthurian Legend." In *King Arthur in Popular Culture,* edited by Elizabeth S. Sklar and Donald L. Hoffman, 9–23. Jefferson, NC: McFarland, 2002.

Smail, R. C. *Crusading Warfare.* 2nd ed. Cambridge, UK: Cambridge University Press, 1995.

Smalley, Beryl. *Historians in the Middle Ages.* London: Thames and Hudson, 1974.

Squire, Kurt. "From Content to Context: Videogames as Designed Experience." *Educational Researcher* 35, no. 8 (2006): 19–29.

Stacey, Robert C. "The Age of Chivalry." In *The Laws of War: Constraints on Warfare in the Western World,* edited by Michael Howard, George J. Andreopoulos, and Mark R. Shulman, 27–39. New Haven: Yale University Press, 1994.

Stafford, Greg. *The Great Pendragon Campaign.* Stone Mountain, GA: White Wolf Publishing, 2006.

———. "Greg Stafford's Pendragon Page." Accessed July 30, 2012. http://www.gspendragon.com/.

———. *King Arthur Pendragon: Chivalric Role-Playing in Arthur's Britain.* Oakland, CA: Chaosium, 1985.

———. *King Arthur Pendragon: Epic Roleplaying in Legendary Britain.* 4th ed. Oakland, CA: Green Knight Publishing, 1999.

———. *Runequest.* Oakland, CA: Chaosium, 1978.

Stam, Robert. "Introduction: The Theory and Practice of Adaptation." In *Literature and Film: A Guide to the Theory and Practice of Film Adaptation.* Edited by Robert Stam and Alessandra Raengo, 1–52. Malden, MA: Blackwell, 2005.

Staniland, Kay. "Medieval Courtly Splendour." *Costume* 14 (1980): 7–23.

Steiner, Rudolf. *Christ and the Spiritual World and the Search for the Holy Grail.* Translated by C. Davy and D. Osmond. London: Rudolf Steiner Press, 1963.

Stern, Eddo. "A Touch of Medieval: Narrative, Magic and Computer Technology in Massively Multiplayer Computer Role-Playing Games." In *Proceedings of Computer Games and Digital Cultures Conference*, edited by Frans Mäyrä, 257–76. Tampere, Finland: Tampere University Press, 2002.

Stewart, Susan. *On Longing: Narratives of the Miniature, the Gigantic, the Souvenir, the Collection*. Durham, NC: Duke University Press, 1993.

Stjerna, Knut. *Essays on Questions Connected with the Old English Poem of Beowulf*. Coventry, UK: Curtis and Beamish, 1912.

Strickland, Matthew. *War and Chivalry: The Conduct and Perception of War in England and Normandy, 1066–1217*. Cambridge, UK: Cambridge University Press, 1996.

Suits, Bernard H. *The Grasshopper: Games, Life, and Utopia*. Toronto: University of Toronto Press, 1978.

Sullivan, C. W. "High Fantasy." In *The International Companion Encyclopedia of Children's Literature*, edited by Peter Hunt, 436–46. London: Routledge, 2004.

"Supreme Court Violent Video Games Ruling: Ban on Sale, Rental to Children Unconstitutional." *The Huffington Post*. Accessed August 19, 2011. http://www.huffingtonpost.com/2011/06/27/supreme-court-violent-video-games_n_884991.html.

Talbert, Richard J. A., and Richard W. Unger, ed. *Cartography in Antiquity and the Middle Ages: Fresh Perspectives, New Methods*. Leiden: Brill, 2008.

Tarnowski, John. "Actual Play: Pendragon." *The RPG Site*. Accessed July 30, 2012. http://www.therpgsite.com/showthread.php?t = 10668.

Taylor, T. L. "Multiple Pleasures: Women and Online Gaming." *Convergence* 9, no. 1 (2003): 21–46.

———. *Play Between Worlds: Exploring Online Game Culture*. Cambridge, MA: MIT Press, 2006.

Taylor, Zach, and Laurie N. Whelan. "Playing the Past: An Introduction." In *Playing the Past: History and Nostalgia in Video Games*, edited by Zach Taylor and Laurie N. Whelan, 1–15. Nashville: Vanderbilt University Press, 2008.

Thacker, Alan. "Bede and History." In *The Cambridge Companion to Bede*, edited by Scott DeGiorgio, 170–89. Cambridge, UK: Cambridge University Press, 2010.

The 13th Warrior. Directed by John McTiernan. Burbank, CA: Touchstone Pictures, 1999.

Tolkien, J. R. R. *The Hobbit*. London: Grafton, 1991.

———. *The Lord of the Rings*. London: HarperCollins, 1993.

Tolmie, Jane. "Medievalism and the Fantasy Heroine." *Journal of Gender Studies* 15 (2006): 145–58.

Tomasch, Sylvia, and Sealy Gilles, ed. *Text and Territory: Geographical Imagination in the Middle Ages*. Philadelphia: University of Pennsylvania Press, 1998.

Torner, Evan, and William J. White, eds. *Immersive Gameplay: Essays on Participatory Media and Role-Playing*. Jefferson, NC: McFarland, 2012.

Toswell, M. J. "The Tropes of Medievalism." *Studies in Medievalism* 17 (2009): 68–76.

Traxel, Oliver. "Medieval and Pseudo-Medieval Elements in Computer Role-Playing Games: Use and Interactivity." *Studies in Medievalism* 16 (2008): 125–42.

Tresca, Michael J. *The Evolution of Fantasy Role-Playing Games*. Jefferson, NC: McFarland, 2011.

Trigg, Stephanie. "Medievalism and Convergence Culture: Researching the Middle Ages for Fiction and Film." *Parergon* 25 (2008): 99–118.

Tuan, Yi-Fu. *Space and Place: The Perspective of Experience*. Minneapolis: University of Minneapolis Press, 2001.

Tyerman, Christopher. *God's War: A New History of the Crusades*. London: Allen Lane, 2006.

The Unofficial Elder Scrolls Page Wiki. "Lore: Books." Accessed July 31 2012. http://www.uesp.net/wiki/Lore:Books.

Utz, Richard. "Preface: A Moveable Feast: Repositionings of 'the Medieval' in Medieval Studies, Medievalism, and Neomedievalism." In *Neomedievalism in the Media: Essays on Film, Television, and Electronic Games*, edited by Carol L. Robinson and Pamela Clements, i-v. Lewiston, ME: Edwin Mellen, 2011.

Van Geel, Ibe. "MMOdata.Net." Accessed October 10, 2012. http://mmodata.net/

van Oostrom, Frits. "Spatial Struggles: Medieval Studies between Nationalism and Globalisation." *Journal of English and Germanic Philology* 105 (2006): 5–24.

Varney, Allen. "Greg Stafford, Mythmaker." *The Escapist,* October 29, 2009. Accessed July 30, 2012. http://www.escapistmagazine.com/articles/view/columns/days-of-high-adventure/6709-Greg-Stafford-Mythmaker#at.

Vegetius. *Epitome of Military Science.* Translated by N. P. Milner. Liverpool: Liverpool University Press, 1993.

Verbruggen, J. F. *The Art of Warfare in Western Europe during the Middle Ages.* Translated by Sumner Willard and R. W. Southern. 2nd ed. Woodbridge, Suffolk: Boydell, 1997.

Verduin, Kathleen. "The Founding and the Founder: Medievalism and the Work of Leslie J. Workman." *Studies in Medievalism* 17 (2009): 1–27.

"Video Games: 14 in the Collection, for Starters." *Inside/Out: Museum of Modern Art Blog.* Accessed January 15, 2013. http://www.moma.org/explore/inside_out/2012/11/29/video-games-14-in-the-collection-for-starters.

"Violent Videogames and Young People." *Harvard Mental Health Letter,* October 2010. Accessed January 15, 2013. http://www.health.harvard.edu/newsletters/Harvard_Mental_Health_Letter/2010/October/violent-video-games-and-young-people.

Wallis, Alistair. "Playing Catch Up: *Gabriel Knight*'s Jane Jensen." *Gamasutra News.* May 17, 2007. Accessed April 29, 2012. http://www.gamasutra.com/php-bin/news_index.php?story=13978.

WarcraftRealms. Census Data. Accessed July 20, 2012. http://www.warcraftrealms.com/census.php?guildid=-1.

Warburg, Aby. *Der Bilderatlas MNEMOSYNE.* In *Gesammelte Schriften* II.1, edited by Martin Warnke. Berlin: Akademie Verlag, 2012.

Warren, W. L. *Henry II.* 2nd ed. New Haven: Yale University Press, 2000.

Weinberger, Garry. "Re: [Dragwars] Fantasy Wargaming." Accessed July 27, 2012. http://games.groups.yahoo.com/group/dragwars/message/4782.

Wells, Herbert George. *Little Wars.* Spring Branch, TX: Skirmisher Publishing, 2011.

Whetter, K. S. *Understanding Genre and Medieval Romance.* Burlington, VT: Ashgate, 2008.

Whitehead, Stephen M. *Men and Masculinities: Key Themes and New Directions.* Cambridge, UK: Polity, 2002.

Whitelock, Dorothy, David C. Douglas, and Susie I. Tucker, ed. and trans. *The Anglo-Saxon Chronicle: A Revised Translation.* London: Eyre and Spottiswoode, 1961.

William of Malmesbury. *Gesta Regum Anglorum: The History of the English Kings.* 2 vols. Edited and translated by R. A. B. Mynors, R. M. Thompson, and M. Winterbottom. Oxford: Clarendon Press, 1998–9.

———. *Willelmi Malmesbiriensis Monachi De Gestis Regum Anglorum Libri Quinque: Historiae Novellae Libri Tres.* Translated by William Stubbs. London: H. M. Stationery Office, 1887.

William of Poitiers. *The Gesta Guillelmi of William of Poitiers.* Edited and translated by R. H. C. Davis and Marjorie Chibnall. Oxford: Clarendon Press, 1998.

William of Tyre. *Historia rerum in partibus transmarinis gestarum.* Translated by James Brundage. In *The Crusades: A Documentary Survey.* Milwaukee: Marquette University Press, 1962.

Williams, David. *Deformed Discourse: The Function of the Monster in Mediaeval Thought and Literature*. Montreal: McGill-Queen's University Press, 1996.

Williams, G. Christopher. "Sorry Dante But Your Princess Is in Another Castle." *PopMatters*. Accessed May 26 2012. http://www.popmatters.com/pm/post/121718-sorry-dante-but-your-princess-is-in-another-castle.

Williams, J. Patrick, Sean Q. Hendricks, and W. Keith Winkler, eds. *Gaming as Culture: Essays on Reality, Identity, and Experience in Fantasy Games*. Jefferson, NC: McFarland, 2006.

Williams, John. "Fantasy Wargaming: Hangins' Too Good fer 'Em!!!" *RPG Geek*. Accessed July 27, 2012. http://rpggeek.com/thread/365078/fantasy-wargaming-hangins-too-good-fer-em.

Willow. Directed by Ron Howard. Culver City, CA: 20th Century Fox, 1988.

Wilson, David M., ed. *The Bayeux Tapestry*. London: Thames and Hudson, 2004.

Wirth, Werner, et al. "A Process Model of the Formation of Spatial Presence Experiences." *Media Psychology* 9 (2007): 493–525.

Wisman, J. A. "*L'Epitoma rei militaris* de Végèce et sa fortune au Moyen Âge." *Le Moyen Âge* 85 (1979): 13–31.

Wolf, Mark J. P. "Z-Axis Development in the Video Game." In *The Video Game Theory Reader 2*, edited by Bernard Perron and Mark J. P. Wolf, 151–67. New York: Routledge, 2009.

Wood, Juliette. "Holy Grail: From Romance Motif to Modern Genre." *Folklore* 111, no. 2 (2000): 169–90.

Woodward, David. "Medieval *Mappaemundi*." In *History of Cartography Vol. I: Prehistoric, Ancient, and Medieval Europe and the Mediterranean*, 286–307. Chicago: University of Chicago, 1987.

Woolf, Henry Bosley. "On the Characterisation of Beowulf." *Journal of English Literary History* 15, no. 2 (June 1948): 85–92.

Woolgar, C.M. *The Senses in Late Medieval England*. London: Yale University Press, 2006.

World of Warcraft. "Formal Dangui." Accessed July 29, 2012. http://us.battle.net/wow/en/item/13895.

———. "Forums." Accessed July 29, 2012. http://us.battle.net/wow/en/forum/.

———. "Game Guide." Accessed July 29, 2012. http://us.battle.net/wow/en/game/.

———. "Gnomeregan." Accessed October 10, 2012. http://us.battle.net/wow/en/zone/gnomeregan/.

World of Warcraft Community Site. "Item Basics." Accessed July 29, 2012. http://wayback.archive.org/web/*/http://www.worldofwarcraft.com/info/items/basics.html.

World of Warcraft Forums. "Plate Bikinis?" Accessed June 20, 2012. http://forums.worldofwarcraft.com/thread.html?topicId=18031368991&sid=1&pageNo=1.

WoW_Ladies. "Formal Dangui." Accessed July 29, 2012. http://wow-ladies.livejournal.com/16155719.html.

———. "Silly Question." July 13, 2012. Accessed July 29, 2012. http://wow-ladies.livejournal.com/1614187.html.

Wowhead. "Barim's Main Gauche." Accessed October 12, 2012. http://www.wowhead.com/item=56390.

———. "Formal Dangui." Accessed July 29, 2012. http://www.wowhead.com/item=13895/formal-dangui.

———. "Thunderfury, Blessed Blade of the Windseeker." Accessed October 13, 2012. http://www.wowhead.com/item=19019.

———. "Unkempt Pants." Accessed October 12, 2012. http://www.wowhead.com/item=21006.

Wowpedia. "Dignified Headmaster's Charge." Accessed October 13, 2012. http://www.wowpedia.org/Dignified_Headmaster's_Charge.

———. "Epic." Accessed July 29, 2012. http://www.wowpedia.org/Epic.

———. "Heirloom." Accessed July 29, 2012. http://www.wowpedia.org/Heirloom.

———. "Legendary." Accessed July 29, 2012. http://www.wowpedia.org/Legendary.

———. "Need Before Greed." Accessed July 29, 2012. http://www.wowpedia.org/Need_Before_Greed.

———. "Profession." Accessed July 29, 2012. http://www.wowpedia.org/Profession.

———. "Quality." Accessed July 29, 2012. http://www.wowpedia.org/Quality.

———. "Rare." Accessed July 29, 2012. http://www.wowpedia.org/Rare.

———. "Thunderfury, Blessed Blade of the Windseeker." Accessed October 13, 2012. http://www.wowpedia.org/Thunderfury.

Wowwiki. "Goblin Rocket Boots." Accessed October 10, 2012. http://www.wowwiki.com/Goblin_Rocket_Boots.

———. "Ultrasafe Transporter: Toshley's Station." Accessed October 10, 2012. http://www.wowwiki.com/Ultrasafe_Transporter:_Toshley's_Station.

———. "Undead Mad Scientists." Accessed October 10, 2012. http://www.wowwiki.com/Mad_scientist.

———. "Venture Trading Company." Accessed October 10, 2012. http://www.wowwiki.com/Venture_Trading_Company.

Wright, Monica L. "Dress for Success: Béroul's *Tristan* and the Restoration of Status through Clothes." *Arthuriana* 18 (2008): 3–16.

Wright, Will. "Sculpting Possibility Space." Keynote presented at Accelerating Change, Stanford University, Palo Alto, CA, November 6, 2004. Accessed May 4, 2012. http://itc.conversationsnetwork.org/shows/detail376.html#.

Yee, Nick. "Maps of Digital Desires: Exploring the Topography of Gender and Play in Online Games." In *Beyond Barbie and Mortal Combat: New Perspectives on Gender and Gaming*, edited by Yasmin B. Kafai, Carrie Heeter, Jill Denner, and Jennifer Y. Sun, 83–95. Cambridge, MA: MIT Press, 2008.

Young, Iris Marion. *Throwing Like a Girl and Other Essays in Feminist Philosophy and Social Theory*. Ann Arbor: UMI Books on Demand, 2002.

Žižek, Slavoj. "Courtly Love, or, Woman as Thing." In *The Metastases of Enjoyment: Six Essays on Woman and Causality*, 89–112. New York: Verso, 1994.

Zomben. "Chivalry & Sorcery—Who Played It? How Was It?" *RPG.net*. Accessed July 23, 2012. http://forum.rpg.net/showthread.php?425109-Chivalry-amp-Sorcery-Who-played-it-How-was-it.

Contributors

Candace Barrington (PhD, Duke University) is Professor of English at Central Connecticut State University, where she specializes in medieval English literature. Her research focuses on the intersection of late-medieval English law and literature, as well as on American medievalism. She has published in *Mediaevalia*, *American Literary History*, and *European Journal of English Studies*; has chapters in *Theorizing Legal Personhood in Late Medieval England* (Brill), *Gower at 600* (Boydell and Brewer), and *Sex and Sexuality in a Feminist World* (Cambridge Scholars); and coedited *Letter of the Law: Legal Practice and Literary Production in Medieval England* (Cornell).

Harry J. Brown (PhD, Lehigh University) specializes in early and Native American literature, literary theory, and digital games. His current research in game studies focuses on counterfactual history, simulated ecologies, and the construction of virtual spaces. He has published three books: *The Native American in Short Fiction in the* Saturday Evening Post (Scarecrow, 2001); *Injun Joe's Ghost: The Indian Mixed-Blood in American Writing* (University of Missouri, 2004); and *Videogames and Education* (M. E. Sharpe, 2008). He has published in *Studies in Medievalism*, *Aether: The Journal of Media Geography*, *Works and Days*, *Paradoxa*, and the *Journal of American and Comparative Cultures*, and he has contributed essays to *The Business of Entertainment* (Praeger, 2008) and *Digital Gameplay: Essays on the Nexus of Games and Gamer* (McFarland, 2005). He is an Associate Professor of English at DePauw University in Indiana.

Oliver Chadwick (PhD candidate, University of Queensland) is the recipient of the inaugural John Hay Scholarship. His research focuses on how medieval masculinities are re-imagined and mobilized in contemporary pop-cultural adaptations of medieval literature. His research aims to challenge medievalist alteritism by examining the gender-constructive relationship between re-imagined images of medieval men and the contemporary receptive subject across a range of pop-cultural media, including video games, comics, and Viking metal.

Teresa Combs is a graduate student in the Master of Arts in English program at University of Alaska Anchorage. This is her first published essay.

Michelle DiPietro (BA [New College of Florida] and MSt [University of Oxford]) earned her BA and MSt in Medieval Studies. In addition to medievalism in popular culture, her scholarly interests include early medieval Ireland and medieval perceptions of the natural world. She has presented at several graduate seminars and the 14th International Congress of Celtic Studies. Her work on Ireland's sacred-tree traditions will appear in *Ríocht na Midhe* (2013).

Tim English (undergraduate student at Central Connecticut State University) has been playing video games his entire life in preparation for this publication. This is his first published academic paper.

Gregory Fedorenko (PhD candidate, Cambridge University) works primarily on the history of France and the Anglo-Norman realm in the twelfth and early thirteenth centuries. He is engaged in a study of the unpublished thirteenth-century prose *Chronique de Normandie*, unraveling the various strands of this complex and multifaceted narrative and considering the reasons for its popularity among medieval aristocratic audiences. He is currently completing doctoral studies and has published in *Nottingham Medieval Studies*.

Jennifer Kavetsky (PhD candidate, University of California, Riverside) specializes in twentieth-century American and British fiction. Her research focuses on the intersections of gender and technology in a variety of media, including print, television, and digital spaces. She has published in *Science Fiction Studies* and has presented her research at several national and regional conferences, including the 2011 Annual MLA Convention and the 2011 Eaton Science Fiction Conference.

Daniel T. Kline (PhD, Indiana University) specializes in Middle English literature and culture, literary and cultural theory, and digital medievalism, and his research concerns children, violence, sacrifice, and ethics in late-medieval England. He has published in *Chaucer Review*, *College Literature*, *Comparative Drama*, the *Journal of English and Germanic Philology*, *Philological Quarterly*, among others, and has chapters in *The Cambridge Companion to Medieval Women's Writing* (Cambridge), *Translating Desire in Medieval and Early Modern Literature* (ACMRS), *Mass Market Medievalism* (McFarland), and *Levinas and Medieval Literature* (Duquesne). He edited *Medieval Literature for Children*

(Routledge) and the *Continuum Handbook of Medieval British Literature* (Continuum). The author/webmaster of *The Electronic Canterbury Tales* (http://www.kankedort.net), Kline is Professor and Chair of English at the University of Alaska Anchorage.

Peter Kudenov completed his MA degree in English at the University of Alaska Anchorage in 2013. This is his first published essay.

Bruno Lessard (PhD, Université de Montréal) is Assistant Professor in the School of Image Arts at Ryerson University in Toronto. He has published extensively on digital media arts and contemporary cinema in journals such as *Parachute, Film-Philosophy, Convergence,* and *Public: Art/Culture/Ideas* and in collections such as *Macbeth: New Critical Essays* (Routledge), *In the Dark Room: Marguerite Duras and Cinema* (Peter Lang), *Sound and Music in Film and Visual Media* (Continuum), *Save ... as Digital Memories* (Palgrave Macmillan), and *Popular Ghosts: The Haunted Spaces of Everyday Culture* (Continuum). He is at work on a book-length publication focusing on adaptation and interactive media.

Elysse T. Meredith (PhD, University of Edinburgh) received her PhD in Medieval Studies in June 2012. Associated with the departments of English literature, French language and literature, and art history, her doctoral thesis examined the use of color and costume in fourteenth- and fifteenth-century Arthuriana, focusing particularly on *Sir Gawain and the Green Knight,* Froissart's *Meliador,* and Parisian illuminations from Arthurian prose manuscripts. In 2009 she was awarded the University of Edinburgh Overseas Research Scholarship and the College of Humanities and Social Sciences Postgraduate Research Award, and in 2011 she received the Beans for Brains Scholarship from Jimmy Beans Wool, which supports knitters and crocheters in tertiary education. For the 2010–11 academic year she served as coeditor of *FORUM,* the University of Edinburgh Postgraduate Journal of Culture and the Arts (http://www.forumjournal.org).

Kristin Noone (PhD candidate at the University of California, Riverside) is working on a dissertation that connects medieval literature, fantasy fiction, and temporal studies. With Audrey Becker, she coedited the collection *Welsh Mythology and Folklore in Popular Culture* (McFarland 2011) and has published articles on ghouls in *Supernatural (Transformative Works and Cultures),* Terry Pratchett and Shakespeare (*Journal of the Fantastic in the Arts*), Neil Gaiman's retellings of *Beowulf (The Weird Fiction Review),* monstrosity in *Tin Man (The Universe of Oz,* McFarland), and Joss Whedon's *Dollhouse (Inside Joss' Dollhouse,* SmartPop).

Serina Patterson (PhD candidate, University of British Columbia) specializes in Middle English literature, medievalism, and digital humanities. Her dissertation research focuses on literary games and gaming in Middle English and Middle French literature. She has published in *New Knowledge Environments* and *LIBER Quarterly: The Journal of European Research Libraries* for her work in developing an online library system for digital-age youth. She is also an associate research assistant for the Electronic Textual Cultures Lab at the University of Victoria.

Jason Pitruzzello (PhD candidate at the University of Houston) specializes in early modern literature, with a secondary focus in medievalisms, both early modern and contemporary. Jason is a teaching fellow at the University of Houston, where he earned the university's highest teaching award, the Teaching Excellence Award, in 2010 while teaching Chaucer, the Beowulf poet, and the Pearl/Gawain poet to upper division undergraduates. He is currently working on his dissertation, which explores Shakespeare's strategies of adapting from his medieval and post-medieval sources.

Thomas Rowland (PhD candidate, Saint Louis University) studies later medieval literature, especially stories of Robin Hood, as well as the intersection of games and narratives in theory and practice. His secondary interests involve video games and how we approach playing them as narratives. Rowland is also involved in the community of researchers of medieval martial arts. He is a contributing member to the International Association of Robin Hood Studies, for which his most current project is hosting the 2013 International Conference. He has published on race and racism in online role-playing video games, and on the literary experience of medieval Robin Hood play-games compared to the experience of video games.

John T. Sebastian (PhD, Cornell University) studies the cultural landscape of late-medieval English devotion across the genres of lyric poetry, mystical prose, and especially religious drama. He is the editor of the forthcoming TEAMS Middle English Text Series edition of *The Croxton Play of the Sacrament* and is with Christina Fitzgerald Co-General Editor of the new *Broadview Anthology of Medieval Drama*. His current project focuses on the tension between faith and knowledge in medieval drama, but he has also published work on Chaucer, Lydgate, the Arthurian legend, and Old Norse literature and culture. He is Associate Professor of Medieval Literature at Loyola University New Orleans, where he serves as the Director of the Medieval Studies Program and was also for several years the Deputy Director of the University Honors Program.

Kevin J. Stevens is a doctoral student in English at Fordham University. He received his BA at Seton Hall University and works as a graduate assistant at Fordham.

Jennifer Stone (PhD, University of Wisconsin–Madison) specializes in sociocultural and critical approaches to literacy education. Her research focuses on young people's out-of-school literacy resources (including digital literacies, popular culture, and linguistic practices), and the implications of such resources for literacy teaching and learning. Stone's recent publications include "Popular websites in adolescents' out-of-school lives: Critical lessons on literacy" in *A New Literacies Sampler,* edited by Knobel & Lankshear (2007); "Textual borderlands: Students' recontextualizations in writing children's books" in *Language Arts* (2005); "Textual tactics of identification" in *Anthropology & Education Quarterly* (2004, co-authored with M. L. Gomez & N. Hobbel); and "Unpacking the social imaginary of literacy education: A case study" in *English Education* (2003).

Angela Tenga (PhD, Purdue University) specializes in Old and Middle English language and literature. Currently, she is Vice President of the Florida College English Association and an Assistant Professor in Humanities at Florida Institute of Technology. Her courses focus on literature, history, writing, and popular culture, while her research interests include early English literature, the literary monstrous, and the virtual self. She has written articles for *Florida Studies* and *Theorizing Twilight: Essays on What's at Stake in a Post-Vampire World*, to be published in fall/winter 2011. She is currently working on a chapter for a collection of essays on vampires and the undead in popular culture.

Nick Webber (PhD, University of Birmingham) has written on identity, cultural history and the relationship of technology and culture, and his current research includes contemporary popular music consumption, online archiving and civic history, and the culture of massively multiplayer online games. He has published a monograph on *The Evolution of Norman Identity 911–1154* (Boydell), and has chapters in *Myth, Rulership, Church and Charters* (Ashgate) and the *Oxford Handbook of Mobile Music and Sound Studies* (OUP). He is a contributor to the *Encyclopedia of Consumer Culture* (Sage), Associate Editor of *The Radio Journal*, and a member of the editorial board of *Midland History.* Webber is Senior Researcher and Research Developer in the Birmingham Centre for Media and Cultural Research at Birmingham City University, UK.

Angela Jane Weisl (PhD, Columbia University) is Professor of English at Seton Hall University, where she specializes in Medieval Literature and Culture, Women's Studies, and History of the English Language. She is the author of *The Persistence of Medievalism: Narrative Adventures in Contemporary Culture* (Palgrave/Macmillan) and *Conquering the Reign of Femeny: Gender and Genre in Chaucer's Romance* (D. S. Brewer), as well as the coeditor of *Constructions of Widowhood and Virginity in the Middle Ages* (Palgrave/Macmillan), with Cindy L. Carlson, and *MLA Approaches to Teaching Chaucer's Troilus and Criseyde and the Shorter Poems* (MLA), with Tison Pugh. She and Tison Pugh also coauthored *Medievalisms: Making the Past in the Present* for Routledge, and she is also working on a project on bodily transformations in medieval narrative. She has articles in several collections on her diverse research interests, including Chaucer, medieval transgendering, and medievalism in reality television.

Timothy Welsh (PhD, University of Washington) works on the intersection of literary theory and new media studies with an emphasis on narrative, virtuality, and interaction. He has chapters in *The Meaning and Culture of Grand Theft Auto* (McFarland) and the forthcoming *Guns, Grenades, and Grunts: The First-Person Shooter* (Continuum). Cofounder of the Critical Gaming Project at the University of Washington, Welsh is currently Assistant Professor of Digital Media at Loyola University New Orleans.

William J. White (PhD, Rutgers University) is interested in the study of games as communication, including the discourse of gaming cultures and communities as well as language and social action in the actual play of games, particularly role-playing games and other interactive fictions. Other areas of investigation include the study of knowledge-producing communities, communication and strategy, and the rhetoric of science fiction. He has published in *Communication Theory, Extrapolation, Human Communication Research*, and the *International Journal of Role-Playing*. He has contributed entries to *Books and Beyond: The Greenwood Encyclopedia of New American Reading* (Greenwood) and chapters on role-playing to *Larp, the Universe, and Everything* (Knutepunkt) and *Journeys to Another World* (Wyrdcon) in addition to a chapter in *Advances in Self-Organizing Systems* (Hampton). Currently coediting a volume on immersive fiction for McFarland, White is Associate Professor of Communication Arts & Sciences at Penn State Altoona.

Kim Wilkins (PhD, University of Queensland) teaches in the Writing, Editing, Publishing Program at University of Queensland. She is a published novelist of more than twenty books, and a researcher in the field of medievalism studies. Publications include articles on writing pedagogy for *Text, English in Australia*, and Cambridge University Press, and articles on Australian popular medievalism for *Journal of Australian Studies, Australian Literary Studies*, and *AustLit*. Her current research project centers on medievalism, adaptation, and Vikings.

Index

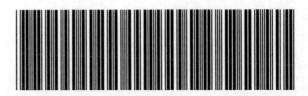